OxBoCh - Granger's 6th

P9-ELF-684

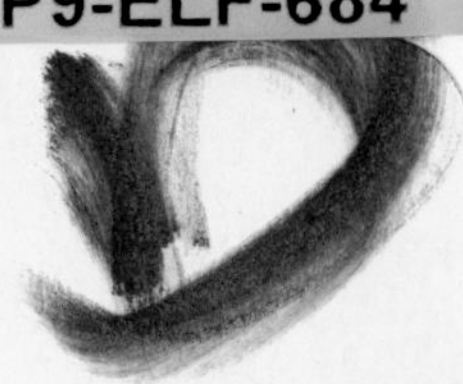

The Oxford Book of Christian Verse

The Oxford Book Of Christian Verse

Chosen and Edited by

Lord David Cecil

Oxford
At the Clarendon Press

Oxford University Press, Ely House, London W. 1
GLASGOW NEW YORK TORONTO MELBOURNE WELLINGTON
CAPE TOWN IBADAN NAIROBI DAR ES SALAAM LUSAKA ADDIS ABABA
DELHI BOMBAY CALCUTTA MADRAS KARACHI LAHORE DACCA
KUALA LUMPUR SINGAPORE HONG KONG TOKYO

First published May 1940
Reprinted July 1940, December 1940
1941, 1951, 1965, 1969, 1973

Printed in Great Britain
at the University Press, Oxford
by Vivian Ridler
Printer to the University

PREFACE

IN composing this anthology I have sometimes had to choose among several poems by one author, of equal literary merit. In such circumstances I have chosen the poem that seemed most significant as an expression of Christian feeling. Again, with the exception of Blake, I have confined my selection to writers whose poems—I do not speak of their private convictions—are consistent with the doctrines of orthodox Christianity. Not to have done so would have been to open my pages to so pressing a concourse of vague mystics as would have swelled the volume to bursting-point. Finally, with one exception, I have kept to poets born in the British Isles. American poetry seemed too wide a field. The one exception is Mr. Eliot. But he is on a different footing. For one thing he is a staunch son of the English church; no other poet speaks for modern Anglicanism with the same authority. In the second place, as the undisputed leader of the modern school of English verse and himself living in England, Mr. Eliot has become, for historical purposes, an English writer.

Authors are arranged chronologically, with a few exceptions, made in order to clarify the course of historical development.

ACKNOWLEDGEMENTS

MY thanks are due to publishers and others for kind permission to include copyright poems by the following:

Hilaire Belloc: Mr. Belloc and Messrs. Gerald Duckworth & Co., Ltd.

Robert Bridges: The Clarendon Press.

ACKNOWLEDGEMENTS

R. W. Buchanan: the Executors of the late W. E. Martyn.

G. K. Chesterton: Miss Collins, Messrs. Methuen & Co., Ltd. (for 'King Alfred Answers the Danes'), and Messrs. Burns, Oates, & Washbourne, Ltd. (for 'Hymn for the Church Militant'); Messrs. Dodd, Mead, & Co., New York.

Mary E. Coleridge: Sir Francis Newbolt and the Executors of the late Sir Henry Newbolt; Messrs. Elkin Mathews, Ltd.

D. M. Dolben: The Oxford University Press.

T. S. Eliot: Messrs. Faber & Faber, Ltd.; Messrs. Harcourt, Brace, & Co. Inc., New York.

Michael Field: Messrs. Grayson & Grayson, Ltd.

G. M. Hopkins: Mr. G. W. S. Hopkins.

Lionel Johnson: Messrs. Ivor Nicholson & Watson, Ltd.

Alice Meynell: Mr. Wilfred Meynell.

F. W. H. Myers: the Executors and Messrs. Longmans Green & Co., Ltd.

Ruth Pitter: The Cresset Press, Ltd., and the Macmillan Co., New York.

C. G. Rossetti: the author's representative and Messrs. Macmillan & Co., Ltd. (for poems 302 to 306, 309, 312, from *The Poetical Works of Christina Rossetti*).

Fredegond Shove: Mrs. Shove.

William Force Stead: Mr. Stead.

Francis Thompson: Mr. Wilfred Meynell.

Charles Williams: Mr. Williams.

Grateful acknowledgement is also made to Mr. Norman Ault for permission to print the following poems from his *Seventeenth Century Lyrics* and *Elizabethan Lyrics*: The Duchess of Newcastle, 'The Soul's Garment'; John Hall, 'Pastoral Hymn'; Patrick Carey, 'Crucifixus pro Nobis'; Clement Paman, 'On Christmas Day'; Samuel Speed, 'Peace', 'The Flower'; Robert Wild, 'An Epitaph'; Francis Quarles, 'On the Infancy of our Saviour'; Phineas Fletcher, 'To my Soul'; William Austin, 'Chanticleer'; and the anonymous piece, 'The Thief', from Mr. Ault's *The Poet's Life of Christ*.

CONTENTS

CONTENTS

CONTENTS

CONTENTS

INTRODUCTION

RELIGIOUS emotion is the most sublime known to man. But, in Christian Europe at any rate, it has not proved the most fertile soil for poetry. Though the great religious poets have been equal to any, they have been fewer in number than the great secular poets. And a large proportion of religious verse is poor stuff. The average hymn is a by-word for forced feeble sentiment, flat conventional expression. And those poets who have invoked both the sacred and the profane muse have, with some striking exceptions, found themselves more comfortable with the profane. Herrick's imagination flowered more freely in *The Hesperides* than in *The Noble Numbers*—Cowper is remembered for *John Gilpin* rather than for *The Olney Hymns*.

All this is more interesting than surprising. The very loftiness of the religious sentiment is in part responsible. A writer's best poetry is usually the expression of his keenest feeling. And though many people have caught a passing whiff of pious emotion, only a few have felt it with the strength and the continuity that they feel sexual love or pleasure in nature. The faintness of their experience reflects itself in the verses in which they seek to communicate it.

Further, those in whom the emotion is strong do not always have the faculty to express it. Rarely, indeed, does humanity produce a Blake gifted with the power to forge new and living symbols for the cosmic mysteries of spiritual experience. Most poets fall back on the traditional symbols of the orthodox liturgy. And these, though magnificently impressive on the lips of their creators, tend to lose their vitality on those of others. It is a poet's essential quality that he speaks with his own voice.

Christian poets are faced by other difficulties. Poetry should be a spontaneous expression of the spirit; the poet lets his personality burst forth without concealment. Primitive writers on religious subjects found no difficulty in doing this. The Hebrew psalmists, for example, spill themselves without shame in their invocations to God; show themselves rancorous or self-pitying or boastful just as the mood dictates. Their mode of expressing themselves is equally uninhibited. 'The Lord awaked out of sleep like a giant refreshed with wine'; no devotional writer of later days would permit himself to use such an image about the All-holy, All-wise object of his adoration. The New Testament conception of God is so much more elevated than that of the Old that the devout person feels it profane to show himself in all his earthy imperfections before Him. He will allow himself to express only unexceptionable sentiments, love, reverence, humility: will voice no aspiration save for a purer soul and stronger faith. As for using any but the most decorous language to express his feelings, the very idea horrifies him. Now very few people live at a sufficiently high moral level to find it natural to express only virtuous sentiments and in the language of impeccable taste, with the consequence that much Christian verse is, by an aesthetic standard, insincere. The writer, that is, does not say what he really feels, but what he thinks he ought to feel: and he speaks not in his own voice but in the solemn tones that seem fitting to his solemn subject.

In spite of these difficulties, however, England has produced a number of magnificent devotional poets; and others, not specifically pious, who have yet found in scripture stimulating subjects for their gifts as didactic or narrative writers. A representative anthology of English Christian Verse has also an additional non-literary interest. Christianity wears a different face to different people and in different periods. As in painting we distinguish the medieval mysticism of a Fra Angelico from the Counter-Reformation mysticism of El Greco, the Catholic piety of Raphael from the Protestant Bible Christianity of Rembrandt, so Donne and Milton, Herbert and Vaughan, Browning and Patmore, Hopkins and Christina Rossetti each express a particular strain of Christian thought, an individual phase of pious feeling. A collection of English Christian Verse is both a history of Christianity in England and an exhibition of the varieties of the religious temperament.

It divides itself into four phases. The first, the pre-Reformation stage, is the least important. For it contains no poet of the first distinction. Before Chaucer neither language nor verse-forms were sufficiently developed to be a vehicle for the finest literature; and none of the best poets of the next age find in religion their most inspiring subject. Langland was a didactic moralist, Chaucer primarily a man of this world. It was a pity. For the period in itself was peculiarly sympathetic to the writing of religious poetry. Naïve and unselfconscious, medieval man approached religion, if not as naturally as a Hebrew psalmist, yet in a less inhibited fashion than any of his descendants. Christian symbols were the recognized language of everyday medieval thought. This coloured literature. Such religious poems as we did produce in the Middle Ages seem at once closer to heaven and more firmly rooted in the earth than those of later times. The mystical poem *The Pearl*, the little carol *I sing of a Maiden*, breathe an ethereal spirituality like the very voice of angels. On the other hand, Chaucer's *Prioress's Tale*, though permeated with Christian sentiment, is yet as easy and natural a piece of narrative as the Rabelaisian anecdote related by the miller. Henryson, too, in his *Bloody Sark*, weaves a fanciful fairy-tale round the doctrine of the atonement; the anonymous author of the carol of *The Seven Virgins* sweeps from heaven to earth as boldly and suddenly as a bird from sky to meadow grass. After a poignant stanza about the Crucifixion—

> 'Oh' [he bursts forth], 'the rose, the gentle rose
> And the fennel that grows so green.
> God give us grace in every place
> To pray for our King and Queen.'

There is nothing unimportant about the next period. In religious verse as elsewhere it is the great age. Its first phase, that of the early Renaissance, is predominantly grand, sumptuous, pictorial, and impersonal. Spenser, the creator of this characteristic manner, did not himself apply it to Christian subjects on any considerable scale. But in brief passages such as the unfinished cantos on mutability which close *The Faerie Queen* he showed this was not from incapacity. A power of clear-cut ideal visualization harmonizes with a rolling organ music to create a majestic sublimity. The possibilities implicit in such a passage were explored more fully by Spenser's successors, Giles Fletcher and Drummond of Hawthornden. Neither had so certain a touch as his master. Drummond's effects are sometimes too obviously calculated, Fletcher is often over-florid. His description of the youthful Christ, with jetty curls and milky skin and sparkling glances, reads for all the world like a portrait of amorous Leander. But both rose to great heights on occasion. Drummond's sonnet on John the Baptist is a fine conception executed with accomplished certainty; while the long description of the New Jerusalem which closes Fletcher's *Christ's Victory and Triumph* moves in a sustained crescendo of celestial magnificence; the parallel, in its elaborate grandeur, of some great religious decoration by Mantegna or Piero della Francesca.

Meanwhile, round this central stream, other poets were trying their hands successfully at other types of religious poetry. The song-writers carolled as gracefully of piety as of shepherds and spring flowers; Campion's hymns are the most refined in English. Sir John Davies wrote a long philosophico-religious poem *Nosce Teipsum*, dull as a whole but with moments of a chaste nobility; Fulke Greville turned a more distinguished intellect, a stronger imagination, to the mysterious problems of redemption and expiation; Southwell, the Roman Catholic martyr, revealed in a handful of verses the flame of a burning lyrical piety.

It was with the seventeenth century, however, with the growth of high Anglicanism on the one hand and Puritanism on the other, that religious poetry rose to its greatest height. The leading figure of the period was Donne. Donne takes first place among English Christian poets. For he alone is equally interesting as Christian and as poet. His style, at once intimate and sublime, the quality of his imagination, lit by unearthly gleams, shadowed by cosmic darkness, alike fitted him to deal with religious matters. And religion was to him so stimulating a subject that there was hardly an aspect of it that did not fire him to poetry. The intricacies of theological argument were to him no dry logic-chopping: they were a positive inspiration to his restless scholastic imagination. And the Christian scheme seemed created to express his personal experience. He did not just believe in the doctrines of sin and expiation and Divine grace, he found them confirmed in his own life. Not that he was a saint. By nature, Donne was rancorous, proud, morbid, and sensual. But this was an advantage to him as a religious poet. For the struggle within him between the natural man and the regenerate gave his work an extraordinary tension. No other of our poets has expressed so poignantly the sense of sin, the straining of the soul to transcend its fleshly tenement, the vision of beatitude all the more ecstatic for the black despair which preceded it, the consciousness of man's utter feebleness, if unstrengthened by the miraculous grace of God. Indeed, to find a parallel among the writers of the world, we have to wait till Dostoievsky.

Donne was also an influence. The Caroline School of devotional poets are his direct descendants. And though none of them was of the calibre to equal him at his best, four among them, Crashaw, Traherne, Vaughan, and Herbert, each made a unique contribution to our religious literature. Traherne is a mystic of happiness; who conveys with a dewy freshness, all radiant with morning light, his perception of the Divine Glory manifest in visible things. Crashaw, the Roman Catholic convert, expresses the devotional spirit of the Counter-Reformation; his poems, like Bernini's sculpture, communicate a semi-erotic mysticism, all pierced hearts and tender flames and ecstatic swoonings. Often hysterical and over-luscious, his inspiration can yet take fire and flare up in a throbbing lyrical rush, unequalled by any other English religious poet. Vaughan is a mystic of nature. Hills and streams, a primrose lurking in the cranny of a river bank, the majestic tranquillity of night, each of these conveys to him some aspect of the Divine spirit. At its best his vision has an extraordinary still intensity; awestruck we seem to watch the very face of God unveiled before us. But Vaughan, too, is unequal; wooden and formless, scarcely ever inspired for more than a stanza at a time.

Herbert cannot be dismissed so briefly. Though less sensationally impressive than Crashaw or Vaughan at their best, in certain qualities he was their superior; in pathos, in variety of fancy, in sense of form. But it is his religious quality that gives him his pre-eminence. Here he can be compared to Donne himself; and not altogether to Donne's advantage. Herbert's religious vision is narrower but of a purer quality. Born with an exquisitely Christian disposition, all humility and spontaneous trusting love, he cultivated it by a lifetime of devotion. Christ was to him as real a personality as any human being. His life-story is the history of his relation to Him. Yet Herbert was not inhumanly spiritual. Sociable and charming, he fully appreciated the attractions of this world; he had experienced the dark night of the soul when he felt himself cut off from any contact with his Divine Master.

But the very beauty of his character prevented his spiritual struggle from achieving the tension of Donne's. Herbert was not tempted to mortal sin. He felt himself exiled from heaven, rather than in hell. And though he had moments of wistful regret for the satisfactions from which his dedication to God had deprived him, yet he never seriously considered turning back. In a little poem *The Quip*, worldly beauty, wit, honour, each in turn parade before him offering their showy prizes; 'But', says Herbert, 'Thou shalt answer, Lord, for me'. And we know he will accept the answer with joyful submission. Herbert has an additional interest as the most complete exponent in our poetry of the peculiar genius of the English Church. His piety is an eminently Anglican piety; refined, dignified, with a delicate appreciation of the value of style and ceremony, but subdued and restrained; its pure outline and quiet tints, a strong contrast to the rich colours and perfumed incense-flames of Crashaw.

Round these four cluster a number of lesser names; notably Quarles, and, in his rare devotional vein, Marvell. From these Herrick stands a little apart. Essentially he was not a Christian but a latter-day pagan; cheerfully innocent of a sense of sin, delightedly abandoning himself to the pleasures of fancy and the senses.

He lays his little garlands of rose and daffodil on the altar of the Virgin as gaily as a classical shepherd making a libation to Aphrodite. But they are very pretty garlands: and their curious mingling of the Christian and the pagan gives them a piquant perfume all their own. Though our spiritual experience may not be enriched thereby, it is a relief to turn now and again from the celestial sublimities of his contemporaries, to linger an instant in Herrick's garden.

A greater name closes the period. Milton—in this alone like Herrick—was not essentially a religious poet. He was a philosopher rather than a devotee. His imagination was lucid and concrete, unlit by heavenly gleams; theology to him was a superior branch of political science, the rule of reason and the moral law as exhibited in the working of the cosmos. Nor was his moral sensibility a Christian one. The Stoic virtues, fortitude, temperance, above all, moral independence, were what he valued. He did not live by faith, scorned hope, and was indisposed to charity; while pride, so far from being the vice which Christianity considers it, was to Milton the mark of a superior nature. As an exponent of the Christian spirit he cannot compare with Donne or Herbert. But if he is not our greatest religious poet, he is the greatest of English poets who have made religion their subject. In so far as his profoundly original achievement had ancestors, it descends from Spenser and Giles Fletcher. His early pieces, the Ode on the Nativity, *Blest Pair of Sirens*, exhibit, though with a more concentrated art and a more fastidious sensibility, the same brocaded beauty, the same elaborately orchestrated harmony. In the epics of his later years these qualities appear, chastened and elevated, in keeping with the height of his great argument. As an exposition of Christian belief *Paradise Lost* and *Paradise Regained* are failures. In *Paradise Lost* All-holy God and innocent Adam are made equally irritable and egotistic; Christ in *Paradise Regained* is an austere, unsympathetic classical philosopher. But for mastery of design, for distinction of style, for sustained grandeur of conception, Milton surpasses every other poet whose works are quoted in this collection.

Milton ends the great period; the next, which begins with the Restoration and goes down to the middle of the nineteenth century, contains nothing to compare with the masterpieces of the preceding century. But it extended the range of religious poetry. Dryden, who presides over its opening, is our only great master of versified theology. In his *Religio Laici* and *The Hind and the Panther*, plain vigorous reasoning is warmed into poetry by the sheer drive and lilt of the author's magnificent versification. None of the leading poets of the phase that followed had so important a contribution to make. But Pope's *Messiah* is a stylish piece of decoration in the baroque manner: Young's *Last Day* is another fine baroque piece, this time in a lurid dramatic vein: and the hymn at the end of Thomson's *Seasons* exhibits a third aspect of Augustan verse, its capacity for landscape-painting, generalized and classical, and here tinged faintly with a religious colour.

Meanwhile, side by side with these gestures of official respect towards Christianity on the part of the leading poets of the period, arose a school of hymn-writers. Hymns are usually a second-rate type of poetry. Composed as they are for the practical purpose of congregational singing, they do not provide a free vehicle for the expression of the poet's imagination, his intimate soul. But for a rare exception like Campion, the Renaissance poets were at once too individual and too fanciful to write successful hymns. The Augustan manner of writing was far more appropriate to their production. And the bulk of our best hymns were written under its influence.

Addison is the first distinguished name among this list of English hymn-writers; he voices admirably the rational piety approved of in the days of Queen Anne. Isaac Watts rises higher; equally straightforward, he had a spontaneous sentiment, a gift of song which raised his best hymns to the level of the true lyric. None of the professional hymn-writers who were his successors was so much of a natural poet. But in the best work of Charles Wesley, of Toplady and John Newton, this lack is compensated for by the creed which inspired them. Evangelicalism, with its emphasis on the mysterious and awful doctrines of the Christian faith, on original sin, redemption by Christ's blood, final perdition, represents a violent reaction against the cool, unenthusiastic common sense of orthodox eighteenth-century devotion. And it imbues their hymns with a passion, a murky thunder-light, that makes them stirring out of all proportion to their strictly literary merits. *Jesu, lover of my Soul*, *Rock of Ages*, these are masterpieces in their minor kind; it is not strange that they have never lost their popularity. Associated with the evangelicals is a greater name, Cowper. Just because he was greater, he was not so successful as a writer of hymns. *Oh for a closer Walk with God*, *The Lord all Happiness Bestow*, in these the emotion is too personal to be appropriate to congregational singing. But in their unemphasized poignancy they are the perfect mirror of their author's religious mood, tender, strained, expressing an agonized longing for faith rather than faith itself.

The next century at first saw no great change of convention. The Oxford Movement did not create a new literary manner to express its new religious attitude. Keble and Newman continue the eighteenth-century tradition of pious writing, earnest and direct in tone, classical and conventionalized in diction. The convention had, by this time, begun to wear a trifle thin; and a certain Victorian mawkishness of tone to insinuate itself. Moreover, the richer symbolism which, in accordance with their convictions, the Tractarians sought to impose on the plain fabric of Augustan style, did not harmonize with it. Newman, it is true, gave distinction to all he touched: if *The Dream of Gerontius* is not a great poem, it is the work of a remarkable writer. But *The Christian Year* is feeble stuff, a sentimental concoction in ecclesiastical Victorian mock-Gothic. For the rest, the leading poets of the first Romantic period showed themselves as little inspired by religious themes as those writers against whom they had reacted. One or two of Wordsworth's ecclesiastical sonnets are beautiful; Coleridge's hymn *In the Vale of Chamouni* is a fine piece of rhetoric, glowing now and again into something more heartfelt. But neither represents its author at his best.

Two names separate themselves from the general survey of this third phase of English Christian verse: Smart and Blake. Smart, in his single remembered piece, *A Song to David*, recaptured the vision of a Divinity universally manifest in creation which is the outstanding glory of the Hebrew psalms. For him, living in the unmystical eighteenth century, God did manage to reveal Himself, not only in the gentle and the serene, but in the strength of the lion, the pride of the peacock, the tumult of the thunder-storm. Blake was yet more original. It is doubtful whether he should appear in a book of Christian verse at all. If he was a Christian, he was certainly a heretic. His surprising gospel, with its admiration for all positive feelings, its horror of any kind of prohibition or asceticism, is at odds both with the doctrines of every important branch of Christianity and also with Christ's own teaching. But Blake, whether he would or no, was soaked through with Christian thought: Christian symbols are an essential part of his native language. And he was exquisitely responsive to certain phases of Christian sentiment. *The Evening Hymn*, *Little Lamb* breathe Christian mercy, Christian humility, Christian compassion. Further, more than any other English poet, more even than Donne or Vaughan, he had the spiritual eye. They have glimpses of the mystic vision; Blake seems to have lived for hours together at the heart of its ineffable light.

The second half of the nineteenth century inaugurates a new phase. The passion and imagination of the Romantic Movement was by that time affecting orthodox believers, and the spiritual impetus given to the English by the various religious revivals of the previous years had begun to bear literary fruit. This is the second outstanding epoch of religious poetry in England. It produced no Donne or Milton, nor yet any writer who expresses the spirit of Anglican Christianity so completely as Herbert. But four poets, Browning, Patmore, Gerard Hopkins, Christina Rossetti, are the equals if not the superiors of Vaughan and Crashaw. Unlike their seventeenth-century prototypes they did not form a school. The rising tide of individualism made impossible any universally accepted tradition of religious verse. None of these poets has much in common with the other. Patmore, a professing Roman Catholic, evolved a religious philosophy of his own, in which sensual and spiritual love fuse together to achieve a mystical union with God. A similarity in spirit to Crashaw shows itself both in the ebullient quality of his emotion and his rich surging style. But he is as much Crashaw's superior in power of mind as he is inferior to him in lyrical talent. Patmore is a titan rather than a god. Torrential, effortful, and extremely idiosyncratic, his work seldom marries word to thought with so compelling a perfection as to make one forget the man in his poem. How high one places him will always depend on how far one is able to sympathize with his personality and point of view. But there is no doubt he is a major writer; charged with passion, untiringly eloquent, and capable of expressing a peculiar intense intellectual ecstasy.

Browning, too, is a personal taste. His idiom is still more individual; cranky, jerky, bristling with deliberately cultivated eccentricities. But he is extraordinarily vital and original. Alone among English Christian poets he is interesting primarily for his ideas. Nearly two thousand years after Christ, Browning was able to restate the doctrines of the gospel so that they sound as fresh as those of a contemporary. Space forbids a detailed analysis of Browning's Christianity. Briefly it centres itself round two beliefs: in the necessary imperfection of man and in the self-sacrificing love of God. Man alone, so Browning seems to sum up the situation, among created beings, feels himself imperfect; weak and erring, he yet perceives in himself fragmentary gleams of higher things, which he recognizes as divine, and towards which he feels impelled to strive.

The brightest gleam within his vision is love. Love, therefore, must be the typical characteristic of God. And since love shows itself most nobly in self-sacrifice, God must be capable of self-sacrifice. These conclusions lead him inevitably to a belief in the central doctrines of Christianity; the fall, the incarnation, the redemption. He conveys these convictions in a queer way, spasmodic, obscure, and inordinately long. But he does it with unforgettable force.

Hopkins and Christina Rossetti are a different type of poet. They are not thinkers but singers. Christina Rossetti, indeed, is the most extreme example in our literature of a purely lyrical talent applied to religion. Her ideas are those of the ordinary pious lady; she shows no signs that her vision was ever illuminated by any unusual mystical experience. All she does is to put into words her simple dreams of heaven, her longing and love for God, her resignation to His will. But to a consummate mastery of her art she joined a unique quality of style and imagination. And her achievement, within its limits, is of the very finest kind. Both imagination and style owe their flavour to a union of incongruities. Her language, save when it is heightened by some traditional piece of symbolism, is plain and colloquial to the verge of prose; her rhythms, on the other hand, are varied, subtle, and intricate in the highest degree. In her imagination a childish feeling for the charm of the pretty and the homely, of spring flowers and golden crowns and comical Hans Andersen animals, joins with a severe Puritan morality and a sense of the tragedy and transience of human life, to create a bitter-sweet poignancy. Finally, behind style and imagination throbs a continuous pulse of passion, which sends her words soaring up to the very zenith of poetry. Her religious sense finds no such fulfilment as her artistic. A sensitive, frustrated character, disillusioned with the world, she turned with a desperate yearning to her faith, as the one beacon light in a universal darkness. But strive as she might, fear and disillusion cast their shadow over all her thoughts. She had faith; she had charity; she lacked hope. This detracts from her value as an aid to devotion; but it makes her poems all the more moving.

Hopkins is also a virtuoso. His effects are not so certain as hers. A natural juggler with words, intoxicated by the fertility of his own invention, he sometimes strained the resources of language beyond their strength; in his efforts to extend the bounds of expression he becomes obscure. But at its best, his verbal invention has a Shakespearian boldness and felicity. And he conveys with extraordinary fire and immediacy the more full-blooded religious emotions; the ecstasy of the rapt worshipper, the black night of the soul cut off from its vision of God. Like Christina Rossetti he had nothing very unusual to say. He voices the typical feelings of a Roman Catholic devotee as she voices those of a high Anglican. But this gives his poems a general appeal of which their eccentricities of expression might otherwise deprive them.

Round these four outstanding pillars of Victorian Christian verse hovered a swarm of lesser names. In the works of that odd Cornish divine, the Reverend Robert Stephen Hawker, orthodox Christian symbols appear, having suffered a sea change into something rich and strange by the action of a primitive Celtic imagination. Mary Coleridge is a minor Christina Rossetti, less accomplished but with her own vein of Gothic fancy. Francis Thompson, like Patmore, is a child of Crashaw, but closer to his father, both in his mental limitations and the jewelled elaboration of his diction. Lionel Johnson adorns a Catholic piety with the lilies and languors of the nineties; Alice Meynell and the two ladies who chose to call themselves Michael Field convey with sincerity and grace the individual quality of their private devotional life; Charles Kingsley's *Drifting* is the poignant cry of a faithful soul desolate in a dissolving world. At the same time, some of the greater poets, not themselves especially

Christian in conviction, turned their hands now and again to Christian themes. Rossetti's *Lady of the Rocks*, Tennyson's *St. Agnes' Eve*, are as pictorial and finished as the rest of their works. Robert Bridges deserves more notice. For though he was a Platonist tinged with Christianity rather than an orthodox believer, he wrote some of the most beautiful poetry about Christianity in the language—the little lyric on Christmas, the peroration which closes *The Testament of Beauty*. Among the poets alive in his time, only Christina Rossetti was a more impeccable craftsman; and her scale was smaller. As Milton is to Crashaw and Vaughan, so, in his lesser degree, is Bridges to Hopkins and Patmore.

There remains our own period. It is an age of doubt, especially among poets. Not many of them write about religion. During the first twenty years of the century little beyond some verses of Mr. Chesterton and Mr. Belloc remains in the memory to-day. But since 1918 Christianity has raised her head again. The Georgian phase of verse produced the sensitive talent of Mr. Force Stead; and since then two of the first poets of the day, Miss Ruth Pitter and Mr. T. S. Eliot, have found in Christianity an inspiration. How far Miss Pitter is an orthodox believer her verses do not reveal. But her whole achievement is full of Christian thought and feeling. And it is lit up by the moonlight of her mystical vision, communicated in language of a fastidious nobility. Mr. Eliot is a still more significant writer. Founder as he is of the modern school of English poets, he combines a revolutionary technique with an Anglicanism as orthodox as that of Donne. His Christianity is superficially a little rigid and joyless: not for him are the celestial intimations that set glowing the heart of Miss Pitter. But, if not seductive, Mr. Eliot's faith is yet compelling; so certain, so heartfelt, so courageous to confront the dark elements in experience. It stands out like a rock amid the onslaught of that squalid sinister contemporary world which he portrays so vividly. Menacing around him lies the dreadful landscape of the waste land; but splendidly he proclaims:

There shall always be the Church and the World,
And the heart of man
Shivering and fluttering between them choosing and
chosen,
Valiant, ignoble, dark, and full of light
Swinging between hell gate and heaven gate
And the gates of hell shall not prevail.

RICHARD ROLLE, OF HAMPOLE

1290?–1349

1 *A Song of the Passion*

MY trewest tresowre sa trayturly was taken,
Sa bytterly bondyn wyth bytand bandes,
How sone of thi seruandes was thou forsaken,
And lathly for my lufe hurld with thair handes.

My well of my wele sa wrangwysly wryed,
Sa pulled owt of preson to pilate at prime;
Thaire dulles and thaire dyntes ful drerely thou dreed
Whan thai schot in thi syght bath slauer and slyme.

My hope of my hele sa hyed to be hanged,
Sa charged with thi crosce and corond with thorne,
Ful sare to thi hert thi steppes tha stanged—
Me thynk thi bak burd breke; it bendes for-borne.

My salue of my sare sa saryful in syght,
Sa naked and nayled thi ryg on the rode,
Ful hydusly hyngand, thai heued the on hyght,
Thai lete the stab in the stane all stekked that thar stode.

My dere-worthly derlyng, sa dolefully dyght,
Sa straytly vpryght streyned on the rode;
For thi mykel mekenes, thi mercy, thi myght,
Thow bete al my bales with bote of thi blode.

bytand] biting. lathly] hatefully. hurld] shoved. well of my wele] source of my joy. wrangwysly wryed] unjustly twisted. dulles] wounds. drerely thou dreed] grievously thou suffered. hele] salvation. hyed] hurried, pushed on. tha stanged] they goaded. burd] must. for-borne] overborne. ryg] back. lete the stab in the stane] caused thee (i.e. the cross) to be thrust into the stone (socket). stekked] fixed. bete al my bales] didst assuage all my sorrows. bote] remedy.

My fender of my fose, sa fonden in the felde,
Sa lufly lyghtand at the euensang tyde;
Thi moder and hir menghe vnlaced thi scheld—
All weped that thar were, thi woundes was sa wyde.

My pereles prynce als pure I the pray,
The mynde of this myrour thou lat me noght mysse;
Bot wynd vp my wylle to won wyth the ay,
That thou be beryd in my brest and bryng me to blysse.
Amen.

ANONYMOUS

2 *The Shepherd upon the Hill*

Can I not syng but hoy
Whan the joly sheperd made so mych joy.

THE Sheperd upon a hill he satt,
He had on hym his tabard and his hat,
His tarbox, hys pype and hys flagat;
Hys name was called joly, joly Wat;
For he was a gud herdes boy,
Vith hoy!
For in hys pype he made so mych joy.

The sheperd upon a hill was layd,
Hys doge to hys gyrdyll was tayd;
He had not slept but a lytill broyd,
But 'Gloria in excelcis' was to hym sayd.
Vith hoy!
For in hys pipe he mad so myche joy.

1 fonden] tested. lufly lyghtand] beautifully descending. menghe] companions. the mynde of this myrour] the purpose of this example. won] dwell.

2 flagat] flageolet. lytill broyd] short time.

ANONYMOUS

The sheperd on a hill he stode,
Rownd a-bowt hym his shepe they yode
He put hys hond vnder hys hode,
He saw a star as rede as blod:
Vith hoy!
For in hys pipe he mad so myche joy.

'Now farwell Mall and also Will,
For my love, go ye all styll
Unto I cum agayn you till,
And euermore, Will, ryng well thy bell.'
Vith hoy!
For in hys pipe he mad so mych joy.

'Now must I go ther Cryst was borne;
Farewell! I cum a-gayn tomorn.
Dog, kepe well my shep fro the corn,
And warn well, warroke, when I blow my horn.'
Vith hoy!
For in hys pipe he made so mych joy.

The sheperd sayd anon ryght:
'I will go se yon farly syght,
Wheras the angell syngith on hight
And the star that shynyth so bryght.'
Vith hoy!
For in [his] pipe he mad so mych joy.

Whan Wat to Bedlem cum was,
He swet; he had gon faster than a pace;
He fownd Jhesu in a sympyll place,
Betwen an ox and an asse.

tomorn] to-morrow. warroke] young boy. farly] marvellous.

Vith hoy!
For in his pipe he mad so mych joy.

'Jhesu! I offer to the here my pype,
My skyrte, my tarbox and my scrype,
Home to my felowes now will I skype,
And also loke unto my shepe.'
Vith hoy!
For in his pipe he mad so myche joy.

'Now farewell, myne own herdesman Wat!'
'Ye, for God, Lady, even so I hat;
Lull well Jhesu in thy lape,
And farewell, Joseph wyth thy rownd cape!'
Vith hoy!
For in hys pipe he mad so myche joy.

'Now may I well both hope and syng,
For I haue bene at Crystis beryng,
Home to my felowes now wyll I flyng;
Cryst of hevyn to his blis vs bryng!'
Vith hoy!
For in his pipe he mad so myche joy.

3 '*Swete Ihesu King of Blisse*'

SWETE ihesu, king of blisse,
Min herte loue, min herte lisse,
Thou art swete mid I-wisse—
Wo is him that the shall misse.

Swete ihesu, min hert light,
Thou art dai with-houten night,
Thou gheue me strengthe and eke might
For-to louien the al right.

2 hat] am called. 3 lisse] joy. mid I-wisse] indeed.

Swete ihesu, mi soule bote,
In min herte thou sette a rote
Of thi loue is so swote,
And wite hit that hit springe mote.

4 *Mary and her Child*

A lovely lady sat and sange
And to her son thus gan she say:
'My son, my lord, my dere derlyng,
Why liggis thou thus in hay?
Myn own dere son,
How art thou cum,
Art thou not God verey?
But neuer the lesse
I will not sese
To syng "by, by, lully, lulley." '

Than spake the child that was so yong
And thus me thowght he said:
'I am knowen as hevyn kyng,
In cribbe thowgh I now be layd;
Thow knowest it is no nay.
Angellis bright
To me shall light;
And of that sight
Ye may be light,
And syng "by, by, lully, lulley." '

3 bote] remedy. thou sette] may thou set. swote] sweet. wite] protect. mote] may.
4 light] glad.

ANONYMOUS

'Jhesu, my son, hevyn kyng,
  Why lyest thou thus in stall?
And why hast thou no riche beddyng
  In sum ryche kyngis hall?
    Me thynkith by right,
    The lord of myght
  Shuld lye in riche aray;
    But neuer the lesse
    I will not sese
  To synge "by, by, lully, lulley." '

'Mary moder, quene of blis,
  Me thynkith it is no lawe
That I shuld go to the kyngis,
  And they not to me drawe;
    But you shall see
    That kyngis thre
  To me will cum on the Twelfth day;
    For this beheste,
    Geve me your brest,
  And syng "by, by, lully, lulley." '

'Jhesu, my son, I pray the, say,
  As thou art to me dere:
How shall I serue the to thy pay,
  And mak the right good chere?
    All thy will
    I wold fulfill,
  Thou knoweste it well, in fay;
    Both rokke the still
    And daunce the ther-till,
  And synge "by, by, lully, lulley." '

pay] contentment.   ther-till] as well.

'Mary, moder, I pray the,
  Take me vp on loft,
And in thyn arme
Thow lappe me warm,
  And daunce me now full ofte;
And yf I wepe,
And will not slepe,
  Than syng "by, by, lully, lulley."'

'Jhesu, my son, hevyn kyng,
Yf it be thy will,
Grant thow me myn askyng,
As reason wold, and skyll:
What so euer they be
That can and will be
  Mery on this day,
To blis them brynge,
And I shall syng:
  "Lulley, by, by, lully, lulley."'

5 *Wynter wakeneth* c. 1300

WYNTER wakeneth al my care,
  Nou thise leves waxeth bare;
Ofte I sike and mourne sare
  When hit cometh in my thoht
  Of this worldes joie, hou hit geth al to noht.

Nou hit is, and nou hit nys,
Al so hit ner nere, ywys;
That moni mon seith, soth hit ys:

4 skyll] right.
5 thise leves] these leaves. sike] sigh. al so hit ner nere] as if it never had been.

Al goth bote Godes wille:
Alle we shule deye, thah us like yllc.

Al that gren me graueth grene
Nou hit faleweth al bydene:
Jhesu, help that hit be sene
And shild us from helle!
For y not whider y shal, ne hou longe her duelle.

GEOFFREY CHAUCER

1340?–1400

6

The Priores's Tale

The Prologe of the Prioresses Tale

Domine, dominus noster.

O LORD our lord, thy name how merveillous
Is in this large worlde y-sprad—quod she:—
For noght only thy laude precious
Parfourned is by men of dignitee,
But by the mouth of children thy bountee
Parfourned is, for on the brest soukinge
Som tyme shewen they thyn heryinge.

Wherfor in laude, as I best can or may,
Of thee, and of the whyte lily flour
Which that thee bar, and is a mayde alway,
To telle a storie I wol do my labour;
Not that I may encresen hir honour;
For she hir-self is honour, and the rote
Of bountee, next hir sone, and soules bote.—

5 thah us like ylle] though it grieve us. bydene] straightway. not] know not. shal] must (go).
6 heryinge] praise. bote] salvation.

O moder mayde! o mayde moder free!
O bush unbrent, brenninge in Moyses sighte,
That ravisedest doun fro the deitee,
Thurgh thyn humblesse, the goost that in th'alighte,
Of whos vertu, whan he thyn herte lighte,
Conceived was the fadres sapience,
Help me to telle it in thy reverence!

Lady! thy bountee, thy magnificence,
Thy vertu, and thy grete humilitee
Ther may no tonge expresse in no science;
For som-tyme, lady, er men praye to thee,
Thou goost biforn of thy benignitee,
And getest us the light, thurgh thy preyere,
To gyden us un-to thy sone so dere.

My conning is so wayk, o blisful quene,
For to declare thy grete worthiness,
That I ne may the weighte nat sustene,
But as a child of twelf monthe old, or lesse,
That can unnethes any word expresse,
Right so fare I, and therfor I yow preye,
Gydeth my song that I shal of yow seye.

Here biginneth the Prioresses Tale.

Ther was in Asie, in a greet citee,
Amonges Cristen folk, a Jewerye,
Sustened by a lord of that contree
For foule usure and lucre of vilanye,
Hateful to Crist and to his companye;
And thurgh the strete men mighte ryde or wende,
For it was free, and open at either ende.

ravisedest] didst draw. science] learned work. unnethes] scarcely.

A litel scole of Cristen folk ther stood
Doun at the ferther ende, in which ther were
Children an heep, y-comen of Cristen blood,
That lerned in that scole yeer by yere
Swich maner doctrine as men used there,
This is to seyn, to singen and to rede,
As smale children doon in hir childhede.

Among thise children was a widwes sone,
A litel clergeon, seven yeer of age,
That day by day to scole was his wone,
And eek also, wher-as he saugh th'image
Of Cristes moder, hadde he in usage,
As him was taught, to knele adoun and seye
His *Ave Marie*, as he goth by the weye.

Thus hath this widwe hir litel sone y-taught
Our blisful lady, Cristes moder dere,
To worshipe ay, and he forgat it naught,
For sely child wol alday sone lere;
But ay, whan I remembre on this matere,
Seint Nicholas stant ever in my presence,
For he so yong to Crist did reverence.

This litel child, his litel book lerninge,
As he sat in the scole at his prymer,
He *Alma redemptoris* herde singe,
As children lerned hir antiphoner;
And, as he dorste, he drough him ner and ner,
And herkned ay the wordes and the note,
Til he the firste vers coude al by rote.

clergeon] schoolboy. wone] wont, custom. sely] good.
alday] always. ner and ner] nearer and nearer. coude] knew.

Noght wiste he what this Latin was to seye,
For he so yong and tendre was of age;
But on a day his felaw gan he preye
T'expounden him this song in his langage,
Or telle him why this song was in usage;
This preyde he him to construe and declare
Ful ofte tyme upon his knowes bare.

His felaw, which that elder was than he,
Answerde him thus: 'this song, I have herd seye,
Was maked of our blisful lady free,
Hir to salue, and eek hir for to preye
To been our help and socour whan we deye.
I can no more expounde in this matere;
I lerne song, I can but smal grammere.'

'And is this song maked in reverence
Of Cristes moder?' seyde this innocent;
'Now certes, I wol do my diligence
To conne it al, er Cristemasse is went;
Though that I for my prymer shal be shent,
And shal be beten thryës in an houre,
I wol it conne, our lady for to honoure.'

His felaw taughte him homward prively,
Fro day to day, til he coude it by rote,
And than he song it wel and boldely
Fro word to word, acording with the note;
Twyës a day it passed thurgh his throte,
To scoleward and homward whan he wente;
On Cristes moder set was his entente.

knowes] knees. shent] scolded.

As I have seyd, thurgh-out the Jewerye
This litel child, as he cam to and fro,
Ful merily than wolde he singe, and crye
O *Alma redemptoris* ever-mo.
The swetnes hath his herte perced so
Of Cristes moder, that, to hir to preye,
He can nat stinte of singing by the weye.

Our firste fo, the serpent Sathanas,
That hath in Jewes herte his waspes nest,
Up swal, and seide, 'O Hebraik peple, allas!
Is this to yow a thing that is honest,
That swich a boy shal walken as him lest
In your despyt, and singe of swich sentence,
Which is agayn your lawes reverence?'

Fro thennes forth the Jewes han conspyred
This innocent out of this world to chace;
An homicyde ther-to han they hyred,
That in an aley hadde a privee place;
And as the child gan for-by for to pace,
This cursed Jew him hente and heeld him faste,
And kitte his throte, and in a pit him caste.

I seye that in a wardrobe they him threwe
Wher-as these Jewes purgen hir entraille.
O cursed folk of Herodes al newe,
What may your yvel entente yow availle?
Mordre wol out, certein, it wol nat faille,
And namely ther th'onour of god shal sprede,
The blood out cryeth on your cursed dede.

up swal] swelled up (in anger). agayn] against. heeld] held. wardrobe] privy. namely ther] especially where.

'O martir, souded to virginitee,
Now maystou singen, folwing ever in oon
The whyte lamb celestial,' quod she,
'Of which the grete evangelist, seint John,
In Pathmos wroot, which seith that they that goon
Biforn this lamb, and singe a song al newe,
That never, fleshly, wommen they ne knewe.'

This povre widwe awaiteth al that night
After hir litel child, but he cam noght;
For which, as sone as it was dayes light,
With face pale of drede and bisy thoght,
She hath at scole and elles-wher him soght,
Til finally she gan so fer espye
That he last seyn was in the Jewerye.

With modres pitee in hir brest enclosed,
She gooth, as she were half out of hir minde,
To every place wher she hath supposed
By lyklihede hir litel child to finde;
And ever on Cristes moder meke and kinde
She cryde, and atte laste thus she wroghte,
Among the cursed Jewes she him soghte.

She frayneth and she preyeth pitously
To every Jew that dwelte in thilke place,
To telle hir, if hir child wente oght for-by.
They seyde, 'nay'; but Jesu, of his grace,
Yaf in hir thought, inwith a litel space,
That in that place after hir sone she cryde,
Wher he was casten in a pit bisyde.

souded to] confirmed in. ever in oon] continually. wroghte] contrived. frayneth] asks. Yaf in hir thought] put it into her mind.

O grete god, that parfournest thy laude
By mouth of innocents, lo heer thy might!
This gemme of chastitee, this emeraude,
And eek of martirdom the ruby bright,
Ther he with throte y-corven lay upright,
He '*Alma redemptoris*' gan to singe
So loude, that al the place gan to ringe.

The Cristen folk, that thurgh the strete wente,
In coomen, for to wondre up-on this thing,
And hastily they for the provost sente;
He cam anon with-outen tarying,
And herieth Crist that is of heven king,
And eek his moder, honour of mankinde,
And after that, the Jewes leet he binde.

This child with pitous lamentacioun
Up-taken was, singing his song alway;
And with honour of greet processioun
They carien him un-to the nexte abbay.
His moder swowning by the bere lay;
Unnethe might the peple that was there
This newe Rachel bringe fro his bere.

With torment and with shamful deth echon
This provost dooth thise Jewes for to sterve
That of this mordre wiste, and that anon;
He nolde no swich cursednesse observe.
Yvel shal have, that yvel wol deserve.
Therfor with wilde hors he dide hem drawe,
And after that he heng hem by the lawe.

leet he binde] he caused to be bound. unnethe] with difficulty. sterve] die.

Up-on his bere ay lyth this innocent
Biforn the chief auter, whyl masse laste,
And after that, the abbot with his covent
Han sped hem for to burien him ful faste;
And whan they holy water on him caste,
Yet spak this child, whan spreynd was holy water,
And song—'*O Alma redemptoris mater!*'

This abbot, which that was an holy man
As monkes been, or elles oghten be,
This yonge child to conjure he bigan,
And seyde, 'o dere child, I halse thee,
In vertu of the holy Trinitee,
Tel me what is thy cause for to singe,
Sith that thy throte is cut, to my seminge?'

'My throte is cut un-to my nekke-boon,'
Seyde this child, 'and, as by wey of kinde,
I sholde have deyed, ye, longe tyme agoon,
But Jesu Crist, as ye in bokes finde,
Wil that his glorie laste and be in minde;
And, for the worship of his moder dere,
Yet may I singe '*O Alma*' loude and clere.

This welle of mercy, Cristes moder swete,
I lovede alwey, as after my conninge;
And whan that I my lyf sholde forlete,
To me she cam, and bad me for to singe
This antem verraily in my deyinge,
As ye han herd, and, whan that I had songe,
Me thoughte, she leyde a greyn up-on my tonge.

spreynd] sprinkled. halse] conjure. sith] since. by wey of kinde] in the course of nature. greyn] grain *or* pearl.

Wherfor I singe, and singe I moot certeyn
In honour of that blisful mayden free,
Til fro my tonge of-taken is the greyn;
And afterward thus seyde she to me,
"My litel child, now wol I fecche thee
Whan that the greyn is fro thy tonge y-take;
Be nat agast, I wol thee nat forsake." '

This holy monk, this abbot, him mene I,
Him tonge out-caughte, and took a-wey the greyn,
And he yaf up the goost ful softely.
And whan this abbot had this wonder seyn,
His salte teres trikled doun as reyn,
And gruf he fil al plat up-on the grounde,
And stille he lay as he had been y-bounde.

The covent eek lay on the pavement
Weping, and herien Cristes moder dere,
And after that they ryse, and forth ben went,
And toke awey this martir fro his bere,
And in a tombe of marbul-stones clere
Enclosen they his litel body swete;
Ther he is now, god leve us for to mete.

O yonge Hugh of Lincoln, slayn also
With cursed Jewes, as it is notable,
For it nis but a litel whyle ago;
Preye eek for us, we sinful folk unstable,
That, of his mercy, god so merciable
On us his grete mercy multiplye,
For reverence of his moder Marye. Amen.

Here is ended the Prioresses Tale.

gruf] on his face. leve] grant.

JOHN LYDGATE

1370?–1450?

7 *Vox ultima Crucis*

TARYE no lenger; toward thyn herytage
Hast on thy weye, and be of ryght good chere.
Go eche day onward on thy pylgrymage;
Thynke howe short tyme thou hast abyden here.
Thy place is bygged above the sterres clere,
Noon erthly palys wrought in so statly wyse.
Come on, my frend, my brother most entere!
For the I offered my blood in sacryfice.

ANONYMOUS

8 *Lullay, lullay*

LULLAY, lullay, litel child,
Thu that were so sterne and wild,
Nou art become meke and mild,
To sauen that was forlore.

But for my senne I wot it is
That godis sone suffret this;
Merci, lord! I haue do mis,
I-wis I wile no more.

Aȝenis my fadris wille I ches
An appel with a reuful res;
Werfore myn heritage I les,
And nou thu wepist therfor.

7 bygged] built. palys] palace.
8 I-wis] certainly. ches] chose. with a reuful res] in grievous rashness. les] lost.

An appel I tok of a tre,
God it hadde for-boden me;
Werfore I sulde dampned be,
    Ȝef thi weping ne wore.

Lullay for wo, thu litel thing,
Thou litel barun, thou litel king;
Mankindde is cause of thi murning,
    That thou hast loued so ȝore.

For man that thu hast ay loued so
Ȝet saltu suffren peines mo,
In heued, in feet, in hondis to,
    And ȝet wepen wel more.

That peine vs make of senne fre,
That peine vs bringge, Jesu, to the,
That peine vs helpe ay to fle,
    The wikkede fendes lore. Amen.

c. 15th Cent.

9 *Adam lay ibowndyn*

ADAM lay ibowndyn,
    bowndyn in a bond
fowr thowsand wynter
    thowt he not to long;
and al was for an appil,
    an appil that he tok,
as clerkes fyndyn
    wretyn in here book.

8 Ȝef thi weping ne wore] if it were not for thy weeping. ȝore] of old. *9* here] their.

ne hadde the appil take ben,
  the appil take ben,
ne hadde never our lady
  a ben Hevene qwen.
blyssid be the tyme
  that appil take was!
therfore we mown syngyn
  Deo gracias.

ROBERT HENRYSON

1430?–1506?

10

The Bludy Serk

THIS hinder yeir I hard be tald
  Thair was a worthy King;
Dukis, Erlis, and Barronis bald,
  He had at his bidding.
The Lord was ancean and ald,
  And sexty yeiris cowth ring;
He had a dochter fair to fald,
  A lusty Lady ying.

Off all fairheid scho bur the flour,
  And eik hir faderis air;
Off lusty laitis and he honour,
  Meik bot and debonair:
Scho wynnit in a bigly bour,
  On fold wes nane so fair,
Princis luvit hir paramour
  In cuntreis our allquhair.

9 mown] may well.
10 cowth ring] did reign. lusty laitis] comely mien. he] high. wynnit] dwelt. fold] earth. paramour] passionately.

Thair dwelt a lyt besyde the King
  A foull Gyand of ane;
Stollin he hes the Lady ying,
  Away with hir is gane,
And kest her in his dungering
  Quhair licht scho micht se nane;
Hungir and cauld and grit thristing
  Scho fand into hir wame.

He wes the laithliest on to luk
  That on the grund mycht gang:
His nailis wes lyk ane hellis cruk,
  Thairwith fyve quarteris lang;
Thair wes nane that he ourtuk,
  In rycht or yit in wrang,
Bot all in schondir he thame schuk,
  The Gyand wes so strang.

He held the Lady day and nycht
  Within his deip dungeoun,
He wald nocht gif of hir a sicht
  For gold nor yit ransoun—
Bot gif the King mycht get a knycht,
  To fecht with his persoun,
To fecht with him beth day and nycht,
  Quhill ane wer dungin doun.

The King gart seik baith fer and neir,
  Beth be se and land,
Off ony knycht gif he mycht heir
  Wald fecht with that Gyand:

foull of ane] most foul. fand into her wame] felt in her belly.
Bot gif] unless Quhill] until. gart] caused, ordered.

A worthy Prince, that had no peir,
  Hes tane the deid on hand
For the luve of the Lady cleir,
  And held full trew cunnand.

That Prince come prowdly to the toun
  Of that Gyand to heir,
And fawcht with him, his awin persoun,
  And tuke him presoneir,
And kest him in his awin dungeoun
  Allane withouttin feir,
With hungir, cauld, and confusioun,
  As full weill worthy weir.

Syne brak the bour, had hame the bricht
  Unto her fadir fre.
Sa evill wondit wes the Knycht
  That he behuvit to de;
Unlusum was his likame dicht,
  His sark was all bludy;
In all the world was thair a wicht
  So peteouss for to se?

The Lady murnyt and maid grit mane,
  With all her mekill mycht—
'I luvit nevir lufe bot ane,
  That dulfully now is dicht;
God sen my lyfe were fra me tane
  Or I had seen yone sicht,
Or ellis in begging evir to gane
  Furth with yone curtass knycht.'

cunnand] covenant. feir] companion. Syne] afterwards. behuvit] must needs. Unlusum] grievously. likame] body. God sen] would to God. Or] before.

He said 'Fair lady, now mone I
  De, trestly ye me trow;
Take ye my serk that is bludy,
  And hing it forrow yow;
First think on it, and syne on me,
  Quhen men cumis yow to wow.'
The Lady said 'Be Mary fre,
  Thairto I mak a vow.'

Quhen that scho lukit to the sark
  Scho thocht on the persoun,
And prayit for him with all hir hart
  That lowsd hir of bandoun,
Quhair scho was wont to sit full merk
  Into that deip dungeoun;
And evir quhill scho wes in quert,
  That was hir a lessoun.

Sa weill the Lady luvit the Knycht
  That no man wald scho tak:
Sa suld we do our God of micht
  That did all for us mak;
Quhilk fullily to deid was dicht,
  For sinfull manis sak,
Sa suld we do beth day and nycht,
  With prayaris to him mak.

This King is lyk the Trinitie,
  Baith in hevin and heir;
The manis saule to the Lady,
  The Gyand to Lucefeir,

mone] must. trestly] truly. of bandoun] from durance.
merk] in darkness. in quert] alive.

The Knycht to Chryst, that deit on tre
  And coft our synnis deir;
The pit to Hell with panis fell,
  The Syn to the woweir.

The Lady was wowd, but scho said nay
  With men that wald hir wed;
Sa suld we wryth all sin away
  That in our breist is bred.
I pray to Jesu Chryst verray,
  For us his blud that bled,
To be our help on domisday
  Quhair lawis ar straitly led.

The saule is Godis dochtir deir,
  And eik his handewerk,
That was betrayit with Lucefeir,
  Quha sittis in hell full merk:
Borrowit with Chrystis angell cleir,
  Hend men, will ye nocht herk?
And for his lufe that bocht us deir
  Think on the BLUDY SERK!

JOHN SKELTON

1460–1529

11 *Woefully Arrayed*

WOFULLY araid
  My blode man for thee ran,
It may not be naid;
My body blo and wan,
  Wofully araid.

10 coft] paid for. woweir] wooer. wryth] turn.
borrowit] redeemed. hend] gentle, courteous.
11 naid] denied blo] livid

Beholde me, I pray thee, with all thi hole reson,
And be not hard hartid, and for this encheson,
That I, for thi saule sake was slayne, in good seson,
Begylde and betraide by Iudas fals treson;
Vnkindly intretid,
With sharp corde sore fretid,
The Iues me thretid,
They mowid, they grynned, they scornyd,
Condemned to deth, as thou maist se.

Thus nakyd am I maked, O man, for thy sake!
I loue thee, then loue me. Why slepist thou? awake!
Remember my tender hart-rote for thee brake,
With paynes my veines constreyned to crake;
Thus was I defasid,
Thus was my flesh rasid,
And I to deth chasid.
Like a lambe led vnto sacrifice,
Slayne I was in most cruell wise.
Wofully araid.

Of sharpe thorne I haue worne a crowne on my hed,
So rubbid, so bobbid, so rufulle, so red,
Sore payned, sore strayned, and for thy loue ded,
Vnfayned, not deined, my blod for to shed,
My fete and handes sore
The sturdy nailis bore;
What myght I suffer more
Than I haue don, O man, for thee?
Cum when thou list, welcome to me.
Wofully araid.

encheson] cause, motive. intretid] treated. thretid] reproved. mowid] made grimaces at. bobbid] beaten.

Deyr brother, non other thyng of thee I desyre,
But geue me thi hert fre, to rewarde myne hire.
I am he that made thee erth, water and fire.
Sathanas, that slouen and right lothely sire,
Hym haue I ouer-caste,
In hell presoune bounde faste,
Wher ay his woo shall laste.
I haue puruaide a place full clere
For mankynde, whom I haue bought dere.

ANONYMOUS

? 15th Cent.

12 *Quia Amore Langueo*

IN the vale of restles mynd
I sowght in mownteyn and in mede,
trustyng a treulove for to fynd:
vpon an hyll than toke I hede;
a voice I herd (and nere I yede)
in gret dolour complaynyng tho,
'see, derë soule, my sydes blede
Quia amore langueo'.

Upon thys mownt I fand a tree;
undir thys tree a man sittyng;
frome hede to fote wowndyd was he,
hys hert blode I saw bledyng;
A semely man to be a kyng,
A graciose face to loke unto.
I askyd hym how he had paynyng,
he said, '*Quia amore langueo*'.

12 nere] nearer.

ANONYMOUS

I am treulove that fals was neuer;
        my sistur, mannys soule, I loued hyr thus;
By-cause I wold on no wyse dissevere,
    I left my kyngdome gloriouse;
    I purveyd hyr a place full preciouse;
        she flytt, I folowyd, I luved her soo;
    that I suffred thes paynès piteuouse
        Quia amore langueo.

My faire love and my spouse bryght,
        I saved hyr fro betyng, and she hath me bett;
I clothed hyr in grace and heuenly lyght,
    this blody surcote she hath on me sett;
    for langyng love, I will not lett,
        swetë strokys be thes, loo;
    I haf loved ever als I hett,
        Quia amore langueo.

I crownyd hyr with blysse and she me with thorne,
        I led hyr to chambre and she me to dye;
I browght hyr to worship and she me to skorne,
    I dyd hyr reverence and she me velanye.
    to love that loveth is no maistrye,
        hyr hate made never my love hyr foo;
    ask than no moo questions whye,
        but *Quia amore langueo.*

Loke vnto myn handys, man!
        thes gloues were geven me whan I hyr sowght;
they be nat white, but rede and wan,
    embrodred with blode my spouse them bowght;

flytt] fled.   hett] promised.

they wyll not of, I lefe them nowght,
    I wowe hyr with them where ever she goo;
thes handes full frendly for hyr fowght,
    Quia amore langueo.

Marvell not, man, thof I sitt styll,
    my love hath shod me wondyr strayte;
she boklyd my fete as was hyr wyll
  with sharp nailes, well thow maist waite!
  in my love was never dissaite,
    for all my membres I haf opynd hyr to;
  my body I made hyr hertys baite,
    Quia amore langueo.

In my syde I haf made hyr nest,
    loke in me, how wyde a wound is here!
this is hyr chambere, here shall she rest,
  that she and I may slepe in fere.
  here may she wasshe, if any filth were;
    here is socour for all hyr woo;
  cum if she will, she shall haf chere,
    Quia amore langueo.

I will abide till she be redy,
    I will to hyr send or she sey nay;
If she be rechelesse I will be redy,
  If she be dawngerouse I will hyr pray.
  If she do wepe, than byd I nay;
    myn armes ben spred to clypp hyr to;
  crye onys, 'I cum!' now, soule, assaye!
    Quia amore langueo.

baite] resting-place. in fere] together. dawngerouse] fastidious.

I sitt on an hille for to see farre,
I loke to the vale, my spouse I see;
now rynne she awayward, now cummyth she narre,
yet fro myn eye syght she may nat be;
sum waite ther pray, to make hyr flee,
I rynne tofore to chastise hyr foo;
recouer my soule agayne to me,
Quia amore langueo.

My swete spouse will we goo play;
apples ben rype in my gardine;
I shall clothe thee in new array,
thy mete shall be mylk, honye, and wyne;
now, dere soule, latt us go dyne,
thy sustenance is in my skrypp, loo!
tary now now, fayre spousë myne,
Quia amore langueo.

yf thow be fowle, I shall make thee clene,
if thow be seke, I shall thee hele;
yf thow owght morne, I shall thee mene,
spouse, why will thow nowght with me dele?
thow fowndyst neuer love so lele;
what wilt thow, sowle, that I shall do?
I may of unkyndnes thee appele,
Quia amore langueo.

What shall I do now with my spouse?
abyde I will hyre iantilnesse,
wold she loke onys owt of hyr howse
of flesshely affeccions and vnclennesse;

narre] nearer. mene] pity. appele] accuse. iantilness] waywardness.

hyr bed is made, hyr bolstar is in blysse,
hyr chambre is chosen, suche are no moo;
loke owt at the wyndows of kyndnesse,
Quia amore langueo.

Long and love thow neuer so hygh,
yit is my love more than thyn may be;
thow gladdyst, thow wepist, I sitt thee by,
yit myght thow, spouse, loke onys at me!
spouse, shuld I alway fedë the
with childys mete? nay, love, nat so!
I pray thee, love, with aduersite,
Quia amore langueo.

My spouse is in chambre, hald your pease!
make no noyse, but lat hyr slepe;
my babe shall sofre noo disease,
I may not here my dere childe wepe,
for with my pappe I shall hyr kepe;
ne wondyr thowgh I tend hyr to,
thys hoole in my side had neuer ben so depe,
but *Quia amore langueo.*

Wax not wery, myn owne dere wyfe,
what mede is aye to lyffe in comfort?
for in tribulacion, I ryñ more ryfe
ofter tymes than in disport;
In welth, in woo, euer I support;
than, derë soule, go neuer me fro!
thy mede is markyd, whan thow art mort,
in blysse; *Quia amore langueo.*

mort] dead.

15th Cent.

13 *Carol*

I SING of a maiden
  That is makeles;
King of all kings
  To her son she ches.

He came al so still
  There his mother was,
As dew in April
  That falleth on the grass.

He came al so still
  To his mother's bour,
As dew in April
  That falleth on the flour.

He came al so still
  There his mother lay,
As dew in April
  That falleth on the spray.

Mother and maiden
  Was never none but she;
Well may such a lady
  Goddes mother be.

15th Cent.

14 *Of a rose, a lovely rose,*
Of a rose is al myn song.

LESTENYT, lordynges, both elde and yinge,
  How this rose began to sprynge;
Swych a rose to myn lykynge
  In al this word ne knowe I non.

13 makeles] matchless. ches] chose.
14 lestenyt] listen. word] world.

ANONYMOUS

The aungil came fro hevene tour
To grete Marye with gret honour,
And seyde sche xuld bere the flour
        That xulde breke the fyndes bond.

The flour sprong in heye Bedlem,
That is bothe bryht and schen:
The rose is Mary, hevene qwyn,
        Out of here bosum the blosme sprong.

The ferste braunche is ful of myht,
That sprong on Crystemesse nyht,
The sterre schon over Bedlem bryht
        That is bothe brod and long.

The secunde braunche sprong to helle,
The fendys power doun to felle:
Therein myht non sowle dwelle;
        Blyssid be the time the rose sprong!

The thredde braunche is good and swote,
It sprang to hevene, crop and rote,
Therein to dwellyn and ben our bote;
        Every day it schewit in prystes hond.

Prey me to here with gret honour,
She that bar the blyssid flowr,
She be our helpe and our socour
        And schyld us fro the fyndes bond.

xuld] was to. fyndes] Devil's. schen] beautiful. bote] salvation.

15th Cent.

15

A Lyke-Wake Dirge

THIS ae nighte, this ae nighte,
—Every nighte and alle,
Fire and fleet and candle-lighte,
And Christe receive thy saule.

When thou from hence away art past,
—Every nighte and alle,
To Whinny-muir thou com'st at last;
And Christe receive thy saule.

If ever thou gavest hosen and shoon,
—Every nighte and alle,
Sit thee down and put them on;
And Christe receive thy saule.

If hosen and shoon thou ne'er gav'st nane
—Every nighte and alle,
The whinnes sall prick thee to the bare bane;
And Christe receive thy saule.

From Whinny-muir when thou may'st pass,
—Every nighte and alle,
To Brig o' Dread thou com'st at last;
And Christe receive thy saule.

From Brig o' Dread when thou may'st pass,
—Every nighte and alle,
To Purgatory fire thou com'st at last;
And Christe receive thy saule.

fleet] house-room.

If ever thou gavest meat or drink,
  —*Every nighte and alle,*
The fire sall never make thee shrink;
  And Christe receive thy saule.

If meat or drink thou ne'er gav'st nane,
  —*Every nighte and alle,*
The fire will burn thee to the bare bane;
  And Christe receive thy saule.

This ae nighte, this ae nighte,
  —*Every nighte and alle,*
Fire and fleet and candle-lighte,
  And Christe receive thy saule.

WILLIAM DUNBAR

1465?–1520?

16 *On the Nativity of Christ*

R*ORATE coeli desuper!*
  Hevins, distil your balmy schouris!
For now is risen the bricht day-ster,
  Fro the rose Mary, flour of flouris:
  The cleir Sone, quhom no cloud devouris,
Surmounting Phebus in the Est,
  Is cumin of his hevinly touris:
    Et nobis Puer natus est.

Archangellis, angellis, and dompnationis,
  Tronis, potestatis, and marteiris seir,
And all ye hevinly operationis,
  Ster, planeit, firmament, and spheir,

16 schouris] showers. cumin] come. seir] various.

WILLIAM DUNBAR

Fire, erd, air, and water cleir,
To Him gife loving, most and lest,
That come in to so meik maneir;
Et nobis Puer natus est.

Synnaris be glad, and penance do,
And thank your Maker hairtfully;
For he that ye micht nocht come to
To you is cumin full humbly
Your soulis with his blood to buy
And loose you of the fiendis arrest—
And only of his own mercy;
Pro nobis Puer natus est.

All clergy do to him inclyne,
And bow unto that bairn benyng,
And do your observance divyne
To him that is of kingis King:
Encense his altar, read and sing
In holy kirk, with mind degest,
Him honouring attour all thing
Qui nobis Puer natus est.

Celestial foulis in the air,
Sing with your nottis upon hicht,
In firthis and in forrestis fair
Be myrthful now at all your mycht;
For passit is your dully nicht,
Aurora has the cloudis perst,
The Son is risen with glaidsum licht,
Et nobis Puer natus est.

erd] earth. loving] praise. lest] least. in to] in. synnaris] sinners. benyng] benign. degest] settled. attour] over, above. perst] pierced.

Now spring up flouris fra the rute,
   Revert you upward naturaly,
In honour of the blissit frute
   That raiss up fro the rose Mary;
   Lay out your levis lustily,
Fro deid take life now at the lest
   In wirschip of that Prince worthy
      Qui nobis Puer natus est.

Sing, hevin imperial, most of hicht!
   Regions of air mak armony!
All fish in flud and fowl of flicht
   Be mirthful and mak melody!
   All *Gloria in excelsis* cry!
Heaven, erd, se, man, bird, and best,—
   He that is crownit abone the sky
      Pro nobis Puer natus est!

17 *Of the Resurrection of Christ*

DONE is a battell on the dragon blak,
   Our campioun Chryst confoundit hes his force;
The yettis of hell ar brokin with a crak,
   The signe triumphall rasit is of the croce,
   The diuillis trymmillis with hiddouss voce,
The saulis ar borrowit and to the bliss can go,
   Chryst with his blud our ransoms dois indoce:
Surrexit Dominus de sepulchro.

16 raiss] rose.   best] beast.
17 yettis] gates.   trymmillis] tremble.   borrowit] redeemed. indoce] endorse.

Dungin is the deidly dragon Lucifer,
  The crewall serpent with the mortall stang;
The auld kene tegir, with his teith on char,
  Quhilk in a wait hes lyne for so lang,
  Thinking to grip ws in his clowis strang;
The mercifull Lord wald nocht that it wer so,
  He maid him for to felye of that fang:
Surrexit Dominus de sepulchro.

He for our saik that sufferit to be slane,
  And lyk a lamb in sacrifice wes dicht,
Is lyk a lyone rissin up agane,
  And as a gyane raxit him on hicht;
  Sprungin is Aurora radius and bricht,
On loft is gone the glorius Apollo,
  The blisfull day departit fro the nycht:
Surrexit Dominus de sepulchro.

The grit victour agane is rissin on hicht,
  That for our querrell to the deth wes woundit;
The sone that wox all paill now schynis bricht,
  And dirknes clerit, our fayth is now refoundit,
  The knell of mercy fra the hevin is soundit,
The Cristin ar deliverit of thair wo,
  The Jowis and thair errour ar confoundit:
Surrexit Dominus de sepulchro.

The fo is chasit, the battell is done ceiss,
  The presone brokin, the jevellouris fleit and flemit;
The weir is gon, confermit is the peis,

dungin] struck down. stang] sting. on char] ajar, open. felye of that fang] fail (to obtain) that prize. raxit him on hicht] stretches himself up. jevellouris fleit and flemit] jailers put to flight and banished.

The fetteris lowsit and the dungeoun temit;
The ransoun maid, the presoneris redemit;
The feild is win, ourcumin is the fo,
Dispulit of the tresur that he yemit:
Surrexit Dominus de sepulchro.

GAVIN DOUGLAS

1474?–1522

18 *From the Prologue to the Tenth Book of the Aeneid*

FREND, farly nocht; na caus is to complene,
Albeit thy wyt gret God may nocht attene:
For, mycht thou comprehend be thyne engyne
The maist excellent maieste dyvyne,
He mycht be reput a pretty god and meyn.

Considir thy raison is so febill and lyte,
And hys knawlage profound and infynyte:
Considir quhon he is onmensurabill.
Hym as he is to knaw, thou art not habill;
It sufficis the beleif thy Creid perfyte.

God is, I grant, in all thing nocht includyt;
Gevis all gudnes, and is of nocht denudyt.
Of hym hes all thing part, and he nocht mynyst:
Hail he is, alquhar, not diuidit ne fynyst:
Without all thing he is, and nocht excludit.

17 temit] emptied. yemit] guarded.

18 farly] marvel. engyne] intelligence. lyte] small. perfyte] perfectly. mynyst] decreased. hail] whole. alquhar] everywhere. without] outside.

O Lord, thy ways beyn investigabill!
Sweit Lord, thy self is sa inestimabill
I can write nocht bot wondris of thy mycht
That lawyt sa far thy maieste and hyght,
To be born man intill ane oxis stabill.

Thou tuke mankynd of ane onwemmyt maid,
Inclosyt within a virginis bosum glaid,
Quham all the hevynys mycht nevir comprehend.
Angellis, scheiphyrdis, and kyngis thy Godheid kend,
Set thou in cryb betwix twa bestis was laid.

Quhat infynyte, excellent hie bonte
Abufe thy warkis, all in wonderfull gre!
Lord, quhen thou man wrocht, to thyne awyn ymage,
That tynt himself throu hys fulych dotage,
Thou man becam, and deit, to mak hym fre.

Maid thou not man first president vnder the,
To dant the bestis, fowlys, and fysch in see?
Subdewit to him the erth and all tharin?
Syne paradice grantit hym and all his kyn,
Gave him fre will, and power nevir to dee?

Enarmyt him with raison and prudence,
Only bad hym kepe thyne obediens,
And to hym suld all creatouris obey?
Bittir was that fruyt for his ofspryng, and fey,
Maid deth onknawin be fund, and lyfe go hens.

lawyt] didst humble. onwemmyt] spotless. kend] recognized. set] although. gre] degree. tynt] ruined. syne] and then. fey] accursed.

O thyne inestimabill luf and cheryte!
Becam a thrall, to mak ws bondis fre;
To quykkyn thy sclavys, tholyt schamfull ded maste fell.
Blissyt be thou, virginal frute, that hereit hell,
And pait the pryce of the forbodin tre!

Thocht thou large stremys sched apon the rude,
A drop had bene sufficient of thy blude
A thousand warldis to have redemyt, I grant;
Bot thou the well of mercy wald nocht skant,
Ws to provoik to lufe the, and be gude.

Our all this, syne, thyne infynyte Godhed,
Thy flesch and blude, in form of wyne and bred,
To be our fuyd of grace, in plege of glor
Thou hest ws geif, in perpetuall memor
Of thy passioun and dolorus paynfull ded.

Quhat thankis dew, or ganȝeld, Lord benyng,
May I, maist wrachit synfull catyve indyng,
Rendir for this souerane peirles hie bonte,
Sen body, saule, and all, I have of the?
Thou art my pryce: mak me thy praye condyng.

My makar, my redemar, and support,
Fra quham all grace and gudness cumis, at schort,
Grant me that grace my mysdedys til amend,
Of this and all my warkis to mak gud end:
Thus I beseik the, Lord; thus I exort,

bondis] bondmen. tholyt] endured. ded] death. hereit] harrowed, despoiled. thocht] though. our] over, besides. ganȝeld] recompense. indyng] unworthy. pryce] prize. til] to.

From the begynyng and end be thow my muse:
All other, Jove and Phebus, I refus.
Lat Virgill hald hys mawmentis to himself:
I wirschip nowder ydoll, stok, nor elf.
Thocht furth I write so as myne autour dois.

Is nane bot thou, the Fader of goddis and men,
Omnipotent, eternal Jove, I ken:
Only the, helply Fader; thar is nane other:
I compt not of thir paygane goddis a fudder,
Quhais power may nocht help a haltand hen.

The Scripture clepys the God, of goddis Lord;
For quha thy mandat kepys in ane accord
Bene ane with the, not in substans, bot grace,
And we our Fader the clepys in euery place:
Mak ws thy sonnys in cherite, but discord.

Thow haldis court our cristall hevynys cleir,
With angellis, sanctis, and hevynly spretis seir,
That but cessyng thy glor and lovyng syngis.
Manifest to the and patent bene all thyngis;
Thy spow and queyn maid, and thy moder deir.

Concord for evir, myrth, rest, and endles blys,
Na feir of hell, nor dreid of ded, thar is
In thy sweit realm, nor na kynd of ennoy,
Bot all weilfair, eys, and euerlestand joy,
Quhais hie plesance, Lord, lat ws neuer mys! Amen.

mawmentis] false gods. thir] those. fudder] load, 'lot.' haltand] lame. clepys] call. but] without. seir] various.

ANONYMOUS

15th–16th Cent.

19 *Mary Modyr, cum and see*

'MARY modyr, cum and se:
  Thi Son is naylyd on a tre.

'His body is wappyd all in wo,
Hand and fot; he may not go;
Thi Son, lady, that thou louyst soo,
  Nakyd is naylyd vpon a tre.

'The blyssyd body that thou hast born
To saue mankynd, that was forlorn,
His body, lady, is al to-torn,
  His hed with thornys, as ye may se.'

Wan Johan this tal began to tell,
Mary wyld not lenger dwell
Tyl sche cam to that hyll
  Ther sche myht her owyn Son see.

'My swet Son, thou art me der;
Qwy haue men hang the her?
Thi hed is closyd wyth a brer;
  Qwy haue men soo doo to the?'

'Johan, this woman I the betake;
Kep this woman for my sake;
On the rod I hyng for mannys sake,
  For synful man, as thou may se.

wappyd] wrapped. closyd wyth a brer] enclosed in a (crown of) thorn. betake] commit.

'This game and loue me must pley
For synfull sowlis that ar to dey;
Ther ys no man that gothe be the wey
That on my peynis wyl lok and se.

'Fadyr, my sowle I the betake;
My body deth for mannys sake;
To hel I go withowtyn wake,
Mannys sole to make fre.'

Prey we al to that blyssyd Son
That he vs help wan we not mon,
And bryng us to blys that is abone.
Amen, amen, amen, for charite.

20 *Saint Stephen and King Herod*

15th Cent.

SEYNT STEVENE was a clerk in Kyng Herowdes halle,
And servyd him of bred and cloth, as every kyng befalle.

Stevyn out of kechone cam, wyth boris hed on honde;
He saw a sterre was fayr and bryht over Bedlem stonde.

He kyst adoun the boris hed and went into the halle.
'I forsak the, Kyng Herowdes, and thi werkes alle.

I forsak the, Kyng Herowdes, and thi werkes alle;
Ther is a chyld in Bedlem born is beter than we alle.'

19 wake] trace (?). we not mon] we may not (help ourselves). abone] above.

20 kyst] cast.

'Quat eylyt the, Stevene? quat is the befalle?
Lakkyt the eyther mete or drynk in Kyng Herowdes halle?'

'Lakit me neyther mete ne drynk in Kyng Herowdes hall;
Ther is a chyld in Bedlem born is beter than we alle.'

'Quat eylyt the, Stevyn? art thu wod, or thu gynnyst to brede?
Lakkyt the eyther gold or fe, or ony ryche wede?'

'Lakyt me neyther gold ne fe, ne non ryche wede;
Ther is a chyld in Bedlem born schal helpyn us at our nede.'

'That is al so soth, Stevyn, al so soth, iwys,
As this capoun crowe schal that lyth here in myn dysh.'

That word was not so sone seyd, that word in that halle,
The capoun crew *Cristus natus est!* among the lordes alle.

'Rysyt up, myn turmentowres, be to and als be on
And ledyt Stevyn out of this town, and stonyt hym wyth ston!'

Tokyn he Stevene, and stonyd hym in the way,
And therfore is his evyn on Crystes owyn day.

21 *The Falcon*

15th Cent.

LULLY, lulley; lully, lulley;
The fawcon hath born my mak away.

He bare hym vp, he bare hym down;
He bare hym into an orchard brown.

20 wod] mad. brede] start out of your mind. schal] shall. be to and als be on] as one man.
21 mak] mate.

In that orchard ther was an hall,
That was hangid with purpill and pall.

And in that hall ther was a bede;
Hit was hangid with gold so rede.

And yn that bed ther lythe a knyght,
His wowndes bledyng day and nyght.

By that bedes side ther kneleth a may,
And she wepeth both nyght and day.

And by that beddes side ther stondith a ston,
'Corpus Christi' wretyn theron.

22 *Here I Sit Alone*

15th Cent.

AS I walked me this endurs day
to the grene wode for to play
and all hevyness to put away
my-self alone.

As I walkyd vndir the grene wode bowe
I sawe a maide fayre i-now;
a child she heppid, she song, she lough—
that child wepid alone.

'Son,' she sayd, 'I have thee borne
to save mankynd that was forlorne;
therfor I pray thee, son, ne morne,
but be still alone.'

'Moder, me thynkith it is ryȝt ill
that men sekyth for to spill.
for them to save it is my will;
therfor I cam hither alone.'

lough] laughed. spill] kill, destroy.

'Sone,' she sayd, 'let it be in thi thought,
for mannys gilt is not with sought;
for thu art he that hath all wrought,
and I thi moder alone.'

23 *God be in my Head*

16th Cent.

GOD be in my head,
And in my understanding;
God be in mine eyes,
And in my looking;
God be in my mouth
And in my speaking;
God be in my heart,
And in my thinking;
God be at my end and at my departing.

24 *The Holly and the Ivy*

16th Cent.

THE holly and the ivy,
When they are both full grown,
Of all the trees that are in the wood,
The holly bears the crown:

The rising of the sun
And the running of the deer,
The playing of the merry organ,
Sweet singing in the choir.

The holly bears a blossom,
As white as the lily flower,
And Mary bore sweet Jesus Christ
To be our sweet Saviour:

The holly bears a berry,
As red as any blood,
And Mary bore sweet Jesus Christ
To do poor sinners good:

The holly bears a prickle,
As sharp as any thorn,
And Mary bore sweet Jesus Christ
On Christmas day in the morn:

The holly bears a bark,
As bitter as any gall,
And Mary bore sweet Jesus Christ
For to redeem us all:

The holly and the ivy,
When they are both full grown,
Of all the trees that are in the wood,
The holly bears the crown:

25 *The Cherry-tree Carol*

16th Cent.

JOSEPH was an old man,
And an old man was he,
When he wedded Mary
In the land of Galilee.

Joseph and Mary walked
Through an orchard good,
Where was cherries and berries
As red as any blood.

ANONYMOUS

Joseph and Mary walked
  Through an orchard green,
Where was berries and cherries
  As thick as might be seen.

O then bespoke Mary,
  With words so meek and mild,
'Pluck me one cherry, Joseph,
  For I am with child.'

O then bespoke Joseph,
  With answer most unkind,
'Let him pluck thee a cherry
  That brought thee now with child.'

O then bespoke the baby
  Within his mother's womb—
'Bow down then the tallest tree
  For my mother to have some.'

Then bowed down the highest tree,
  Unto his mother's hand.
Then she cried, 'See, Joseph,
  I have cherries at command.'

O then bespake Joseph—
  'I have done Mary wrong;
But now cheer up, my dearest,
  And do not be cast down.

'O eat your cherries, Mary,
  O eat your cherries now,
O eat your cherries, Mary,
  That grow upon the bough.'

Then Mary plucked a cherry,
  As red as any blood;
Then Mary she went homewards
  All with her heavy load.

As Joseph was a-walking,
  He heard an angel sing:
'This night there shall be born
  On earth our heavenly King;

'He neither shall be born
  In housen nor in hall,
Nor in the place of Paradise,
  But in an ox's stall.

'He neither shall be clothèd
  In purple nor in pall,
But all in fair linen
  As wear the babies all.

'He neither shall be rockèd
  In silver nor in gold,
But in a wooden cradle
  That rocks upon the mould.

'He neither shall be christened
  In white wine nor red,
But with fair spring water
  As we were christenéd.'

Then Mary took her young son,
  And set him on her knee:
Saying, 'My dear son, tell me,
  Tell how this world shall be.'

mould] ground.

'O I shall be as dead, mother,
As stones are in the wall;
O the stones in the streets, mother,
Shall sorrow for me all.

'On Easter-day, dear mother,
My rising up shall be;
O the sun and the moon, mother,
Shall both arise with me.'

26 *I saw Three Ships*

16th Cent.

I SAW three ships come sailing in,
On Christmas Day, on Christmas Day,
I saw three ships come sailing in,
On Christmas Day in the morning.
And what was in those ships all three?
Our Saviour Christ and his lady.
Pray, whither sailed those ships all three?
O, they sailed into Bethlehem.
And all the bells on earth shall ring,
And all the angels in Heaven shall sing,
And all the souls on earth shall sing.
Then let us all rejoice amain!

27 *The Holy Well*

16th Cent.

AS it fell out one May morning,
And upon a bright holiday,
Sweet Jesus asked of his dear mother
If he might go to play.

ANONYMOUS

'To play, to play, sweet Jesus shall go,
  And to play now get you gone;
And let me hear of no complaint
  At night when you come home.'

Sweet Jesus went down to yonder town,
  As far as the Holy Well,
And there did see as fine childrén
  As any tongue can tell.
He said, 'God bless you every one,
  And your bodies Christ save and see!
And now, little children, I'll play with you,
  And you shall play with me.'

But they made answer to him, 'No!
  Thou art meaner than us all;
Thou art but a simple fair maid's child,
  Born in an ox's stall.'
Sweet Jesus turned him round about,
  Neither laughed, nor smiled, nor spoke;
But the tears came trickling from his eyes
  Like waters from the rock.

Sweet Jesus turned him round about,
  To his mother's dear home went he,
And said, 'I have been in yonder town,
  As after you may see:
I have been down in yonder town,
  As far as the Holy Well;
There did I meet with as fine childrén
  As any tongue can tell.

'I said, "God bless you every one,
  And your bodies Christ save and see!
And now, little children, I'll play with you,
  And you shall play with me."
But they made answer to me "No";
  They were lords' and ladies' sons,
And I the meanest of them all,
  Born in an ox's stall.'

'Though you are but a maiden's child,
  Born in an ox's stall,
Thou art the Christ, the King of Heaven,
  And the Saviour of them all!
Sweet Jesus, go down to yonder town,
  As far as the Holy Well,
And take away those sinful souls,
  And dip them deep in hell.'

'Nay, nay,' sweet Jesus smiled and said;
  'Nay, nay, that may not be,
For there are too many sinful souls
  Crying out for the help of me.'
Then up spoke the angel Gabriel,
  Upon a good set steven,
'Although you are but a maiden's child,
  You are the King of Heaven!'

28 *The Seven Virgins* 16th Cent.

ALL under the leaves, the leaves of life,
  I met with virgins seven,
And one of them was Mary mild,
  Our Lord's mother from heaven.

upon a good set steven] in a firm voice.

ANONYMOUS

'O what are you seeking, you seven fair maids,
  All under the leaves of life?
Come tell, come tell me what seek you
  All under the leaves of life.'

'We're seeking for no leaves, Thomas,
  But for a friend of thine;
We're seeking for sweet Jesus Christ,
  To be our guide and thine.'

'Go you down, go you down to yonder town,
  And sit in the gallery;
And there you'll find sweet Jesus Christ,
  Nailed to a big yew-tree.'

So down they went to yonder town,
  As fast as foot could fall,
And many a grievous bitter tear,
  From the virgins' eyes did fall.

'O peace, mother, O peace, mother,
  Your weeping doth me grieve;
O I must suffer this,' he said,
  'For Adam and for Eve.'

'O how can I my weeping leave,
  Or my sorrows undergo,
Whilst I do see my own Son die,
  When sons I have no mo?'

'Dear mother, dear mother, you must take John,
  All for to be your son,
And he will comfort you sometimes,
  Mother, as I have done.'

'O, come, thou John Evangelist,
  Thou'rt welcome unto me,
But more welcome my own dear son,
  That I nursed upon my knee.'

Then he laid his head on his right shoulder,
  Seeing death it struck him nigh:
'The Holy Ghost be with your soul,—
  I die, mother dear, I die.'

Oh the rose, the rose, the gentle rose,
  And the fennel that grows so green!
God give us grace in every place,
  To pray for our king and queen.

Furthermore for our enemies all
  Our prayers they should be strong.
Amen, Good Lord! your charity
  Is the ending of my song.

WILLIAM BALDWIN

fl. 1547

29 *Christ, my beloved*

CHRIST, my Beloved which still doth feed
  Among the flowers, having delight
    Among his faithful lilies,
Doth take great care for me indeed,
  And I again with all my might
    Will do what so his will is.

My Love in me and I in him,
  Conjoined by love, who still abide
    Among the faithful lilies
Till day do break, and truth do dim
  All shadows dark and cause them slide,
    According as his will is.

WILLIAM BALDWIN

30 *Christ to his Spouse*

LO, thou, my love, art fair;
Myself hath made thee so:
Yea, thou art fair indeed,
Wherefore thou shalt not need
In beauty to despair;
For I accept thee so,
For fair.

For fair, because thine eyes
Are like the culvers' white,
Whose simpleness in deed
All others do exceed:
Thy judgement wholly lies
In true sense of sprite
Most wise.

JAMES, JOHN, AND ROBERT WEDDERBURN

c. 1567

31 *Balulalow*

O MY deir hert, young Jesus sweit,
Prepare thy creddil in my spreit,
And I sall rock thee in my hert
And never mair from thee depart.

But I sall praise thee evermoir
With sangis sweit unto thy gloir;
The knees of my hert sall I bow,
And sing that richt *Balulalow!*

30 culvers] doves. 31 spreit] spirit.

RICHARD STANYHURST

1547–1618

32 *To the Trinity*

TRINITY blessed, deity coequal,
 Unity sacred, God one eke in essence,
Yield to thy servant, pitifully calling
 Merciful hearing.

Virtuous living did I long relinquish,
Thy will and precepts miserably scorning,
Grant to me, sinful patient, repenting,
 Healthful amendment.

Blessed I judge him, that in heart is healed:
Cursed I know him, that in health is harmed:
Thy physic therefore, to me, wretch unhappy,
 Send, my Redeemer.

Glory to God, the Father, and his only
Son, the protector of us earthly sinners,
The sacred spirit, labourers refreshing,
 Still be renowned. Amen.

EDMUND SPENSER

1552–1599

33

AND is there care in heaven? and is there love
 In heavenly spirits to these creatures base,
That may compassion of their evils move?
There is: else much more wretched were the case

Of men, than beasts. But O, th'exceeding grace
Of highest God, that loves his creatures so,
And all his workes with mercy doth embrace,
That blessed Angels he sends to and fro,
To serve to wicked man, to serve his wicked foe.

How oft do they their silver bowers leave,
To come to succour us, that succour want?
How oft do they with golden pineons, cleave
The flitting skys, like flying Pursuivant,
Against foul fiends to aid us militant?
They for us fight, they watch and duely ward,
And their bright Squadrons round about us plant,
And all for love, and nothing for reward:
O why should heavenly God to men have such regard?

34 *Mutability*

WHEN I bethink me on that speech whilere,
Of *Mutability*, and well it weigh:
Me seems, that though she all unworthy were
Of the Heav'ns Rule; yet very sooth to say,
In all things else she bears the greatest sway.
Which makes me loathe this state of life so tickle,
And love of things so vain to cast away;
Whose flow'ring pride, so fading and so fickle,
Short *Time* shall soon cut down with his consuming sickle.

Then gin I think on that which Nature said.
Of that same time when no more *Change* shall be,
But steadfast rest of all things firmly stayed
Vpon the pillars of Eternity,

tickle] insecure.

That is contrare to *Mutability:*
For, all that moveth, doth in *Change* delight:
But thence-forth all shall rest eternally
With Him that is the God of Sabbaoth hight:
O that great Sabbaoth God, grant me that Sabbaoth's sight.

35 *Amoretti. Sonnet lxviii*

MOST glorious Lord of life, that on this day,
didst make thy triumph over death and sin:
and having harrowed hell, didst bring away
captivity thence captive us to win:
This ioyous day, dear Lord, with ioy begin,
and grant that we for whom thou diddest die
being with thy dear blood clean washed from sin,
may live for ever in felicity.
And that thy love we weighing worthily,
may likewise love thee for the same again:
and for thy sake that all like dear didst buy,
with love may one another entertain.
So let us love, dear love, like as we ought,
love is the lesson which the Lord us taught.

HUMFREY GIFFORD

fl. 1580

36 *A Prayer*

O MIGHTY God, Which for us men
Didst suffer on the Cross
The painful pangs of bitter death,
To save our souls from loss,

hight] is called.

HUMFREY GIFFORD

I yield thee here most hearty thanks,
  In that thou dost vouchsafe,
Of me most vile and sinful wretch,
  So great regard to have.
Alas, none ever had more cause
  To magnify thy name,
Than I, to whom thy mercies shew'd
  Do witness well the same.
So many brunts of fretting foes
  Who ever could withstand,
If thou had'st not protected me,
  With thy most holy hand?
A thousand times in shameful sort
  My sinful life had ended,
If by thy gracious goodness, Lord,
  I had not been defended.
In stinking pools of filthy vice
  So deeply was I drown'd,
That none there was but thee alone,
  To set my foot on ground.
When as the fiend had led my soul
  E'en to the gates of hell,
Thou call'dst me back, and dost me choose
  In heaven with thee to dwell:—
Let furies now fret on their fill,
  Let Satan rage, and roar,
As long as thou art on my side,
  What need I care for more?

brunts] assaults.

SIR WALTER RALEGH

1552?–1618

37 *The Passionate Man's Pilgrimage*

Supposed to be written by One at the Point of Death

GIVE me my scallop shell of quiet,
My staff of faith to walk upon,
My scrip of joy, immortal diet,
My bottle of salvation:
My gown of glory, hope's true gage,
And thus i'll take my pilgrimage.

Blood must be my body's balmer,
No other balm will there be given,
Whilst my soul like a white Palmer
Travels to the land of heaven,
Over the silver mountains,
Where spring the Nectar fountains;
And there i'll kiss
The bowl of bliss,
And drink my eternal fill
On every milken hill.
My soule will be a-dry before,
But after it, will ne'er thirst more.

And by the happy blisful way
More peaceful pilgrims I shall see,
That have shook off their gowns of clay,
And go apparelled fresh like me.
I'll bring them first
To slake their thirst,

And then to tast those nectar suckets
At the clear wells
Where sweetness dwells,
Drawn up by Saints in crystal buckets.

And when our bottles and all we,
Are filled with immortality:
Then the holy paths we'll travel
Strewed with rubies thick as gravel,
Ceilings of diamonds, saphire floors,
High walls of coral and pearl bowers.

From thence to heaven's bribeless hall
Where no corrupted voices brawl,
No conscience molten into gold,
Nor forg'd accusers bought and sold,
No cause deferd, nor vain spent jorney,
For there Christ is the King's Attourney:
Who pleads for all without degrees,
And he hath Angels, but no fees.

When the grand twelve million jury,
Of our sinns with sinful fury,
Gainst our souls black verdicts give,
Christ pleads his death, and then we live,
Be thou my speaker, taintless pleader,
Unblotted lawyer, true proceeder,
Thou movest salvation even for alms:
Not with a bribèd lawyers palms.

And this is my eternal plea,
To him that made heaven, earth and sea,
Seeing my flesh must die so soon,
And want a head to dine next noon,

Just at the stroke when my veins start and spread
Set on my soul an everlasting head.
Then am I ready like a palmer fit,
To tread those blest paths which before I writ.

38 *The Author's Epitaph, made by Himselfe*

EVEN such is Time, which takes in trust
Our youth, our joys, and all we have,
And pays us but with age and dust,
Who in the dark and silent grave,
When we have wandered all our ways,
Shuts up the story of our days:
And from which earth, and grave, and dust,
The Lord shall raise me up I trust.

FULKE GREVILLE, LORD BROOKE

1554–1628

39 *Caelica*

LXXXVIII

WHENAS man's life, the light of human lust,
In socket of his earthly lantern burns,
That all his glory unto ashes must:
And generations to corruption turns;
Then fond desires that only fear their end,
Do vainly wish for life, but to amend.

But when this life is from the body fled,
To see itself in that eternal glass,
Where Time doth end, and thoughts accuse the dead,
Where all to come is one with all that was;
Then living men ask how he left his breath,
That while he livèd never thought of death.

FULKE GREVILLE, LORD BROOKE

40 *Caelica*

XCVIII

ETERNAL Truth, almighty, infinite,
Only exilèd from man's fleshly heart,
Where Ignorance and Disobedience fight,
In hell and sin, which shall have greatest part:
When thy sweet mercy opens forth the light,
Of grace, which giveth eyes unto the blind,
And with the Law even ploughest up our sprite
To faith, wherein flesh may salvation find:
Thou bidst us pray, and we do pray to thee,
But as to power and God without us plac'd,
Thinking a wish may wear out vanity,
Or habits be by miracles defac'd:
One thought to God we give, the rest to sin;
Quickly unbent is all desire of good;
True words pass out, but have no being within,
We pray to Christ, yet help to shed His blood;
For while we say 'believe', and feel it not,
Promise amends, and yet despair in it,
Hear Sodom judged, and go not out with Lot,
Make Law and Gospels riddles of the wit:
We with the Jews even Christ still crucify,
As not yet come to our impiety.

41 *Caelica*

XCIX

WRAPP'D up, O Lord, in man's degeneration
The glories of Thy truth, Thy joys eternal,
Reflect upon my soul's dark desolation.
And ugly prospects o'er the spirits infernal.

'Lord, I have sinn'd, and mine iniquity,
'Deserves this Hell; yet Lord deliver me.'

Thy power and mercy never comprehended,
Rest lively imag'd in my conscience wounded;
Mercy to grace, and power to fear extended,
Both infinite, and I in both confounded;
'Lord, I have sinn'd, and mine iniquity,
'Deserves this hell; yet Lord deliver me.'

If from this depth of sin, this hellish grave,
And fatal absence from my Saviour's glory,
I could implore His mercy Who can save,
And for my sins, not pains of sin, be sorry:
Lord from this horror of iniquity,
And hellish grave, Thou wouldst deliver me.

42 *Caelica*

CIV

O FALSE and treacherous Probability,
Enemy of truth, and friend to wickedness
With whose blear eyes Opinion learns to see,
Truth's feeble party here, and barrenness.
When thou hast thus misled Humanity,
And lost obedience in the pride of wit,
With reason dar'st thou judge the Deity,
And in thy flesh make bold to fashion it.

Vain thought, the word of Power a riddle is,
And till the vails be rent, the flesh new-born
Reveals no wonders of that inward bliss,
Which but where faith is, everywhere finds scorn;
'Who therefore censures God with fleshly sp'rit
'As well in time may wrap up infinite.'

43

Caelica

CX

SION lies waste, and Thy Jerusalem,
O Lord, is fallen to utter desolation;
Against thy prophets and thy holy men,
The sin hath wrought a fatal combination;
Profaned thy name, thy worship overthrown,
And made thee, living Lord, a God unknown.

Thy powerful laws, thy wonders of creation,
Thy word incarnate, glorious heaven, dark hell,
Lie shadowed under man's degeneration;
Thy Christ still crucified for doing well;
Impiety, O Lord, sits on thy throne,
Which makes thee, living Lord, a God unknown.

Man's superstition hath thy truth entombed,
His atheism again her pomps defaceth;
That sensual unsatiable vast womb
Of thy seen Church, thy unseen Church disgraceth;
There lives no truth with them that seem thine own,
Which make thee, living Lord, a God unknown.

Yet unto thee, Lord—mirror of transgression—
We who for earthly idols have forsaken
Thy heavenly image—sinless, pure impression—
And so in nets of vanity lie taken,
All desolate implore that to thine own,
Lord, thou no longer live a God unknown.

Yet, Lord, let Israel's plagues not be eternal,
Nor sin for ever cloud thy sacred mountains,
Nor with false flames spiritual but infernal,
Dry up thy Mercy's ever springing fountains:
  Rather, sweet Jesus, fill up time and come,
  To yield the sin her everlasting doom.

SIR PHILIP SIDNEY

1554–1586

44 *Leave me O Love*

LEAVE me, O Love, which reachest but to dust,
  And thou, my mind, aspire to higher things!
Grow rich in that which never taketh rust:
Whatever fades, but fading pleasure brings.
Draw in thy beams, and humble all thy might
To that sweet yoke where lasting freedoms be;
Which breaks the clouds and opens forth the light
That doth both shine and give us sight to see.
O take fast hold! let that light be thy guide
In this small course which birth draws out to death,
And think how evil becometh him to slide
Who seeketh Heaven, and comes of heavenly breath.
  Then farewell, world! thy uttermost I see:
  Eternal Love, maintain thy life in me!

ROBERT SOUTHWELL

c. 1561–1595

45 *The Burning Babe*

AS I in hoary winter's night stood shivering in the snow,
  Surprised I was with sudden heat which made my heart to glow;
And lifting up a fearful eye to view what fire was near,
A pretty Babe all burning bright did in the air appear;

Who, scorched with excessive heat, such floods of tears did
 shed,
As though his floods should quench his flames which with his
 tears were fed.
'Alas!' quoth he, 'but newly born in fiery heats I fry,
Yet none approach to warm their hearts or feel my fire but I.
My faultless breast the furnace is, the fuel wounding thorns;
Love is the fire, and sighs the smoke, the ashes shame and
 scorns;
The fuel justice layeth on, and mercy blows the coals;
The metal in this furnace wrought are men's defiled souls:
For which, as now on fire I am to work them to their good,
So will I melt into a bath to wash them in my blood.'
With this he vanished out of sight and swiftly shrunk away,
And straight I called unto mind that it was Christmas day.

46 *A Child my Choice*

LET folly praise that fancy loves, I praise and love that
 Child
Whose heart no thought, Whose tongue no word, Whose
 hand no deed defiled.
I praise Him most, I love Him best, all praise and love is His;
While Him I love, in Him I live, and cannot live amiss.
Love's sweetest mark, laud's highest theme, man's most
 desired light,
To love Him life, to leave Him death, to live in Him de-
 light.
He mine by gift, I His by debt, thus each to other due,
First friend He was, best friend He is, all times will try Him
 true.

46 that] what.

Though young, yet wise, though small, yet strong; though man, yet God He is;
As wise He knows, as strong He can, as God He loves to bliss.
His knowledge rules, His strength defends, His love doth cherish all;
His birth our joy, His life our light, His death our end of thrall.
Alas! He weeps, He sighs, He pants, yet do His angels sing;
Out of His tears, His sighs and throbs, doth bud a joyful spring.
Almighty Babe, Whose tender arms can force all foes to fly,
Correct my faults, protect my life, direct me when I die!

47 *Times go by Turns*

THE lopped tree in time may grow again,
Most naked plants renew both fruit and flower;
The sorriest wight may find release of pain,
The driest soil suck in some moistening shower.
Times go by turns, and chances change by course,
From foul to fair, from better hap to worse.

The sea of Fortune doth not ever flow,
She draws her favours to the lowest ebb;
Her tides hath equal times to come and go,
Her loom doth weave the fine and coarsest web.
No joy so great but runneth to an end,
No hap so hard but may in fine amend.

Not always fall of leaf, nor ever spring,
No endless night, yet not eternal day;
The saddest birds a season find to sing,
The roughest storm a calm may soon allay.
Thus, with succeeding turns, God tempereth all,
That man may hope to rise, yet fear to fall.

47 in fine] at last.

A chance may win that by mischance was lost;
The net, that holds no great, takes little fish;
In some things all, in all things none are crossed;
Few all they need, but none have all they wish.
Unmeddled joys here to no man befall;
Who least, hath some; who most, hath never all.

48 *Before my Face the Picture hangs*

BEFORE my face the picture hangs,
That daily should put me in mind
Of those cold qualms and bitter pangs,
That shortly I am like to find:
But yet, alas, full little I
Do think hereon that I must die.

I often look upon a face
Most ugly, grisly, bare, and thin;
I often view the hollow place,
Where eyes and nose had sometimes been;
I see the bones across that lie,
Yet little think that I must die.

I read the label underneath,
That telleth me whereto I must;
I see the sentence eke that saith
'Remember, man, that thou art dust!'
But yet, alas, but seldom I
Do think indeed that I must die.

Continually at my bed's head
A hearse doth hang, which doth me tell,
That I ere morning may be dead,
Though now I feel myself full well:

47 that] that which.

But yet, alas, for all this, I
Have little mind that I must die.

The gown which I do use to wear,
The knife wherewith I cut my meat,
And eke that old and ancient chair
Which is my only usual seat;
All these do tell me I must die,
And yet my life amend not I.

My ancestors are turned to clay,
And many of my mates are gone;
My youngers daily drop away,
And can I think to 'scape alone?
No, no, I know that I must die,
And yet my life amend not I.

Not Solomon, for all his wit,
Nor Samson, though he were so strong,
No king nor person ever yet
Could 'scape, but death laid him along:
Wherefore I know that I must die,
And yet my life amend not I.

Though all the East did quake to hear
Of Alexander's dreadful name,
And all the West did likewise fear
To hear of Julius Caesar's fame,
Yet both by death in dust now lie.
Who then can 'scape, but he must die?

If none can 'scape death's dreadful dart,
  If rich and poor his beck obey,
If strong, if wise, if all do smart,
  Then I to 'scape shall have no way.
    Oh! grant me grace, O God, that I
    My life may mend, sith I must die.

49 *Come to your Heaven, you heavenly Choirs!*

COME to your heaven, you heavenly choirs!
  Earth hath the heaven of your desires;
Remove your dwelling to your God,
A stall is now his best abode;
Sith men their homage do deny,
Come, angels, all their fault supply.

His chilling cold doth heat require,
Come, seraphins, in lieu of fire;
This little ark no cover hath,
Let cherubs' wings his body swathe;
Come, Raphael, this Babe must eat,
Provide our little Toby meat.

Let Gabriel be now his groom,
That first took up his earthly room;
Let Michael stand in his defence,
Whom love hath linked to feeble sense;
Let graces rock when he doth cry,
And angels sing his lullaby.

sith] since.

The same you saw in heavenly seat,
Is he that now sucks Mary's teat;
Agnize your King a mortal wight,
His borrowed weed lets not your sight;
Come, kiss the manger where he lies,
That is your bliss above the skies.

This little Babe, so few days old,
Is come to rifle Satan's fold;
All hell doth at his presence quake,
Though he himself for cold do shake;
For in this weak unarmed wise
The gates of hell he will surprise.

With tears he fights and wins the field,
His naked breast stands for a shield;
His battering shot are babish cries,
His arrows looks of weeping eyes,
His martial ensigns cold and need,
And feeble flesh his warrior's steed.

His camp is pitched in a stall,
His bulwark but a broken wall;
The crib his trench, hay-stalks his stakes,
Of shepherds he his muster makes;
And thus, as sure his foe to wound,
The angels' trumps alarum sound.

My soul, with Christ join thou in fight;
Stick to the tents that he hath pight;
Within his crib is surest ward,
This little Babe will be thy guard;
If thou wilt foil thy foes with joy,
Then flit not from this heavenly boy.

MARY HERBERT, COUNTESS OF PEMBROKE

1561–1621

50

Psalm 139

O LORD, in me there lieth nought
But to thy search revealed lies;
For when I sit
Thou markest it;
No less thou notest when I rise;
Yea, closest closet of my thought
Hath open windows to thine eyes.

Thou walkest with me when I walk;
When to my bed for rest I go,
I find thee there
And everywhere;
Not youngest thought in me doth grow,
No, not one word I cast to talk,
But, yet unuttered, thou dost know.

If forth I march, thou goest before;
If back I turn, thou comest behind;
So forth nor back
Thy guard I lack;
Nay, on me too thy hand I find.
Well I thy wisdom may adore,
But never reach with earthy mind.

To shun thy notice, leave thine eye,
O! whither might I take my way?
To starry sphere?
Thy throne is there.
To dead men's undelightsome stay?
There is thy walk, and there to lie
Unknown in vain I should assay.

O sun, whom light nor flight can match,
  Suppose thy lightful flightful wings
    Thou lend to me,
    And I could flee
  So far as thee the evening brings,
Even led to west he would me catch,
  Nor should I lurk with western things.

Do thou thy best, O secret night,
  In sable veil to cover me,
    Thy sable veil
    Shall vainly fail;
  With day unmasked my night shall be;
For night is day, and darkness light,
  O Father of all lights, to thee.

HENRY CONSTABLE

1562–1613

51 *O Gracious Shepherd*

O GRACIOUS Shepherd! for Thy simple flock
  By guileful goats to ravening wolves misled,
  Who Thine own dear heart's precious blood didst shed,
And lamb-like offered to the butcher's block:
O gracious Shepherd! unremoving Rock
  Of succour to all such as thither fled,
  Respect one of Thy flock which followèd
These cursèd goats, and doth repentant knock,
  To be with mercy taken to Thy fold.
I know Thy grace doth still for wanderers look;
  I was a lost sheep once: dear Lord! behold,
And in compassion take me with Thy hook.
  In one lost sheep new found, Thou dost rejoice;
  Then know Thy sheep, which knows his Shepherd's voice.

WILLIAM SHAKESPEARE

1564–1616

52 *Sonnet CXLVI*

POOR soul, the centre of my sinful earth,
Fooled by these rebel powers that thee array,
Why dost thou pine within and suffer dearth,
Painting thy outward walls so costly gay?
Why so large cost, having so short a lease,
Dost thou upon thy fading mansion spend?
Shall worms, inheritors of this excess,
Eat up thy charge? Is this thy body's end?
Then, soul, live thou upon thy servant's loss,
And let that pine to aggravate thy store;
Buy terms divine in selling hours of dross;
Within be fed, without be rich no more:
So shalt thou feed on Death, that feeds on men,
And Death once dead, there's no more dying then.

THOMAS CAMPION

1567–1620

53 *Out of my Soul's Depth*

OUT of my soul's depth to thee my cries have sounded:
Let thine ears my plaints receive, on just fear grounded.
Lord, shouldst thou weigh our faults, who 's not confounded?

But with grace thou censur'st thine when they have erred,
Therefore shall thy blessed name be lov'd and feared.
Ev'n to thy throne my thoughts and eyes are reared.

Thee alone my hopes attend, on thee relying;
In thy sacred word I'll trust, to thee fast flying,
Long ere the watch shall break, the morn descrying.

In the mercies of our God who live secured,
May of full redemption rest in him assured,
Their sin-sick souls by him shall be recured.

54 *View me, Lord, a work of Thine*

VIEW me, Lord, a work of thine:
Shall I then lie drown'd in night?
Might thy grace in me but shine,
I should seem made all of light.

But my soul still surfeits so
On the poisoned baits of sin,
That I strange and ugly grow,
All is dark and foul within.

Cleanse me, Lord, that I may kneel
At thine altar, pure and white:
They that once thy mercies feel,
Gaze no more on earth's delight.

Worldly joys like shadows fade,
When the heav'nly light appears;
But the cov'nants thou hast made,
Endless, know nor days, nor years.

In thy word, Lord, is my trust,
To thy mercies fast I fly;
Though I am but clay and dust,
Yet thy grace can lift me high.

55 *To Music bent is my retired Mind*

TO Music bent is my retired mind,
And fain would I some song of pleasure sing;
But in vain joys no comfort now I find,
From heav'nly thoughts all true delight doth spring.
Thy power, O God, thy mercies, to record,
Will sweeten ev'ry note and ev'ry word.

All earthly pomp or beauty to express,
Is but to carve in snow, on waves to write.
Celestial things, though men conceive them less,
Yet fullest are they in themselves of light:
Such beams they yield as know no means to die,
Such heat they cast as lifts the Spirit high.

56 *Never weather-beaten Sail*

NEVER weather-beaten Sail more willing bent to shore,
Never tired Pilgrim's limbs affected slumber more,
Than my wearied sprite now longs to fly out of my troubled breast.
O come quickly, sweetest Lord, and take my soul to rest.

Ever-blooming are the joys of Heav'n's high paradise,
Cold age deafs not there our ears, nor vapour dims our eyes:
Glory there the sun outshines, whose beams the blessed only see;
O come quickly, glorious Lord, and raise my sprite to thee.

57 *Seek the Lord*

SEEK the Lord, and in his ways perséver.
  O faint not, but as Eagles fly;
  For his steep hill is high;
Then striving gain the top, and triumph ever.

When with glory there thy brows are crowned,
  New joys so shall abound in thee,
  Such sights thy soul shall see,
That worldly thoughts shall by their beams be drowned.

Farewell, World, thou mass of mere confusion,
  False light, with many shadows dimm'd,
  Old witch, with new foils trimm'd,
Thou deadly sleep of soul, and charm'd illusion.

I the King will seek, of Kings adored;
  Spring of light, tree of grace and bliss,
  Whose fruit so sov'reign is
That all who taste it are from death restored.

SIR HENRY WOTTON

1568–1639

58 *D. O. M.*

ETERNAL Mover, whose diffuséd glory,
  To show our grovelling reason what Thou art,
Unfolds itself in clouds of nature's story,
  Where Man, Thy proudest creature, acts his part;
Whom yet, alas, I know not why, we call
The world's contracted sum, the little all;

For what are we but lumps of walking clay?
    Why should we swell? whence should our spirits rise?
Are not brute beasts as strong, and birds as gay,—
    Trees longer lived, and creeping things as wise?
Only our souls were left an inward light,
To feel our weakness, and confess Thy might.

Thou then, our strength, Father of life and death,
    To whom our thanks, our vows, ourselves we owe,
From me, Thy tenant of this fading breath,
    Accept those lines which from Thy goodness flow;
And Thou, that wert Thy regal Prophet's muse,
Do not Thy praise in weaker strains refuse!

Let these poor notes ascend unto Thy throne,
    Where majesty doth sit with mercy crown'd,
Where my Redeemer lives, in Whom alone
    The errors of my wandering life are drown'd:
Where all the choir of Heaven resound the same,
That only Thine, Thine is the saving Name!

Well, then, my soul, joy in the midst of pain;
    Thy CHRIST, that conquer'd Hell, shall from above
With greater triumph yet return again,
    And conquer His own justice with His love;
Commanding earth and seas to render those
Unto His bliss, for whom He paid His woes.

Now have I done; now are my thoughts at peace;
    And now my joys are stronger than my grief:
I feel those comforts, that shall never cease,
    Future in hope, but present in belief;
Thy words are true, Thy promises are just,
And Thou wilt find Thy dearly-bought in dust!

59 *A Dialogue betwixt God and the Soul*

Soul. WHILST my Soul's eye beheld no light
But what stream'd from thy gracious sight,
To me the world's greatest king
Seem'd but some little vulgar thing.

God. Whilst thou prov'dst pure; and that in thee
I could glass all my deity:
How glad did I from Heaven depart,
To find a lodging in thy heart!

Soul. Now fame and greatness bear the sway,
('Tis they that hold my prison's key:)
For whom my soul would die, might she
Leave them her immortality.

God. I, and some few pure souls conspire,
And burn both in a mutual fire,
For whom I'd die once more, ere they
Should miss of Heaven's eternal day.

Soul. But Lord! what if I turn again,
And with an adamantine chain,
Lock me to thee? What if I chase
The world away to give thee place?

God. Then though these souls in whom I joy
Are Seraphims, Thou but a toy,
A foolish toy, yet once more I
Would with thee live, and for thee die.

BARNABE BARNES

1568–1609

60 *The World's bright Comforter*

THE world's bright comforter, whose beamsome light
Poor creatures cheereth, mounting from the deep,
His course doth in prefixed compass keep;
And, as courageous giant, takes delight
To run his race and exercise his might,
Till him, down galloping the mountain's steep,
Clear Hesperus, smooth messenger of sleep,
Views; and the silver ornament of night
Forth brings, with stars past number in her train,
All which with sun's long borrowed splendour shine.
The seas, with full tide swelling, ebb again;
All years to their old quarters new resign;
The winds forsake their mountain-chambers wild,
And all in all things with God's virtue filled.

SIR JOHN DAVIES

1569–1626

61 *An Acclamation*

O IGNORANT poor man! what dost thou bear
Locked up within the casket of thy breast?
What jewels, and what riches hast thou there!
What heavenly treasure in so weak a chest!

Look in thy soul, and thou shalt beauties find,
Like those which drowned Narcissus in the flood;
Honour and pleasure both are in thy mind,
And all that in the world is counted good.

Think of her worth, and think that God did mean
  This worthy mind should worthy things embrace;
  Blot not her beauties with thy thoughts unclean,
  Nor her dishonour with thy passions base;

Kill not her quickening power with surfeitings,
  Mar not her sense with sensuality;
  Cast not her serious wit on idle things:
  Make not her free-will, slave to vanity.

And when thou think'st of her eternity,
  Think not that death against her nature is,
  Think it a birth; and when thou goest to die,
  Sing like a swan, as if thou went'st to bliss.

And if thou, like a child, didst fear before,
  Being in the dark, where thou didst nothing see;
  Now I have brought thee torch-light, fear no more;
  Now, when thou diest, thou canst not hood-winked be.

And thou, my soul, which turn'st thy curious eye,
  To view the beams of thine own form divine;
  Know, that thou canst know nothing perfectly,
  While thou art clouded with this flesh of mine.

Take heed of over-weening, and compare
  Thy peacock's feet with thy gay peacock's train;
  Study the best, and highest things that are,
  But of thy self an humble thought retain.

Cast down thy self, and only strive to raise
  The glory of thy Maker's sacred name;
  Use all thy powers that blessed power to praise,
  Which gives thee power to be, and use the same.

JOHN DONNE

1572–1631

62 *Hymn to God my God, in my Sickness*

SINCE I am coming to that holy room,
  Where, with thy choir of saints for evermore,
I shall be made thy music; as I come
  I tune the instrument here at the door,
  And what I must do then, think here before.

Whilst my physicians by their love are grown
  Cosmographers, and I their map, who lie
Flat on this bed, that by them may be shown
  That this is my south-west discovery
  Per fretum febris, by these straits to die,

I joy, that in these straits, I see my west;
  For, though their currents yield return to none,
What shall my west hurt me? As west and east
  In all flat maps (and I am one) are one,
  So death doth touch the resurrection.

Is the pacific sea my home? Or are
  The eastern riches? Is Jerusalem?
Anyan, and Magellan, and Gibraltar,
  All straits, and none but straits, are ways to them,
  Whether where Japhet dwelt, or Cham, or Sem.

We think that Paradise and Calvary,
  Christ's Cross, and Adam's tree, stood in one place;
Look Lord, and find both Adams met in me;
  As the first Adam's sweat surrounds my face,
  May the last Adam's blood my soul embrace.

So, in his purple wrapp'd receive me, Lord,
By these his thorns give me his other crown;
And as to others' souls I preach'd thy word,
Be this my text, my sermon to mine own,
Therefore that he may raise the Lord throws down.

63 *A Hymn to Christ, at the Author's last going into Germany*

IN what torn ship soever I embark,
That ship shall be my emblem of thy ark;
What sea soever swallow me, that flood
Shall be to me an emblem of thy blood;
Though thou with clouds of anger do disguise
Thy face; yet through that mask I know those eyes,
Which, though they turn away sometimes,
They never will despise.

I sacrifice this island unto thee,
And all whom I lov'd there, and who lov'd me;
When I have put our seas twixt them and me,
Put thou thy sea betwixt my sins and thee.
As the trees' sap doth seek the root below
In winter, in my winter now I go,
Where none but thee, th'eternal root
Of true Love I may know.

Nor thou nor thy religion dost control,
The amorousness of an harmonious soul,
But thou wouldst have that love thy self: as thou
Art jealous, Lord, so I am jealous now,
Thou lov'st not, till from loving more, thou free
My soul: Who ever gives, takes liberty:

O, if thou car'st not whom I love
  Alas, thou lov'st not me.

Seal then this bill of my divorce to all,
On whom those fainter beams of love did fall;
Marry those loves, which in youth scattered be
On Fame, Wit, Hopes (false mistresses) to thee.
Churches are best for prayer, that have least light:
To see God only, I go out of sight:
  And to 'scape stormy days, I choose
    An everlasting night.

64 *A Hymn to God the Father*

WILT thou forgive that sin where I begun,
  Which was my sin, though it were done before?
Wilt thou forgive that sin, through which I run,
  And do run still: though still I do deplore?
    When thou hast done, thou hast not done,
      For, I have more.

Wilt thou forgive that sin which I have won
  Others to sin? and, made my sin their door?
Wilt thou forgive that sin which I did shun
  A year, or two: but wallowed in, a score?
    When thou hast done, thou hast not done,
      For I have more.

I have a sin of fear, that when I have spun
  My last thread, I shall perish on the shore;
But swear by thyself, that at my death thy son
  Shall shine as he shines now, and heretofore;
    And, having done that, Thou hast done,
      I fear no more.

JOHN DONNE

65 *Holy Sonnets*

(i)

THOU hast made me, and shall thy work decay?
Repair me now, for now mine end doth haste,
I run to death, and death meets me as fast,
And all my pleasures are like yesterday;
I dare not move my dim eyes any way,
Despair behind, and death before doth cast
Such terror, and my feeble flesh doth waste
By sin in it, which it t'wards hell doth weigh;
Only thou art above, and when towards thee
By thy leave I can look, I rise again;
But our old subtle foe so tempteth me,
That not one hour my self I can sustain;
Thy Grace may wing me to prevent his art,
And thou like adamant draw mine iron heart.

(ii)

I am a little world made cunningly
Of elements, and an angelic sprite,
But black sin hath betray'd to endless night
My world's both parts, and (oh) both parts must die.
You which beyond that heaven which was most high
Have found new spheres, and of new lands can write,
Pour new seas in mine eyes, that so I might
Drown my world with my weeping earnestly,
Or wash it, if it must be drown'd no more:
But oh it must be burnt! alas the fire
Of lust and envy have burnt it heretofore,
And made it fouler; Let their flames retire,
And burn me, O Lord, with a fiery zeal
Of thee and thy house, which doth in eating heal.

JOHN DONNE

(iii)

This is my play's last scene, here heavens appoint
My pilgrimage's last mile; and my race
Idly, yet quickly run, hath this last pace,
My span's last inch, my minute's latest point,
And gluttonous death, will instantly unjoint
My body, and soul, and I shall sleep a space,
But my ever-waking part shall see that face,
Whose fear already shakes my every joint:
Then, as my soul, to heaven her first seat, takes flight,
And earth-borne body, in the earth shall dwell,
So, fall my sins, that all may have their right,
To where they are bred, and would press me, to hell.
Impute me righteous, thus purg'd of evil,
For thus I leave the world, the flesh, the devil.

(iv)

At the round earth's imagin'd corners, blow
Your trumpets, Angels, and arise, arise
From death, you numberless infinities
Of souls, and to your scatter'd bodies go,
All whom the flood did, and fire shall o'erthrow,
All whom war, dearth, age, agues, tyrannies,
Despair, law, chance, hath slain, and you whose eyes,
Shall behold God, and never taste death's woe.
But let them sleep, Lord, and me mourn a space,
For, if above all these, my sins abound,
'Tis late to ask abundance of thy grace,
When we are there; here on this lowly ground,
Teach me how to repent; for that's as good
As if thou hadst seal'd my pardon, with thy blood.

(*v*)

Spit in my face you Jews, and pierce my side,
Buffet, and scoff, scourge, and crucify me,
For I have sinn'd, and sinn'd, and only he,
Who could do no iniquity, hath died:
But by my death cannot be satisfied
My sins, which pass the Jews' impiety:
They kill'd once an inglorious man, but I
Crucify him daily, being now glorified.
Oh let me then, his strange love still admire:
Kings pardon, but he bore our punishment.
And Jacob came cloth'd in vile harsh attire
But to supplant, and with gainful intent:
God cloth'd himself in vile man's flesh, that so
He might be weak enough to suffer woe.

(*vi*)

Batter my heart, three-person'd God; for, you
As yet but knock, breathe, shine, and seek to mend;
That I may rise, and stand, o'erthrow me, and bend
Your force, to break, blow, burn and make me new.
I, like an usurped town, to another due,
Labour to admit you, but O, to no end.
Reason, your viceroy in me, me should defend,
But is captiv'd, and proves weak or untrue.
Yet dearly I love you, and would be loved fain,
But am betroth'd unto your enemy:
Divorce me, untie, or break that knot again,
Take me to you, imprison me, for I
Except you enthrall me, never shall be free,
Nor ever chaste, except you ravish me.

66 *Good Friday, 1613. Riding Westward*

LET man's soul be a sphere, and then, in this,
The intelligence that moves, devotion is,
And as the other Spheres, by being grown
Subject to foreign motions, lose their own,
And being by others hurried every day,
Scarce in a year their natural form obey:
Pleasure or business, so, our souls admit
For their first mover, and are whirl'd by it.
Hence is 't, that I am carried towards the west
This day, when my soul's form bends toward the east.
There I should see a sun, by rising set,
And by that setting endless day beget;
But that Christ on this cross, did rise and fall,
Sin had eternally benighted all.
Yet dare I almost be glad, I do not see
That spectacle of too much weight for me.
Who sees God's face, that is self life, must die;
What a death were it then to see God die?
It made his own lieutenant, Nature, shrink,
It made his footstool crack, and the sun wink.
Could I behold those hands which span the poles,
And turn all spheres at once, pierc'd with those holes?
Could I behold that endless height which is
Zenith to us, and our Antipodes,
Humbled below us? or that blood which is
The seat of all our souls, if not of his,
Made dirt of dust, or that flesh which was worn
By God, for his apparel, ragg'd, and torn?
If on these things I durst not look, durst I
Upon his miserable mother cast mine eye,

Who was God's partner here, and furnish'd thus
Half of that sacrifice, which ransom'd us?
Though these things, as I ride, be from mine eye,
They are present yet unto my memory,
For that looks towards them; and thou look'st towards me,
O Saviour, as thou hang'st upon the tree;
I turn my back to thee, but to receive
Corrections, till thy mercies bid thee leave.
O think me worth thine anger, punish me,
Burn off my rusts, and my deformity,
Restore thine image, so much, by thy grace,
That thou may'st know me, and I'll turn my face.

67 *From The Litany*

(i)

FROM being anxious, or secure,
Dead clods of sadness, or light squibs of mirth,
From thinking, that great courts immure
All, or no happiness, or that this earth
Is only for our prison fram'd,
Or that thou art covetous
To them whom thou lovest, or that they are maim'd
From reaching this world's sweet, who seek thee thus,
With all their might, Good Lord deliver us.

(ii)

From needing danger, to be good,
From owing thee yesterday's tears to-day,
From trusting so much to thy blood,
That in that hope, we wound our soul away,

From bribing thee with alms, to excuse
Some sin more burdenous,
From light affecting, in religion, news,
From thinking us all soul, neglecting thus
Our mutual duties, Lord deliver us.

(iii)

Hear us, O hear us Lord; to thee
A sinner is more music, when he prays,
Than spheres, or angels' praises be,
In panegyric Allelujahs;
Hear us, for till thou hear us, Lord
We know not what to say;
Thine ear to our sighs, tears, thoughts gives voice and word.
O Thou who Satan heard'st in Job's sick day,
Hear thyself now, for thou in us dost pray.

(iv)

That we may change to evenness
This intermitting aguish piety;
That snatching cramps of wickedness
And apoplexies of fast sin, may die;
That music of thy promises,
Not threats in thunder may
Awaken us to our just offices;
What in thy book, thou dost, or creatures say,
That we may hear, Lord hear us, when we pray.

JOHN DONNE

68 *The Progress of the Soul*

GREAT Destiny the Commissary of God,
That hast mark'd out a path and period
For every thing; who, where we offspring took
Our ways and ends, seest at one instant; Thou
Knot of all causes, thou whose changeless brow
Ne'er smiles nor frowns, O vouch thou safe to look
And show my story, in thy eternal book:
That (if my prayer be fit) I may understand
So much myself, as to know with what hand,
How scant, or liberal this my life's race is spanned.

To my six lustres almost now outwore,
Except thy book owe me so many more,
Except my legend be free from the lets
Of steep ambition, sleepy poverty,
Spirit-quenching sickness, dull captivity,
Distracting business, and from beauty's nets,
And all that calls from this, and to others whets,
O let me not launch out, but let me save
Th'expense of brain and spirit; that my grave
His right and due, a whole unwasted man may have.

But if my days be long, and good enough,
In vain this sea shall enlarge, or enrough
Itself; for I will through the wave, and foam,
And shall, in sad lone ways a lively sprite,
Make my dark heavy poem light, and light.
For though through many straits, and lands I roam,
I launch at paradise, and I sail towards home;
The course I there began, shall here be stay'd,
Sails hoisted there, struck here, and anchors laid
In Thames, which were at Tigris, and Euphrates weighed

For the great soul which here amongst us now
Doth dwell, and moves that hand, and tongue, and brow,
Which, as the moon the sea, moves us; to hear
Whose story, with long patience you will long;
(For 'tis the crown, and last strain of my song)
This soul to whom Luther, and Mahomet were
Prisons of flesh; this soul which oft did tear,
And mend the wrecks of th'Empire, and late Rome,
And liv'd when every great change did come,
    Had first in paradise, a low, but fatal room.

69 *From 'The Second Anniversary'*

THINK then, my soul, that death is but a groom,
    Which brings a taper to the outward room,
Whence thou spiest first a little glimmering light,
And after brings it nearer to thy sight;
For such approaches doth heaven make in death.
Think thyself labouring now with broken breath,
And think those broken and soft notes to be
Division, and thy happiest harmony.
Think thee laid on thy death-bed, loose and slack,
And think that but unbinding of a pack,
To take one precious thing, thy soul, from thence.
Think thyself parch'd with fever's violence;
Anger thine ague more, by calling it
Thy physic; chide the slackness of the fit.
Think that thou hear'st thy knell, and think no more,
But that, as bells call'd thee to church before,
So this to the triumphant church calls thee.
Think Satan's sergeants round about thee be,

And think that but for legacies they thrust;
Give one thy pride, to another give thy lust;
Give them those sins which they gave thee before,
And trust th'immaculate blood to wash thy score.
Think thy friends weeping round, and think that they
Weep but because they go not yet thy way.
Think that they close thine eyes, and think in this,
That they confess much in the world amiss,
Who dare not trust a dead man's eye with that
Which they from God and angels cover not.
Think that they shroud thee up, and think from thence
They reinvest thee in white innocence.
Think that thy body rots, and—if so low,
Thy soul exalted so, thy thoughts can go—
Think thee a prince, who of themselves create
Worms, which insensibly devour their state.
Think that they bury thee, and think that rite
Lays thee to sleep but a Saint Lucy's night. . . .
Think further on thyself, my soul, and think
How thou at first wast made but in a sink.
Think that it argued some infirmity,
That those two souls, which then thou found'st in me,
Thou fed'st upon, and drew'st into thee both
My second soul of sense, and first of growth.
Think but how poor thou wast, how obnoxious;
Whom a small lump of flesh could poison thus.
This curded milk, this poor unlitter'd whelp,
My body, could, beyond escape or help,
Infect thee with original sin, and thou
Could'st neither then refuse, nor leave it now.
Think that no stubborn, sullen anchorite,
Which fix'd to a pillar, or a grave, doth sit

Bedded and bathed in all his ordures, dwells
So foully as our souls in their first-built cells.
Think in how poor a prison thou didst lie,
After, enabled but to suck, and cry,
Think, when 'twas grown to most, 'twas a poor inn,
A province pack'd up in two yards of skin;
And that usurp'd, or threaten'd with a rage
Of sicknesses, or their true mother, age.
But think that death hath now enfranchised thee;
Thou hast thy expansion now, and liberty.
Think that a rusty piece, discharged, is flown
In pieces, and the bullet is his own,
And freely flies; this to thy soul allow.
Think thy shell broke, think thy soul hatch'd but now.
And think this slow-paced soul which late did cleave
To a body, and went but by the body's leave,
Twenty perchance, or thirty mile a day,
Dispatches in a minute all the way
'Twixt heaven and earth; she stays not in the air,
To look what meteors there themselves prepare;
She carries no desire to know, nor sense,
Whether th'air's middle region be intense;
For th'element of fire, she doth not know,
Whether she pass'd by such a place or no;
She baits not at the moon, nor cares to try
Whether in that new world men live, and die;
Venus retards her not to inquire, how she
Can—being one star—Hesper and Vesper be;
He that charm'd Argus' eyes, sweet Mercury,
Works not on her, who now is grown all eye;
Who if she meet the body of the sun,
Goes through, not staying till his course be run;

Who finds in Mars his camp no corps of guard,
Nor is by Jove, nor by his father barr'd;
But ere she can consider how she went,
At once is at, and through the firmament;
And as these stars were but so many beads
Strung on one string, speed undistinguish'd leads
Her through those spheres, as through the beads a string.
Whose quick succession makes it still one thing.
As doth the pith, which, lest our bodies slack,
Strings fast the little bones of neck and back,
So by the soul doth death string heaven and earth;
For when our soul enjoys this her third birth
—Creation gave her one, a second, grace—
Heaven is as near and present to her face
As colours are and objects, in a room,
Where darkness was before, when tapers come. . . .
But 'twere but little to have changed our room,
If, as we were in this our living tomb
Oppress'd with ignorance, we still were so.
Poor soul, in this thy flesh what dost thou know?
Thou know'st thyself so little, as thou know'st not
How thou didst die, nor how thou wast begot.
Thou neither know'st how thou at first cam'st in,
Nor how thou took'st the poison of man's sin;
Nor dost thou—though thou know'st that thou art so—
By what way thou art made immortal, know.
Thou art too narrow, wretch, to comprehend
Even thyself, yea though thou wouldst but bend
To know thy body. Have not all souls thought
For many ages, that our body is wrought
Of air, and fire, and other elements?
And now they think of new ingredients;

And one soul thinks one, and another way
Another thinks, and 'tis an even lay.
Know'st thou but how the stone doth enter in
The bladder's cave, and never break the skin?
Know'st thou how blood, which to the heart doth flow,
Doth from one ventricle to th'other go?
And for the putrid stuff which thou dost spit,
Know'st thou how thy lungs have attracted it?
There are no passages, so that there is
—For aught thou know'st—piercing of substances.
And of those many opinions which men raise
Of nails and hairs, dost thou know which to praise?
What hope have we to know ourselves, when we
Know not the least things which for our use be?
We see in authors, too stiff to recant,
A hundred controversies of an ant;
And yet one watches, starves, freezes, and sweats,
To know but catechisms and alphabets
Of unconcerning things, matters of fact,
How others on our stage their parts did act,
What Caesar did, yea, and what Cicero said.
Why grass is green, or why our blood is red,
Are mysteries which none have reach'd unto.
In this low form, poor soul, what wilt thou do?
When wilt thou shake off this pedantery,
Of being taught by sense and fantasy?
Thou look'st through spectacles; small things seem great
Below; but up unto the watch-tower get,
And see all things despoil'd of fallacies;
Thou shalt not peep through lattices of eyes,
Nor hear through labyrinths of ears, nor learn
By circuit or collections to discern.

In heaven thou straight know'st all concerning it,
And what concerns it not shalt straight forget. . . .
Return not, my soul, from this ecstasy
And meditation of what thou shalt be,
To earthly thoughts, till it to thee appear
With whom thy conversation must be there.
With whom wilt thou converse? what station
Canst thou choose out, free from infection,
That will not give thee theirs, nor drink in thine?
Shalt thou not find a spongy slack divine
Drink and suck in th'instructions of great men,
And for the word of God vent them again?
Are there not some courts—and then, no things be
So like as courts—which in this let us see
That wits and tongues of libellers are weak,
Because they do more ill than these can speak?
The poison's gone through all; poisons affect
Chiefly the chiefest parts, but some effect
In nails, and hairs, yea excrements, will show;
So lies the poison of sin in the most low.
Up, up, my drowsy soul, where thy new ear
Shall in the angels' songs no discord hear;
Where thou shalt see the blessed mother-maid
Joy in not being that which men have said;
Where she's exalted, more for being good
Than for her interest of motherhood;
Up to those patriarchs, which did longer sit
Expecting Christ, than they've enjoy'd Him yet;
Up to those prophets, which now gladly see
Their prophecies grown to be history;
Up to th'apostles, who did bravely run
All the sun's course, with more light than the sun;

Up to those martyrs, who did calmly bleed
Oil to th'apostles' lamps, dew to their seed; . . .
But pause, my soul, and study, ere thou fall
On accidental joys, th'essential.
Still, before accessories do abide
A trial, must the principal be tried.
And what essential joy canst thou expect
Here upon earth? what permanent effect
Of transitory causes? Dost thou love
Beauty—and beauty worthiest is to move—?
Poor cozened cozener, that she, and that thou,
Which did begin to love, are neither now;
You are both fluid, changed since yesterday;
Next day repairs—but ill—last day's decay.
Nor are—although the river keep the name—
Yesterday's waters and to-day's the same.
So flows her face, and thine eyes; neither now
That saint nor pilgrim, which your loving vow
Concern'd, remains; but whilst you think you be
Constant, you're hourly in inconstancy.
Honour may have pretence unto our love,
Because that God did live so long above
Without this honour, and then loved it so,
That He at last made creatures to bestow
Honour on Him, not that He needed it,
But that to His hands man might grow more fit.
But since all honours from inferiors flow,
—For they do give it; princes do but show
Whom they would have so honour'd—and that this
On such opinions and capacities
Is built, as rise and fall to more and less;
Alas! 'tis but a casual happiness.

Hath ever any man to himself assigned
This or that happiness to arrest his mind,
But that another man which takes a worse,
Thinks him a fool for having ta'en that course?
They who did labour Babel's tower to erect,
Might have considered, that for that effect
All this whole solid earth could not allow
Nor furnish forth materials enow;
And that his centre, to raise such a place,
Was far too little to have been the base.
No more affords this world foundation
To erect true joy, were all the means in one;
But as the heathen made them several gods
Of all God's benefits, and all His rods
—For as the wine, and corn, and onions are
Gods unto them, so agues be, and war—
And as by changing that whole precious gold
To such small copper coins, they lost the old,
And lost their only God, who ever must
Be sought alone, and not in such a thrust;
So much mankind true happiness mistakes;
No joy enjoys that man, that many makes.
Then, soul, to thy first pitch work up again;
Know that all lines which circles do contain,
For once that they the centre touch, do touch
Twice the circumference; and be thou such,
Double on heaven thy thoughts on earth employ'd.
—All will not serve; only who have enjoy'd
The sight of God in fullness can think it;
For it is both the object and the wit.
This is essential joy, where neither He
Can suffer diminution, nor we; . . .

All casual joy doth loud and plainly say,
Only by coming, that it can away.
Only in heaven joy's strength is never spent,
And accidental things are permanent.
Joy of a soul's arrival ne'er decays,
For that soul ever joys and ever stays.
Joy that their last great consummation
Approaches in the resurrection,
When earthly bodies more celestial
Shall be, than angels' were, for they could fall;
This kind of joy doth every day admit
Degrees of growth, but none of losing it.

BEN JONSON

1573?–1637

70 *A Hymn to God the Father*

HEAR me, O God!
  A broken heart
  Is my best part:
Use still thy rod,
  That I may prove
  Therein, thy love.

If thou hadst not
  Been stern to me,
  But left me free,
I had forgot
  Myself and thee.

For sin's so sweet,
  As minds ill bent
  Rarely repent,
Until they meet
  Their punishment.

Who more can crave
    Than thou hast done:
    That gav'st a Son,
To free a slave?
    First made of nought;
    With all since bought.

Sin, Death, and Hell,
    His glorious Name
    Quite overcame;
Yet I rebel,
    And slight the same.

But I'll come in,
    Before my loss,
    Me farther toss,
As sure to win
    Under His Cross.

71 *Good and Great God!*

GOOD and great God! can I not think of Thee,
    But it must straight my melancholy be?
Is it interpreted in me disease,
That laden with my sins, I seek for ease?
O! be Thou witness, that the reins dost know
And hearts of all, if I be sad for show,
And judge me after, if I dare pretend
To aught but grace, or aim at other end.
As Thou art all, so be Thou all to me,
First, midst, and last, converted One and Three;
My Faith, my Hope, my Love; and in this state,
My Judge, my Witness, and my Advocate.

Where have I been this while exiled from Thee,
And whither rapt, now Thou but stoop'st to me?
Dwell, dwell here still! O! being everywhere,
How can I doubt to find Thee ever here?
I know my state, both full of shame and scorn,
Conceived in sin, and unto labour born,
Standing with fear, and must with horror fall,
And destined unto judgment after all.
I feel my griefs too, and there scarce is ground
Upon my flesh to inflict another wound.
Yet dare I not complain or wish for death,
With holy Paul, lest it be thought the breath
Of discontent; or that these prayers be
For weariness of life, not love of Thee.

EDMUND BOLTON

1575?–1633?

72 *A Carol*

SWEET Music, sweeter far
Than any song is sweet:
Sweet Music heavenly rare,
Mine ears, (O peers) doth greet.
Yon gentle flocks, whose fleeces, pearl'd with dew,
Resemble heaven, whom golden drops make bright:
Listen, O listen, now;—O not to you
Our pipes make sport to shorten weary night:—
But voices most divine
Make blissful harmony:
Voices that seem to shine,
For what else clears the sky?
Tunes can we hear, but not the singers see;
The tunes divine, and so the singers be.

peers] mates.

EDMUND BOLTON

Lo, how the firmament
Within an azure fold
The flock of stars hath pent,
That we might them behold.
Yet from their beams proceedeth not this light,
Nor can their crystals such reflection give.
What then doth make the element so bright?
The heavens are come down upon earth to live.
But hearken to the song:
Glory to glory's King,
And peace all men among,
These queristers do sing.
Angels they are, as also (Shepherds) He,
Whom in our fear we do admire to see.

Let not amazement blind
Your souls, (said he) annoy:
To you and all mankind,
My message bringeth joy.
For lo! the world's great Shepherd now is born,
A blesséd babe, an infant full of power:
After long night, up-risen is the morn,
Renowning Bethlem in the Saviour.
Sprung is the perfect day,
By prophets seen afar:
Sprung is the mirthful May,
Which Winter cannot mar.
In David's city doth this Sun appear,
Clouded in flesh;—yet, Shepherds! sit we here.

element] ethereal sky.

PHINEAS FLETCHER

1582–1650

73 *To My Soul*

HOW is 't, my Soul, that thou giv'st eyes their sight
  To view their objects, yet hast none
    To see thine own?
Earth's, air's, heaven's beauties they discern: their light
  Fair flowers admires, their several dresses,
    Their golden tresses;
The lily, rose, the various tulip, scorning
The pride of princes in their choice adorning.

They joy to view the aïr's painted nations:
  The peacock's train which the head outvies
    With fairer eyes,
And emulates the heavenly constellations;
  The ostrich whose fair plume embraves
    Kings, captains, slaves;
The halcyons whose Triton-bills appease
Curled waves, and with their eggs lay stormy seas.

Pilots' fixed eyes observe the arctic Bear
  With all her unwashed starry trains
    In heavenly plains;
Night-travellers behold the moon to steer
  Her ship, sailing, while Eol raves,
    Through cloudy waves;
Our less world's suns with pleasure view the light
Which gives all beauties beauty, them their sight.

Thou that giv'st sight to clay, to blackness light,
  How art so dull, so dim in duty
    To view his beauty
Who quickens every life, lights every light?

His height those eagles' eyes surpasses:
Thou want'st thy glasses:
Take up that pèrspective and view those streams
Of light, and fill thy waning orb with beams.

Then see the flowers clad in his liveries,
And from his cheek and lovely face
Steal all their grace:
See fowls from him borrow their braveries,
And all their feather-painted dresses
From his fair tresses:
See stars, and moon, the sun and all perfection
Beg light and life from his bright eyes' reflection.

Look on his lips: heaven's gate there open lies,
Thence that grace-breathing Spirit blows,
Thence honey flows.
Look on his hands: the world's full treasuries.
Fix all thy looks his heart upon:
Love's highest throne.
And, when thy sight that radiant beauty blears
And dazzles thy weak eyes, see with thine ears.

74 *A Litany*

DROP, drop, slow tears,
And bathe those beauteous feet
Which brought from Heaven
The news and Prince of Peace:
Cease not, wet eyes,
His mercy to entreat;
To cry for vengeance
Sin doth never cease.

In your deep floods
    Drown all my faults and fears;
Nor let His eye
    See sin, but through my tears.

GILES FLETCHER

1588?–1623

75 *On the Crucifixion*

IT was but now their sounding clamours sung,
Blessed is he, that comes from the most high,
And all the mountains with Hosanna rung,
And now, away with him, away they cry,
And nothing can be heard but crucify:
  It was but now, the crown itself they save,
  And golden name of king unto him gave,
And now, no king, but only Caesar, they will have:

It was but now they gathered blooming May,
And of his arms disrob'd the branching tree,
To strew with boughs, and blossoms all thy way,
And now, the branchless trunk a cross for thee,
And May, dismayed, thy coronet must be:
  It was but now they were so kind, to throw
  Their own best garments, where thy feet should go,
And now, thyself they strip, and bleeding wounds they show.

See where the author of all life is dying:
O fearful day! he dead, what hope of living?
See where the hopes of all our lives are buying:
O cheerful day! they bought, what fear of grieving?

Love love for hate, and death for life is giving:
Lo how his arms are stretch'd abroad to grace thee,
And, as they open stand, call to embrace thee,
Why stay'st thou then my soul; ô fly, fly, thither haste thee.

From *Christ's Triumph over Death.*

76 *The Heavenly Jerusalem*

HERE may the band, that now in triumph shines,
And that (before they were invested thus)
In earthly bodies carried heavenly minds,
Pitched round about in order glorious,
Their sunny tents, and houses luminous,
All their eternal day in songs employing,
Joying their end, without end of their joying,
While their almighty prince destruction is destroying.

How can such joy as this want words to speak?
And yet what words can speak such joy as this?
Far from the world, that might their quiet break,
Here the glad souls the face of beauty kiss,
Pour'd out in pleasure, on their beds of bliss.
And drunk with nectar torrents, ever hold
Their eyes on him, whose graces manifold,
The more they do behold, the more they would behold.

No sorrow now hangs clouding on their brow,
No bloodless malady empales their face,
No age drops on their hairs his silver snow,
No nakedness their bodies doth embase,

No poverty themselves, and theirs, disgrace,
  No fear of death the joy of life devours,
  No unchaste sleep their precious time deflowers,
No loss, no grief, no change wait on their winged hours.

But now their naked bodies scorn the cold,
And from their eyes joy looks, and laughs at pain,
The infant wonders how he came so old,
And old man how he came so young again;
Still resting, though from sleep they still refrain,
  Where all are rich, and yet no gold they owe,
  And all are kings, and yet no subjects know,
All full, and yet no time on food they do bestow.

For things that pass are past, and in this field,
The indeficient spring no winter fears,
The trees together fruit, and blossom yield,
Th'unfading lily leaves of silver bears,
And crimson rose a scarlet garment wears:
  And all of these on the saints' bodies grow,
  Not, as they wont, on baser earth below;
Three rivers here of milk, and wine, and honey flow.

About the holy City rolls a flood
Of molten crystal, like a sea of glass,
On which weak stream a strong foundation stood,
Of living diamonds the building was,
That all things else, besides it self, did pass.
  Her streets, instead of stones, the stars did pave,
  And little pearls, for dust, it seem'd to have,
On which soft-streaming manna, like pure snow, did wave.

GILES FLETCHER

In mid'st of this City celestial,
Where the eternal temple should have rose,
Lighten'd th' idea beatifical:
End, and beginning of each thing that grows,
Whose self no end, nor yet beginning knows,
  That hath no eyes to see, nor ears to hear,
  Yet sees, and hears, and is all eye, all ear,
That no where is contain'd, and yet is everywhere.

Changer of all things, yet immutable,
Before, and after all, the first, and last,
That moving all, is yet immovable,
Great without quantity, in whose forecast,
Things past are present, things to come are past
  Swift without motion, to whose open eye
  The hearts of wicked men unbreasted lie,
At once absent, and present to them, far and nigh.

It is no flaming lustre, made of light,
No sweet consent, or well-tim'd harmony,
Ambrosia, for to feast the Appetite,
Or flowery odour, mixed with spicery.
No soft embrace, or pleasure bodily,
  And yet it is a kind of inward feast,
  A harmony, that sounds within the breast,
An odour, light, embrace, in which the soul doth rest.

A heav'nly feast, no hunger can consume,
A light unseen, yet shines in every place,
A sound, no time can steal, a sweet perfume,
No winds can scatter, an entire embrace,

That no satiety can ere unlace,
  Ingraced into so high a favour, there
  The saints, with their beau-peers whole worlds outwear,
And things unseen do see, and things unheard do hear.

Ye blessed souls, grown richer by your spoil,
Whose loss, though great, is cause of greater gains,
Here may your weary spirits rest from toil,
Spending your endless ev'ning, that remains,
Among those white flocks, and celestial trains,
  That feed upon their shepherds' eyes, and frame
  That heav'nly music of so wondrous fame,
Psalming aloud the holy honours of his name.

Had I a voice of steel to tune my song,
Were every verse as smoothly filed as glass,
And every member turnèd to a tongue,
And every tongue were made of sounding brass,
Yet all that skill, and all this strength, alas,
  Should it presume to gild, were misadvis'd,
  The place, where David hath new songs devis'd,
As in his burning throne he sits emparadis'd.

From *Christ's Triumph after Death.*

THOMAS PESTEL

1584?–1659?

77 *Psalm for Christmas Day*

FAIREST of morning lights appear,
  Thou blest and gaudy day,
On which was born our Saviour dear;
  Arise and come away!

gaudy day] festival.

THOMAS PESTEL

This day prevents His day of doom;
His mercy now is nigh;
The mighty God of Love is come,
The Dayspring from on high!

Behold the great Creator makes
Himself a house of clay,
A robe of Virgin-flesh He takes
Which He will wear for aye.

Hark, hark, the wise Eternal Word
Like a weak infant cries:
In form of servant is the Lord,
And God in cradle lies.

This wonder struck the world amazed,
It shook the starry frame;
Squadrons of Spirits stood and gazed,
Then down in troops they came.

Glad Shepherds ran to view this sight;
A quire of Angels sings;
And eastern Sages with delight
Adore this King of kings.

Join then, all hearts that are not stone,
And all our voices prove,
To celebrate this Holy One,
The God of peace and love.

78 *A Psalm for Sunday Night*

O SING the glories of our LORD;
His grace and truth resound,
And His stupendous acts record,
Whose mercies have no bound!

He made the all-informing light
And hosts of Angels fair;
'Tis He with shadows clothes the night,
He clouds or clears the air.

Those restless skies with stars enchased
He on firm hinges set;
The wave-embracéd earth He placed
His hanging cabinet.

We in His summer-sunshine stand,
And by His favour grow;
We gather what His bounteous hand
Is pleaséd to bestow.

When He contracts His brow, we mourn,
And all our strength is vain;
To former dust in death we turn,
Till He inspire again.

79 *The Relief on Easter Eve*

LIKE an hart, the livelong day
That in thorns and thickets lay,
Rouse thee, soul, thy flesh forsake,
Got to relief from thy brake;
Shudd'ring I would have thee part,
And at every motion start.

Look behind thee still to see
If thy frailties follow thee.
Deep in silence of the night,
Take a sweet and stoln delight.
Graze on clover by this calm,
Precious spring of bleeding balm.
Thou remembrest how it ran
From his side, that 's God and man.
Taste the pleasures of this stream,
Thou wilt think thy flesh a dream.
Nightly this repast go take,
Got to relief from thy brake.

WILLIAM DRUMMOND OF HAWTHORNDEN

1585–1649

80 *Love which is here a care*

LOVE which is here a care,
That wit and will doth mar,
Uncertain truce, and a most certain war;
A shrill tempestuous wind,
Which doth disturb the mind,
And, like wild waves, all our designs commove;
Among those sprites above
Which see their Maker's face,
It a contentment is, a quiet peace,
A pleasure void of grief, a constant rest,
Eternal joy which nothing can molest.

81 *For the Baptist*

THE last and greatest herald of heaven's King,
Girt with rough skins, hies to the deserts wild,
Among that savage brood the woods forth bring,
Which he than man more harmless found and mild:
His food was locusts, and what young doth spring,
With honey that from virgin hives distilled;
Parched body, hollow eyes, some uncouth thing
Made him appear long since from earth exiled.
There burst he forth: 'All ye, whose hopes rely
On God, with me amidst these deserts mourn;
Repent, repent, and from old errors turn.'
Who listened to his voice, obeyed his cry?
Only the echoes, which he made relent,
Rung from their marble caves, 'Repent, repent!'

82 *The Angels for the Nativity of Our Lord*

RUN, shepherds, run where Bethlem blest appears,
We bring the best of news, be not dismayed,
A Saviour there is born more old than years,
Amidst heaven's rolling heights this earth who stayed.
In a poor cottage inned, a virgin maid
A weakling did him bear, who all upbears;
There is he, poorly swaddled, in manger laid,
To whom too narrow swaddlings are our spheres:
Run, shepherds run, and solemnize his birth,
This is that night—no, day, grown great with bliss,
In which the power of Satan broken is;
In heaven be glory, peace unto the earth!
Thus singing, through the air the angels swam,
And cope of stars re-echoèd the same.

WILLIAM DRUMMOND OF HAWTHORNDEN

83 *Change should breed Change*

NEW doth the sun appear,
The mountains' snows decay,
Crowned with frail flowers forth comes the baby year.
My soul, time posts away,
And thou yet in that frost
Which flower and fruit hath lost,
As if all here immortal were, dost stay:
For shame! thy powers awake,
Look to that heaven which never night makes black,
And there, at that immortal sun's bright rays,
Deck thee with flowers which fear not rage of days.

WILLIAM AUSTIN

1587–1634

84 *Chanticleer*

ALL this night shrill chanticleer,
Day's proclaiming trumpeter,
Claps his wings and loudly cries,
Mortals, mortals, wake and rise!
See a wonder
Heaven is under;
From the earth is risen a Sun
Shines all night, though day be done.

Wake, O earth, wake everything!
Wake and hear the joy I bring;
Wake and joy; for all this night
Heaven and every twinkling light,
All amazing,
Still stand gazing.
Angels, Powers, and all that be,
Wake, and joy this Sun to see.

Hail, O Sun, O blessèd Light,
Sent into the world by night!
Let thy rays and heavenly powers
Shine in these dark souls of ours;
For most duly
Thou art truly
God and man, we do confess:
Hail, O Sun of Righteousness!

85

A Lullaby

SWEET baby, sleep! what ails my dear,
What ails my darling thus to cry?
Be still, my child, and lend thine ear,
To hear me sing thy lullaby:
My pretty lamb, forbear to weep;
Be still, my dear; sweet baby, sleep.

Thou blessèd soul, what canst thou fear
What thing to thee can mischief do?
Thy God is now thy Father dear,
His holy Spouse, thy Mother too.
Sweet baby, then forbear to weep;
Be still, my babe; sweet baby, sleep.

Sweet baby, sleep, and nothing fear;
For whosoever thee offends
By thy Protector threaten'd are,
And God and Angels are thy friends.
Sweet baby, then forbear to weep;
Be still, my babe; sweet baby, sleep.

WILLIAM AUSTIN

When God with us was dwelling here,
  In little babes He took delight;
Such innocents as thou, my dear,
  Are ever precious in His sight.
Sweet baby, then forbear to weep;
Be still, my babe; sweet baby, sleep.

A little infant once was He;
  And strength in weakness then was laid
Upon His Virgin Mother's knee,
  That power to thee might be convey'd.
Sweet baby, then forbear to weep;
Be still, my babe; sweet baby, sleep.

The King of kings, when He was born,
  Had not so much for outward ease;
By Him such dressings were not worn,
  Nor such-like swaddling-clothes as these.
Sweet baby, then forbear to weep;
Be still, my babe; sweet baby, sleep.

Within a manger lodged thy Lord,
  Where oxen lay, and asses fed:
Warm rooms we do to thee afford,
  An easy cradle or a bed.
Sweet baby, then forbear to weep;
Be still, my babe; sweet baby, sleep.

Thou hast, yet more, to perfect this,
  A promise and an earnest got
Of gaining everlasting bliss,
  Though thou, my babe, perceiv'st it not;
Sweet baby, then forbear to weep;
Be still, my babe; sweet baby, sleep.

86 *To a Musician*

Many musicians are more out of order than their instruments; such as are so, may by singing this Ode become reprovers of their own untunable affections: they who are better tempered, are hereby remembered what music is most acceptable to God, and most profitable to themselves.

WHAT helps it those,
Who skill in song have found,
Well to compose
Of disagreeing notes,
By artful choice,
A sweetly pleasing sound,
To fit their voice,
And their melodious throats?
What helps it them
That they this cunning know,
If most condemn
The way in which they go?
What will he gain
By touching well his lute,
Who shall disdain
A grave advice to hear?
What from the sounds
Of organ, fife, or lute,
To him redounds,
Who doth no sin forbear?
A mean respect,
By tuning strings he hath,
Who doth neglect
A rectified path.
Therefore, O Lord!
So tuned let me be

Unto Thy Word,
　　　　And Thy ten-stringed law,
That in each part
　　　　I may thereto agree,
And feel my heart
　　　　Inspired with loving awe;
He sings and plays
　　　　The songs which best thou lovest,
Who does and says
　　　　The things which Thou approvest.
Teach me the skill
　　　　Of him whose harp assuaged
Those passions ill
　　　　Which oft afflicted Saul;
Teach me the strain
　　　　Which calmeth minds enraged,
And which from vain
　　　　Affections doth recall:
So to the choir
　　　　Where angels music make,
I may aspire
　　　　When I this life forsake.

ROBERT HERRICK

1591–1674

87 *His Prayer for Absolution*

FOR those my unbaptized rhymes,
Writ in my wild unhallowed times;
For every sentence, clause and word,
That's not inlaid with thee (my Lord),
Forgive me, God, and blot each line
Out of my book, that is not thine.

But if, 'mongst all, thou find'st here one
Worthy thy benediction;
That one of all the rest, shall be
The glory of my work, and me.

88 *His Litany, to the Holy Spirit*

IN the hour of my distress,
When temptations me oppress,
And when I my sins confess,
Sweet Spirit comfort me!

When I lie within my bed,
Sick in heart, and sick in head,
And with doubts discomforted,
Sweet Spirit comfort me!

When the house doth sigh and weep,
And the world is drown'd in sleep,
Yet mine eyes the watch do keep;
Sweet Spirit comfort me!

When the artless doctor sees
No one hope, but of his fees,
And his skill runs on the lees;
Sweet Spirit comfort me!

When his potion and his pill,
Has, or none, or little skill,
Meet for nothing, but to kill;
Sweet Spirit comfort me!

ROBERT HERRICK

When the passing-bell doth toll,
And the furies in a shoal
Come to fright a parting soul;
Sweet Spirit comfort me!

When the tapers now burn blue,
And the comforters are few,
And that number more than true;
Sweet Spirit comfort me!

When the priest his last hath pray'd,
And I nod to what is said,
'Cause my speech is now decay'd;
Sweet Spirit comfort me!

When (God knows) I'm toss'd about,
Either with despair, or doubt;
Yet before the glass be out,
Sweet Spirit comfort me!

When the tempter me pursu'th
With the sins of all my youth,
And half damns me with untruth;
Sweet Spirit comfort me!

When the flames and hellish cries
Fright mine ears, and fright mine eyes,
And all terrors me surprise;
Sweet Spirit comfort me!

When the judgement is reveal'd,
And that open'd which was seal'd,
When to Thee I have appeal'd;
Sweet Spirit comfort me!

89 *To his Saviour, a Child; a Present, by a Child*

GO pretty child, and bear this flower
Unto thy little Saviour;
And tell him, by that bud now blown,
He is the *Rose of Sharon* known:
When thou hast said so, stick it there
Upon his bib, or stomacher:
And tell him, (for good handsel too)
That thou hast brought a whistle new,
Made of a clean straight oaten reed,
To charm his cries, (at time of need:)
Tell him, for coral, thou hast none;
But if thou hadst, he should have one;
But poor thou art, and known to be
Even as moneyless, as he.
Lastly, if thou canst win a kiss
From those mellifluous lips of his.
Then never take a second one,
To spoil the first impression.

90 *To God, on his Sickness*

WHAT though my harp, and viol be
Both hung upon the willow-tree?
What though my bed be now my grave,
And for my house I darkness have?
What though my healthful days are fled,
And I lie numbered with the dead?
Yet I have hope, by thy great power,
To spring; though now a wither'd flower.

91 *To his Conscience*

CAN I not sin, but thou wilt be
My private protonotary?
Can I not woo thee to pass by
A short and sweet iniquity?
I'll cast a mist and cloud upon
My delicate transgression,
So utter dark, as that no eye
Shall see the hugg'd impiety:
Gifts blind the wise, and bribes do please,
And wind all other witnesses:
And wilt not thou, with gold, be tied
To lay thy pen and ink aside?
That in the mirk and tongueless night,
Wanton I may, and thou not write?
It will not be: And, therefore, now,
For times to come, I'll make this vow,
From aberrations to live free;
So I'll not fear the judge, or thee.

92 *Grace for Children*

WHAT God gives, and what we take,
'Tis a gift for Christ his sake:
Be the meal of beans and peas,
God be thank'd for those, and these.
Have we flesh, or have we fish.
All are fragments from his dish.
He his church save, and the king,
And our peace here, like a spring,
Make it ever flourishing.

93 *Another Grace for a Child*

HERE a little child I stand,
Heaving up my either hand;
Cold as paddocks though they be,
Here I lift them up to thee,
For a benison to fall
On our meat, and on us all.

94 *The Star-Song: A Carol to the King; sung at White-Hall*

The Flourish of Music: then followed the Song.

TELL us, thou clear and heavenly tongue,
Where is the babe but lately sprung?
Lies he the lily-banks among?

Or say, if this new birth of ours
Sleeps, laid within some ark of flowers,
Spangled with dew-light; thou canst clear
All doubts, and manifest the where.

Declare to us, bright star, if we shall seek
Him in the morning's blushing cheek,
Or search the beds of spices through,
To find him out?

Star. No, this ye need not do;
But only come, and see Him rest
A princely babe in 's mother's breast.

Chor. He's seen, he's seen, why then a round,
Let's kiss the sweet and holy ground;
And all rejoice, that we have found
A King, before conception crown'd.

Come then, come then, and let us bring
Unto our pretty Twelfth-tide king,
Each one his several offering;

Chor. And when night comes, we'll give him wassailing:
And that his treble honours may be seen,
We'll choose him king, and make his mother queen.

95 *His Wish to God*

I WOULD to God, that mine old age might have
Before my last, but here a living grave,
Some one poor alms-house; there to lie, or stir,
Ghost-like, as in my meaner sepulchre;
A little piggin, and a pipkin by,
To hold things fitting my necessity;
Which, rightly us'd, both in their time and place,
Might me excite to fore, and after-grace.
Thy cross, my *Christ*, fixed 'fore mine eyes should be,
Not to adore that, but to worship thee.
So, here the remnant of my days I'd spend,
Reading thy bible, and my book; so end.

96 *The White Island: or Place of the Blest*

IN this world (the *Isle of Dreams*)
While we sit by sorrow's streams,
Tears and terrors are our themes
Reciting:

But when once from hence we fly,
More and more approaching nigh
Unto young Eternity
Uniting:

In that whiter Island, where
Things are evermore sincere;
Candour here, and lustre there
Delighting:

There no monstrous fancies shall
Out of hell an horror call,
To create (or cause at all)
Affrighting.

There in calm and cooling sleep
We our eyes shall never steep;
But eternal watch shall keep,
Attending

Pleasures, such as shall pursue
Me immortaliz'd, and you;
And fresh joys, as never too
Have ending.

97 *No coming to God without Christ*

GOOD and great God! How should I fear
To come to Thee, if Christ not there!
Could I but think, He would not be
Present, to plead my cause for me;
To Hell I'd rather run, than I
Would see Thy face, and He not by.

THOMAS HEYWOOD

d. 1650?

98

The Search for God

I SOUGHT Thee round about, O Thou my God,
To find Thy abode:
I said unto the Earth, 'Speak, art thou He?'
She answered me,
'I am not.' I enquired of creatures all,
In general,
Contained therein: they with one voice proclaim
That none amongst them challenged such a name.

I asked the seas, and all the deeps below,
My God to know:
I asked the reptiles, and whatever is
In the abyss:
Even from the shrimp to the leviathan
My enquiry ran:
But in those deserts, which no line can sound,
The God I sought for was not to be found.

I asked the Air, if that were He, but know
It told me, 'No':
I from the towering eagle to the wren
Demanded then,
If any feathered fowl 'mong them were such:
But they, all much
Offended at my question, in full quire
Answered, to find my God I must look higher.

. . . . .

And now, my God, by Thy illumining grace,
Thy glorious face
(So far forth as Thou wilt discovered be)
Methinks I see:
And though invisible and infinite,
To human sight
Thou in Thy Mercy, Justice, Truth, appearest,
In which to our frail senses Thou com'st nearest.

O, make us apt to seek and quick to find,
Thou God most kind:
Give us Love, Hope, and Faith in Thee to trust,
Thou God most just:
Remit all our offences, we entreat,
Most Good, most Great:
Grant that our willing though unworthy quest
May, through Thy grace, admit us 'mongst the blest.

FRANCIS QUARLES

1592–1644

99 *Like to the Arctic Needle*

LIKE to the arctic needle, that doth guide
The wand'ring shade by his magnetic pow'r,
And leaves his silken gnomon to decide
The question of the controverted hour,
First frantics up and down from side to side,
And restless beats his crystal'd iv'ry case,
With vain impatience jets from place to place,
And seeks the bosom of his frozen bride;
At length he slacks his motion, and doth rest
His trembling point at his bright pole's beloved breast.

E'en so my soul, being hurried here and there,
  By ev'ry object that presents delight,
Fain would be settled, but she knows not where;
  She likes at morning what she loathes at night:
She bows to honour; then she lends an ear
    To that sweet swan-like voice of dying pleasure,
    Then tumbles in the scatter'd heaps of treasure;
Now flatter'd with false hope; now foil'd with fear:
    Thus finding all the world's delight to be
But empty toys, good God, she points alone to thee.

But hath the virtued steel a power to move?
  Or can the untouch'd needle point aright?
Or can my wand'ring thoughts forbear to rove,
  Unguided by the virtue of thy sprite?
O hath my leaden soul the art t'improve
    Her wasted talent, and, unrais'd, aspire
    In this sad moulting time of her desire?
Not first belov'd, have I the power to love;
    I cannot stir, but as thou please to move me,
Nor can my heart return thee love, until thou love me.

The still commandress of the silent night
  Borrows her beams from her bright brother's eye;
His fair aspect fills her sharp horns with light,
  If he withdraw, her flames are quench'd and die:
E'en so the beams of thy enlight'ning sprite,
    Infus'd and shot into my dark desire,
    Inflame my thoughts, and fill my soul with fire,
That I am ravish'd with a new delight;
    But if thou shroud thy face, my glory fades,
And I remain a nothing, all compos'd of shades.

Eternal God! O thou that only art
  The sacred fountain of eternal light,
And blessed loadstone of my better part,
  O thou, my heart's desire, my soul's delight!
Reflect upon my soul, and touch my heart,
    And then my heart shall prize no good above thee;
    And then my soul shall know thee; knowing, love thee;
And then my trembling thoughts shall never start
    From thy commands, or swerve the least degree,
Or once presume to move, but as they move in thee.

100 *O whither shall I fly?*

O WHITHER shall I fly? what path untrod
Shall I seek out to 'scape the flaming rod
Of my offended, of my angry God?

Where shall I sojourn? what kind sea will hide
My head from thunder? where shall I abide,
Until his flames be quench'd or laid aside?

What, if my feet should take their hasty flight,
And seek protection in the shade of night?
Alas! no shades can blind the God of light.

What if my soul should take the wings of day,
And find some desert? If she springs away,
The wings of vengeance clip as fast as they.

What, if some solid rock should entertain
My frighted soul? can solid rocks restrain
The stroke of Justice, and not cleave in twain?

clip] cleave the air.

FRANCIS QUARLES

Nor sea, nor shade, nor shield, nor rock, nor cave,
Nor silent deserts, nor the sullen grave,
What flame-eyed fury means to smite, can save.

The seas will part, graves open, rocks will split;
The shield will cleave; the frighted shadows flit;
Where Justice aims, her fiery darts must hit.

No, no, if stern-brow'd vengeance means to thunder,
There is no place above, beneath, or under,
So close, but will unlock or rive in sunder.

'Tis vain to flee; 'tis neither here nor there
Can 'scape that hand, until that hand forbear;
Ah me! where is he not, that's ev'rywhere?

'Tis vain to flee, till gentle mercy show
Her better eye; the farther off we go,
The swing of Justice deals the mightier blow.

Th'ingenuous child, corrected, doth not fly
His angry mother's hand, but clings more nigh,
And quenches with his tears her flaming eye.

Shadows are faithless, and the rocks are false;
No trust in brass, no trust in marble walls;
Poor cots are e'en as safe as princes' halls.

Great God! there is no safety here below;
Thou art my fortress, thou that seem'st my foe.
'Tis thou, that strik'st the stroke, must guard the blow.

Thou art my God, by thee I fall or stand;
Thy grace hath given me courage to withstand
All tortures, but my conscience and thy hand.

I know thy justice is thyself; I know,
Just God, thy very self is mercy too;
If not to thee, where, whither shall I go?

Then work thy will; if passion bid me flee,
My reason shall obey; my wings shall be
Stretch'd out no further than from thee to thee.

101 *My Glass is half unspent*

MY glass is half unspent; forbear t'arrest
My thriftless day too soon: my poor request
Is, that my glass may run but out the rest.

My time-devoured minutes will be done
Without thy help; see, see how swift they run:
Cut not my thread before my thread be spun.

The gain's not great I purchase by this stay;
What loss sustain'st thou by so small delay,
To whom ten thousand years are but a day?

My following eye can hardly make a shift
To count my winged hours; they fly so swift,
They scarce deserve the bounteous name of gift.

The secret wheels of hurrying time do give
So short a warning, and so fast they drive,
That I am dead before I seem to live.

And what's a life? a weary pilgrimage,
Whose glory in one day doth fill thy stage
With childhood, manhood, and decrepit age.

FRANCIS QUARLES

And what's a life? the flourishing array
Of the proud summer-meadow, which to-day
Wears her green plush, and is to-morrow hay.

And what's a life? a blast sustain'd with clothing,
Maintain'd with food, retain'd with vile self-loathing,
Then weary of itself, again to nothing.

Read on this dial, how the shades devour
My short-liv'd winter's day; hour eats up hour;
Alas! the total's but from eight to four.

Behold these lilies, (which thy hands have made
Fair copies of my life, and open laid
To view,) how soon they droop, how soon they fade!

Shade not that dial, night will blind too soon;
My non-ag'd day already points to noon;
How simple is my suit! how small my boon!

Nor do I beg this slender inch, to while
The time away, or safely to beguile
My thoughts with joy, there's nothing worth a smile.

No, no: 'tis not to please my wanton ears
With frantic mirth, I beg but hours, not years:
And what thou giv'st me, I will give to tears.

Draw not that soul which would be rather led!
That seed has yet not broke my serpent's head;
O shall I die before my sins are dead?

Behold these rags; am I a fitting guest
To taste the dainties of thy royal feast,
With hands and face unwash'd, ungirt, unblest?

First, let the Jordan streams, that find supplies
From the deep fountain of my heart, arise,
And cleanse my spots, and clear my lep'rous eyes.

I have a world of sins to be lamented;
I have a sea of tears that must be vented:
O spare till then; and then I die contented.

102 *Why dost thou shade thy lovely Face?*

WHY dost thou shade thy lovely face? O why
Does that eclipsing hand so long deny
The sunshine of thy soul-enlivening eye?

Without that light, what light remains in me?
Thou art my life, my way, my light; in thee
I live, I move, and by thy beams I see.

Thou art my life; if thou but turn away,
My life's a thousand deaths: thou art my way;
Without thee, Lord, I travel not, but stray.

My light thou art; without thy glorious sight,
Mine eyes are darken'd with perpetual night.
My God, thou art my way, my life, my light.

Thou art my way; I wander, if thou fly:
Thou art my light; if hid, how blind am I!
Thou art my life; if thou withdraw, I die.

Mine eyes are blind and dark, I cannot see;
To whom, or whither should my darkness flee,
But to the light? and who's that light but thee?

FRANCIS QUARLES

My path is lost, my wand'ring steps do stray;
I cannot safely go, nor safely stay;
Whom should I seek but thee, my path, my way?

O, I am dead: to whom shall I, poor I,
Repair? to whom shall my sad ashes fly
For life? and where is life but in thine eye?

And yet thou turn'st away thy face, and fly'st me;
And yet I sue for grace, and thou deny'st me;
Speak, art thou angry, Lord, or only try'st me?

Unscreen those heav'nly lamps, or tell me why
Thou shad'st thy face? perhaps thou think'st no eye
Can view those flames, and not drop down and die.

If that be all, shine forth and draw thee nigher;
Let me behold and die, for my desire
Is, phoenix-like, to perish in that fire.

Death-conquer'd Lazarus was redeem'd by thee;
If I am dead, Lord, set death's pris'ner free;
Am I more spent, or stink I worse than he?

If my puff'd life be out, give leave to tine
My shameless snuff at that bright lamp of thine;
O what's thy light the less for lighting mine?

If I have lost my path, great Shepherd say,
Shall I still wander in a doubtful way?
Lord, shall a lamb of Israel's sheep-fold stray?

Thou art the pilgrim's path, the blind man's eye;
The dead man's life: on thee my hopes rely;
If thou remove, I err, I grope, I die.

Disclose thy sun-beams, close thy wings and stay;
See, see how I am blind and dead, and stray,
O thou that art my light, my life, my way.

103 *On the Infancy of Our Saviour*

HAIL, blessed Virgin, full of heavenly grace,
Blest above all that sprang from human race;
Whose heaven-saluted womb brought forth in one,
A blessed Saviour, and a blessed son:
Oh! what a ravishment 't had been to see
Thy little Saviour perking on thy knee!
To see him nuzzle in thy virgin breast,
His milk-white body all unclad, undressed!
To see thy busy fingers clothe and wrap
His spradling limbs in thy indulgent lap!
To see his desperate eyes, with childish grace,
Smiling upon his smiling mother's face!
And, when his forward strength began to bloom,
To see him diddle up and down the room!
Oh, who would think so sweet a babe as this
Should e'er be slain by a false-hearted kiss!
Had I a rag, if sure thy body wore it,
Pardon, sweet Babe, I think I should adore it:
Till then, O grant this boon (a boon far dearer),
The weed not being, I may adore the wearer.

GEORGE HERBERT

1593–1632

104 *Love*

LOVE bade me welcome; yet my soul drew back,
Guilty of dust and sin.
But quick-ey'd Love, observing me grow slack
From my first entrance in,

Drew nearer to me, sweetly questioning,
    If I lack'd anything.
'A guest,' I answer'd, 'worthy to be here':
    Love said, 'You shall be he.'
'I, the unkind, ungrateful? Ah, my dear
    I cannot look on Thee.'
Love took my hand, and smiling did reply,
    'Who made the eyes but I?'
'Truth, Lord, but I have marr'd them; let my shame
    Go where it doth deserve.'
'And know you not,' says Love, 'Who bore the blame?'
    'My dear, then I will serve.'
'You must sit down,' says Love, 'and taste My meat.'
    So I did sit and eat.

105

Affliction

WHEN first Thou didst entice to Thee my heart,
    I thought the service brave:
So many joys I writ down for my part,
        Besides what I might have
Out of my stock of natural delights,
Augmented with Thy gracious benefits.

I lookèd on Thy furniture so fine,
        And made it fine to me;
Thy glorious household-stuff did me entwine,
        And 'tice me unto Thee;
Such stars I counted mine: both heav'n and earth
Paid me my wages in a world of mirth.

What pleasures could I want, whose King I served,
Where joys my fellows were?
Thus argu'd into hopes, my thoughts reserved
No place for grief or fear,
Therefore my sudden soul caught at the place,
And made her youth and fierceness seek Thy face.

At first thou gav'st me milk and sweetnesses;
I had my wish and way;
My days were strew'd with flow'rs and happiness;
There was no month but May.
But with my years sorrow did twist and grow,
And made a party unawares for woe.

My flesh began unto my soul in pain,
Sicknesses cleave my bones,
Consuming agues dwell in ev'ry vein,
And tune my breath to groans;
Sorrow was all my soul; I scarce believed,
Till grief did tell me roundly, that I lived.

When I got health, Thou took'st away my life,
And more,—for my friends die;
My mirth and edge was lost, a blunted knife
Was of more use than I:
Thus thin and lean, without a fence or friend,
I was blown through with ev'ry storm and wind.

Whereas my birth and spirit rather took
The way that takes the town,
Thou didst betray me to a ling'ring book,
And wrap me in a gown.
I was entangled in the world of strife
Before I had the power to change my life.

Yet, for I threatened oft the siege to raise,
Not simpering all mine age,
Thou often didst with academic praise
Melt and dissolve my rage.
I took Thy sweetened pill till I came near;
I could not go away, nor persevere.

Yet lest perchance I should too happy be
In my unhappiness,
Turning my purge to food, Thou throwest me
Into more sicknesses:
Thus doth Thy power cross-bias me, not making
Thine own gift good, yet me from my ways taking.

Now I am here, what Thou wilt do with me
None of my books will show:
I read, and sigh, and wish I were a tree,—
For sure then I should grow
To fruit or shade; at least some bird would trust
Her household to me, and I should be just.

Yet, though Thou troublest me, I must be meek;
In weakness must be stout.
Well, I will change the service, and go seek
Some other master out.
Ah, my dear God, though I am clean forgot,
Let me not love Thee, if I love Thee not.

106 *Prayer*

PRAYER, the Church's banquet, Angels' age,
God's breath in man returning to his birth,
The soul in paraphrase, heart in pilgrimage,
The Christian plummet sounding heav'n and earth;

Engine against th'Almighty, sinner's tower,
  Reversèd thunder, Christ-side-piercing spear,
The six-days-world transposing in an hour,
  A kind of tune which all things hear and fear;

Softness, and peace, and joy, and love, and bliss,
  Exalted Manna, gladness of the best,
  Heaven in ordinary, man well dressed,
The milky way, the bird of Paradise,

  Church-bells beyond the stars heard, the soul's blood,
  The land of spices, something understood.

107 *The Temper*

HOW should I praise Thee, Lord? how should my rhymes
  Gladly engrave Thy love in steel,
  If, what my soul doth feel sometimes,
    My soul might ever feel!

Although there were some forty heav'ns or more,
  Sometimes I peer above them all;
  Sometimes I hardly reach a score,
    Sometimes to Hell I fall.

O, rack me not to such a vast extent,
  Those distances belong to Thee;
  The world's too little for Thy tent,
    A grave too big for me.

Wilt Thou meet arms with man, that Thou dost stretch
  A crumb of dust from heav'n to hell?
  Will great God measure with a wretch?
    Shall he Thy stature spell?

O, let me, when Thy roof my soul hath hid,
  O, let me roost and nestle there;
  Then of a sinner Thou art rid,
    And I of hope and fear.

Yet take Thy way; for sure Thy way is best:
  Stretch or contract me, Thy poor debtor;
  This is but tuning of my breast,
    To make the music better.

Whether I fly with angels, fall with dust,
  Thy hands made both, and I am there;
  Thy power and love, my love and trust,
    Make one place ev'rywhere.

108 *Frailty*

LORD, in my silence how do I despise
    What upon trust
Is stylèd honour, riches, or fair eyes,
    But is fair dust!
  I surname them gilded clay,
  Dear earth, fine grass or hay;
In all, I think my foot doth ever tread
    Upon their head.

But when I view abroad both regiments,
    The world's and Thine,—
Thine clad with simpleness and sad events;
    The other fine,
  Full of glory and gay weeds,
  Brave language, braver deeds,—
That which was dust before doth quickly rise,
    And prick mine eyes.

O, brook not this, lest if what even now
My foot did tread
Affront those joys wherewith Thou didst endow
And long since wed
My poor soul, ev'n sick of love,—
It may a Babel prove,
Commodious to conquer heav'n and Thee,
Planted in me.

109 *Employment*

HE that is weary, let him sit;
My soul would stir
And trade in courtesies and wit,
Quitting the fur
To cold complexions needing it.

Man is no star, but a quick coal
Of mortal fire:
Who blows it not, nor doth control
A faint desire,
Lets his own ashes choke his soul.

When th' elements did for place contest
With Him whose will
Ordain'd the highest to be best,
The earth sat still,
And by the others is oppress'd.

Life is a business, not good-cheer;
Ever in wars.
The sun still shineth there or here,
Whereas the stars
Watch an advantage to appear.

Oh that I were an orange-tree,
That busy plant!
Then should I ever laden be,
And never want
Some fruit for him that dressed me.

But we are still too young or old;
The man is gone
Before we do our wares unfold;
So we freeze on,
Until the grave increase our cold.

110

The Pearl

Matt. xiii

I KNOW the ways of learning; both the head
And pipes that feed the press, and make it run;
What reason hath from nature borrowèd,
Or of itself, like a good housewife, spun
In laws and policy; what the stars conspire,
What willing nature speaks, what forc'd by fire;
Both th' old discoveries and the new-found seas,
The stock and surplus, cause and history,—
All these stand open, or I have the keys:
Yet I love Thee.

I know the ways of honour, what maintains
The quick returns of courtesie and wit;
In vies of favours whether party gains;
When glory swells the heart, and mouldeth it
To all expressions both of hand and eye;
Which on the world a true-love knot may tie,

And bear the bundle, wheresoe'er it goes;
How many drams of spirit there must be
To sell my life unto my friends or foes:
Yet I love Thee.

I know the ways of pleasure, the sweet strains,
The lullings and the relishes of it;
The propositions of hot blood and brains;
What mirth and music mean; what love and wit
Have done these twenty hundred years and more;
I know the projects of unbridled store:
My stuff is flesh, not brass; my senses live,
And grumble oft that they have more in me
Than he that curbs them, being but one to five:
Yet I love Thee.

I know all these, and have them in my hand:
Therefore not sealèd, but with open eyes
I fly to Thee, and fully understand
Both the main sale and the commodities;
And at what rate and price I have Thy love,
With all the circumstances that may move:
Yet through the labyrinths, not my grovelling wit,
But Thy silk-twist let down from heav'n to me,
Did both conduct and teach me how by it
To climb to Thee.

111

The Quip

THE merry World did on a day
With his train-bands and mates agree
To meet together where I lay,
And all in sport to jeer at me.

First Beauty crept into a rose,
Which when I plucked not, 'Sir', said she,
'Tell me, I pray, whose hands are those?'
But Thou shalt answer, Lord, for me.

Then Money came, and chinking still,
'What tune is this, poor man?' said he;
'I heard in Music you had skill':
But Thou shalt answer, Lord, for me.

Then came brave Glory puffing by
In silks that whistled, who but he!
He scarce allowed me half an eye:
But Thou shalt answer, Lord, for me.

Then came quick Wit and Conversation,
And he would needs a comfort be,
And, to be short, make an oration:
But Thou shalt answer, Lord, for me.

Yet when the hour of Thy design
To answer these fine things shall come,
Speak not at large, say, I am Thine,
And then they have their answer home.

112 *Peace*

SWEET Peace, where dost thou dwell? I humbly crave,
Let me once know.
I sought thee in a secret cave,
And ask'd if Peace were there.
A hollow wind did seem to answer, 'No;
Go seek elsewhere.'

I did; and going did a rainbow note:
Surely, thought I,
This is the lace of Peace's coat:
I will search out the matter.
But while I look'd, the clouds immediately
Did break and scatter.

Then went I to a garden, and did spy
A gallant flower,
The Crown Imperial. Sure, said I,
Peace at the root must dwell.
But when I digg'd, I saw a worm devour
What show'd so well.

At length I met a rev'rend good old man,
Whom when for Peace
I did demand, he thus began:
'There was a Prince of old
At Salem dwelt, Who liv'd with good increase
Of flock and fold.

'He sweetly liv'd; yet sweetness did not save
His life from foes.
But after death out of His grave
There sprang twelve stalks of wheat;
Which many wond'ring at, got some of those
To plant and set.

'It prosper'd strangely, and did soon disperse
Through all the earth;
For they that taste it do rehearse
That virtue lies therein;
A secret virtue, bringing peace and mirth
By flight of sin.

'Take of this grain, which in my garden grows,
And grows for you;
Make bread of it; and that repose
And peace, which ev'ry where
With so much earnestness you do pursue,
Is only there.'

113 *The Collar*

I STRUCK the board, and cry'd, 'No more,
I will abroad.'
What, shall I ever sigh and pine?
My lines and life are free; free as the road,
Loose as the wind, as large as store.
Shall I be still in suit?
Have I no harvest but a thorn
To let me blood, and not restore
What I have lost with cordial fruit?
Sure there was wine
Before my sighs did dry it; there was corn
Before my tears did drown it;
Is the year only lost to me?
Have I no bays to crown it?
No flowers, no garlands gay? all blasted,
All wasted?
Not so, my heart; but there is fruit,
And thou hast hands.
Recover all thy sigh-blown age
On double pleasures; leave thy cold dispute
Of what is fit and not; forsake thy cage,
Thy rope of sands
Which petty thoughts have made: and made to thee

Good cable, to enforce and draw,
And be thy law,
While thou didst wink and wouldst not see.
Away: take heed:
I will abroad.
Call in thy death's-head there, tie up thy fears.
He that forbears
To suit and serve his need
Deserves his load.
But as I rav'd and grew more fierce and wild
At every word,
Methought I heard one calling, 'Child':
And I replied, 'My Lord'.

114 *Assurance*

O SPITEFUL bitter thought,
Bitterly spiteful thought! Couldst thou invent
So high a torture? is such poison bought?
Doubtless, but in the way of punishment;
When wit contrives to meet with thee,
No such rank poison can there be.

Thou saidst but even now
That all was not so fair as I conceiv'd
Betwixt my God and me. That I allow,
And coin large hopes, but that I was deceiv'd:
Either the league was broke, or near it
And that I had great cause to fear it.

And what to this? what more
Could poison, if it had a tongue, express?
What is thy aim? wouldst thou unlock the door

To cold despairs and gnawing pensiveness?
Wouldst thou raise devils? I see, I know;
I writ thy purpose long ago.

But I will to my Father,
Who heard thee say it. O most gracious Lord,
If all the hope and comfort that I gather
Were from myself, I had not half a word,
Not half a letter to oppose
What is objected by my foes.

But Thou art my desert:
And in this league, which now my foes invade,
Thou art not only to perform Thy part,
But also mine; as when the league was made,
Thou didst at once Thyself indite,
And hold my hand while I did write.

Wherefore, if Thou canst fail,
Then can Thy truth and I: but while rocks stand
And rivers stir, Thou canst not shrink or quail;
Yea, when both rocks and all things shall disband,
Then shalt Thou be my rock and tower,
And make their ruin praise Thy power.

Now, foolish thought, go on,
Spin out thy thread, and make thereof a coat
To hide thy shame; for thou hast cast a bone
Which bounds on thee, and will not down thy throat:
What for it self Love once began,
Now Love and Truth will end in man.

115
The Flower

HOW fresh, O Lord, how sweet and clean
Are Thy returns! ev'n as the flowers in Spring,
To which, besides their own demesne,
The late-past frosts tributes of pleasure bring;
Grief melts away
Like snow in May,
As if there were no such cold thing.

Who would have thought my shrivell'd heart
Could have recover'd greenness? It was gone
Quite under ground; as flowers depart
To see their mother-root, when they have blown,
Where they together
All the hard weather,
Dead to the world, keep house unknown.

These are Thy wonders, Lord of power,
Killing and quick'ning, bringing down to Hell
And up to Heaven in an hour;
Making a chiming of a passing-bell.
We say amiss
This or that is;
Thy word is all, if we could spell.

O that I once past changing were,
Fast in Thy Paradise, where no flower can wither;
Many a spring I shoot up fair,
Off'ring at Heav'n, growing and groaning thither;
Nor doth my flower
Want a spring-shower,
My sins and I joining together.

But while I grow in a straight line,
Still upwards bent, as if Heav'n were mine own,
Thy anger comes, and I decline:
What frost to that? what pole is not the zone
Where all things burn,
When Thou dost turn,
And the least frown of Thine is shown?

And now in age I bud again,
After so many deaths I live and write;
I once more smell the dew and rain,
And relish versing: O, my only Light,
It cannot be
That I am he
On whom Thy tempests fell all night.

These are Thy wonders, Lord of love,
To make us see we are but flow'rs that glide;
Which when we once can find and prove,
Thou hast a garden for us where to bide;
Who would be more,
Swelling through store,
Forfeit their Paradise by their pride.

116 *A True Hymn*

MY Joy, my Life, my Crown!
My heart was meaning all the day,
Somewhat it fain would say,
And still it runneth mutt'ring up and down
With only this, my Joy, my Life, my Crown!

Yet slight not these few words;
If truly said, they may take part
Among the best in art:
The fineness which a hymn or psalm affords
Is when the soul into the lines accords.

He who craves all the mind,
And all the soul, and strength, and time
If the words only rhyme,
Justly complains that somewhat is behind
To make his verse, or write a hymn in kind.

Whereas, if th' heart be moved,
Although the verse be somewhat scant,
God doth supply the want;
As when th' heart says, sighing to be approved,
'O could I love!' and stops, God writeth 'Loved'.

117 *Bitter-Sweet*

AH, my dear angry Lord,
Since Thou dost love, yet strike;
Cast down, yet help afford;
Sure I will do the like.

I will complain, yet praise,
I will bewail, approve;
And all my sour-sweet days
I will lament, and love.

118 *Discipline*

THROW away Thy rod,
Throw away Thy wrath;
O my God,
Take the gentle path.

For my heart's desire
Unto Thine is bent:
I aspire
To a full consent.

Nor a word or look
I affect to own,
But by book,
And Thy Book alone.

Though I fail, I weep;
Though I halt in pace,
Yet I creep
To the throne of grace.

Then let wrath remove,
Love will do the deed;
For with love
Stony hearts will bleed.

Love is swift of foot;
Love 's a man of war,
And can shoot,
And can hit from far.

Who can scape his bow?
That which wrought on Thee,
Brought Thee low,
Needs must work on me.

Throw away Thy rod:
Though man frailties hath,
Thou art God:
Throw away Thy wrath.

119 *Christmas*

ALL after pleasures as I rid one day,
  My horse and I, both tired, body and mind,
With full cry of affections, quite astray,
  I took up in the next inn I could find.

There when I came, whom found I but my dear,
  My dearest Lord, expecting till the grief
Of pleasures brought me to Him, ready there
  To be all passengers' most sweet relief.

O Thou, Whose glorious yet contracted light,
  Wrapt in Night's mantle, stole into a manger,
Since my dark soul and brutish is Thy right,
  To man, of all beasts, be not Thou a stranger:

Furnish and deck my soul, that Thou mayst have
A better lodging than a rack or grave.

THE shepherds sing; and shall I silent be?
    My God, no hymn for Thee?
My soul 's a shepherd too; a flock it feeds
    Of thoughts and words and deeds:
The pasture is Thy Word; the streams Thy grace,
    Enriching all the place.

Shepherd and flock shall sing, and all my powers
    Out-sing the daylight hours;
Then we will chide the Sun for letting Night
    Take up his place and right:
We sing one common Lord; wherefore he should
    Himself the candle hold.

I will go searching till I find a sun
        Shall stay till we have done;
A willing shiner, that shall shine as gladly
        As frost-nipped suns look sadly:
Then we will sing, and shine all our own day,
        And one another pay:

His beams shall cheer my breast, and both so twine,
Till ev'n His beams sing, and my music shine.

120 *The Pulley*

WHEN God at first made man,
        Having a glass of blessings standing by,
'Let us,' said He, 'pour on him all we can;
Let the world's riches, which dispersèd lie,
        Contract into a span.'

        So strength first made a way;
Then beauty flow'd, then wisdom, honour, pleasure;
When almost all was out, God made a stay,
Perceiving that, alone of all His treasure,
        Rest in the bottom lay.

        'For if I should,' said He,
'Bestow this jewel also on My creature,
He would adore My gifts instead of Me,
And rest in Nature, not the God of Nature:
        So both should losers be.

        'Yet let him keep the rest,
But keep them with repining restlessness;
Let him be rich and weary, that at least,
If goodness lead him not, yet weariness
        May toss him to My breast.'

JAMES SHIRLEY

1596–1666

121 *O fly my Soul*

O FLY my soul, what hangs upon
thy drooping wings,
and weighs them down,
With love of gaudy mortal things?
The Sun is now i' th' East, each shade
as he doth rise,
is shorter made,
That Earth may lessen to our eyes:
Oh be not careless then, and play
until the Star of peace
Hide all his beams in dark recess;
Poor Pilgrims needs must lose their way,
When all the shadows do increase.

CHRISTOPHER HARVEY

1597–1663

122 *Comfort in Extremity*

ALAS! my LORD is going,
Oh my woe!
It will be mine undoing;
If He go,
I'll run and overtake Him;
If He stay,
I'll cry aloud, and make Him
Look this way.
O stay, my LORD, my Love, 'tis I;
Comfort me quickly, or I die.

'Cheer up thy drooping spirits;
                    I am here.
Mine all-sufficient merits
                    Shall appear
Before the throne of glory
                    In thy stead:
I'll put into thy story
                    What I did.
  Lift up thine eyes, sad soul, and see
  Thy Saviour here. Lo, I am He.'

Alas! shall I present
                    My sinfulness
To Thee? Thou wilt resent
                    The loathsomeness.
'Be not afraid, I'll take
                    Thy sins on Me,
And all My favour make
                    To shine on thee.'
  LORD, what Thou'lt have me, Thou must make me.
  'As I have made thee now, I take thee.'

WILLIAM HABINGTON

1605–1654

123 *'What am I who dare to call Thee, God!'*

WHAT am I who dare to call Thee, GOD!
  And raise my fancy to discourse Thy power?
    To whom dust is the period,
Who am not sure to farm this very hour?

farm] possess or rent.

For how know I the latest sand
In my frail glass of life, doth not now fall?
And while I thus astonish'd stand
I but prepare for my own funeral?
Death doth with man no order keep:
It reckons not by the expense of years,
But makes the Queen and beggar weep,
And ne'er distinguishes between their tears.
He who the victory doth gain
Falls as he him pursues, who from him flies,
And is by too good fortune slain:
The lover in his amorous courtship dies;
The statesman suddenly expires
While he for others ruin doth prepare:
And the gay Lady while she admires
Her pride, and curls in wanton nets her hair.
No state of man is fortified
'Gainst the assault of th' universal doom:
But who the Almighty fear, deride
Pale Death, and meet with triumph in the tomb.

124 *'Welcome, thou safe Retreat!'*

WELCOME, thou safe retreat!
Where th' injured man may fortify
'Gainst the invasions of the great:
Where the lean slave, who th' oar doth ply,
Soft as his admiral may lie.

expense] expenditure.

Great statist! 'tis your doom,
Though your designs swell high and wide,
To be contracted in a tomb!
And all your happy cares provide
But for your heir authórized pride.

Nor shall your shade delight
I' th' pomp of your proud obsequies:
And should the present flattery write
A glorious epitaph, the wise
Will say, 'The poet's wit here lies.'

How reconciled to fate
Will grow the aged villager,
When he shall see your funeral state!
Since death will him as warm inter
As you in your gay sepulchre.

The great decree of God
Makes every path of mortals lead
To this dark common period.
For what by-ways soe'er we tread,
We end our journey 'mong the dead.

125 *'Time! where didst thou those years inter'*

TIME! where didst thou those years inter
Which I have seen decease?
My soul 's at war, and truth bids her
Find out their hidden sepulchre,
To give her troubles peace.

WILLIAM HABINGTON

Pregnant with flowers doth not the Spring
Like a late bride appear?
Whose feather'd music only bring
Caresses, and no requiem sing
On the departed year?

The Earth, like some rich wanton heir
Whose parents coffin'd lie,
Forgets it once look'd pale and bare,
And doth for vanities prepare,
As the Spring ne'er should die.

The present hour, flatter'd by all,
Reflects not on the last;
But I, like a sad factor, shall
To account my life each moment call,
And only weep the past.

My memory tracks each several way
Since reason did begin
Over my actions her first sway:
And teacheth me that each new day
Did only vary sin.

Poor bankrupt Conscience! where are those
Rich hours but farm'd to thee?
How carelessly I some did lose,
And other to my lust dispose,
As no rent-day should be!

I have infected with impure
Disorders my first years.
But I'll to penitence inure
Those that succeed. There is no cure
Nor antidote but tears.

WILLIAM HABINGTON

126 *'When I survey the bright'*

WHEN I survey the bright
Celestial sphere;
So rich with jewels hung, that night
Doth like an Ethiop bride appear:

My soul her wings doth spread
And heaven-ward flies,
The Almighty's mysteries to read
In the large volumes of the skies.

For the bright firmament
Shoots forth no flame
So silent, but is eloquent
In speaking the creator's name.

No unregarded star
Contracts its light
Into so small a character,
Removed far from our human sight,

But if we steadfast look
We shall discern
In it, as in some holy book,
How man may heavenly knowledge learn.

It tells the conqueror,
That far-stretch'd power,
Which his proud dangers traffic for,
Is but the triumph of an hour:

That from the farthest north,
Some nation may,
Yet undiscover'd, issue forth,
And o'er his new-got conquest sway:

Some nation yet shut in
With hills of ice
May be let out to scourge his sin,
Till they shall equal him in vice.

And then they likewise shall
Their ruin have;
For as yourselves your empires fall,
And every kingdom hath a grave.

Thus those celestial fires,
Though seeming mute,
The fallacy of our desires
And all the pride of life confute:—

For they have watch'd since first
The world had birth:
And found sin in itself accurst,
And nothing permanent on Earth.

SIR THOMAS BROWNE

1605–1682

127 *Evening Hymn*

THE night is come like to the day,
Depart not Thou, great God, away;
Let not my sins, black as the night,
Eclipse the lustre of Thy light.
Keep still in my horizon, for to me
The sun makes not the day, but Thee.
Thou whose nature cannot sleep,
On my temples sentry keep;
Guard me 'gainst those watchful foes,
Whose eyes are open while mine close.

Let no dreams my head infest,
But such as Jacob's temples blest.
While I do rest, my soul advance,
Make my sleep a holy trance:
That I may, my rest being wrought,
Awake into some holy thought.
And with as active vigour run
My course, as doth the nimble sun.
Sleep is a death, O make me try
By sleeping what it is to die.
And as gently lay my head
On my grave, as now my bed.
Now ere I rest, great God, let me
Awake again at last with Thee.
And thus assured, behold I lie
Securely, or to wake or die.
These are my drowsy days, in vain
I do now wake to sleep again.
O come that hour, when I shall never
Sleep again, but wake for ever!

EDMUND WALLER

1606–1687

128 *Last Verses*

THE seas are quiet when the winds give o'er;
So calm are we when passions are no more.
For then we know how vain it was to boast
Of fleeting things, so certain to be lost.
Clouds of affection from our younger eyes
Conceal that emptiness which age descries.

The soul's dark cottage, batter'd and decay'd,
Lets in new light through chinks that Time hath made:
Stronger by weakness, wiser, men become
As they draw near to their eternal home.
Leaving the old, both worlds at once they view
That stand upon the threshold of the new.

THOMAS WASHBOURNE

1606–1687

129 *Casting all your Care upon God, for He careth for you*

COME, heavy souls, oppressed that are
With doubts, and fears, and carking care.
Lay all your burthens down, and see
Where's One that carried once a tree
Upon His back, and, which is more,
A heavier weight, your sins, He bore.
Think then how easily He can
Your sorrows bear that's God and Man;
Think too how willing He's to take
Your care on Him, Who for your sake
Sweat bloody drops, prayed, fasted, cried,
Was bound, scourged, mocked and crucified
He that so much for you did do,
Will do yet more, and care for you.

JOHN MILTON

1608–1674

130 *On the Morning of Christ's Nativity*

Compos'd 1629

I

THIS is the month, and this the happy morn,
  Wherein the Son of Heav'n's eternal King,
Of wedded maid and virgin mother born,
Our great redemption from above did bring;
For so the holy sages once did sing,
  That he our deadly forfeit should release,
And with his Father work us a perpetual peace.

II

That glorious form, that light unsufferable,
And that far-beaming blaze of majesty,
Wherewith he wont at Heav'n's high council-table
To sit the midst of Trinal Unity,
He laid aside; and here with us to be,
  Forsook the courts of everlasting day,
And chose with us a darksome house of mortal clay.

III

Say Heavenly Muse, shall not thy sacred vein
Afford a present to the Infant God?
Hast thou no verse, no hymn, or solemn strain,
To welcome him to this his new abode;
Now while the Heav'n by the sun's team untrod
  Hath took no print of the approaching light,
And all the spangled host keep watch in squadrons bright?

IV

See how from far upon the eastern road
The star-led wizards haste with odours sweet:
O run, prevent them with thy humble ode,
And lay it lowly at his blessed feet;
Have thou the honour first thy Lord to greet,
  And join thy voice unto the Angel Quire,
From out his secret altar touch'd with hallow'd fire.

The Hymn

I

It was the winter wild,
While the Heav'n-born child,
  All meanly wrapp'd in the rude manger lies:
Nature in awe to him
Had doff'd her gaudy trim,
  With her great Master so to sympathize:
It was no season then for her
To wanton with the sun her lusty paramour.

II

Only with speeches fair
She woos the gentle air
  To hide her guilty front with innocent snow,
And on her naked shame,
Pollute with sinful blame,
  The saintly veil of maiden white to throw;
Confounded, that her Maker's eyes
Should look so near upon her foul deformities.

III

But he, her fears to cease,
Sent down the meek-ey'd Peace;
  She crown'd with olive green, came softly sliding
Down through the turning sphere
His ready harbinger,
  With turtle wing the amorous clouds dividing,
And waving wide her myrtle wand,
She strikes a universal peace through sea and land.

IV

No war, or battle's sound
Was heard the world around:
  The idle spear and shield were high up hung;
The hooked chariot stood
Unstain'd with hostile blood,
  The trumpet spake not to the armed throng;
And kings sat still with awful eye,
As if they surely knew their sovran Lord was by.

V

But peaceful was the night
Wherein the Prince of light
  His reign of peace upon the earth began:
The winds with wonder whist
Smoothly the waters kist,
  Whispering new joys to the mild ocean,
Who now hath quite forgot to rave,
While birds of calm sit brooding on the charmed wave

VI

The stars with deep amaze
Stand fix'd in steadfast gaze,
Bending one way their precious influence;
And will not take their flight,
For all the morning light,
Or Lucifer that often warn'd them thence;
But in their glimmering orbs did glow,
Until their Lord himself bespake, and bid them go.

VII

And though the shady gloom
Had given day her room,
The sun himself withheld his wonted speed;
And hid his head for shame,
As his inferior flame
The new-enlightn'd world no more should need;
He saw a greater Sun appear
Than his bright throne, or burning axletree could bear.

VIII

The shepherds on the lawn,
Or ere the point of dawn,
Sat simply chatting in a rustic row;
Full little thought they than
That the mighty Pan
Was kindly come to live with them below;
Perhaps their loves, or else their sheep,
Was all that did their silly thoughts so busy keep.

IX

When such music sweet
Their hearts and ears did greet,
  As never was by mortal finger strook;
Divinely warbled voice
Answering the stringed noise,
  As all their souls in blissful rapture took:
The air such pleasure loth to lose,
With thousand echoes still prolongs each heav'nly close.

X

Nature that heard such sound
Beneath the hollow round
  Of Cynthia's seat, the airy region thrilling,
Now was almost won
To think her part was done,
  And that her reign had here its last fulfilling;
She knew such harmony alone
Could hold all Heav'n and Earth in happier union.

XI

At last surrounds their sight
A globe of circular light,
  That with long beams the shame-fac'd night array'd;
The helmed cherubim
And sworded seraphim
  Are seen in glittering ranks with wings display'd,
Harping in loud and solemn quire,
With unexpressive notes to Heav'n's new-born Heir.

XII

Such music (as 'tis said)
Before was never made,
  But when of old the sons of morning sung;
While the Creator Great
His constellations set,
  And the well-balanc'd world on hinges hung,
And cast the dark foundations deep,
And bid the welt'ring waves their oozy channel keep.

XIII

Ring out ye crystal spheres,
Once bless our human ears,
  (If ye have power to touch our senses so),
And let your silver chime
Move in melodious time;
  And let the base of Heav'n's deep organ blow;
And with your ninefold harmony
Make up full consort to th' angelic symphony.

XIV

For if such holy song
Enwrap our fancy long,
  Time will run back, and fetch the age of gold;
And speckl'd Vanity
Will sicken soon and die,
  And leprous Sin will melt from earthly mould;
And Hell itself will pass away,
And leave her dolorous mansions to the peering day.

XV

Yea, Truth and Justice then
Will down return to men,
  Orb'd in a rainbow; and like glories wearing
Mercy will sit between,
Thron'd in celestial sheen,
  With radiant feet the tissu'd clouds down steering;
And Heav'n as at some festival
Will open wide the gates of her high palace hall.

XVI

But wisest Fate says no,
This must not yet be so,
  The Babe lies yet in smiling infancy,
That on the bitter cross
Must redeem our loss,
  So both himself and us to glorify:
Yet first to those ychain'd in sleep,
The wakeful trump of doom must thunder through the deep,

XVII

With such a horrid clang
As on mount Sinai rang
  While the red fire and smould'ring clouds out brake
The aged Earth aghast
With terror of that blast,
  Shall from the surface to the centre shake;
When at the world's last session,
The dreadful Judge in middle air shall spread his throne.

XVIII

And then at last our bliss
Full and perfect is,
  But now begins; for from this happy day
Th' old Dragon under ground
In straiter limits bound,
  Not half so far casts his usurped sway;
And wrath to see his kingdom fail,
Swinges the scaly horror of his folded tail.

XIX

The oracles are dumb,
No voice or hideous hum
  Runs through the arched roof in words deceiving.
Apollo from his shrine
Can no more divine,
  With hollow shriek the steep of Delphos leaving.
No nightly trance, or breathed spell,
Inspires the pale-ey'd priest from the prophetic cell.

XX

The lonely mountains o'er,
And the resounding shore,
  A voice of weeping heard, and loud lament;
From haunted spring, and dale
Edg'd with poplar pale,
  The parting Genius is with sighing sent.
With flower-inwov'n tresses torn
The nymphs in twilight shade of tangled thickets mourn.

XXI

In consecrated earth,
And on the holy hearth,
  The Lars and Lemures moan with midnight plaint;
In urns and altars round,
A drear and dying sound
  Affrights the Flamens at their service quaint;
And the chill marble seems to sweat,
While each peculiar power forgoes his wonted seat.

XXII

Peor and Baälim
Forsake their temples dim,
  With that twice-batter'd god of Palestine;
And mooned Ashtaroth,
Heav'n's queen and mother both,
  Now sits not girt with tapers' holy shine;
The Libyc Hammon shrinks his horn,
In vain the Tyrian maids their wounded Thammuz mourn.

XXIII

And sullen Moloch fled,
Hath left in shadows dread
  His burning idol all of blackest hue;
In vain with cymbals' ring,
They call the grisly king,
  In dismal dance about the furnace blue;
The brutish gods of Nile as fast,
Isis and Orus, and the dog Anubis haste.

XXIV

Nor is Osiris seen
In Memphian grove, or green,
   Trampling the unshowr'd grass with lowings loud;
Nor can he be at rest
Within his sacred chest,
   Naught but profoundest Hell can be his shroud;
In vain with timbrell'd anthems dark
The sable-stoled sorcerers bear his worshipp'd ark.

XXV

He feels from Juda's land
The dreaded Infant's hand,
   The rays of Bethlehem blind his dusky eyn;
Nor all the gods beside
Longer dare abide,
   Not Typhon huge ending in snaky twine:
Our Babe, to show his Godhead true,
Can in his swaddling bands control the damned crew.

XXVI

So when the sun in bed,
Curtain'd with cloudy red,
   Pillows his chin upon an orient wave;
The flocking shadows pale
Troop to th' infernal jail,
   Each fetter'd ghost slips to his several grave;
And the yellow-skirted fays
Fly after the night-steeds, leaving their moon-lov'd maze.

XXVII

But see the Virgin blest,
Hath laid her Babe to rest.
  Time is our tedious song should here have ending:
Heav'n's youngest teemed star,
Hath fix'd her polish'd car,
  Her sleeping Lord with handmaid lamp attending.
And all about the courtly stable,
Bright-harness'd angels sit in order serviceable.

131 *On Time*

FLY envious *Time*, till thou run out thy race,
Call on the lazy leaden-stepping hours,
Whose speed is but the heavy plummet's pace;
And glut thyself with what thy womb devours,
Which is no more than what is false and vain,
And merely mortal dross;
So little is our loss,
So little is thy gain.
For when as each thing bad thou hast entomb'd,
And last of all, thy greedy self consum'd,
Then long Eternity shall greet our bliss
With an individual kiss;
And joy shall overtake us as a flood,
When everything that is sincerely good
And perfectly divine,
With truth, and peace, and love shall ever shine
About the supreme Throne
Of him, t'whose happy-making sight alone,

When once our heav'nly-guided soul shall climb,
Then all this earthy grossness quit,
Attir'd with stars, we shall for ever sit,
Triumphing over death, and chance, and thee, O Time.

132 *'Blest Pair of Sirens'*

BLEST pair of Sirens, pledges of Heav'n's joy,
Sphere-born harmonious sisters, Voice, and Verse,
Wed your divine sounds, and mixed power employ
Dead things with inbreath'd sense able to pierce,
And to our high-rais'd phantasy present,
That undisturbed song of pure content,
Ay sung before the sapphire-colour'd throne
To him that sits theron
With saintly shout, and solemn jubilee,
Where the bright seraphim in burning row
Their loud up-lifted angel trumpets blow,
And the cherubic host in thousand choirs
Touch their immortal harps of golden wires,
With those just spirits that wear victorious palms,
Hymns devout and holy psalms
Singing everlastingly;
That we on earth with undiscording voice
May rightly answer that melodious noise;
As once we did, till disproportion'd sin
Jarr'd against nature's chime, and with harsh din
Broke the fair music that all creatures made
To their great Lord, whose love their motion sway'd
In perfect diapason, whilst they stood
In first obedience, and their state of good.

O may we soon again renew that song,
And keep in tune with Heav'n, till God ere long
To his celestial consort us unite,
To live with him, and sing in endless morn of light.

133 *On his Blindness*

WHEN I consider how my light is spent,
Ere half my days, in this dark world and wide,
And that one talent which is death to hide
Lodg'd with me useless, though my soul more bent
To serve therewith my Maker, and present
My true account, lest he returning chide;
'Doth God exact day-labour, light deni'd?'
I fondly ask: but Patience, to prevent
That murmur, soon replies, 'God doth not need
Either man's work, or his own gifts; who best
Bear his mild yoke, they serve him best: his state
Is kingly; thousands at his bidding speed,
And post o'er land and ocean without rest;
They also serve who only stand and wait.'

134 *Morning Hymn of Adam and Eve*

THESE are thy glorious works Parent of good,
Almighty, thine this universal frame,
Thus wondrous fair; thyself how wondrous then!
Unspeakable, who sitst above these Heavens
To us invisible or dimly seen
In these thy lowest works, yet these declare
Thy goodness beyond thought, and Power Divine:
Speak ye who best can tell, ye sons of light,

Angels, for ye behold him, and with songs
And choral symphonies, day without night,
Circle his throne rejoicing, ye in Heav'n,
On earth join all ye creatures to extol
Him first, him last, him midst, and without end.
Fairest of stars, last in the train of night,
If better thou belong not to the dawn,
Sure pledge of day, that crownst the smiling morn
With thy bright circlet, praise him in thy sphere
While day arises, that sweet hour of prime.
Thou sun, of this great world both eye and soul,
Acknowledge him thy greater, sound his praise
In thy eternal course, both when thou climb'st,
And when high noon has gaind, and when thou fall'st.
Moon, that now meet'st the orient sun, now fli'st
With the fixed stars, fixed in their orb that flies,
And ye five other wandering fires that move
In mystic dance not without song, resound
His praise, who out of darkness call'd up light.
Air, and ye elements the eldest birth
Of nature's womb, that in quaternion run
Perpetual circle, multiform; and mix
And nourish all things, let your ceaseless change
Vary to our great maker still new praise.
Ye mists and exhalations that now rise
From hill or steaming lake, dusky or grey,
Till the sun paint your fleecy skirts with gold,
In honour to the world's great author rise,
Whether to deck with clouds the uncoloured sky,
Or wet the thirsty earth with falling showers,
Rising or falling still advance his praise.
His praise ye winds, that from four quarters blow,

Breath soft or loud; and wave your tops, ye pines,
With every plant, in sign of worship wave.
Fountains and ye, that warble, as ye flow,
Melodious murmurs, warbling tune his praise.
Join voices all ye living souls, ye birds,
That singing up to Heaven gate ascend,
Bear on your wings and in your notes his praise;
Ye that in waters glide, and ye that walk
The earth, and stately tread, or lowly creep;
Witness if I be silent, morn or even,
To hill, or valley, fountain, or fresh shade
Made vocal by my song, and taught his praise.
Hail universal Lord, be bounteous still
To give us only good; and if the night
Have gathered aught of evil or concealed,
Disperse it, as now light dispels the dark.

Paradise Lost, V. 153–208.

135 *The First Day of Creation*

SO sang the hierarchies: meanwhile the Son
On his great expedition now appear'd,
Girt with omnipotence, with radiance crown'd
Of majesty divine, sapience and love
Immense, and all his Father in him shone.
About his chariot numberless were pour'd
Cherub and Seraph, Potentates and Thrones,
And Virtues, winged spirits, and chariots wing'd,
From the armoury of God, where stand of old
Myriads between two brazen mountains lodg'd

Against a solemn day, harnessed at hand,
Celestial equipage; and now came forth
Spontaneous, for within them Spirit lived,
Attendant on their Lord: Heav'n open'd wide
Her ever-during gates, harmonious sound
On golden hinges moving, to let forth
The King of Glory in his powerful word
And spirit coming to create new worlds.
On heav'nly ground they stood, and from the shore
They view'd the vast immeasurable abyss
Outrageous as a sea, dark, wasteful, wild,
Up from the bottom turn'd by furious winds
And surging waves, as mountains to assault
Heav'n's highth, and with the centre mix the pole.
  Silence, ye troubl'd waves, and thou deep, peace,
Said then th' Omnific Word, your discord end:
  Nor staid, but on the wings of Cherubim
Uplifted, in paternal glory rode
Far into Chaos, and the world unborn;
For Chaos heard his voice: him all his train
Follow'd in bright procession to behold
Creation, and the wonders of his might.
Then staid the fervid wheels, and in his hand
He took the golden compasses, prepar'd
In God's eternal store, to circumscribe
This universe, and all created things:
One foot he center'd, and the other turn'd:
Round through the vast profundity obscure,
And said, thus far extend, thus far thy bounds,
This be thy just circumference, O World.
Thus God the Heav'n created, thus the earth,
Matter unform'd and void: darkness profound

Cover'd th' abyss: but on the watery calm
His brooding wings the spirit of God outspred,
And vital virtue infus'd, and vital warmth
Throughout the fluid mass, but downward purg'd
The black tartareous cold infernal dregs
Adverse to life; then founded, then conglob'd
Like things to like, the rest to several place
Disparted, and between spun out the air,
And earth self-ballanc'd on her centre hung.
  Let there be light, said God, and forthwith light
Ethereal, first of things, quintessence pure
Sprung from the deep, and from her native east
To journey through the airy gloom began,
Spher'd in a radiant cloud, for yet the sun
Was not; she in a cloudy tabernacle
Sojourn'd the while. God saw the light was good;
And light from darkness by the hemisphere
Divided: light the day, and darkness night
He nam'd. Thus was the first day ev'n and morn:
Nor past uncelebrated, nor unsung
By the celestial choirs, when orient light
Exhaling first from darkness they beheld:
Birth-day of Heav'n and earth; with joy and shout
The hollow universal orb they fill'd,
And touch'd their golden harps, and hymning prais'd
God and his works, creator him they sung,
Both when first ev'ning was, and when first morn.

Paradise Lost, VII. 192–260.

136 *The First Temptation*

FULL forty days he pass'd, whether on hill
Sometimes, anon in shady vale, each night
Under the covert of some ancient oak,
Or cedar, to defend him from the dew,
Or harbour'd in one cave, is not reveal'd;
Nor tasted human food, nor hunger felt
Till those days ended, hunger'd then at last
Among wild beasts: they at his sight grew mild,
Nor sleeping him nor waking harm'd, his walk
The fiery serpent fled, and noxious worm,
The lion and fierce tiger glar'd aloof.
But now an aged man in rural weeds,
Following, as seem'd, the quest of some stray ewe,
Or wither'd sticks to gather; which might serve
Against a winter's day when winds blow keen,
To warm him wet return'd from field at eve,
He saw approach, who first with curious eye
Perus'd him, then with words thus uttered spake.
  Sir, what ill chance hath brought thee to this place
So far from path or road of men, who pass
In troop or caravan, for single none
Durst ever, who return'd, and dropp'd not here
His carcass, pin'd with hunger and with drought?
I ask the rather, and the more admire,
For that to me thou seem'st the man, who late
Our new baptizing prophet at the ford
Of Jordan honour'd so, and call'd thee son
Of God; I saw and heard, for we sometimes
Who dwell this wild, constrain'd by want, come forth
To town or village nigh (nighest is far)

Where ought we hear, and curious are to hear,
What happ'ns new; fame also finds us out.
To whom the Son of God. Who brought me hither
Will bring me hence, no other guide I seek.
By miracle he may, reply'd the swain,
What other way I see not, for we here
Live on tough roots and stubs, to thirst inur'd
More then the camel, and to drink go far,
Men to much misery and hardship born;
But if thou be the Son of God, command
That out of these hard stones be made thee bread;
So shalt thou save thy self and us relieve
With food, whereof we wretched seldom taste.
He ended, and the Son of God reply'd.
Think'st thou such force in bread? is it not written
(For I discern thee other than thou seem'st)
Man lives not by bread only, but each word
Proceeding from the mouth of God; who fed
Our fathers here with manna; in the Mount
Moses was forty days, nor eat nor drank,
And forty days Eliah without food
Wandered this barren waste, the same I now:
Why dost thou then suggest to me distrust,
Knowing who I am, as I know who thou art?
Whom thus answer'd th' Arch Fiend now undisguis'd.
'Tis true, I am that spirit unfortunate,
Who leagued with millions more in rash revolt
Kept not my happy station, but was driv'n
With them from bliss to the bottomless deep,
Yet to that hideous place not so confin'd
By rigour unconniving, but that oft
Leaving my dolorous prison I enjoy

Large liberty to round this globe of earth,
Or range in th' air, nor from the Heav'n of Heav'ns
Hath he excluded my resort sometimes.
I came among the sons of God, when he
Gave up into my hands Uzzean Job
To prove him, and illustrate his high worth;
And when to all his angels he propos'd
To draw the proud King Ahab into fraud
That he might fall in Ramoth, they demurring,
I undertook that office, and the tongues
Of all his flattering prophets glibb'd with lies
To his destruction, as I had in charge.
For what he bids I do; though I have lost
Much lustre of my native brightness, lost
To be belov'd of God, I have not lost
To love, at least contemplate and admire
What I see excellent in good, or fair,
Or vertuous, I should so have lost all sense.
What can be then less in me than desire
To see thee and approach thee, whom I know
Declar'd the Son of God, to hear attent
Thy wisdom, and behold thy God-like deeds?
Men generally think me much a foe
To all mankind: why should I? they to me
Never did wrong or violence, by them
I lost not what I lost, rather by them
I gain'd what I have gain'd, and with them dwell
Co-partner in these regions of the world,
If not disposer; lend them oft my aid,
Oft my advice by presages and signs,
And answers, oracles, portents and dreams,
Whereby they may direct their future life.

Envy they say excites me, thus to gain
Companions of my misery and woe.
At first it may be; but long since with woe
Nearer acquainted, now I feel by proof,
That fellowship in pain divides not smart,
Nor lightens aught each man's peculiar load.
Small consolation then, were man adjoin'd:
This wounds me most (what can it less) that man,
Man fall'n shall be restor'd, I never more.
  To whom our Saviour sternly thus replied.
Deservedly thou griev'st, compos'd of lies
From the beginning, and in lies wilt end;
Who boast'st release from Hell, and leave to come
Into the Heav'n of Heavens; thou com'st indeed,
As a poor miserable captive thrall,
Comes to the place where he before had sat
Among the prime in splendour, now depos'd,
Ejected, emptied, gaz'd, unpitied, shun'd,
A spectacle of ruin or of scorn
To all the host of Heaven; the happy place
Imparts to thee no happiness, no joy,
Rather inflames thy torment, representing
Lost bliss, to thee no more communicable,
So never more in Hell than when in Heaven.
But thou art serviceable to Heaven's King.
Wilt thou impute to obedience what thy fear
Extorts, or pleasure to do ill excites?
What but thy malice mov'd thee to misdeem
Of righteous Job, then cruelly to afflict him
With all inflictions, but his patience won?
The other service was thy chosen task,
To be a liar in four hundred mouths;

For lying is thy sustenance, thy food.
Yet thou pretend'st to truth; all oracles
By thee are giv'n, and what confessed more true
Among the nations? that hath been thy craft,
By mixing somewhat true to vent more lies.
But what have been thy answers, what but dark
Ambiguous and with double sense deluding,
Which they who ask'd have seldom understood,
And not well understood as good not known?
Who ever by consulting at thy shrine
Return'd the wiser, or the more instruct
To fly or follow what concern'd him most,
And run not sooner to his fatal snare?
For God hath justly giv'n the nations up
To thy delusions; justly, since they fell
Idolatrous, but when his purpose is
Among them to declare his providence
To thee not known, whence hast thou then thy truth,
But from him or his angels president
In every province, who themselves disdaining
To approach thy temples, give thee in command
What to the smallest tittle thou shalt say
To thy adorers; thou with trembling fear,
Or like a fawning parasite obey'st;
Then to thy self ascrib'st the truth fore-told.
But this thy glory shall be soon retrench'd;
No more shalt thou by oracling abuse
The Gentiles; henceforth oracles are ceased,
And thou no more with pomp and sacrifice
Shalt be enquir'd at Delphos or elsewhere,
At least in vain, for they shall find thee mute.
God hath now sent his living oracle

Into the world, to teach his final will,
And sends his spirit of truth henceforth to dwell
In pious hearts, an inward oracle
To all truth requisite for men to know.
  So spake our Saviour; but the subtle Fiend,
Though inly stung with anger and disdain,
Dissembl'd, and this answer smooth return'd.
  Sharply thou hast insisted on rebuke,
And urg'd me hard with doings, which not will
But misery hath wrested from me; where
Easily canst thou find one miserable,
And not inforc'd oft-times to part from truth;
If it may stand him more instead to lie,
Say and unsay, feign, flatter, or abjure?
But thou art plac'd above me, thou art Lord;
From thee I can and must submiss endure
Check or reproof, and glad to scape so quit.
Hard are the ways of truth, and rough to walk,
Smooth on the tongue discoursed, pleasing to th' ear,
And tuneable as silvan pipe or song;
What wonder then if I delight to hear
Her dictates from thy mouth? most men admire
Virtue, who follow not her lore: permit me
To hear thee when I come (since no man comes)
And talk at least, though I despair to attain.
Thy Father, who is holy, wise and pure,
Suffers the hypocrite or atheous priest
To tread his sacred courts, and minister
About his altar, handling holy things,
Praying or vowing, and vouchsaf'd his voice
To Balaam reprobate, a prophet yet
Inspir'd; disdain not such access to me.

To whom our Saviour with unalter'd brow.
Thy coming hither, though I know thy scope,
I bid not or forbid; do as thou find'st
Permission from above; thou canst not more.
He added not; and Satan bowing low
His gray dissimulation, disappear'd
Into thin air diffus'd: for now began
Night with her sullen wing to double-shade
The desert, fowls in their clay nests were couch'd;
And now wild beasts came forth the woods to roam.

Paradise Regained, I. 303–502.

ROBERT WILD

1609–1679

137 *An Epitaph*

for a godly man's tomb

HERE lies a piece of Christ; a star in dust;
A vein of gold; a china dish that must
Be used in heaven, when God shall feast the just.

SIDNEY GODOLPHIN

1610–1643

138 *Wise Men and Shepherds*

LORD when the wise men came from far
Led to thy cradle by a star,
Then did the shepherds too rejoice,
Instructed by thy angel's voice,
Blest were the wisemen in their skill,
And shepherds in their harmless will.

SIDNEY GODOLPHIN

Wisemen in tracing nature's laws
Ascend unto the highest cause,
Shepherds with humble fearfulness
Walk safely, though their light be less:
Though wisemen better know the way,
It seems no honest heart can stray.

There is no merit in the wise
But love, (the shepherds' sacrifice).
Wisemen, all ways of knowledge past,
To th' shepherds' wonder come at last;
To know, can only wonder breed,
And not to know, is wonder's seed.

A wiseman at the altar bows
And offers up his studied vows
And is received; may not the tears,
Which spring too from a shepherd's fears,
And sighs upon his frailty spent,
Though not distinct, be eloquent?

'Tis true, the object sanctifies
All passions which within us rise,
But since no creature comprehends
The cause of causes, end of ends,
He who himself vouchsafes to know
Best pleases his creator so.

When then our sorrows we apply
To our own wants and poverty,
When we look up in all distress
And our own misery confess,
Sending both thanks and prayers above,
Then though we do not know, we love.

RICHARD CRASHAW

1613?–1649

139 *Against Irresolution*

WHAT Heaven-besiegèd heart is this
Stands trembling at the gate of bliss:
Holds fast the door, yet dares not venture
Fairly to open and to enter?
Whose definition is a doubt
'Twixt life and death, 'twixt in and out.
Ah! linger not, loved soul: a slow
And late consent was a long No,
Who grants at last, a great while tried
And did his best, to have denied:
  What magic-bolts, what mystic bars
Maintain the will in these strange wars?
What fatal, yet fantastic, bands
Keep the free heart from his own hands?
Say, lingering fair, why comes the birth
Of your brave soul so slowly forth?
Plead your pretences (O you strong
In weakness!) why you choose so long
In labour of yourself to lie,
Not daring quite to live nor die.
  So when the year takes cold we see
Poor waters their own prisoners be:
Fetter'd and lock'd up fast they lie
In a cold self-captivity.
Th' astonish'd nymphs their flood's strange fate
    deplore
To find themselves their own severer shore.
  Love, that lends haste to heaviest things,
In you alone hath lost his wings.

Look round and read the world's wide face,
The field of nature or of grace;
Where can you fix, to find excuse
Or pattern for the pace you use?
Mark with what faith fruits answer flowers,
And know the call of Heaven's kind showers:
Each mindful plant hastes to make good
The hope and promise of his bud.
Seed-time 's not all: there should be harvest too.
Alas! and has the year no spring for you?
Both winds and waters urge their way,
And murmur if they meet a stay.
Mark how the curled waves work and wind,
All hating to be left behind.
Each big with business thrusts the other,
And seems to say: "Make haste, my brother."
The aery nation of neat doves,
That draw the chariot of chaste loves,
Chide your delay: yea, those dull things,
Whose ways have least to do with wings,
Make wings, at least, of their own weight,
And by their love control their fate.
So lumpish steel, untaught to move,
Learn'd first his lightness by his love.
  Whate'er Love's matter be, he moves
By th' even wings of his own doves,
Lives by his own laws, and does hold
In grossest metals his own gold.
  All things swear friends to fair and good,
Yea suitors: man alone is wooed,
Tediously wooed, and hardly won:
Only not slow to be undone;

As if the bargain had been driven
So hardly betwixt earth and Heaven,
Our God would thrive too fast, and be
Too much a gainer by 't, should we
Our purchased selves too soon bestow
On Him, who has not loved us so.
When love of us called Him to see
If we'd vouchsafe His company,
He left His Father's court, and came
Lightly as a lambent flame,
Leaping upon the hills, to be
The humble King of you and me.
Nor can the cares of His whole crown
(When one poor sigh sends for Him down)
Detain Him, but He leaves behind
The late wings of the lazy wind,
Spurns the tame laws of time and place,
And breaks thro' all ten heavens to our embrace.
Yield to His siege, wise soul, and see
Your triumph in His victory.
Disband dull fears, give faith the day:
To save your life, kill your delay.
'Tis cowardice that keeps this field;
And want of courage not to yield.
Yield then, O yield, that love may win
The fort at last, and let life in.
Yield quickly, lest perhaps you prove
Death's prey before the prize of love.
This fort of your fair self, if 't be not won,
He is repulsed indeed; but you're undone.

140

Hymn to St. Theresa

LOVE, thou art absolute sole lord
Of life and death. To prove the word,
We'll now appeal to none of all
Those thy old soldiers, great and tall,
Ripe men of martyrdom, that could reach down
With strong arms, their triumphant crown;
Such as could with lusty breath
Speak loud into the face of death
Their great Lord's glorious name, to none
Of those whose spacious bosoms spread a throne
For Love at large to fill: spare blood and sweat;
And see him take a private seat,
Making his mansion in the mild
And milky soul of a soft child.
Scarce has she learn't to lisp the name
Of martyr; yet she thinks it shame
Life should so long play with that breath
Which spent can buy so brave a death.
She never undertook to know
What death with love should have to do;
Nor has she e're yet understood
Why to show love, she should shed blood.
Yet though she cannot tell you why,
She can love, and she can die.
Scarce has she blood enough to make
A guilty sword blush for her sake;
Yet has she a heart dares hope to prove
How much less strong is death then love.
Be love but there; let poor six years
Be pos'd with the maturest fears

Man trembles at, you straight shall find
Love knows no nonage, nor the mind.
'Tis love, not years or limbs that can
Make the martyr, or the man.
   Love touch'd her heart, and lo, it beats
High, and burns with such brave heats;
Such thirsts to die, as dares drink up
A thousand cold deaths in one cup.
Good reason. For she breathes all fire.
Her weak breast heaves with strong desire
Of what she may with fruitless wishes
Seek for amongst her Mother's kisses.
   Since 'tis not to be had at home
She'll travel to a martyrdom.
No home for here confesses she
But where she may a martyr be.
   She'll to the Moors; and trade with them,
For this unvalued diadem.
She'll offer them her dearest breath,
With Christ's name in't, in change for death.
She'll bargain with them; and will give
Them God; teach them how to live
In him: or, if they this deny,
For him she'll teach them how to die.
So shall she leave amongst them sown
Her Lord's blood; or at least her own.
   Farewell then, all the world! Adieu.
Teresa is no more for you.
Farewell, all pleasures, sports, and joys,
(Never till now esteemed toys)
Farewell what ever dear may be,
Mother's arms or Father's knee.

Farewell house, and farewell home!
She's for the Moors, and martyrdom.
  Sweet, not so fast! lo thy fair Spouse
Whom thou seekst with so swift vows,
Calls thee back, and bids thee come
T'embrace a milder martyrdom.
  Blest powers forbid, thy tender life
Should bleed upon a barbarous knife;
Or some base hand have power to raze
Thy breast's chaste cabinet, and uncase
A soul kept there so sweet, oh no;
Wise heav'n will never have it so
Thou art love's victim; and must die
A death more mystical and high.
Into love's arms thou shalt let fall
A still-surviving funeral.
His is the dart must make the death
Whose stroke shall taste thy hallow'd breath;
A dart thrice dip'd in that rich flame
Which writes thy spouse's radiant name
Upon the roof of heav'n; where aye
It shines, and with a sovereign ray
Beats bright upon the burning faces
Of souls which in that name's sweet graces
Find everlasting smiles. So rare,
So spiritual, pure, and fair
Must be th'immortal instrument
Upon whose choice point shall be sent
A life so lov'd; and that there be
Fit executioners for Thee,
The fair'st and first-born sons of fire
Blest Seraphim, shall leave their choir

And turn love's soldiers, upon thee
To exercise their archery.
   O how oft shalt thou complain
Of a sweet and subtle pain.
Of intolerable joys;
Of a death, in which who dies
Loves his death, and dies again.
And would for ever so be slain.
And lives, and dies; and knows not why
To live, but that he thus may never leave to die.
   How kindly will thy gentle heart
Kiss the sweetly-killing dart!
And close in his embraces keep
Those delicious wounds, that weep
Balsam to heal themselves with. Thus
When these thy deaths, so numerous,
Shall all at last die into one,
And melt thy soul's sweet mansion;
Like a soft lump of incense, hasted
By too hot a fire, and wasted
Into perfuming clouds, so fast
Shalt thou exhale to Heav'n at last
In a resolving sigh, and then
O what? Ask not the tongues of men.
Angels cannot tell, suffice,
Thy self shall feel thine own full joys
And hold them fast for ever. There
So soon as thou shalt first appear,
The Moon of maiden stars, thy white
Mistress, attended by such bright
Souls as thy shining self, shall come
And in her first ranks make thee room;

Where 'mongst her snowy family
Immortal welcomes wait for thee.
O what delight, when reveal'd life shall stand
And teach thy lips heav'n with his hand;
On which thou now may'st to thy wishes
Heap up thy consecrated kisses.
What joys shall seize thy soul, when she
Bending her blessed eyes on thee
(Those second smiles of Heav'n) shall dart
Her mild rays through thy melting heart!
Angels, thy old friends, there shall greet thee
Glad at their own home now to meet thee.
All thy good works which went before
And waited for thee, at the door,
Shall own thee there; and all in one
Weave a constellation
Of crowns, with which the king thy spouse
Shall build up thy triumphant brows.
All thy old woes shall now smile on thee
And thy pains sit bright upon thee,
All thy sorrows here shall shine,
All thy suff'rings be divine.
Tears shall take comfort, and turn gems
And wrongs repent to diadems.
Ev'n thy deaths shall live; and new
Dress the soul that erst they slew.
Thy wounds shall blush to such bright scars
As keep account of the lamb's wars.
Those rare works where thou shalt leave writ,
Love's noble history, with wit
Taught thee by none but him, while here
They feed our souls, shall clothe thine there.

Each heav'nly word by whose hid flame
Our hard hearts shall strike fire, the same
Shall flourish on thy brows and be
Both fire to us and flame to thee;
Whose light shall live bright in thy face
By glory, in our hearts by grace.
  Thou shalt look round about, and see
Thousands of crown'd souls throng to be
Themselves thy crown. Sons of thy vows
The virgin-births with which thy sovereign spouse
Made fruitful thy fair soul, go now
And with them all about thee bow
To Him, put on (he'll say) put on
(My rosy love) That thy rich zone
Sparkling with the sacred flames
Of thousand souls, whose happy names
Heav'n keeps upon thy score. (Thy bright
Life brought them first to kiss the light
That kindled them to stars.) and so
Thou with the lamb, thy lord, shalt go;
And wheresoe'er he sets his white
Steps, walk with him those ways of light
Which who in death would live to see,
Must learn in life to die like thee.

141 *The Flaming Heart*

Upon the book and picture of the Seraphical Saint Teresa (as she is usually expressed with a Seraphim beside her).

WELL meaning readers! you that come as friends
And catch the precious name this piece pretends;
Make not too much haste to admire
That fair-cheek'd fallacy of fire.

That is a seraphim, they say
And this the great Teresia.
Readers, be rul'd by me; and make
Here a well-plac'd and wise mistake.
You must transpose the picture quite,
And spell it wrong to read it right;
Read Him for her, and her for Him;
And call the Saint the Seraphim.
Painter, what did'st thou understand
To put her dart into his hand!
See, even the years and size of him
Shows this the mother Seraphim.
This is the mistress flame; and duteous he
Her happy fire-works, here, comes down to see.
O most poor-spirited of men!
Had thy cold pencil kissed her pen
Thou could'st not so unkindly err
To show us this faint shade for her.
Why man, this speaks pure mortal frame;
And mocks with female frost love's manly flame.
One would suspect thou meant'st to paint
Some weak, inferior, woman saint.
But had thy pale-faced purple took
Fire from the burning cheeks of that bright book
Thou would'st on her have heaped up all
That could be found seraphical;
What e'er this youth of fire wears fair,
Rosy fingers, radiant hair,
Glowing cheek, and glistering wings,
All those fair and flagrant things,
But before all, that fiery dart
Had fill'd the hand of this great heart.

Do then as equal right requires,
Since His the blushes be, and her's the fires,
Resume and rectify thy rude design;
Undress thy Seraphim into mine.
Redeem this injury of thy art;
Give Him the veil, give her the dart.
Give Him the veil; that he may cover
The red cheeks of a rival'd lover.
Asham'd that our world, now, can show
Nests of new Seraphims here below.
Give her the dart, for it is she
(Fair youth) shoots both thy shaft and Thee.
Say, all ye wise and well-pierc'd hearts
That live and die amidst her darts,
What is 't your tasteful spirits do prove
In that rare life of her, and love?
Say and bear witness. Sends she not
A Seraphim at every shot?
What magazines of immortal arms there shine!
Heavn's great artillery in each love-spun line.
Give then the dart to her who gives the flame;
Give him the veil, who kindly takes the shame.
But if it be the frequent fate
Of worst faults to be fortunate;
If all's prescription; and proud wrong
Hearkens not to an humble song;
For all the gallantry of him,
Give me the suffering Seraphim.
His be the bravery of all those bright things,
The glowing cheeks, the glistering wings;
The rosy hand, the radiant dart;
Leave her alone The Flaming Heart.

Leave her that; and thou shalt leave her
Not one loose shaft but love's whole quiver.
For in love's field was never found
A nobler weapon than a wound.
Love's passives are his activ'st part.
The wounded is the wounding heart.
O heart! the equal poise of love's both parts
Big alike with wounds and darts.
Live in these conquering leaves; live all the same;
And walk through all tongues one triumphant flame.
Live here, great heart; and love and die and kill;
And bleed and wound; and yield and conquer still.
Let this immortal life where'er it comes
Walk in a crowd of loves and martyrdoms.
Let mystic deaths wait on't; and wise souls be
The love-slain witnesses of this life of thee.
O sweet incendiary! show here thy art,
Upon this carcass of a hard, cold, heart,
Let all thy scatter'd shafts of light, that play
Among the leaves of thy large books of day,
Combin'd against this breast at once break in
And take away from me my self and sin,
This gracious robbery shall thy bounty be;
And my best fortunes such fair spoils of me.
O thou undaunted daughter of desires!
By all thy dower of lights and fires;
By all the eagle in thee, all the dove;
By all thy lives and deaths of love;
By thy large draughts of intellectual day,
And by thy thirsts of love more large than they;
By all thy brim-fill'd bowls of fierce desire,
By thy last morning's draught of liquid fire;

By the full kingdom of that final kiss
That seiz'd thy parting soul, and seal'd thee his;
By all the heav'ns thou hast in him,
Fair sister of the Seraphim!
By all of him we have in thee;
Leave nothing of my self in me.
Let me so read thy life, that I
Unto all life of mine may die.

142 *The Nativity*

COME we shepherds whose blest sight
Hath met love's noon in Nature's night;
 Come lift we up our loftier song
And wake the sun that lies too long.

To all our world of well-stol'n joy
 He slept; and dreamt of no such thing.
While we found out Heaven's fairer eye
 And kiss'd the cradle of our King.
Tell him he rises now, too late
To show us aught worth looking at.

Tell him we now can show him more
 Than he e'er show'd to mortal sight;
Than he himself e'er saw before;
 Which to be seen needs not his light.
Tell him, Tityrus, where th' hast been
Tell him, Thyrsis, what th' hast seen.

Tityrus. Gloomy night embrac'd the place
 Where the noble infant lay.
The babe look'd up and show'd his face;
 In spite of darkness, it was day.

It was thy day, sweet! and did rise
Not from the East, but from thine eyes.

Thyrs. Winter chid aloud; and sent
  The angry North to wage his wars.
The North forgot his fierce intent;
  And left perfumes in stead of scars.
By those sweet eyes' persuasive pow'rs
Where he meant frost, he scatter'd flow'rs.

Both. We saw thee in thy balmy nest,
  Young dawn of our eternal day!
We saw thine eyes break from their East
  And chase the trembling shades away.
We saw thee; and we blest the sight,
We saw thee by thine own sweet light.

Tit. Poor world (said I) what wilt thou do
  To entertain this starry stranger?
Is this the best thou canst bestow?
  A cold, and not too cleanly, manger?
Contend, ye pow'rs of heav'n and earth
To fit a bed for this huge birth.

Thyr. Proud world, said I; cease your conte
  And let the mighty babe alone.
The Phoenix builds the Phoenix' nest.
  Love's architecture is his own.
The babe whose birth embraves this morn,
Made his own bed e'er he was born.

Tit. I saw the curl'd drops, soft and slow,
  Come hovering o'er the place's head;

Off'ring their whitest sheets of snow
  To furnish the fair infant's bed.
Forbear, said I; be not too bold.
Your fleece is white but 'tis too cold.

Thyr. I saw the obsequious Seraphims
  Their rosy fleece of fire bestow.
For well they now can spare their wings
  Since Heav'n itself lies here below.
Well done, said I: but are you sure
Your down so warm, will pass for pure?

Tit. No no, your King's not yet to seek
  Where to repose his royal head;
See see, how soon his new-bloom'd cheek
  Twixt mother's breasts is gone to bed.
Sweet choice, said we! no way but so
Not to lie cold, yet sleep in snow.

Both. We saw thee in thy balmy nest,
  Bright dawn of our eternal day!
We saw thine eyes break from their East
  And chase the trembling shades away.
We saw thee: and we blest the sight.
We saw thee, by thine own sweet light.

Full Chorus.

Welcome, all wonders in one sight!
  Eternity shut in a span.
Summer in winter. Day in night.
  Heaven in earth, and God in man.
Great little one! whose all-embracing birth
Lifts earth to heaven, stoops heav'n to earth.

Welcome. Though nor to gold nor silk.
  To more then Caesar's birthright is;
Two sister-seas of Virgin-Milk,
  With many a rarely-temper'd kiss
That breathes at once both maid and mother,
Warms in the one, cools in the other.

Welcome, though not to those gay flies,
  Guilded i' th' beams of earthly kings;
Slippery souls in smiling eyes;
  But to poor shepherds, home-spun things:
Whose wealth 's their flock; whose wit, to be
  Well read in their simplicity.
Yet when young April's husband show'rs
  Shall bless the fruitful Maya's bed
We'll bring the first-born of her flow'rs
  To kiss thy feet and crown thy head.
To thee, dread lamb! whose love must keep
  The shepherds, more than they the sheep.
To thee, meek majesty! soft king
  Of simple graces and sweet loves.
Each of us his lamb will bring
  Each his pair of silver doves;
Till burnt at last in fire of thy fair eyes,
  Our selves become our own best sacrifice.

143

Charitas Nimia,
or The Dear Bargain

LORD, what is man? why should he cost thee
  So dear? what had his ruin lost thee?
Lord what is man? that thou hast overbought
    So much a thing of nought?

RICHARD CRASHAW

Love is too kind, I see; and can
Make but a simple merchant man.
'Twas for such sorry merchandise
Bold painters have put out his eyes.

Alas, sweet lord, what wer't to thee
If there were no such worms as we?
Heav'n ne'er the less still heav'n would be,
Should mankind dwell
In the deep hell.
What have his woes to do with thee?

Let him go weep
O'er his own wounds;
Seraphims will not sleep
Nor spheres let fall their faithful rounds.

Still would the youthful Spirits sing;
And still thy spacious palace ring.
Still would those beauteous ministers of light
Burn all as bright,

And bow their flaming heads before thee;
Still thrones and dominions would adore thee,
Still would those ever-wakeful sons of fire
Keep warm thy praise
Both nights and days,
And teach thy lov'd name to their noble lyre.

Let froward dust then do its kind;
And give itself for sport to the proud wind.
Why should a piece of peevish clay plead shares
In the Eternity of thy old cares?
Why should'st thou bow thy awful breast to see
What mine own madnesses have done with me?

RICHARD CRASHAW

Should not the king still keep his throne
Because some desperate fool's undone?
Or will the world's illustrious eyes
Weep for every worm that dies?

Will the gallant sun
E'er the less glorious run?
Will he hang down his golden head
Or e'er the sooner seek his western bed,
Because some foolish fly
Grows wanton, and will die?

If I were lost in misery,
What was it to thy heav'n and thee?
What was it to thy precious blood
If my foul heart call'd for a flood?

What if my faithless soul and I
Would needs fall in
With guilt and sin,
What did the lamb, that he should die?
What did the lamb, that he should need,
When the wolf sins, himself to bleed?

If my base lust,
Bargain'd with death and well-beseeming dust
Why should the white
Lamb's bosom write
The purple name
Of my sin's shame?

Why should his unstain'd breast make good
My blushes with his own heart-blood?

O my Saviour, make me see
How dearly thou hast paid for me

That lost again my life may prove
As then in death, so now in love.

144 *The Widow's Mites*

TWO mites, two drops (yet all her house and land),
Falls from a steady heart, though trembling hand:
The other's wanton wealth foams high, and brave,
The other cast away, she only gave.

145 *On Mr. G. Herbert's Book*

intitled the Temple of Sacred Poems, sent to a Gentlewoman

KNOW you, fair, on what you look;
Divinest love lies in this book:
Expecting fire from your eyes,
To kindle this his sacrifice.
When your hands untie these strings,
Think you have an angel by th' wings.
One that gladly will be nigh,
To wait upon each morning sigh.
To flutter in the balmy air,
Of your well perfumed prayer.
These white plumes of his he'll lend you,
Which every day to heaven will send you:
To take acquaintance of the sphere,
And all the smooth faced kindred there.

And though Herbert's name do owe
These devotions, fairest; know
That while I lay them on the shrine
Of your white hand, they are mine.

JOHN AUSTIN

1613–1669

146 *Hark, my Soul*

HARK, my soul, how every thing
Strives to serve our bounteous King;
Each a double tribute pays;
Sings its part, and then obeys.

Nature's sweet and chiefest quire
Him with cheerful notes admire;
Chanting every day their lauds,
While the grove their song applauds.

Though their voices lower be,
Streams have too their melody;
Night and day they warbling run,
Never pause, but still sing on.

All the flowers that gild the spring
Hither their still music bring;
If Heaven bless them, thankful they
Smell more sweet, and look more gay.

Only we can scarce afford
This short office to our Lord;
We,—on whom His bounty flows,
All things gives, and nothing owes.

Wake, for shame, my sluggish heart,
Wake, and gladly sing thy part:
Learn of birds, and springs, and flowers,
How to use thy noble powers.

Call whole Nature to thy aid,
Since 'twas He whole Nature made;
Join in one eternal song,
Who to one God all belong.

Live for ever, glorious Lord,
Live, by all Thy works adored;
One in Three, and Three in One,
Thrice we bow to Thee alone.

147 *Fain would my Thoughts*

FAIN would my thoughts fly up to Thee,
  Thy peace, sweet Lord, to find;
But when I offer, still the world
  Lays clogs upon my mind.

Sometimes I climb a little way
  And thence look down below;
How nothing, there, do all things seem,
  That here make such a show!

Then round about I turn my eyes
  To feast my hungry sight;
I meet with Heaven in every thing,
  In every thing delight.

When I have thus triumph'd awhile,
  And think to build my nest,
Some cross conceits come fluttering by,
  And interrupt my rest.

Then to the earth again I fall,
  And from my low dust cry,
'Twas not in my wing, LORD, but Thine,
  That I got up so high.

And now, my God, whether I rise,
  Or still lie down in dust,
Both I submit to Thy blest will;
  In both, on Thee I trust.

Guide Thou my way, who art Thyself
  My everlasting end,
That every step, or swift, or slow,
  Still to Thyself may tend!

To Father, Son, and Holy Ghost,
  One consubstantial Three,
All highest praise, all humblest thanks,
  Now and for ever be!

JEREMY TAYLOR

1613–1667

148 *The Penitent*

LORD, I have sinn'd, and the black number swells
  To such a dismal sum,
That should my stony heart and eyes,
And this whole sinful trunk a flood become,

And melt to tears, their drops could not suffice
        To count my score,
        Much less to pay:
But Thou, my God, hast blood in store,
Yet, since the balsam of thy blood,
Although it can, will do no good,
Unless the wound be cleans'd in tears before;
Thou in whose sweet, but pensive face,
Laughter could never steal a place,
        Teach but my heart and eyes
        To melt away,
And then one drop of balsam will suffice.

HENRY MORE

1614–1687

149 *Resolution:*

the Song of Hylobaris concerning Divine Providence

WHERE'S now the object of thy fears;
Needless sighs and fruitless tears?
They be all gone like idle dream
Suggested from the body's steam.
O cave of horror black as pitch!
Dark den of spectres that bewitch
The weaken'd fancy, sore affright
With the grim shades of grisly night.
What's plague and prison? Loss of friends?
War, dearth, and death that all things ends?
Mere bug-bears for the childish mind:
Pure panic terrors of the blind.

HENRY MORE

Collect thy soul into one sphere
Of light, and 'bove the earth it rear:
Those wild scatter'd thoughts that erst
Lay loosely in the world dispersed
Call in: thy spirit thus knit in one
Fair lucid orb; those fears be gone
Like vain impostures of the night
That fly before the morning bright.
Then with pure eyes thou shalt behold
How the first Goodness doth infold
All things in loving tender arms:
That deemèd mischiefs are no harms,
But sovereign salves, and skilful cures
Of greater woes the world endures;
That man's stout soul may win a state
Far raised above the reach of Fate.

Then wilt thou say, God rules the world,
Though mountain over mountain hurl'd
Be pitch'd amid the foaming main,
Which busy winds to wrath constrain.
His fall doth make the billows start
And backward skip from every part,
Quite sunk; then o'er his senseless side
The waves in triumph proudly ride.
Though inward tempests fiercely rock
The tottering earth, that with the shock
High spires and heavy rocks fall down
With their own weight drove into ground;
Though pitchy blasts from Hell up-borne
Stop the outgoings of the morn,

And nature play her fiery games
In this forced night, with fulgurant flames,
Baring by fits for more affright
The pale dead visages, ghastly sight
Of men astonish'd at the stoure
Of Heaven's great rage, the rattling showers
Of hail, the hoarse bellowing of thunder,
Their own loud shrieks made mad with wonder:
All this confusion cannot move
The purgèd mind, freed from the love
Of commerce with her body dear,
Cell of sad thoughts, sole spring of fear.

Whate'er I feel or hear or see
Threats but these parts that mortal be.
Nought can the honest heart dismay
Unless the love of living clay,
And long acquaintance with the light
Of this out-world, and what to sight
Those too officious beams discover
Of forms that round about us hover.

Power, Wisdom, Goodness sure did frame
This Universe, and still guide the same.
But thoughts from passions sprung, deceive
Vain mortals. No man can contrive
A better course than what's been run
Since the first circuit of the sun.

He that beholds all from on high
Knows better what to do than I.

fulgurant] lightning. stoure] tumult.

I'm not mine own: should I repine
If He dispose of what's not mine?
Purge but thy soul of blind self-will,
Thou straight shalt see God doth no ill.
The world He fills with the bright rays
Of His free goodness. He displays
Himself throughout. Like common air
That spirit of life through all doth fare.
Suck'd in by them as vital breath
That willingly embrace not death.
But those that with that living law
Be unacquainted, cares do gnaw;
Mistrust of God's good providence
Doth daily vex their wearied sense.

150 *Hymn to Charity and Humility*

FAR have I clamber'd in my mind
But nought so great as love I find:
Deep-searching wit, mount-moving might
Are nought compar'd to that good spright.
Light of delight and soul of bliss!
Sure source of lasting happiness!
Higher than Heaven! lower than hell!
What is thy tent? where may'st thou dwell?
  My mansion hight humility,
Heaven's vastest capability.
The further it doth downward tend
The higher up it doth ascend;
If it go down to utmost nought
It shall return with that it sought.

Lord stretch thy tent in my strait breast,
Enlarge it downward, that sure rest
May there be pight; for that pure fire
Wherewith thou wontest to inspire
All self-dead souls. My life is gone,
Sad solitude's my irksome wonne.
Cut off from men and all this world
In Lethe's lonesome ditch I am hurl'd.
Nor might nor sight doth ought me move,
Nor do I care to be above.
O feeble rays of mental light!
That best be seen in this dark night,
What are you? what is any strength
If it be not laid in one length
With pride or love? I nought desire
But a new life or quite t'expire.
Could I demolish with mine eye
Strong towers, stop the fleet Stars in sky,
Bring down to earth the pale-fac'd Moon,
Or turn black midnight to bright noon:
Though all things were put in my hand,
As parch'd as dry as th' Libyan sand
Would be my life if Charity
Were wanting. But Humility
Is more than my poor soul durst crave
That lies intomb'd in lowly grave.
But if't were lawful up to send
My voice to Heaven, this should it rend:
  Lord thrust me deeper into dust
That thou may'st raise me with the just.

RICHARD BAXTER

1615–1691

151 *Lord, it belongs not to my Care*

LORD, it belongs not to my care,
  Whether I die or live;
To love and serve Thee is my share,
  And this Thy grace must give.

If life be long I will be glad,
  That I may long obey;
If short—yet why should I be sad
  To soar to endless day?

Christ leads me through no darker rooms
  Than He went through before;
He that unto God's kingdom comes,
  Must enter by this door.

Come, Lord, when grace has made me meet
  Thy blessèd face to see;
For if Thy work on earth be sweet,
  What will Thy glory be!

Then I shall end my sad complaints,
  And weary, sinful days;
And join with the triumphant saints,
  To sing Jehovah's praise.

My knowledge of that life is small,
  The eye of faith is dim;
But 'tis enough that Christ knows all,
  And I shall be with Him.

JOSEPH BEAUMONT

1615–1699

152 *Morning Hymn*

WHAT'S this morn's bright eye to me,
If I see not Thine and Thee,
Fairer Jesu; in whose face
All my Heaven is spread!—Alas,
Still I grovel in dead night,
Whilst I want Thy living light;
Dreaming with wide open eyes
Fond fantastic vanities.

Shine, my only Day-Star, shine:
So mine eyes shall wake by Thine;
So the dreams I grope in now
To clear visions all shall grow;
So my day shall measured be
By Thy Grace's clarity;
So shall I discern the path
Thy sweet law prescribed hath;
For Thy ways cannot be shown
By any light but by Thine own.

153 *The Ascension*

LIFT up your heads, great gates, and sing,
Now Glory comes, and Glory's King;
Now by your high all-golden way
The fairer Heaven comes home to-day.

Hark! now the gates are ope, and hear
The tune of each triumphant sphere;

Where every Angel as he sings
Keeps time with his applauding wings,
And makes Heaven's loftiest roof rebound
The echoes of the noble sound.

154 *Whit Sunday*

FOUNTAIN of Sweets! Eternal Dove!
Which leav'st Thy glorious perch above,
And hovering down, vouchsafest thus
To make Thy nest below with us.

Soft as Thy softest feathers, may
We find Thy love to us to-day;
And in the shelter of Thy wing
Obtain Thy leave and grace to sing.

155 *The Garden*

THE Garden's quit with me: as yesterday
I walked in that, to day that walks in me;
Through all my memory
It sweetly wanders, and has found a way
To make me honestly possess
What still another's is.

Yet this gain's dainty sense doth gall my mind
With the remembrance of a bitter loss.
Alas, how odd and cross
Are earth's delights, in which the soul can find
No honey, but withal some sting
To check the pleasing thing!

For now I'm haunted with the thought of that
Heav'n-planted garden, where felicity
Flourished on every tree.
Lost, lost it is; for at the guarded gate
A flaming sword forbiddeth Sin
(That's I,) to enter in.

O Paradise! when I was turned out
Hadst thou but kept the serpent still within,
My banishment had been
Less sad and dangerous: but round about
This wide world runneth raging he
To banish me from me:

I feel that through my soul he death hath shot;
And thou, alas, hast locked up life's tree.
O miserable me,
What help were left, had Jesus's pity not
Shewed me another tree, which can
Enliven dying man.

That tree, made fertile by his own dear blood;
And by his death with quick'ning virtue fraught.
I now dread not the thought
Of barracado'd Eden, since as good
A Paradise I planted see
On open Calvary.

ABRAHAM COWLEY

1618–1667

156

Hell

from *Davideis*. *Book I*

BENEATH the silent chambers of the earth,
Where the sun's fruitful beams give metals birth,
Where he the growth of fatal gold does see,
Gold which above more influence has than he.
Beneath the dens where unfletched tempests lie,
And infant winds their tender voices try,
Beneath the mighty ocean's wealthy caves,
Beneath th'eternal fountain of all waves,
Where their vast court the mother-waters keep,
And undisturb'd by moons in silence sleep,
There is a place deep, wondrous deep below,
Which genuine night and horror does o'erflow;
No bound controls th'unwearied space, but hell
Endless as those dire pains that in it dwell.
Here no dear glimpse of the sun's lovely face,
Strikes through the solid darkness of the place;
No dawning morn does her kind reds display;
One slight weak beam would here be thought the day.
No gentle stars with their fair gems of light
Offend the tyrannous and unquestion'd night.
Here Lucifer the mighty captive reigns:
Proud, 'midst his woes, and tyrant in his chains.
Once general of a gilded host of sprights,
Like Hesper, leading forth the spangled nights.
But down like lightning, which him struck, he came,
And roar'd at his first plunge into the flame.

Myriads of spirits fell wounded round him there;
With dropping lights thick shone the singed air.
Since when the dismal solace of their woe,
Has only been weak mankind to undo.

157 *The Annunciation*

from *Davideis. Book II*

FAIR Angels pass'd by next in seemly Bands,
All gilt, with gilded baskets in their hands.
Some as they went the blue-ey'd violets strew,
Some spotless lilies in loose order threw.
Some did the way with full-blown roses spread;
Their smell divine, and colour strangely red;
Not such as our dull gardens proudly wear,
Whom weathers taint, and winds' rude kisses tear.
Such, I believe, was the first rose's hue,
Which, at God's word, in beauteous Eden grew.
Queen of the flowers, which made that orchard gay,
The morning blushes of the spring's new day.
With sober pace an heav'nly maid walks in,
Her looks all fair; no sign of native sin
Through her whole body writ; immod'rate grace
Spoke things far more than human in her face.
It casts a dusky gloom o'er all the flow'rs;
And with full beams their mingled light devours.
An angel strait broke from a shining cloud,
And press'd his wings, and with much rev'rence bow'd.
Again he bow'd, and grave approach he made,
And thus his sacred message sweetly said:
Hail, full of grace, thee the whole world shall call
Above all Bles'd; thee, who shalt bless them all.

Thy Virgin womb in wondrous sort shall shroud
Jesus the God; (and then again he bow'd)
Conception the great Spirit shall breathe on thee;
Hail thou, who must God's wife, God's mother be!
With that, his seeming form to heav'n he rear'd;
She low obeisance made, and disappear'd.

SIR EDWARD SHERBURNE

1618–1702

158 *And she washed his Feet with her Tears, and wiped them with the Hairs of her Head*

THE proud Ægyptian Queen, her Roman guest,
(T'express her love in height of state, and pleasure)
With pearl dissolv'd in gold, did feast,
Both food, and treasure.

And now (dear Lord!) thy lover, on the fair
And silver tables of thy feet, behold!
Pearl in her tears, and in her hair,
Offers thee gold.

ANDREW MARVELL

1621–1678

159 *The Coronet*

WHEN for the thorns with which I long, too long,
With many a piercing wound,
My Saviour's head have crown'd,
I seek with garlands to redress that wrong:
Through every garden, every mead,
I gather flow'rs (my fruits are only flow'rs)

Dismantling all the fragrant towers
That once adorn'd my shepherdess's head.
And now when I have summ'd up all my store,
Thinking (so I myself deceive)
So rich a chaplet thence to weave
As never yet the king of glory wore:
Alas I find the serpent old
That, twining in his speckled breast,
About the flow'rs disguised does fold,
With wreaths of fame and interest.
Ah, foolish Man, that would'st debase with them,
And mortal glory, Heaven's diadem!
But thou who only could'st the serpent tame,
Either his slipp'ry knots at once untie,
And disentangle all his winding snare:
Or shatter too with him my curious frame
And let these wither, so that he may die,
Though set with skill and chosen out with care.
That they, while Thou on both their spoils dost tread,
May crown thy feet, that could not crown thy head.

160 *Song of the Emigrants*

WHERE the remote Bermudas ride
In th' ocean's bosom unespied,
From a small boat, that row'd along,
The list'ning winds receiv'd this song.
What should we do but sing his praise
That led us through the wat'ry maze,
Unto an isle so long unknown,
And yet far kinder than our own

When he the huge sea-monsters wracks,
That lift the deep upon their backs,
He lands us on a grassy stage;
Safe from the storms, and prelate's rage.
He gave us this eternal spring,
Which here enamels every thing;
And sends the fowls to us in care,
On daily visits through the air.
He hangs in shades the orange bright,
Like golden lamps in a green night.
And does in the pomegranates close
Jewels more rich than Ormus shows.
He makes the figs our mouths to meet;
And throws the melons at our feet.
But apples plants of such a price,
No tree could ever bear them twice.
With cedars, chosen by his hand,
From Lebanon, he stores the land.
And makes the hollow seas, that roar,
Proclaim the ambergris on shore.
He cast (of which we rather boast)
The Gospels' pearl upon our coast.
And in these rocks for us did frame
A temple, where to sound his name.
Oh let our voice his praise exalt,
Till it arrive at Heaven's vault:
Which thence (perhaps) rebounding, may
Echo beyond the Mexique Bay.
Thus sung they, in the English boat,
An holy and a cheerful note,
And all the way, to guide their chime,
With falling oars they kept the time.

161

On a Drop of Dew

SEE how the Orient dew,
Shed from the bosom of the morn
Into the blowing roses,
Yet careless of its mansion new;
For the clear region where 'twas born
Round in its self incloses:
And in its little globe's extent,
Frames as it can its native element.
How it the purple flow'r does slight,
Scarce touching where it lies,
But gazing back upon the skies,
Shines with a mournful light;
Like its own tear,
Because so long divided from the sphere.
Restless it rolls and unsecure,
Trembling lest it grow impure:
Till the warm sun pity its pain,
And to the skies exhale it back again.
So the soul, that drop, that ray
Of the clear fountain of eternal day,
Could it within the human flow'r be seen,
Rememb'ring still its former height,
Shuns the sweet leaves and blossoms green;
And, recollecting its own light,
Does, in its pure and circling thoughts, express
The greater heaven in an heaven less.
In how coy a figure wound,
Every way it turns away:
So the world excluding round,
Yet receiving in the day.

Dark beneath, but bright above:
Here disdaining, there in love,
How loose and easy hence to go:
How girt and ready to ascend.
Moving but on a point below,
It all about does upwards bend.
Such did the manna's sacred dew distil;
White, and entire, though congeal'd and chill.
Congeal'd on earth: but does, dissolving, run
Into the glories of th' almighty sun.

162 *A Dialogue between the Soul and Body*

Soul.

O WHO shall, from this dungeon, raise
A soul enslav'd so many ways?
With bolts of bones, that fetter'd stands
In feet; and manacled in hands.
Here blinded with an eye; and there
Deaf with the drumming of an ear.
A soul hung up, as 'twere, in chains
Of nerves, and arteries, and veins.
Tortur'd, besides each other part,
In a vain head, and double heart.

Body.

O who shall me deliver whole,
From bonds of this tyrannic soul?
Which, stretched upright, impales me so,
That mine own precipice I go;
And warms and moves this needless frame:
(A fever could but do the same.)

And, wanting where its spite to try,
Has made me live to let me die.
A body that could never rest,
Since this ill spirit it possessed.

Soul.

What magic could me thus confine
Within another's grief to pine?
Where whatsoever it complain,
I feel, that cannot feel, the pain.
And all my care itself employs,
That to preserve, which me destroys:
Constrain'd not only to endure
Diseases, but, what's worse, the cure:
And ready oft the port to gain,
Am shipwrecked into health again.

Body.

But physic yet could never reach
The maladies thou me dost teach;
Whom first the cramp of hope does tear:
And then the palsy shakes of fear.
The pestilence of love does heat:
Or hatred's hidden ulcer eat.
Joy's cheerful madness does perplex:
Or sorrow's other madness vex.
Which knowledge forces me to know;
And memory will not forgo.
What but a soul could have the wit
To build me up for sin so fit?
So architects do square and hew
Green trees that in the forest grew.

HENRY VAUGHAN

1622–1695

163 *Childhood*

I CANNOT reach it; and my striving eye
Dazzles at it, as at eternity.
Were now that chronicle alive,
Those white designs which children drive,
And the thoughts of each harmless hour,
With their content, too, in my pow'r,
Quickly would I make my path even,
And by mere playing go to Heaven.
Why should men love
A wolf, more than a lamb or dove?
Or choose hell-fire and brimstone streams
Before bright stars, and God's own beams?
Who kisseth thorns, will hurt his face,
But flowers do both refresh and grace,
And sweetly living (fie on men!)
Are when dead, medicinal then.
If seeing much should make staid eyes,
And long experience should make wise;
Since all that age doth teach, is ill,
Why should I not love childhood still?
Why if I see a rock or shelf,
Shall I from thence cast down my self,
Or by complying with the world,
From the same precipice be hurl'd?
Those observations are but foul
Which make me wise to lose my soul.

And yet the practice worldlings call
Business and weighty action all,

Checking the poor child for his play,
But gravely cast themselves away.

Dear, harmless age! the short, swift span,
Where weeping virtue parts with man;
Where love without lust dwells, and bends
What way we please, without self-ends.

An age of mysteries! which he
Must live twice, that would God's face see;
Which Angels guard, and with it play,
Angels! which foul men drive away.

How do I study now, and scan
Thee, more than e'er I studied man,
And only see through a long night
Thy edges, and thy bordering light!
O for thy centre and mid-day!
For sure that is the narrow way.

164 *The Night*

John 2. 3

THROUGH that pure Virgin-shrine,
That sacred veil drawn o'er thy glorious noon
That men might look and live as glow-worms shine,
And face the Moon:
Wise Nicodemus saw such light
As made him know his God by night.

Most blest believer he!
Who in that land of darkness and blind eyes
Thy long expected healing wings could see,
When thou didst rise,

And what can never more be done,
Did at midnight speak with the sun!

O who will tell me, where
He found thee at that dead and silent hour!
What hallow'd solitary ground did bear
So rare a flower,
Within whose sacred leaves did lie
The fullness of the deity.

No mercy-seat of gold,
No dead and dusty Cherub, nor carv'd stone,
But his own living works did my Lord hold
And lodge alone;
Where trees and herbs did watch and peep
And wonder, while the Jews did sleep.

Dear night! this world's defeat;
The stop to busy fools; care's check and curb;
The day of Spirits; my soul's calm retreat
Which none disturb!
Christ's progress, and his prayer time;
The hours to which high heaven doth chime.

God's silent, searching flight:
When my Lord's head is fill'd with dew, and all
His locks are wet with the clear drops of night;
His still, soft call;
His knocking time; the soul's dumb watch,
When Spirits their fair kindred catch.

Were all my loud, evil days
Calm and unhaunted as is thy dark tent,
Whose peace but by some Angel's wing or voice
Is seldom rent;
Then I in Heaven all the long year
Would keep, and never wander here.

But living where the sun
Doth all things wake, and where all mix and tire
Themselves and others, I consent and run
To ev'ry mire,
And by this world's ill-guiding light,
Err more than I can do by night.

There is in God (some say)
A deep, but dazzling darkness; as men here
Say it is late and dusky, because they
See not all clear;
O for that night! where I in him
Might live invisible and dim.

165 *The World*

I SAW Eternity the other night,
Like a great ring of pure and endless light,
All calm, as it was bright;
And round beneath it, Time, in hours, days, years,
Driven by the spheres,
Like a vast shadow moved; in which the world
And all her train were hurl'd.

The doting Lover in his quaintest strain
Did there complain;
Near him, his lute, his fancy, and his slights,
Wit's sour delights;

With gloves and knots, the silly snares of pleasure;
Yet his dear treasure
All scatter'd lay, while he his eyes did pour
Upon a flower.

The darksome Statesman hung with weights and woe,
Like a thick midnight-fog, moved there so slow,
He did not stay, nor go;
Condemning thoughts—like sad eclipses—scowl
Upon his soul,
And clouds of crying witnesses without
Pursued him with one shout;
Yet digg'd the mole, and lest his ways be found,
Work'd under ground,
Where he did clutch his prey; but One did see
That policy;
Churches and altars fed him; perjuries
Were gnats and flies;
It rain'd about him blood and tears, but he
Drank them as free.

The fearful Miser on a heap of rust
Sate pining all his life there; did scarce trust
His own hands with the dust;
Yet would not place one piece above, but lives
In fear of thieves:
Thousands there were as frantic as himself,
And hugg'd each one his pelf.

The down-right Epicure placed heaven in sense,
And scorn'd pretence;
While others, slipped into a wide excess,
Said little less;

The weaker sort, slight, trivial wares enslave,
Who think them brave;
And poor, despisèd Truth sat counting by
Their victory.

Yet some, who all this while did weep and sing,
And sing, and weep, soar'd up into the ring;
But most would use no wing.
O fools—said I—thus to prefer dark night
Before true light!
To live in grots, and caves, and hate the day
Because it shews the way:—
The way, which from this dead and dark abode
Leads up to God;
A way where you might tread the Sun, and be
More bright than he!
But as I did their madness so discuss,
One whisper'd thus,—
This ring the Bride-groom did for none provide
But for His Bride.

166 *The Morning-Watch*

O JOYS! Infinite sweetness! with what flowers,
And shoots of glory, my soul breaks, and buds!
All the long hours
Of night, and rest
Through the still shrouds
Of sleep, and clouds,
This dew fell on my breast;
O how it bloods,

And spirits all my Earth! hark! In what rings,
And hymning circulations the quick world
Awakes, and sings;
The rising winds,
And falling springs,
Birds, beasts, all things
Adore him in their kinds.
Thus all is hurl'd
In sacred hymns, and order, the great chime
And symphony of nature. Prayer is
The world in tune,
A spirit-voice,
And vocal joys
Whose echo is heav'n's bliss.
O let me climb
When I lie down! The pious soul by night
Is like a clouded star, whose beams though said
To shed their light
Under some cloud
Yet are above,
And shine, and move
Beyond that misty shroud.
So in my bed
That curtain'd grave, though sleep, like ashes, hide
My lamp, and life, both shall in thee abide.

167 *The Dawning*

AH! what time wilt thou come? when shall that cry,
The bridegroom 's coming! fill the sky?
Shall it in the evening run
When our words and works are done?

Or will thy all-surprising light
    Break at midnight?
When either sleep, or some dark pleasure
Possesseth mad man without measure;
Or shall these early, fragrant hours
    Unlock thy bow'rs?
And with their blush of light descry
Thy locks crown'd with eternity;
Indeed, it is the only time
That with thy glory doth best chime;
All now are stirring, ev'ry field
    Full hymns doth yield,
The whole creation shakes off night,
And for thy shadow looks the light;
Stars now vanish without number,
Sleepy planets set, and slumber,
The pursy clouds disband, and scatter;
All expect some sudden matter,
Not one beam triumphs, but from far
    That morning-star.

O at what time soever thou
(Unknown to us) the heavens wilt bow,
And, with thy angels in the van,
Descend to judge poor careless man,
Grant, I may not like puddle lie
In a corrupt security,
Where, if a traveller water crave,
He finds it dead, and in a grave;
But as this restless, vocal spring
All day and night doth run, and sing,

And though here born, yet is acquainted
Elsewhere, and flowing keeps untainted;
So let me all my busy age
In thy free services engage,
And though (while here) of force I must
Have commerce sometimes with poor dust,
And in my flesh, though vile, and low,
As this doth in her channel, flow,
Yet let my course, my aim, my love,
And chief acquaintance be above;
So when that day and hour shall come
In which thy self will be the sun,
Thou'lt find me dressed and on my way,
Watching the break of thy great day.

168 *Ascension-Day*

LORD Jesus! with what sweetness and delights,
Sure, holy hopes, high joys and quick'ning flights
Dost thou feed thine! O thou! the hand that lifts
To him, who gives all good and perfect gifts.
Thy glorious, bright Ascension (though remov'd
So many ages from me) is so prov'd
And by thy spirit seal'd to me, that I
Feel me a sharer in thy victory.
I soar and rise
Up to the skies,
Leaving the world their day,
And in my flight,
For the true light
Go seeking all the way;

I greet thy sepulchre, salute thy grave,
That blest enclosure, where the angels gave
The first glad tidings of thy early light,
And resurrection from the earth and night.
I see that morning in thy convert's tears,
Fresh as the dew, which but this dawning wears?
I smell her spices, and her ointment yields,
As rich a scent as the now primros'd-fields:
The day-star smiles, and light, with thee deceas'd,
Now shines in all the chambers of the east.
What stirs, what posting intercourse and mirth
Of saints and angels glorify the earth?
What sighs, what whispers, busy stops and stays;
Private and holy talk fill all the ways?
They pass as at the last great day, and run
In their white robes to seek the risen sun;
I see them, hear them, mark their haste, and move
Amongst them, with them, wing'd with faith and love.
Thy forty days' more secret commerce here,
After thy death and funeral, so clear
And indisputable, shows to my sight
As the sun doth, which to those days gave light.
I walk the fields of Bethani which shine
All now as fresh as Eden, and as fine.
Such was the bright world, on the first seventh day,
Before man brought forth sin, and sin decay;
When like a virgin clad in flowers and green
The pure earth sat, and the fair woods had seen
No frost, but flourish'd in that youthful vest,
With which their great creator had them dress'd:
When heav'n above them shin'd like molten glass,
While all the planets did unclouded pass;

And springs, like dissolv'd pearls their streams did pour
Ne'er marr'd with floods, nor anger'd with a show'r.
With these fair thoughts I move in this fair place,
And the last steps of my mild master trace;
I see him leading out his chosen train,
All sad with tears, which like warm summer-rain
In silent drops steal from their holy eyes,
Fix'd lately on the cross, now on the skies.
And now (eternal Jesus!) thou dost heave
Thy blessed hands to bless, these thou dost leave;
The cloud doth now receive thee, and their sight
Having lost thee, behold two men in white!
Two and no more: *what two attest, is true*,
Was thine own answer to the stubborn Jew.
Come then thou faithful witness! come dear Lord
Upon the clouds again to judge this world!

169 *The Revival*

UNFOLD, unfold! take in his light,
Who makes thy cares more short than night.
The joys, which with his day-star rise,
He deals to all, but drowsy eyes:
And what the men of this world miss,
Some drops and dews of future bliss.
  Hark! how his winds have chang'd their note,
And with warm whispers call thee out.
The frosts are past, the storms are gone:
And backward life at last comes on.
The lofty groves in express joys
Reply unto the turtle's voice,
And here in dust and dirt, O here
The lilies of his love appear!

170 *The Seed growing secretly*

S. Mark 4. 26

IF this world's friends might see but once
What some poor man may often feel,
Glory, and gold, and crowns and thrones
They would soon quit and learn to kneel.

My dew, my dew! my early love,
My soul's bright food, thy absence kills!
Hover not long, eternal dove!
Life without thee is loose and spills.

Something I had, which long ago
Did learn to suck, and sip, and taste,
But now grown sickly, sad and slow,
Doth fret and wrangle, pine and waste.

O spread thy sacred wings and shake
One living drop! one drop life keeps!
If pious griefs heaven's joys awake,
O fill his bottle! thy child weeps!

Slowly and sadly doth he grow,
And soon as left, shrinks back to ill;
O feed that life, which makes him blow
And spread and open to thy will!

For thy eternal, living wells
None stain'd or wither'd shall come near:
A fresh, immortal green there dwells,
And spotless white is all the wear.

HENRY VAUGHAN

Dear, secret greenness! nurs'd below
Tempest and winds, and winter-nights,
Vex not, that but one sees thee grow,
That one made all these lesser lights.

If those bright joys he singly sheds
On thee, were all met in one crown,
Both sun and stars would hide their heads;
And moons, though full, would get them down.

Let glory be their bait, whose minds
Are all too high for a low cell:
Though hawks can prey through storms and winds,
The poor bee in her hive must dwell.

Glory, the crowd's cheap tinsel still
To what most takes them, is a drudge;
And they too oft take good for ill,
And thriving vice for virtue judge.

What needs a conscience calm and bright
Within itself an outward test?
Who breaks his glass to take more light,
Makes way for storms into his rest.

Then bless thy secret growth, nor catch
At noise, but thrive unseen and dumb;
Keep clean, bear fruit, earn life and watch
Till the white winged reapers come!

171 *I walked the other Day*

I WALK'D the other day (to spend my hour)
Into a field
Where I sometimes had seen the soil to yield
A gallant flow'r,
But winter now had ruffled all the bow'r
And curious store
I knew there heretofore.

Yet I whose search lov'd not to peep and peer
I'th' face of things
Thought with my self, there might be other springs
Besides this here
Which, like cold friends, sees us but once a year,
And so the flow'r
Might have some other bow'r.

Then taking up what I could nearest spy
I digg'd about
That place where I had seen him to grow out,
And by and by
I saw the warm recluse alone to lie
Where fresh and green
He lived of us unseen.

Many a question intricate and rare
Did I there strow,
But all I could extort was, that he now
Did there repair
Such losses as befel him in this air
And would e'er long
Come forth most fair and young.

This past, I threw the clothes quite o'er his head,
And stung with fear
Of my own frailty dropped down many a tear
Upon his bed,
Then sighing whisper'd, Happy are the dead!
What peace doth now
Rock him asleep below?

And yet, how few believe such doctrine springs
From a poor root
Which all the winter sleeps here under foot
And hath no wings
To raise it to the truth and light of things,
But is still trod
By ev'ry wand'ring clod.

O thou! whose spirit did at first inflame
And warm the dead,
And by a sacred incubation fed
With life this frame
Which once had neither being, form, nor name,
Grant I may so
Thy steps track here below,

That in these masques and shadows I may see
Thy sacred way,
And by those hid ascents climb to that day
Which breaks from thee
Who art in all things, though invisibly;
Show me thy peace,
Thy mercy, love, and ease,

And from this care, where dreams and sorrows reign
Lead me above
Where light, joy, leisure, and true comforts move
Without all pain,
There, hid in thee, show me his life again
At whose dumb urn
Thus all the year I mourn.

172 *They are all gone into the World of Light*

THEY are all gone into the world of light!
And I alone sit ling'ring here;
Their very memory is fair and bright,
And my sad thoughts doth clear.

It glows and glitters in my cloudy breast
Like stars upon some gloomy grove,
Or those faint beams in which this hill is dress'd,
After the sun's remove.

I see them walking in an air of glory,
Whose light doth trample on my days:
My days, which are at best but dull and hoary,
Mere glimmering and decays.

O holy hope! and high humility,
High as the Heavens above!
These are your walks, and you have show'd them me
To kindle my cold love,

Dear, beauteous death! the Jewel of the Just,
Shining nowhere, but in the dark;
What mysteries do lie beyond thy dust;
Could man outlook that mark!

He that hath found some fledg'd bird's nest, may know
At first sight, if the bird be flown;
But what fair well, or grove he sings in now,
That is to him unknown.

And yet, as angels in some brighter dreams
Call to the soul, when man doth sleep:
So some strange thoughts transcend our wonted themes,
And into glory peep.

If a star were confin'd into a tomb
Her captive flames must needs burn there;
But when the hand that lock'd her up, gives room,
She'll shine through all the sphere.

O Father of eternal life, and all
Created glories under thee!
Resume thy spirit from this world of thrall
Into true liberty.

Either disperse these mists, which blot and fill
My perspective (still) as they pass,
Or else remove me hence unto that hill,
Where I shall need no glass.

173 *The Dwelling-Place*

S. John, chap. 1. *ver.* 38, 39

WHAT happy, secret fountain,
Fair shade, or mountain,
Whose undiscover'd virgin glory
Boasts it this day, though not in story,
Was then thy dwelling? did some cloud
Fix'd to a tent, descend and shroud

My distress'd Lord? or did a star
Beckon'd by thee, though high and far,
In sparkling smiles haste gladly down
To lodge light, and increase her own?
My dear, dear God! I do not know
What lodg'd thee then, nor where, nor how;
But I am sure, thou dost now come
Oft to a narrow, homely room,
Where thou too hast but the least part,
My God, I mean my sinful heart.

174

Religion

MY God, when I walk in those groves,
And leaves thy spirit doth still fan,
I see in each shade that there grows
An angel talking with a man.

Under a juniper, some house,
Or the cool myrtle's canopy,
Others beneath an oak's green boughs,
Or at some fountain's bubbling eye;

Here Jacob dreams, and wrestles; there
Elias by a raven is fed,
Another time by th' angel, where
He brings him water with his bread;

In Abr'ham's tent the winged guests
(O how familiar then was heaven!)
Eat, drink, discourse, sit down, and rest
Until the cool and shady even;

Nay thou thyself, my God, in fire,
Whirlwinds, and clouds, and the soft voice
Speak'st there so much, that I admire
We have no conf'rence in these days;

Is the truce broke? or 'cause we have
A mediator now with thee,
Dost thou therefore old treaties waive
And by appeals from him decree?

Or is't so, as some green heads say
That now all miracles must cease?
Though thou hast promis'd they should stay
The tokens of the Church, and peace;

No, no; religion is a spring
That from some secret, golden mine
Derives her birth, and thence doth bring
Cordials in every drop, and wine;

But in her long, and hidden course
Passing through the earth's dark veins,
Grows still from better unto worse,
And both her taste, and colour stains,

Then drilling on, learns to increase
False echoes, and confused sounds,
And unawares doth often seize
On veins of sulphur under ground;

So poison'd, breaks forth in some clime,
And at first sight doth many please,
But drunk, is puddle, or mere slime
And 'stead of physic, a disease;

Just such a tainted sink we have
Like that Samaritan's dead well,
Nor must we for the kernel crave
Because most voices like the shell.

Heal then these waters, Lord; or bring thy flock,
Since these are troubled, to the springing rock,
Look down great Master of the feast; O shine,
And turn once more our water into wine!

175 *Quickness*

FALSE life! a foil and no more, when
Wilt thou be gone?
Thou foul deception of all men
That would not have the true come on.

Thou art a moonlike toil; a blind
Self-posing state;
A dark contest of waves and wind;
A mere tempestuous debate.

Life is a fix'd, discerning light,
A knowing joy;
No chance, or fit: but ever bright,
And calm and full, yet doth not cloy.

'Tis such a blissful thing, that still
Doth vivify,
And shine and smile, and hath the skill
To please without Eternity.

Thou art a toilsome mole, or less,
A moving mist,
But life is, what none can express,
A quickness, which my God hath kiss'd.

176 *Corruption*

SURE, it was so. Man in those early days
Was not all stone, and earth,
He shin'd a little, and by those weak rays
Had some glimpse of his birth.
He saw heaven o'er his head, and knew from whence
He came (condemned) hither,
And, as first love draws strongest, so from hence
His mind sure progress'd thither.
Things here were strange unto him: sweat, and till,
All was a thorn, or weed,
Nor did those last, but (like himself) died still
As soon as they did seed,
They seem'd to quarrel with him; for that act
That fell him, foil'd them all,
He drew the curse upon the world, and crack'd
The whole frame with his fall.
This made him long for home, as loath to stay
With murmurers, and foes;
He sigh'd for Eden, and would often say
Ah! what bright days were those?
Nor was heav'n cold unto him; for each day
The valley, or the mountain
Afforded visits, and still paradise lay
In some green shade, or fountain.
Angels lay leiger here; each bush, and cell,
Each oak, and highway knew them,
Walk but the fields, or sit down at some well,
And he was sure to view them.

lay leiger] were present.

Almighty love! where art thou now? mad man
Sits down, and freezeth on,
He raves, and swears to stir nor fire, nor fan,
But bids the thread be spun.
I see, thy curtains are close-drawn; thy bow
Looks dim too in the cloud,
Sin triumphs still, and man is sunk below
The centre, and his shroud;
All's in deep sleep, and night; thick darkness lies
And hatcheth o'er thy people;
But hark! what trumpet's that? what angel cries
Arise! Thrust in thy sickle.

SAMUEL CROSSMAN

1624?–1684

177 '*I said sometimes with Tears*'

I SAID sometimes with tears,
Ah me! I'm loth to die!
LORD, silence Thou these fears:
My life's with Thee on high.
Sweet truth to me!
I shall arise,
And with these eyes
My Saviour see.

My life's a shade, my days
Apace to death decline;
My LORD is Life; He'll raise
My dust again, ev'n mine.
My peaceful grave shall keep
My bones till, that sweet day
I wake from my long sleep
And leave my bed of clay.

SAMUEL CROSSMAN

My Lord His angels shall
Their golden trumpets sound;
At whose most welcome call
My grave shall be unbound.
    Sweet truth to me!
        I shall arise,
        And with these eyes
    My Saviour see.

MARGARET CAVENDISH, DUCHESS OF NEWCASTLE

1625–1673

178 *The Soul's Garment*

GREAT Nature clothes the soul, which is but thin,
With fleshly garments, which the Fates do spin;
And when these garments are grown old and bare,
With sickness torn, Death takes them off with care,
And folds them up in peace and quiet rest,
And lays them safe within an earthly chest:
Then scours them well and makes them sweet and clean,
Fit for the soul to wear those clothes again.

PATRICK CAREY

fl. 1651

179 *Hymn: Crucifixus pro nobis*

CHRIST IN THE CRADLE

LOOK, how he shakes for cold!
How pale his lips are grown!
Wherein his limbs to fold
Yet mantle has he none.

His pretty feet and hands
(Of late more pure and white
Than is the snow
That pains them so)
Have lost their candour quite.
His lips are blue
(Where roses grew),
He's frozen everywhere:
All th' heat he has
Joseph, alas,
Gives in a groan; or Mary in a tear.

CHRIST IN THE GARDEN

Look, how he glows for heat!
What flames come from his eyes!
'Tis blood that he does sweat,
Blood his bright forehead dyes:
See, see! It trickles down:
Look, how it showers amain!
Through every pore
His blood runs o'er,
And empty leaves each vein.
His very heart
Burns in each part;
A fire his breast doth sear:
For all this flame,
To cool the same
He only breathes a sigh, and weeps a tear.

candour] whiteness.

PATRICK CAREY

CHRIST IN HIS PASSION

What bruises do I see!
What hideous stripes are those!
Could any cruel be
Enough, to give such blows?
Look, how they bind his arms
And vex his soul with scorns,
Upon his hair
They make him wear
A crown of piercing thorns.
Through hands and feet
Sharp nails they beat:
And now the cross they rear:
Many look on;
But only John
Stands by to sigh, Mary to shed a tear.

Why did he shake for cold?
Why did he glow for heat?
Dissolve that frost he could,
He could call back that sweat.
Those bruises, stripes, bonds, taunts,
Those thorns, which thou didst see,
Those nails, that cross,
His own life's loss,
Why, oh, why suffered he?
'Twas for thy sake.
Thou, thou didst make
Him all those torments bear:
If then his love
Do thy soul move,
Sigh out a groan, weep down a melting tear.

JOHN HALL

180 *Pastoral Hymn* 1627–1656

HAPPY choristers of air,
Who by your nimble flight draw near
His throne, whose wondrous story,
And unconfinèd glory
Your notes still carol, whom your sound
And whom your plumy pipes rebound.

Yet do the lazy snails no less
The greatness of our Lord confess.
And those whom weight hath chained,
And to the earth restrained,
Their ruder voices do as well,
Yea, and the speechless fishes tell.

Great Lord, from whom each tree receives,
Then pays again, as rent, his leaves;
Thou dost in purple set
The rose and violet
And gir'st the sickly lily white;
Yet in them all thy name dost write.

ANONYMOUS

181 *The Guest*

YET if His Majesty, our sovereign lord,
Should of his own accord
Friendly himself invite,
And say 'I'll be your guest to-morrow night,'
How should we stir ourselves, call and command
All hands to work! 'Let no man idle stand!

gir'st] dost clothe.

'Set me fine Spanish tables in the hall;
See they be fitted all;
Let there be room to eat
And order taken that there want no meat.
See every sconce and candlestick made bright,
That without tapers they may give a light.

'Look to the presence: are the carpets spread,
The dazie o'er the head,
The cushions in the chairs,
And all the candles lighted on the stairs?
Perfume the chambers, and in any case
Let each man give attendance in his place!'

Thus, if a king were coming, would we do;
And 'twere good reason too;
For 'tis a duteous thing
To show all honour to an earthly king,
And after all our travail and our cost,
So he be pleased, to think no labour lost.

But at the coming of the King of Heaven
All's set at six and seven;
We wallow in our sin,
Christ cannot find a chamber in the inn.
We entertain Him always like a stranger,
And, as at first, still lodge Him in the manger.

182 *'The New Jerusalem'*

HIERUSALEM, my happy home,
When shall I come to thee?
When shall my sorrows have an end,
Thy joys when shall I see?

dazie] dais, canopy.

ANONYMOUS

O happy harbour of the Saints!
  O sweet and pleasant soil!
In thee no sorrow may be found,
  No grief, no care, no toil.

There lust and lucre cannot dwell,
  There envy bears no sway;
There is no hunger, heat, nor cold,
  But pleasure every way.

Thy walls are made of precious stones,
  Thy bulwarks diamonds square;
Thy gates are of right orient pearl,
  Exceeding rich and rare.

Thy turrets and thy pinnacles
  With carbuncles do shine;
Thy very streets are paved with gold,
  Surpassing clear and fine.

Ah, my sweet home, Hierusalem,
  Would God I were in thee!
Would God my woes were at an end,
  Thy joys that I might see!

Thy garden and thy gallant walks
  Continually are green;
There grows such sweet and pleasant flowers
  As nowhere else are seen.

Quite through the streets, with silver sound,
  The flood of Life doth flow;
Upon whose banks on every side
  The wood of Life doth grow.

There trees for evermore bear fruit,
  And evermore do spring;
There evermore the angels sit,
  And evermore do sing.

Our Lady sings *Magnificat*
  With tones surpassing sweet;
And all the virgins bear their part,
  Sitting about her feet.

Hierusalem, my happy home,
  Would God I were in thee!
Would God my woes were at an end,
  Thy joys that I might see!

183 *O that I had Wings like a Dove*

O GRACIOUS God, O Saviour sweet,
  O Jesus, think on me,
And suffer me to kiss Thy feet,
  Though late I come to Thee.

Behold, dear Lord, I come to Thee
  With sorrow and with shame,
For when Thy bitter wounds I see,
  I know I caused the same.

Sweet Jesu, who shall lend me wings
  Of peace and perfect love,
That I may rise from earthly things
  To rest with Thee above?

For sin and sorrow overflow
  All earthly things so high,
That I can find no rest below,
  But unto Thee I fly.

Wherefore my soul doth loathe the things
  Which gave it once delight,
And unto Thee, the King of kings,
  Would mount with all her might.

And yet the weight of flesh and blood
  Doth so my wings restrain,
That oft I strive and gain no good,
  But rise, to fall again.

Yet when this fleshly misery
  Is master'd by the mind,
I cry, 'avaunt, all vanity':
  And 'Satan, stand behind.'

So thus, sweet LORD, I fly about
  In weak and weary case
Like the lone dove which Noah sent [out],
  And found no resting place.

My weary wings, sweet JESU, mark,
  And when Thou thinkest best
Stretch forth Thy arm from out the ark,
  And take me to Thy rest.

184 *'Let not the sluggish sleep'*

LET not the sluggish sleep
  Close up thy waking eye,
Until with judgement deep
  Thy daily deeds thou try:

He that one sin in conscience keeps
When he to quiet goes,
More vent'rous is than he that sleeps
With twenty mortal foes!

185 *'If I could shut the Gate'*

IF I could shut the gate against my thoughts
And keep out sorrow from this room within,
Or memory could cancel all the notes
Of my misdeeds, and I unthink my sin:
How free, how clear, how clean my soul should lie,
Discharged of such a loathsome company!

Or were there other rooms without my heart
That did not to my conscience join so near,
Where I might lodge the thoughts of sin apart
That I might not their clamorous crying hear,
What peace, what joy, what ease should I possess,
Freed from their horrors that my soul oppress!

But, O my Saviour, Who my refuge art,
Let Thy dear mercies stand 'twixt them and me,
And be the wall to separate my heart
So that I may at length repose me free;
That peace, and joy, and rest may be within,
And I remain divided from my sin.

186 *The Farewell*

METHINKS I draw but sickly breath:
Who knows but I
Before next night may sleeping lie,
Rock'd in the arms of death?

The swift-foot minutes pass away;
For Time hath wings,
That flag not for the breath of kings,
Nor brook the least delay.

And what a parcel of my sand
Is yet to pass,
Or what may break the crazy glass,
How shall I understand?

Then, base delights and dunghill joys!
Farewell, adieu!
While yet I live I'm dead to you,
And such-like toys.

I would not longer own a thought
That crawls so low,
Or lavish out my wishes so
In quest of less than nought.

My soul is wing'd with quick desires
To pass the sky;
Nothing below what is most high
Allays those noble fires.

LORD, as the kindling is from Thee,
So Thine the breath
That must continue it, till death
Be dead and cease to be.

187 *'But art Thou come, dear Saviour?'*

BUT art Thou come, dear Saviour? hath Thy love
Thus made Thee stoop, and leave Thy throne above

Thy lofty heavens, and thus Thyself to dress
In dust to visit mortals? Could no less

A condescension serve? and after all
The mean reception of a cratch and stall?

Dear Lord, I'll fetch Thee thence! I have a room
('Tis poor, but 'tis my best) if Thou wilt come

Within so small a cell, where I would fain
Mine and the world's Redeemer entertain,

I mean, my heart: 'tis sluttish, I confess,
And will not mend Thy lodging, Lord, unless

Thou send before Thy harbinger, I mean
Thy pure and purging Grace, to make it clean

And sweep its nasty corners; then I'll try
To wash it also with a weeping eye.

And when 'tis swept and wash'd, I then will go
And, with Thy leave, I'll fetch some flowers that grow

In Thine own garden, Faith and Love, to Thee;
With these I'll dress it up, and these shall be

My rosemary and bays. Yet when my best
Is done, the room's not fit for such a guest.

But here's the cure; Thy presence, Lord, alone
Will make a stall a court, a cratch a throne.

cratch] crib, manger.

188 *The Invitation*

LORD, what unvalued pleasures crown'd
The days of old;
When Thou wert so familiar found,
Those days were gold;—

When Abram wish'd Thou couldst afford
With him to feast;
When Lot but said, 'Turn in, my LORD,'
Thou wert his guest.

But, ah! this heart of mine doth pant,
And beat for Thee;
Yet Thou art strange, and wilt not grant
Thyself to me.

What, shall Thy people be so dear
To Thee no more?
Or is not heaven to earth as near
As heretofore?

The famish'd raven's hoarser cry
Finds out Thine ear;
My soul is famish'd, and I die
Unless Thou hear.

O Thou great ALPHA! King of kings
Or bow to me,
Or lend my soul seraphic wings,
To get to Thee.

189 *'Rise, O my Soul!'*

RISE, O my soul! with thy desires to heaven,
  And with divinest contemplation use
Thy time, where Time's eternity is given,
  And let vain thoughts no more thy thoughts abuse;
But down in [midnight] darkness let them lie;
So live thy better, let thy worse thoughts die!

And thou, my soul, inspired with holy flame,
  View and review, with most regardful eye,
That holy Cross, whence thy salvation came,
  On which thy Saviour and thy sin did die!
For in that sacred object is much pleasure,
And in that Saviour is my life, my treasure.

To thee, O JESU! I direct my eyes;
  To Thee my hands, to Thee my humble knees;
To Thee my heart shall offer sacrifice;
  To Thee my thoughts, Who my thoughts only sees:
To Thee myself,—myself and all I give;
To Thee I die; to Thee I only live!

190 *God our Help*

WITH floods and storms thus we be tossed,
  Awake, good Lord, to Thee we cry.
Our ship is almost sunk and lost.
Thy mercy help our misery.
  Man's strength is weak: man's wit is dull:
Man's reason's blind. These things t'amend,
Thy hand, O Lord, of might is full;
Awake betime, and help us send.

In Thee we trust, and in no wight:
Save us as chickens under the hen.
Our crookedness Thou canst make right,
Glory to Thee for aye. Amen.

191 *'And art Thou come, Blest Babe?'*

AND art Thou come, blest Babe, and come to me?
Come down to teach me how to come to Thee?

Welcome, thrice welcome to my panting soul,
Which, as it loves, doth grieve that 'tis so foul.

The less 'tis fit for Thee come from above,
The more it needs Thee, and the more I love.

192 *'Show me more Love'*

SHOW me more love, my dearest LORD;
Oh turn away Thy clouded face,
Give me some secret look or word
That may betoken love and grace;
No day or time is black to me
But that wherein I see not Thee.
Show me more love: a clouded face
Strikes deeper than an angry blow;
Love me and kill me by Thy grace,
I shall not much bewail my woe.
But even to be
In heaven unloved of Thee,
Were hell in heaven for to see.
Then hear my cry and help afford:
Show me more love, my dearest LORD!

ANONYMOUS

Show me more love, my dearest LORD,—
I cannot think, nor speak, nor pray;
Thy work stands still, my strength is stored
In Thee alone. Oh come away,
Show me Thy beauties, call them mine,
My heart and tongue will soon be Thine.
Show me more love; or if my heart
Too common be for such a guest,
Let Thy good Spirit, by Its art,
Make entry and put out the rest;
For 'tis Thy nest.
Then he's of heaven possest,
That heaven hath in his breast.
Then hear me cry, and help afford;
Show me more love, my dearest LORD!

193

The Thief

'SAY bold but blessed thief,
That in a trice
Slipped into paradise,
And in plain day
Stol'st heaven away,
What trick couldst thou invent
To compass thy intent?
What arms?
What charms?'
'Love and belief.'

'Say bold but blessed thief,
How couldst thou read
A crown upon that head?

What text, what gloss,
A kingdom on a cross?
How couldst thou come to spy
God in a man to die?
What light?
What sight?'
'The sight of grief—

'I sight to God his pain;
And by that sight
I saw the light;
Thus did my grief
Beget relief.
And take this rule from me,
Pity thou him, he'll pity thee.
Use this,
Ne'er miss,
Heaven may be stol'n again.'

JOHN BUNYAN

1628–1688

194 *The Shepherd's Song*

HE that is down needs fear no fall,
He that is low, no pride;
He that is humble ever shall
Have God to be his guide.

I am content with what I have,
Little be it or much:
And, Lord, contentment still I crave,
Because Thou savest such.

Fullness to such a burden is
That go on pilgrimage:
Here little, and hereafter bliss,
Is best from age to age.

NATHANIEL WANLEY

1634–1680

195 *Royal Presents*

THE off'rings of the Eastern kings of old
Unto our lord were incense, myrrh and gold;
Incense because a God; gold as a king;
And myrrh as to a dying man they bring.
Instead of incense (Blessed Lord) if we
Can send a sigh or fervent prayer to thee,
Instead of myrrh if we can but provide
Tears that from penitential eyes do slide,
And though we have no gold; if for our part
We can present thee with a broken heart
Thou wilt accept: and say those Eastern kings
Did not present thee with more precious things.

196 *The Sigh*

AH! with what freedom could I once have pray'd,
And drench'd in tears my supplications made,
Wing'd 'em with sighs, to send 'em how I strove
By wind or water to my God above;
But now of late methinks I feel
Myself transforming into steel.
Nothing that's hard but doth impart
Its stubborn hardness to my heart.

NATHANIEL WANLEY

Ah! with what ardour could I once have heard,
How hath this heart of mine been sweetly stirr'd,
Quick'ned and rais'd to such a lively frame
That I have wondered how and whence it came!
  But now alas those days are done,
  There is more life in stocks or stone;
  Nothing more indispos'd can be,
  Ah! lead itself is light to me.

Ah! when the beams of light on me did shine
How did I gaze on heav'n and think it mine.
Then could I spurn at earth as at a toy,
No such poor limits then could bound my Joy
  But ah! how are those white hours fled,
  That earth I spurn'd now fills my head,
  And I that aim'd than stars more high
  Now grov'ling in a dust-heap lie.

Ah me! my God, if a deep sigh or groan
May find thy gracious ear or reach thy throne,
Oh thence dispatch a word, speak till I hear:
Hence-forth be this your posture; AS YOU WERE.

SAMUEL SPEED

d. 1681

197 *Peace*

I SOUGHT for Peace, but could not find;
  I sought it in the city,
But they were of another mind,
  The more's the pity!

I sought for Peace of country swain,
  But yet I could not find;
So I, returning home again,
  Left Peace behind.

Sweet Peace, where dost thou dwell? said I.
  Methought a voice was given:
'Peace dwelt not here, long since did fly
  To God in heaven.'

Thought I, this echo is but vain,
  To folly 'tis of kin;
Anon I heard it tell me plain,
  'Twas killed by sin.

Then I believed the former voice,
  And rested well content,
Laid down and slept, rose, did rejoice,
  And then to heaven went.
There I enquired for Peace, and found it true,
An heavenly plant it was, and sweetly grew.

198 *The Flower*

OH, that I were a lovely flower
  In Christ his bower;
Or that I were a weed, to fade
  Under his shade.
But how can I a weed become
If I am shadowed with the Son?

CLEMENT PAMAN

fl. 1660

199

On Christmas Day

To my heart

TO-DAY,
Hark! Heaven sings;
Stretch, tune, my heart!
(For hearts have strings
May bear their part)
And though thy lute were bruised i' the fall,
Bruised hearts may reach an humble pastoral.

To-day,
Shepherds rejoice,
And angels do
No more: thy voice
Can reach that too:
Bring them at least thy pipe along,
And mingle consort with the angels' song.

To-day,
A shed that's thatched
(Yet straws can sing)
Holds God; God matched
With beasts; beasts bring
Their song their way: for shame then raise
Thy notes! lambs bleat, and oxen bellow praise.

To-day,
God honoured man
Not angels: yet
They sing; and can
Raised man forget?

CLEMENT PAMAN

Praise is our debt to-day, now shall
Angels (man's not so poor) discharge it all?

To-day,
Then, screw thee high,
My heart, up to
The angels' cry;
Sing 'glory', do:
What if thy strings all crack and fly?
On such a ground, music 'twill be to die.

THOMAS TRAHERNE

200 *From 'The Salutation'* 1636?–1674

THESE little limbs,
These eyes and hands which here I find,
These rosy cheeks wherewith my life begins;
Where have ye been? Behind
What curtain were ye from me hid so long!
Where was, in what abyss, my speaking tongue?

When silent I
So many thousand thousand years
Beneath the dust did in a chaos lie,
How could I smiles, or tears,
Or lips, or hands, or eyes, or ears perceive?
Welcome ye Treasures which I now receive.

I that so long
Was nothing from eternity,
Did little think such joys as ear and tongue
To celebrate or see:
Such sounds to hear, such hands to feel, such feet,
Beneath the skies, on such a ground to meet.

New burnish'd joys!
Which yellow gold and pearl excel!
Such sacred treasures are the limbs in boys
In which a soul doth dwell:
Their organized joints and azure veins
More wealth include than the dead world contains.

From dust I rise
And out of nothing now awake;
These brighter regions which salute mine eyes
A gift from God I take:
The earth, the seas, the light, the day, the skies,
The sun and stars are mine; if those I prize.

Long time before
I in my mother's womb was born,
A God preparing did this glorious store,
The world for me adorn.
Into this Eden so divine and fair,
So wide and bright, I come, his son and heir.

A stranger here
Strange things doth meet, strange glories see,
Strange treasures lodg'd in this fair World appear,
Strange all and new to me:
But that they mine should be who nothing was,
That strangest is of all; yet brought to pass.

201

Desire

I

FOR giving me desire,
An eager thirst, a burning ardent fire,
A virgin infant flame,
A Love with which into the world I came,

An inward hidden Heavenly love,
Which in my soul did work and move,
And ever ever me inflame
With restless longing, Heavenly avarice,
That never could be satisfied,
That did incessantly a Paradise
Unknown suggest, and something undescried
Discern, and bear me to it; be
Thy Name for ever praised by me.

II

My parched and withered bones
Burnt up did seem: my soul was full of groans:
My thoughts extensions were:
Like paces, reaches, steps they did appear:
They somewhat hotly did pursue,
Knew that they had not all their due,
Nor ever quiet were:
But made my flesh like hungry, thirsty ground,
My heart a deep profound abyss,
And every joy and pleasure but a wound,
So long as I my blessedness did miss.
O Happiness! A famine burns,
And all my life to anguish turns!

III

Where are the silent streams,
The living waters and the glorious beams,
The sweet reviving bowers,
The shady groves, the sweet and curious flowers,
The springs and trees, the Heavenly days,
The flow'ry meads, and glorious rays,
The gold and silver towers?

Alas! all these are poor and empty things!
  Trees, waters, days, and shining beams,
Fruits, flowers, bowers, shady groves and springs,
No joy will yield, no more than silent streams;
  These are but dead material toys,
  And cannot make my Heavenly joys.

IV

      O Love! Ye Amities,
And friendships that appear above the skies!
      Ye feasts and living pleasures!
Ye senses, honours, and imperial treasures!
  Ye bridal joys! ye high delights
  That satisfy all appetites!
      Ye sweet affections, and
Ye high respects! Whatever joys there be
  In triumphs, whatsoever stand
In amicable sweet society,
Whatever pleasures are at His right hand,
  Ye must before I am divine,
  In full propriety be mine.

V

      This soaring, sacred thirst,
Ambassador of bliss, approached first,
      Making a place in me
That made me apt to prize, and taste, and see.
  For not the objects but the sense
  Of things doth bliss to souls dispense,
      And make it, Lord, like thee.

Sense, feeling, taste, complacency, and sight,
  These are the true and real joys,
The living, flowing, inward, melting, bright,
And Heavenly pleasures; all the rest are toys:
  All which are founded in desire,
  As light in flame and heat in fire.

202 *The Approach*

THAT childish thoughts such joys inspire
  Doth make my wonder and his glory higher;
  His bounty and my wealth more great;
It shows his kingdom and his work complete,
  In which there is not anything
Not meet to be the joy of Cherubim.

  He in our childhood with us walks,
And with our thoughts mysteriously he talks
  He often visiteth our minds,
But cold acceptance in us ever finds:
  We send him often griev'd away,
Else he would oft'ner come and stay.

  O Lord, I wonder at thy love
Which did my infancy so early move:
  But more at that which did forbear
And mov'd so long, tho' slighted many a year:
  But most of all, at last, that thou
Shouldst me thyself convert I scarce know how.

  Thy gracious motions oft in vain
Assaulted me: my heart did hard remain

Long time: I sent my God away
Griev'd much that he could not impart his joy.
I careless was, nor did regard
The end for which he all these thoughts prepar'd.

But now with new and open eyes
I see beneath as if above the skies:
And as I backward look again
See all his thoughts and mine most clear and plain;
He did approach, he me did woo;
I wonder that my God this thing would do.

From nothing taken first I was:
What wondrous things his glory brought to pass.
Now in this world I him discern,
And me enveloped in more than gold;
In deep abysses of delights
In present hidden precious benefits.

Those thoughts his goodness long before
Prepar'd as precious and celestial store;
With curious art in me inlaid,
That childhood might itself alone be said
My tutor, teacher, guide to be;
Instructed then even by the Deity.

203 *Poverty*

As in the house I sate
Alone and desolate,
No creature but the fire and I,
The chimney and the stool, I lift mine eye
Up to the wall,
And in the silent hall

Saw nothing mine
But some few cups and dishes shine:
The table and the wooden stools
Where people us'd to dine:
A painted cloth there was
Wherein some ancient story wrought
A little entertain'd my thought
Which light discover'd through the glass.

I wonder'd much to see
That all my wealth should be
Confin'd in such a little room,
Yet hope for more I scarcely durst presume.
It griev'd me sore
That such a scanty store
Should be my all:
For I forgot my ease and health,
Nor did I think of hands or eyes,
Nor soul nor body prize;
I neither thought the sun,
Nor moon, nor stars, nor people, mine,
Though they did round about me shine;
And therefore was I quite undone.

Some greater things I thought
Must needs for me be wrought,
Which till my craving mind could see
I ever should lament my poverty:
I fain would have
Whatever bounty gave;
Nor could there be
Without, or love or deity:

For, should not he be infinite
Whose hand created me?
Ten thousand absent things
Did vex my poor and wanting mind,
Which, till I be no longer blind,
Let me not see the King of Kings.

His love must surely be
Rich, infinite, and free;
Nor can he be thought a God
Of grace and pow'r, that fills not his abode,
His Holy Court,
In kind and liberal sort;
Joys and pleasures,
Plenty of jewels, goods, and treasures,
(To enrich the poor, cheer the forlorn)
His palace must adorn,
And given all to me:
For till His works my wealth became,
No love, or peace, did me enflame:
But now I have a deity.

204 *From 'On Christmas Day'*

SHAKE off thy sloth, my drowsy soul, awake;
With angels sing
Unto thy king,
And pleasant music make;
Thy lute, thy harp, or else thy heartstrings take,
And with thy music let thy sense awake.
See how each one the other calls
To fix his ivy on the walls,

Transplanted there it seems to grow
As if it rooted were below:
Thus he, who is thy King,
Makes winter, spring.

'Tis he that life and spirit doth infuse:
Let ev'ry thing
The praises sing
Of Christ the King of Jews;
Who makes things green, and with a spring infuse
A season which to see it doth not use:
Old winter's frost and hoary hair,
With garlands crowned, bays doth wear;
The nipping frost of wrath being gone,
To him the manger made a throne,
Due praises let us sing,
Winter and spring.

See how, their bodies clad with finer clothes,
They now begin
His praise to sing
Who purchas'd their repose:
Whereby their inward joy they do disclose;
Their dress alludes to better works than those:
His gayer weeds and finer band,
New suit and hat, into his hand
The ploughman takes; his neatest shoes,
And warmer gloves, he means to use:
And shall not I, my King,
Thy praises sing?

See how their breath doth smoke, and how they haste
His praise to sing
With Cherubim;
They scarce a breakfast taste;
But through the streets, lest precious time should waste,
When service doth begin, to church they haste.
And shall not I, Lord, come to thee,
The beauty of thy temple see?
Thy name with joy I will confess,
Clad in my Saviour's righteousness;
'Mong all thy servants sing
To thee my King.

'Twas thou that gav'st us cause for fine attires;
Ev'n thou, O King,
As in the spring,
Dost warm us with thy fires
Of love: thy blood hath bought us new desires;
Thy righteousness doth clothe with new attires.
Both fresh and fine let me appear
This day divine, to close the year;
Among the rest let me be seen
A living branch and always green,
Think it a pleasant thing
Thy praise to sing.

At break of day, O how the bells did ring!
To thee, my King,
The bells did ring;
To thee the angels sing:
Thy goodness did produce this other spring,
For this it is they make the bells to ring:

The sounding bells do through the air
Proclaim thy welcome far and near;
While I alone with thee inherit
All these joys, beyond my merit.
Who would not always sing
To such a King?

I all these joys, above my merit, see
By thee, my King,
To whom I sing,
Entire convey'd to me.
My treasure, Lord, thou mak'st the people be
That I with pleasure might thy servants see.
Ev'n in their rude external ways
They do set forth my Saviour's praise,
And minister a light to me;
While I by them do hear to thee
Praises, my Lord and King,
Whole churches ring.

Hark how remoter parishes do sound!
Far off they ring
For thee, my King,
Ev'n round about the town:
The churches scatter'd over all the ground
Serve for thy praise, who art with glory crown'd.
This city is an engine great
That makes my pleasure more complete;
The sword, the mace, the magistrate,
To honour thee attend in state;
The whole assembly sings;
The minster rings.

205 *Insatiableness*

I

NO walls confine! Can nothing hold my mind?
Can I no rest nor satisfaction find?
Must I behold eternity
And see
What things above the Heav'ns be?
Will nothing serve the turn?
Nor earth, nor seas, nor skies?
Till I what lies
In time's beginning find;
Must I till then for ever burn?

Not all the crowns; not all the heaps of gold
On earth; not all the tales that can be told,
Will satisfaction yield to me:
Nor tree,
Nor shade, nor sun, nor Eden, be
A joy: nor gems in gold,
(Be't pearl or precious stone,)
Nor spring, nor flowers,
Answer my craving powers,
Nor anything that eyes behold.

Till I what was before all time descry,
The world's beginning seems but vanity.
My soul doth there long thoughts extend;
No end
Doth find, or being comprehend:
Yet somewhat sees that is

The obscure shady face
Of endless space,
All room within; where I
Expect to meet eternal bliss.

II

This busy, vast, inquiring soul
Brooks no control,
No limits will endure,
Nor any rest: it will all see,
Not time alone, but ev'n eternity.
What is it? Endless sure.

'Tis mean ambition to desire
A single world:
To many I aspire,
Though one upon another hurl'd:
Nor will they all, if they be all confin'd,
Delight my mind.

This busy, vast, inquiring soul
Brooks no control:
'Tis very curious too.
Each one of all those worlds must be
Enriched with infinite variety
And worth; or 'twill not do.

'Tis nor delight nor perfect pleasure
To have a purse
That hath a bottom in its treasure,
Since I must thence endless expense disburse.
Sure there's a God (for else there's no delight)
One infinite.

206

The Preparative

My body being dead, my limbs unknown;
Before I skill'd to prize
Those living stars, mine eyes;
Before my tongue or cheeks were to me shewn,
Before I knew my hands were mine,
Or that my sinews did my members join;
When neither nostril, foot, nor ear,
As yet was seen, or felt, or did appear;
I was within
A house I knew not, newly cloth'd with skin.

Then was my Soul my only all to me,
A living endless eye,
Scarce bounded with the sky,
Whose power, whose act, whose essence was to see;
I was an inward sphere of light,
Or an interminable orb of sight,
An endless and a living day,
A vital sun that round about did ray:
All life, all sense,
A naked, simple, pure intelligence.

I then no thirst nor hunger did perceive;
No dull necessity,
No want was known to me:
Without disturbance then I did receive
The fair ideas of all things,
And had the honey even without the stings.
A meditating inward eye
Gazing at quiet did within me lie,
And every thing
Delighted me that was their heavenly king.

For sight inherits beauty; hearing, sounds;
The nostril, sweet perfumes,
All tastes have hidden rooms
Within the tongue; the feeling feeling wounds
With pleasure and delight: but I
Forgot the rest, and was all sight or eye,
Unbody'd and devoid of care,
Just as in heav'n the holy angels are:
For simple sense
Is lord of all created excellence.

Being thus prepar'd for all felicity;
Not prepossess'd with dross,
Nor basely glued to gross
And dull materials that might ruin me,
Not fetter'd by an iron fate,
With vain affections in my earthy state,
To anything that might seduce
My sense, or else bereave it of its use;
I was as free
As if there were nor sin nor misery.

Pure empty powers that did nothing loathe,
Did, like the fairest glass
Or spotless polish'd brass,
Themselves soon in their object's image clothe:
Divine impressions, when they came,
Did quickly enter and my soul inflame.
'Tis not the object, but the light,
That maketh heav'n: 'tis a truer sight.
Felicity
Appears to none but them that purely see.

A disentangled and a naked sense,
　　A mind that's unpossess'd,
　　A disengaged breast,
An empty and a quick intelligence
　　Acquainted with the golden mean,
An even spirit, pure, and serene,
　　Is that where beauty, excellence
And pleasure keep their court of residence.
　　　　My soul retire,
Get free, and so thou shalt even all admire.

Christian Ethics

207 ***For man to act***

FOR man to act as if his soul did see
The very brightness of eternity;
For man to act as if his love did burn
Above the spheres, even while it's in its urn;
For man to act even in the wilderness,
As if he did those sovereign joys possess,
Which do at once confirm, stir up, enflame,
And perfect angels; having not the same!
It doth increase the value of his deeds,
In this a man a Seraphim exceeds:
　To act on obligations yet unknown,
To act upon rewards as yet unshown,
To keep commands whose beauty's yet unseen,
To cherish and retain a zeal between
Sleeping and waking; shows a constant care;
And that a deeper love, a love so rare,
That no eye-service may with it compare.

The angels, who are faithful while they view
His glory, know not what themselves would do,
Were they in our estate! A dimmer light
Perhaps would make them err as well as we;
And in the coldness of a darker night,
Forgetful and lukewarm themselves might be.
Our very rust shall cover us with gold,
Our dust shall sprinkle while their eyes behold
The glory springing from a feeble state,
Where mere belief doth, if not conquer fate,
Surmount, and pass what it doth antedate.

208 *Mankind is sick*

MANKIND is sick, the world distemper'd lies,
Oppressed with sins and miseries.
Their sins are woes; a long corrupted train
Of poison, drawn from Adam's vein,
Stains all his seed, and all his kin
Are one disease of life within.
They all torment themselves!
The world's one bedlam, or a greater cave
Of madmen, that do always rave.

The wise and good like kind physicians are,
That strive to heal them by their care.
They physic and their learning calmly use,
Although the patient them abuse.
For since the sickness is (they find)
A sad distemper of the mind;
All railings they impute,
All injuries, unto the sore disease,
They are expressly come to ease!

If we would to the world's distemper'd mind
  Impute the rage which there we find,
We might, even in the midst of all our foes,
  Enjoy and feel a sweet repose.
  Might pity all the griefs we see,
  Anointing every malady
    With precious oil and balm;
And while our selves are calm, our art improve
  To rescue them, and show our love.

But let's not fondly our own selves beguile;
  If we revile 'cause they revile,
Our selves infected with their sore disease,
  Need others' helps to give us ease.
  For we more mad than they remain,
  Need to be cut, and need a chain
    Far more than they. Our brain
Is craz'd; and if we put our wit to theirs,
  We may be justly made their heirs.

But while with open eyes we clearly see
  The brightness of his majesty;
While all the world, by sin to Satan sold,
  In daily wickedness grows old,
  Men in chains of darkness lie,
  In bondage and iniquity,
    And pierce and grieve themselves!
The dismal woes wherein they crawl, enhance
  The peace of our inheritance.

We wonder to behold ourselves so nigh
  To so much sin and misery,
And yet to see ourselves so safe from harm!
  What amulet, what hidden charm

Could fortify and raise the soul
So far above them; and control
Such fierce malignity!
The brightness and the glory which we see
Is made a greater mystery.

And while we feel how much our God doth love
The peace of sinners, how much move,
And sue, and thirst, intreat, lament and grieve,
For all the crimes in which they live,
And seek and wait, and call again,
And long to save them from the pain
Of sin, from all their woe!
With greater thirst, as well as grief we try,
How to relieve their misery.

The life and splendour of felicity,
Whose floods so overflowing be,
The streams of joy which round about his throne,
Enrich and fill each holy one,
Are so abundant, that we can
Spare all, even all to any man!
And have it all ourselves!
Nay, have the more! We long to make them see
The sweetness of felicity.

While we contemplate their distresses, how,
Blind wretches, they in bondage bow,
And tear and wound themselves, and vex and groan,
And chafe and fret so near his throne,

And know not what they ail, but lie
Tormented in their misery
(Like madmen that are blind)
In works of darkness nigh such full delight:
That they might find and see the sight,

What would we give! that they might likewise see
The glory of his majesty!
The joy and fullness of that high delight,
Whose blessedness is infinite!
We would even cease to live, to gain
Them from their misery and pain,
And make them with us reign.
For they themselves would be our greatest treasures
When sav'd, our own most heavenly pleasures.

O holy Jesus who didst for us die,
And on the altar bleeding lie,
Bearing all torment, pain, reproach and shame,
That we by virtue of the same,
Though enemies to God, might be
Redeem'd, and set at liberty.
As thou didst us forgive,
So meekly let us love to others show,
And live in heaven on earth below!

Let's prize their souls, and let them be our gems,
Our temples and our diadems,
Our brides, our friends, our fellow-members, eyes,
Hands, hearts and souls, our victories,

And spoils and trophies, our own joys!
Compar'd to souls all else are toys!
O Jesus let them be
Such unto us as they are unto thee,
Vessels of glory and felicity!

How will they love us, when they find our care
Brought them all thither where they are!
When they conceive, what terror 'tis to dwell
In all the punishments of Hell:
And in a lively manner see,
O Christ, eternal joys in thee!
How will they all delight
In praising thee for us, with all their might,
How sweet a grace, how infinite!

209 *Contentment is a sleepy Thing*

CONTENTMENT is a sleepy thing!
If it in death alone must die;
A quiet mind is worse than poverty!
Unless it from enjoyment spring!
That's blessedness alone that makes a king!
Wherein the joys and treasures are so great,
They all the powers of the soul employ,
And fill it with a work complete,
While it doth all enjoy.
True joys alone contentment do inspire,
Enrich content, and make our courage higher.
Content alone's a dead and silent stone:
The real life of bliss
Is glory reigning in a throne,

Where all enjoyment is
The soul of man is so inclin'd to see,
Without his treasures no man's soul can be,
Nor rest content uncrown'd!
Desire and love
Must in the height of all their rapture move,
Where there is true felicity.

BISHOP THOMAS KEN

1637–1711

210 *'Awake, my Soul'*

AWAKE, my Soul, and with the sun,
Thy daily stage of duty run;
Shake off dull sloth, and joyful rise,
To pay thy morning sacrifice.

Thy precious time misspent, redeem;
Each present day thy last esteem;
Improve thy talent with due care,
For the great day thyself prepare.

Let all thy converse be sincere,
Thy conscience as the noon-day clear;
Think how all-seeing God thy ways,
And all thy secret thoughts, surveys.

By influence of the light divine,
Let thy own light to others shine;
Reflect all heaven's propitious rays,
In ardent love, and cheerful praise.

Wake, and lift up thyself, my heart,
And with the Angels bear thy part,
Who all night long unwearied sing
High praise to the eternal King.

BISHOP THOMAS KEN

Awake, awake! ye heavenly choir,
May your devotion me inspire,
That I, like you, my age may spend;
Like you, may on my God attend.

May I, like you, in God delight,
Have all day long my God in sight,
Perform, like you, my Maker's will—
O, may I never more do ill!

Had I your wings, to heaven I'd fly;
But God shall that defect supply;
And my soul, wing'd with warm desire,
Shall all day long to heaven aspire.

Glory to Thee, who safe hast kept,
And hast refresh'd me whilst I slept:—
Grant, Lord, when I from death shall wake,
I may of endless light partake.

I would not wake, nor rise again,
E'en Heaven itself I would disdain,
Wert not Thou there to be enjoy'd,
And I in hymns to be employ'd.

Heaven is, dear Lord, where'er Thou art;
O never then from me depart;
For to my soul, 'tis hell to be,
But for one moment, without Thee.

Lord, I my vows to Thee renew,
Scatter my sins as morning dew;
Guard my first springs of thought and will,
And with Thyself my spirit fill.

Direct, control, suggest, this day,
All I design, or do, or say;
That all my powers, with all their might,
In Thy sole glory may unite.

Praise God, from whom all blessings flow,
Praise Him, all creatures here below;
Praise Him above, ye heavenly host,
Praise Father, Son, and Holy Ghost.

211

Now

THE *Past* can be no more—
Whose misemploying I deplore:
The *Future* is to me
An absolute uncertainty:
The *Now*, which will not with me stay,
Within a second flies away.

I heard God often say,
Now, of salvation is the day,—
But turn'd from heaven my view,
I still had something else to do;
Till God a dream instructive sent,
To warn me timely to repent.

Methought Death, with his dart,
Had mortally transfix'd my heart;
And devils round about,
To seize my spirit flying out,
Cried—'*Now*, of which you took no care,
Is turn'd to *Never* and despair!'

I gave a sudden start,
And waked, with *Never* in my heart:
Still I that *Never* felt,
Never upon my spirit dwelt;—
A thousand thanks to God I paid,
That my sad *Never* was delay'd.

212

An Anodyne

As in the night I restless lie,
I the watch-candle keep in eye;
The innocent I often blame,
For the slow wasting of its flame.
Sweet ease!—O whither are you fled!—
With one short slumber ease my head!

My curtain oft I draw away,
Eager to see the morning ray;
But when the morning gilds the skies,
The morning no relief supplies.
To me, alas! the morning light
Is as afflictive as the night.

My vigorous cries to God ascend,
Oh!—will not God my cries attend?
Can God paternal love forbear—
Can God reject a filial prayer?
Is there in Heaven for me no cure—
Why do I then such pains endure?

My flesh in torture oft repines
At what God for my good designs;

My spirit the repiner chides,
Submissive to God's will abides:
God my disease and temper weighs;
No pang superfluous on me lays.

Why should I then my pains decline,
Inflicted by pure love divine?
Let them run out their destined course,
And spend upon me all their force:
Short pains can never grievous be,
Which work a blest eternity.

JOHN DRYDEN

1631–1700

213 *From 'Religio Laici'*

DIM, as the borrow'd beams of moon and stars
To lonely, weary, wandering travellers
Is reason to the soul: And as on high
Those rolling fires discover but the sky
Not light us here; so reason's glimmering ray
Was lent, not to assure our doubtful way,
But guide us upward to a better day.
And as those nightly tapers disappear
When day's bright Lord ascends our hemisphere;
So pale grows reason at religion's sight;
So dies, and so dissolves in supernatural light.
Some few, whose lamp shone brighter, have been led
From cause to cause to nature's secret head;
And found that one first principle must be;
But what, or who, that universal He;
Whether some Soul incompassing this ball,
Unmade, unmov'd; yet making, moving all;

Or various atoms, interfering dance
Leapt into form (the noble work of chance,)
Or this great all was from eternity;
Not ev'n the Stagirite himself could see;
And Epicurus guess'd as well as he.
As blindly grop'd they for a future state,
As rashly judg'd of Providence and Fate:
But least of all could their endeavours find
What most concern'd the good of human kind:
For happiness was never to be found;
But vanish'd from 'em, like enchanted ground.
One thought content the good to be enjoyed:
This, every little accident destroyed:
The wiser madmen did for virtue toil,
A thorny, or at best a barren soil:
In pleasure some their glutton souls would steep,
But found their line too short, the well too deep,
And leaky vessels which no bliss could keep.
Thus, anxious thoughts in endless circles roll,
Without a centre where to fix the soul:
In this wild maze their vain endeavours end:
How can the less the greater comprehend?
Or finite reason reach infinity?
For what could fathom God were more than he.

The deist thinks he stands on firmer ground,
Cries *εὗρεκα*: the mighty secret's found:
God is that spring of good, supreme and best;
We, made to serve, and in that service blest;
If so, some rules of worship must be given,
Distributed alike to all by Heaven:

Else God were partial, and to some denied
The means His justice should for all provide.
This general worship is to praise, and pray:
One part to borrow blessings, one to pay:
And when frail nature slides into offence,
The sacrifice for crimes is penitence.
Yet, since th' effects of providence, we find,
Are variously dispensed to human kind;
That vice triumphs and virtue suffers here,
(A brand that sovereign justice cannot bear;)
Our reason prompts us to a future state,
The last appeal from fortune, and from fate,
Where God's all-righteous ways will be declar'd,
The bad meet punishment, the good, reward.

Thus Man by his own strength to Heaven would soar:
And would not be obliged to God for more.
Vain, wretched creature, how art thou misled
To think thy wit these God-like notions bred!
These truths are not the product of thy mind,
But dropped from heaven, and of a nobler kind.
Reveal'd religion first inform'd thy sight,
And reason saw not till faith sprung the light.
Hence all thy natural worship takes the source:
'Tis revelation what thou thinkst discourse.
Else how com'st thou to see these truths so clear,
Which so obscure to heathens did appear?
Not Plato these, nor Aristotle found.
Nor he whose wisdom oracles renown'd.
Hast thou a wit so deep, or so sublime,
Or canst thou lower dive, or higher climb?

JOHN DRYDEN

Canst thou, by reason, more of god-head know
Than Plutarch, Seneca, or Cicero?
Those giant wits, in happier ages born,
(When arms and arts did Greece and Rome adorn,)
Knew no such system: no such piles could raise
Of natural worship, built on prayer and praise,
To one sole God:
Nor did remorse, to expiate sin, prescribe:
But slew their fellow creatures for a bribe:
The guiltless victim groan'd for their offence;
And cruelty and blood was penitence.
If sheep and oxen could atone for men
Ah! at how cheap a rate the rich might sin!
And great oppressors might Heaven's wrath beguile
By offering his own creatures for a spoil!

Dar'st thou, poor worm, offend Infinity?
And must the terms of peace be given by thee?
Then thou art justice in the last appeal;
Thy easy God instructs thee to rebel:
And, like a King remote, and weak, must take
What satisfaction thou art pleased to make.

But if there be a power too just, and strong
To wink at crimes and bear unpunish'd wrong;
Look humbly upward, see his will disclose
The forfeit first, and then the fine impose,
A mulct thy poverty could never pay
Had not eternal wisdom found the way
And with cœlestial wealth supplied thy store;
His justice makes the fine, his mercy quits the score.

See God descending in thy human frame;
Th' offended, suffering in th' offender's name:
All thy misdeeds to Him imputed see,
And all his righteousness devolv'd on thee.

For granting we have sinned, and that th' offence
Of man, is made against omnipotence,
Some price, that bears proportion, must be paid
And Infinite with Infinite be weigh'd.
See then the Deist lost: remorse for vice
Not paid, or paid, inadequate in price:
What farther means can reason now direct,
Or what relief from human wit expect?

JOHN NORRIS OF BEMERTON

1657–1711

214 *Hymn to Darkness*

HAIL thou most sacred venerable thing!
What Muse is worthy thee to sing?
Thee, from whose pregnant universal womb
All things, even Light thy rival, first did come.
What dares he not attempt that sings of thee,
Thou first and greatest mystery?
Who can the secrets of thy essence tell?
Thou like the light of God art inaccessible.

Before great Love this monument did raise,
This ample theatre of praise.
Before the folding circles of the sky
Were tun'd by Him who is all harmony.
Before the morning stars their hymn began,
Before the council held for man.
Before the birth of either Time or Place,
Thou reign'st unquestion'd monarch in the empty space.

Thy native lot thou didst to Light resign,
  But still half of the globe is thine.
Here with a quiet, and yet aweful hand,
Like the best emperors thou dost command.
To thee the stars above their brightness owe,
  And mortals their repose below.
To thy protection Fear and Sorrow flee,
And those that weary are of light, find rest in thee.

Tho' light and glory be th' Almighty's throne,
  Darkness is His pavilion.
From that His radiant beauty, but from thee
He has His terror and His majesty.
Thus when He first proclaim'd His sacred Law,
  And would His rebel subjects awe,
Like princes on some great solemnity,
He appear'd in's robes of State, and clad Himself with thee.

The blest above do thy sweet umbrage prize,
  When cloy'd with light, they veil their eyes.
The vision of the Deity is made
More sweet and beatifick by thy shade.
But we poor tenants of this orb below
  Don't here thy excellencies know,
Till Death our understandings does improve,
And then our wiser ghosts thy silent night-walks love.

But thee I now admire, thee would I choose
  For my religion, or my Muse.
'Tis hard to tell whether thy reverend shade
Has more good votaries or poets made,

umbrage] shade.

From thy dark caves were inspirations given,
  And from thick groves went vows to Heaven.
Hail then thou Muse's and Devotion's spring,
'Tis just we should adore, 'tis just we should thee sing.

215 *The Aspiration*

HOW long, great God, how long must I
  Immured in this dark prison lie;
Where at the grates and avenues of sense,
My soul must watch to have intelligence;
Where but faint gleams of Thee salute my sight,
Like doubtful moonshine in a cloudy night:
    When shall I leave this magic sphere,
    And be all mind, all eye, all ear?

    How cold this clime! And yet my sense
    Perceives e'en here Thy influence.
E'en here Thy strong magnetic charms I feel,
And pant and tremble like the amorous steel.
To lower good, and beauties less divine,
Sometimes my erroneous needle does decline,
    But yet, so strong the sympathy,
    It turns, and points again to Thee.

    I long to see this excellence
    Which at such distance strikes my sense.
My impatient soul struggles to disengage
Her wings from the confinement of her cage.
Wouldst thou, great Love, this prisoner once set free,
How would she hasten to be link'd to Thee!
    She'd for no angels' conduct stay,
    But fly, and love-on, all the way.

THOMAS SHEPHERD

1665–1739

216 ### '*Alas, my God*'

ALAS, my GOD, that we should be
Such strangers to each other!
O that as friends we might agree,
And walk and talk together!

May I taste that communion, LORD,
Thy people have with Thee?
Thy Spirit daily talks with them,
O let It talk with me!

Like Enoch, let me walk with GOD,
And thus walk out my day,
Attended with the heavenly Guards,
Upon the King's highway.

When wilt Thou come unto me, LORD?
O come, my LORD most dear!
Come near, come nearer, nearer still:
I'm well when Thou art near.

There's no such thing as pleasure here;
My JESUS is my all:
As Thou dost shine or disappear,
My pleasures rise and fall.

When wilt Thou come unto me, LORD?
For, till Thou dost appear,
I count each moment for a day,
Each minute for a year.

JOSEPH ADDISON

1672–1719

217

Ode

THE spacious firmament on high,
With all the blue ethereal sky,
And spangled heav'ns, a shining frame,
Their great original proclaim:
Th' unwearied sun, from day to day,
Does his creator's power display,
And publishes to every land
The work of an almighty hand.

Soon as the evening shades prevail,
The moon takes up the wondrous tale,
And nightly to the listening earth
Repeats the story of her birth:
Whilst all the stars that round her burn,
And all the planets, in their turn,
Confirm the tidings as they roll,
And spread the truth from pole to pole.

What though, in solemn silence, all
Move round the dark terrestrial ball?
What tho' nor real voice nor sound
Amid their radiant orbs be found?
In reason's ear they all rejoice,
And utter forth a glorious voice,
For ever singing, as they shine,
'The hand that made us is divine.'

218 *How are thy Servants blest*

HOW are Thy servants blest, O Lord!
How sure is their defence!
Eternal wisdom is their guide,
Their help Omnipotence.

In foreign realms, and lands remote,
Supported by Thy care,
Through burning climes I pass'd unhurt,
And breath'd in tainted air.

Thy mercy sweeten'd every soil,
Made every region please;
The hoary Alpine hills it warm'd,
And smooth'd the Tyrrhene seas.

Think, O my soul, devoutly think,
How, with affrighted eyes,
Thou saw'st the wide-extended deep
In all its horrors rise.

Confusion dwelt in every face,
And fear in every heart,
When waves on waves, and gulfs in gulfs,
O'ercame the pilot's art.

Yet then from all my griefs, O Lord!
Thy mercy set me free;
Whilst in the confidence of prayer
My soul took hold on Thee.

For though in dreadful whirls we hung
High on the broken wave,
I knew Thou wert not slow to hear,
Nor impotent to save.

The storm was laid, the winds retir'd,
  Obedient to Thy will;
The sea, that roar'd at Thy command,
  At Thy command was still.

In midst of dangers, fears and death,
  Thy goodness I'll adore;
And praise Thee for Thy mercies past,
  And humbly hope for more.

My life, if Thou preserv'st my life,
  Thy sacrifice shall be;
And death, if death must be my doom,
  Shall join my soul to Thee.

219 *'When all Thy Mercies'*

WHEN all Thy mercies, O my God,
  My rising soul surveys;
Transported with the view, I'm lost
  In wonder, love and praise.

O how shall words with equal warmth
  The gratitude declare,
That glows within my ravish'd heart!
  But Thou canst read it there.

Thy providence my life sustain'd,
  And all my wants redress'd,
When in the silent womb I lay,
  And hung upon the breast.

To all my weak complaints and cries,
  Thy mercy lent an ear,
Ere yet my feeble thoughts had learnt
  To form themselves in prayer.

Unnumber'd comforts to my soul
  Thy tender care bestow'd,
Before my infant heart conceiv'd
  From whom these comforts flow'd.

When in the slippery path of youth
  With heedless steps I ran.
Thine arm unseen convey'd me safe
  And led me up to man.

ISAAC WATTS

1674–1748

220 ### *From 'A Cradle Song'*

HUSH! my dear, lie still and slumber,
  Holy Angels guard thy bed!
Heavenly blessings without number
  Gently falling on thy head.

Sleep, my babe; thy food and raiment,
  House and home, thy friends provide;
All without thy care or payment,
  All thy wants are well supplied.

How much better thou'rt attended
  Than the Son of God could be,
When from heaven He descended,
  And became a child like thee!

Soft and easy is thy cradle:
  Coarse and hard thy Saviour lay:
When His birthplace was a stable,
  And His softest bed was hay.

See the kinder shepherds round Him,
  Telling wonders from the sky!
Where they sought Him, there they found Him,
  With His Virgin-Mother by.

See the lovely Babe a-dressing;
  Lovely Infant, how He smiled!
When he wept, the Mother's blessing
  Soothed and hush'd the holy Child.

Lo, He slumbers in His manger,
  Where the hornèd oxen fed;
—Peace, my darling, here's no danger;
  Here's no ox a-near thy bed!

May'st thou live to know and fear Him,
  Trust and love Him all thy days;
Then go dwell for ever near Him,
  See His face, and sing His praise!

I could give thee thousand kisses,
  Hoping what I most desire;
Not a mother's fondest wishes
  Can to greater joys aspire.

221 *'Where-e'er my flatt'ring Passions rove'*

WHERE-E'ER my flatt'ring passions rove
  I find a lurking snare;
'Tis dangerous to let loose our love
  Beneath th' eternal fair.

Souls whom the tie of friendship binds,
  And partners of our blood,
Seize a large portion of our minds,
  And leave the less for God.

Nature has soft but powerful bands,
  And reason she controls;
While children with their little hands
  Hang closest to our souls.

Thoughtless they act th' old serpent's part;
  What tempting things they be!
Lord, how they twine about our heart,
  And draw it off from thee!

Dear Sovereign, break these fetters off,
  And set our spirits free;
God in himself is bliss enough,
  For we have all in Thee.

222

Felicity

NO, 'tis in vain to seek for bliss;
  For bliss can ne'er be found
'Till we arrive where Jesus is,
  And tread on heav'nly ground.

There's nothing round these painted skies,
  Or round this dusty clod;
Nothing, my soul, that's worth thy joys,
  Or lovely as thy God.

'Tis heav'n on earth to taste his love,
  To feel his quick'ning grace;
And all the Heav'n I hope above
  Is but to see his face.

223

'O God, our Help'

O GOD, our help in ages past,
  Our hope for years to come,
Our shelter from the stormy blast,
  And our eternal home:

Under the shadow of Thy Throne
  Thy saints have dwelt secure;
Sufficient is Thine arm alone,
  And our defence is sure.

Before the hills in order stood,
  Or earth received her frame,
From everlasting Thou art God,
  To endless years the same.

Thy word commands our flesh to dust,
  'Return ye sons of men':
All nations rose from earth at first,
  And turn to earth again.

A thousand ages in Thy sight
  Are like an evening gone;
Short as the watch that ends the night
  Before the rising sun.

The busy tribes of flesh and blood
  With all their lives and cares
Are carried downward by thy flood
  And lost in following years.

Time, like an ever-rolling stream,
  Bears all its sons away;
They fly forgotten, as a dream
  Dies at the opening day.

Like flowery fields the nations stand
  Pleased with the morning light;
The flowers, beneath the Mower's hand,
  Lie withering ere 'tis night.

Our God, our help in ages past;
  Our hope for years to come;
Be Thou our guard while troubles last,
  And our eternal home!

224 *'Sweet Muse'*

SWEET Muse, descend and bless the shade,
  And bless the evening grove;
Business, and noise, and day are fled,
  And every care, but love.

But hence, ye wanton young and fair,
  Mine is a purer flame;
No Phyllis shall infect the air,
  With her unhallowed name.

Jesus has all my Powers possessed,
  My hopes, my fears, my joys:
He, the dear Sovereign of my breast,
  Shall still command my voice.

Some of the fairest choirs above
  Shall flock around my song,
With joy to hear the name they love
  Sound from a mortal tongue.

His charms shall make my numbers flow,
 And hold the falling floods,
While silence sits on every bough,
 And bends the list'ning woods.

I'll carve our passion on the bark,
 And every wounded tree
Shall drop and bear some mystic mark
 That Jesus died for me.

The swains shall wonder when they read,
 Inscrib'd on all the grove,
That Heaven itself came down, and bled
 To win a mortal's love.

EDWARD YOUNG

1683–1765

225 ### *The Day of Judgement*

NOW the descending triumph stops its flight
From earth full twice a planetary height.
There all the clouds condens'd, two columns raise
Distinct with orient veins, and golden blaze.
One fix'd on earth, and one in sea, and round
Its ample foot the swelling billows sound.
These an immeasurable arch support,
The grand tribunal of this awful court.
Sheets of bright azure, from the purest sky,
Stream from the crystal arch, and round the columns fly.
Death, wrapt in chains, low at the basis lies,
And on the point of his own arrow dies.
 Here high enthron'd th' eternal Judge is plac'd,
With all the grandeur of his godhead grac'd;

Stars on his robes in beauteous order meet,
And the sun burns beneath his awful feet.
Now an archangel eminently bright,
From off his silver staff of wondrous height,
Unfurls the Christian flag, which waving flies,
And shuts and opens more than half the skies:
The cross so strong a red, it sheds a stain,
Where'er it floats, on earth, and air, and main;
Flushes the hill, and sets on fire the wood,
And turns the deep-dy'd ocean into blood.
Oh formidable glory! dreadful bright!
Refulgent torture to the guilty sight.
Ah turn, unwary muse, nor dare reveal
What horrid thoughts with the polluted dwell.
Say not, (to make the sun shrink in his beam)
Dare not affirm, they wish it all a dream;
Wish, or their souls may with their limbs decay,
Or God be spoil'd of his eternal sway.
But rather, if thou know'st the means, unfold
How they with transport might the scene behold.
Ah how! but by repentance, by a mind
Quick, and severe its own offence to find?
By tears, and groans, and never-ceasing care,
And all the pious violence of prayer?
Thus then, with fervency till now unknown,
I cast my heart before th' eternal throne,
In this great temple, which the skies surround,
For homage to its lord, a narrow bound.
'O thou! whose balance does the mountains weigh,
Whose will the wild tumultuous seas obey,
Whose breath can turn those watery worlds to flame,
That flame to tempest, and that tempest tame;

Earth's meanest son, all trembling, prostrate falls,
And on the boundless of thy goodness calls.
 'Oh! give the winds all past offence to sweep,
To scatter wide, or bury in the deep:
Thy power, my weakness, may I ever see,
And wholly dedicate my soul to thee: . . .
 'Grant I may ever, at the morning ray,
Open with prayer the consecrated day;
Tune thy great praise, and bid my soul arise,
And with the mounting sun ascend the skies:
As that advances, let my zeal improve,
And glow with ardour of consummate love;
Nor cease at eve, but with the setting sun
My endless worship shall be still begun.
 'And, oh! permit the gloom of solemn night
To sacred thought may forcibly invite.
When this world's shut, and awful planets rise,
Call on our minds, and raise them to the skies;
Compose our souls with a less dazzling sight,
And show all nature in a milder light;
How every boisterous thought in calm subsides!
How the smooth'd spirit into goodness glides!
O how divine! to tread the milky way,
To the bright palace of the lord of day;
His court admire, or for his favour sue,
Or leagues of friendship with his saints renew;
Pleas'd to look down, and see the world asleep,
While I long vigils to its founder keep!
 'Canst thou not shake the centre? Oh! control,
Subdue by force, the rebel in my soul:
Thou, who canst still the raging of the flood,
Restrain the various tumults of my blood;

Teach me, with equal firmness, to sustain
Alluring pleasure, and assaulting pain.
O may I pant for thee in each desire!
And with strong faith foment the holy fire!
Stretch out my soul in hope, and grasp the prize,
Which in eternity's deep bosom lies!
At the great day of recompense behold,
Devoid of fear, the fatal book unfold!
Then wafted upward to the blissful seat,
From age to age, my grateful song repeat;
My light, my life, my God, my Saviour see,
And rival angels in the praise of thee.'

226 *The Lament of the Damned in Hell*

'WHO burst the barriers of my peaceful grave?
Ah! cruel death, that would no longer save,
But grudg'd me e'en that narrow dark abode,
And cast me out into the wrath of God;
Where shrieks, the roaring flame, the rattling chain,
And all the dreadful eloquence of pain,
Our only song; black fire's malignant light,
The sole refreshment of the blasted sight.
Must all those pow'rs, heaven gave me to supply
My soul with pleasure, and bring in my joy,
Rise up in arms against me, join the foe,
Sense, reason, memory, increase my woe?
And shall my voice, ordain'd on hymns to dwell,
Corrupt to groans, and blow the fires of hell?
Oh! must I look with terror on my gain,
And with existence only measure pain?

What! no reprieve, no least indulgence given,
No beam of hope, from any point of heaven!
Ah mercy! mercy! art thou dead above?
Is love extinguish'd in the source of love?
 'Bold that I am, did heaven stoop down to hell?
Th' expiring Lord of life my ransom seal?
Have I not been industrious to provoke?
From his embraces obstinately broke?
Pursu'd and panted for his mortal hate,
Earn'd my destruction, labour'd out my fate?
And dare I on extinguish'd love exclaim?
Take, take full vengeance, rouse the slack'ning flame;
Just is my lot—but oh! must it transcend
The reach of time, despair a distant end?
With dreadful growth shoot forward, and arise,
Where thought can't follow, and bold fancy dies?
 'Never! where falls the soul at that dread sound?
Down an abyss how dark, and how profound?
Down, down, (I still am falling, horrid pain!)
Ten thousand thousand fathoms still remain;
My plunge but still begun—And this for sin?
Could I offend, if I had never been,
But still increas'd the senseless happy mass,
Flow'd in the stream, or shiver'd in the grass?
 'Father of mercies! why from silent earth
Didst thou awake, and curse me into birth?
Tear me from quiet, ravish me from night,
And make a thankless present of thy light?
Push into being a reverse of thee,
And animate a clod with misery?
 'The beasts are happy; they come forth, and keep
Short watch on earth, and then lie down to sleep.

Pain is for man; and oh! how vast a pain
For crimes, which made the Godhead bleed in vain!
Annull'd his groans, as far as in them lay,
And flung his agonies, and death, away!
As our dire punishment for ever strong,
Our constitution too for ever young.
Curs'd with returns of vigour, still the same
Powerful to bear, and satisfy the flame:
Still to be caught, and still to be pursu'd!
To perish still, and still to be renew'd!
  'And this, my help! my God! at thy decree?
Nature is chang'd, and hell should succour me.
And canst thou then look down from perfect bliss,
And see me plunging in the dark abyss?
Calling thee Father, in a sea of fire?
Or pouring blasphemies at thy desire?
With mortals' anguish wilt thou raise thy name,
And by my pangs omnipotence proclaim?
  'Thou, who canst toss the planets to and fro,
Contract not thy great vengeance to my woe;
Crush worlds; in hotter flames fall'n angels lay;
On me Almighty wrath is cast away.
Call back thy thunders, Lord, hold in thy rage,
Nor with a speck of wretchedness engage:
Forget me quite, nor stoop a worm to blame;
But lose me in the greatness of thy name.
Thou art all love, all mercy, all divine,
And shall I make those glories cease to shine?
Shall sinful man grow great by his offence,
And from its course turn back Omnipotence?
  'Forbid it! and oh! grant, great God, at least
This one, this slender, almost no request;

When I have wept a thousand lives away,
When torment is grown weary of its prey,
When I have rav'd ten thousand years in fire,
Ten thousand thousand, let me then expire.'

ALEXANDER POPE

1688–1744

227 *Messiah*

YE Nymphs of Solyma! begin the song:
To heav'nly themes sublimer strains belong.
The mossy fountains, and the sylvan shades,
The dreams of Pindus and th' Aonian maids,
Delight no more—O thou my voice inspire
Who touch'd Isaiah's hallow'd lips with fire!
  Rapt into future times, the Bard begun:
A Virgin shall conceive, a Virgin bear a Son!
From Jesse's root behold a branch arise,
Whose sacred flow'r with fragrance fills the skies:
Th' Aethereal spirit o'er its leaves shall move,
And on its top descends the mystic Dove.
Ye Heav'ns! from high the dewy nectar pour,
And in soft silence shed the kindly show'r!
The sick and weak the healing plant shall aid,
From storms a shelter, and from heat a shade.
All crimes shall cease, and ancient fraud shall fail;
Returning Justice lift aloft her scale;
Peace o'er the World her olive wand extend,
And white-rob'd Innocence from heav'n descend.
Swift fly the years, and rise th' expected morn!
Oh spring to light, auspicious Babe, be born!
See Nature hastes her earliest wreaths to bring,
With all the incense of the breathing spring:

See lofty Lebanon his head advance,
See nodding forests on the mountains dance:
See spicy clouds from lowly Saron rise,
And Carmel's flow'ry top perfumes the skies!
Hark! a glad voice the lonely desert cheers;
Prepare the way! a God, a God appears:
A God, a God! the vocal hills reply,
The rocks proclaim th' approaching Deity.
Lo, earth receives him from the bending skies!
Sink down ye mountains, and ye valleys rise,
With heads declin'd, ye cedars homage pay;
Be smooth, ye rocks, ye rapid floods, give way!
The Saviour comes! by ancient bards foretold:
Hear him, ye deaf, and all ye blind, behold!
He from thick films shall purge the visual ray,
And on the sightless eye-ball pour the day:
'Tis he th' obstructed paths of sound shall clear,
And bid new music charm th' unfolding ear:
The dumb shall sing, the lame his crutch forego,
And leap exulting like the bounding roe.
No sigh, no murmur the wide world shall hear,
From ev'ry face he wipes off ev'ry tear.
In adamantine chains shall Death be bound,
And Hell's grim Tyrant feel th' eternal wound.
As the good shepherd tends his fleecy care,
Seeks freshest pasture and the purest air,
Explores the lost, the wand'ring sheep directs,
By day o'ersees them, and by night protects,
The tender lambs he raises in his arms,
Feeds from his hand, and in his bosom warms;
Thus shall mankind his guardian care engage,
The promis'd father of the future age.

No more shall nation against nation rise,
Nor ardent warriors meet with hateful eyes,
Nor fields with gleaming steel be cover'd o'er,
The brazen trumpets kindle rage no more;
But useless lances into scythes shall bend,
And the broad falchion in a plough-share end.
Then palaces shall rise; the joyful Son
Shall finish what his short-liv'd Sire begun;
Their vines a shadow to their race shall yield,
And the same hand that sow'd, shall reap the field.
The swain in barren deserts with surprise
Sees lilies spring, and sudden verdure rise;
And starts, amidst the thirsty wilds to hear
New falls of water murm'ring in his ear.
On rifted rocks, the dragon's late abodes,
The green reed trembles, and the bulrush nods.
Waste sandy valleys, once perplex'd with thorn,
The spiry fir and shapely box adorn:
To leafless shrubs the flow'ring palms succeed,
And od'rous myrtle to the noisome weed.
The lambs with wolves shall graze the verdant mead,
And boys in flow'ry bands the tiger lead;
The steer and lion at one crib shall meet,
And harmless serpents lick the pilgrim's feet
The smiling infant in his hand shall take
The crested basilisk and speckled snake,
Pleas'd the green lustre of the scales survey,
And with their forky tongues shall innocently play.
Rise, crown'd with light, imperial Salem, rise!
Exalt thy tow'ry head, and lift thy eyes!
See, a long race thy spacious courts adorn;
See future sons, and daughters yet unborn,

In crowding ranks on ev'ry side arise,
Demanding life, impatient for the skies!
See barb'rous nations at thy gates attend,
Walk in thy light, and in thy temple bend;
See thy bright altars throng'd with prostrate kings,
And heap'd with products of Sabaean springs!
For thee Idume's spicy forests blow,
And seeds of gold in Ophir's mountains glow.
See heav'n its sparkling portals wide display,
And break upon thee in a flood of day!
No more the rising Sun shall gild the morn,
Nor ev'ning Cynthia fill her silver horn;
But lost, dissolv'd in thy superior rays
One tide of glory, one unclouded blaze
O'erflow thy courts: the light himself shall shine
Reveal'd, and God's eternal day be thine!
The seas shall waste, the skies in smoke decay,
Rocks fall to dust, and mountains melt away;
But fix'd his word, his saving pow'r remains;—
Thy realm for ever lasts, thy own Messiah reigns!

SAMUEL WESLEY

1691–1739

228 *Hymn to God the Father*

HAIL, Father! whose creating call
  Unnumber'd worlds attend;
Jehovah! comprehending all,
  Whom none can comprehend.

In light unsearchable enthron'd,
  Which Angels dimly see;
The Fountain of the Godhead own'd,
  And foremost of the Three.

From whom through an eternal Now
  The Son Thy offspring flow'd,
An everlasting Father Thou,
  An everlasting God!

Nor quite display'd to worlds above,
  Nor quite on earth conceal'd;
By wondrous unexhausted Love
  To mortal man reveal'd!

Supreme and all-sufficient God,
  When nature shall expire;
When worlds, created by Thy nod,
  Shall perish by Thy fire.

Thy Name, Jehovah! be ador'd
  By creatures without end!
Whom none but Thy essential Word
  And Spirit comprehend.

JOHN BYROM

1692–1763

229 *'My Spirit longeth for Thee'*

MY spirit longeth for Thee,
  Within my troubled breast
Altho' I be unworthy
  Of so divine a Guest.

Of so divine a Guest,
  Unworthy tho' I be,
Yet has my heart no rest,
  Unless it come from Thee.

Unless it come from Thee,
  In vain I look around;
In all that I can see,
  No rest is to be found.

No rest is to be found,
  But in Thy blessèd love;
O! let my wish be crown'd,
  And send it from above!

JAMES THOMSON

1700–1748

230 *A Hymn on the Seasons*

THESE, as they change, Almighty Father! these
  Are but the varied God. The rolling year
Is full of thee. Forth in the pleasing Spring
Thy beauty walks, thy tenderness and love.
Wide flush the fields; the softening air is balm;
Echo the mountains round; the forest smiles;
And every sense, and every heart, is joy.
Then comes thy glory in the Summer-months,
With light and heat refulgent. Then thy sun
Shoots full perfection through the swelling year:
And oft thy voice in dreadful thunder speaks,
And oft, at dawn, deep noon, or falling eve,
By brooks and groves, in hollow-whispering gales.
Thy bounty shines in Autumn unconfined,
And spreads a common feast for all that lives.
In Winter awful thou! with clouds and storms
Around thee thrown, tempest o'er tempest rolled,
Majestic darkness! On the whirlwind's wing
Riding sublime, thou bidst the world adore,
And humblest nature with thy northern blast.

Mysterious round! what skill, what force divine,
Deep-felt in these appear! a simple train,
Yet so delightful mixed, with such kind art,
Such beauty and beneficence combined,
Shade unperceived so softening into shade,
And all so forming an harmonious whole
That, as they still succeed, they ravish still.
But, wandering oft with brute unconscious gaze,
Man marks not thee, marks not the mighty hand
That, ever busy, wheels the silent spheres,
Works in the secret deep, shoots steaming thence
The fair profusion that o'erspreads the Spring,
Flings from the sun direct the flaming day,
Feeds every creature, hurls the tempest forth,
And, as on earth this grateful change revolves,
With transport touches all the springs of life.

Nature, attend! join, every living soul
Beneath the spacious temple of the sky,
In adoration join; and ardent raise
One general song! To him, ye vocal gales,
Breathe soft, whose spirit in your freshness breathes:
Oh! talk of him in solitary glooms,
Where, o'er the rock, the scarcely-waving pine
Fills the brown shade with a religious awe.
And ye, whose bolder note is heard afar,
Who shake the astonished world, lift high to Heaven
The impetuous song, and say from whom you rage.
His praise, ye brooks, attune, ye trembling rills;
And let me catch it as I muse along.
Ye headlong torrents, rapid and profound;
Ye softer floods, that lead the humid maze

Along the vale; and thou, majestic main,
A secret world of wonders in thyself,
Sound his stupendous praise, whose greater voice
Or bids you roar or bids your roarings fall.
Soft roll your incense, herbs, and fruits, and flowers,
In mingled clouds to him, whose sun exalts,
Whose breath perfumes you, and whose pencil paints.
Ye forests, bend; ye harvests, wave to him—
Breathe your still song into the reaper's heart
As home he goes beneath the joyous moon.
Ye that keep watch in heaven, as earth asleep
Unconscious lies, effuse your mildest beams,
Ye constellations! while your angels strike
Amid the spangled sky the silver lyre.
Great source of day! best image here below
Of thy Creator, ever pouring wide
From world to world the vital ocean round!
On nature write with every beam his praise.
The thunder rolls: be hushed the prostrate world,
While cloud to cloud returns the solemn hymn.
Bleat out afresh, ye hills; ye mossy rocks,
Retain the sound; the broad responsive low,
Ye valleys, raise; for the Great Shepherd reigns,
And his unsuffering kingdom yet will come.
Ye woodlands all, awake: a boundless song
Burst from the groves; and, when the restless day,
Expiring, lays the warbling world asleep,
Sweetest of birds, sweet Philomela! charm
The listening shades, and teach the night his praise!
Ye, chief, for whom the whole creation smiles,
At once the head, the heart, the tongue of all,
Crown the great hymn! In swarming cities vast,

Assembled men, to the deep organ join
The long-resounding voice, oft breaking clear
At solemn pauses through the swelling bass;
And, as each mingling flame increases each,
In one united ardour rise to heaven.
Or, if you rather choose the rural shade,
And find a fane in every sacred grove,
There let the shepherd's flute, the virgin's lay,
The prompting seraph, and the poet's lyre
Still sing the God of Seasons as they roll.
For me, when I forget the darling theme,
Whether the blossom blows, the summer-ray
Russets the plain, inspiring autumn gleams,
Or winter rises in the blackening east,
Be my tongue mute, may fancy paint no more,
And, dead to joy, forget my heart to beat!

Should fate command me to the farthest verge
Of the green earth, to distant barbarous climes,
Rivers unknown to song, where first the sun
Gilds Indian mountains, or his setting beam
Flames on the Atlantic isles, 'tis nought to me;
Since God is ever present, ever felt,
In the void waste as in the city full,
And where he vital spreads there must be joy.
When even at last the solemn hour shall come,
And wing my mystic flight to future worlds,
I cheerful will obey; there, with new powers,
Will rising wonders sing: I cannot go
Where universal love not smiles around,
Sustaining all yon orbs and all their sons;
From seeming evil still educing good,

And better thence again, and better still,
In infinite progression. But I lose
Myself in him, in light ineffable!
Come then, expressive Silence, muse his praise.

PHILIP DODDRIDGE

1702–1751

231 *'Live while you live'*

'LIVE while you live,' the Epicure would say,
'And seize the pleasures of the present day.'
'Live while you live,' the sacred Preacher cries,
'And give to God each moment as it flies.'
Lord, in my views let both united be;
I live in pleasure, when I live to Thee.

232 *'Ye Golden Lamps of Heaven'*

YE golden lamps of Heaven, farewell,
With all your feeble light;
Farewell, thou ever-changing moon,
Pale empress of the night.

And thou, refulgent orb of day,
In brighter flames array'd;
—My soul, that springs beyond thy sphere,
No more demands thine aid.

Ye stars are but the shining dust
Of my Divine abode,
The pavement of those heavenly courts
Where I shall reign with God.

The Father of eternal light
  Shall there His beams display;
Nor shall one moment's darkness mix
  With that unvaried day.

No more the drops of piercing grief
  Shall swell into mine eyes;
Nor the meridian sun decline
  Amidst those brighter skies.

CHARLES WESLEY

1707–1788

233 *'Jesu, Lover of my Soul'*

JESU, Lover of my soul,
  Let me to Thy bosom fly,
While the nearer waters roll,
  While the tempest still is high:
Hide me, O my Saviour, hide
  Till the storm of life is past,
Safe into the haven guide,
  O receive my soul at last!

Other refuge have I none;
  Hangs my helpless soul on Thee;
Leave, ah! leave me not alone,
  Still support and comfort me!
All my trust on Thee is stay'd,
  All my help from Thee I bring:
Cover my defenceless head
  With the shadow of Thy wing!

Wilt Thou not regard my call?
  Wilt Thou not accept my prayer?
Lo! I sink, I faint, I fall—
  Lo! on Thee I cast my care!
Reach me out Thy gracious hand:
  While I of Thy strength receive,
Hoping against hope I stand,
  Dying, and behold I live!

Plenteous grace with Thee is found,
  Grace to cover all my sin;
Let the healing streams abound;
  Make and keep me pure within:—
Thou of Life the Fountain art,
  Freely let me take of Thee;
Spring Thou up within my heart,—
  Rise to all eternity!

234 *'Come, O thou Traveller unknown'*

COME, O Thou Traveller unknown,
  Whom still I hold, but cannot see,
My company before is gone,
  And I am left alone with Thee;
With Thee all night I mean to stay,
And wrestle till the break of day.

I need not tell Thee who I am,
  My misery or sin declare;
Thyself hast call'd me by my name;
  Look on Thy hands, and read it there!
But Who, I ask Thee, Who art Thou?
Tell me Thy name, and tell me now.

In vain Thou strugglest to get free,
  I never will unloose my hold;
Art Thou the Man that died for me?
  The secret of Thy love unfold.
Wrestling, I will not let Thee go,
Till I Thy Name, Thy Nature know.

Wilt Thou not yet to me reveal
  Thy new, unutterable Name?
Tell me, I still beseech Thee, tell:
  To know it now, resolved I am:
Wrestling, I will not let Thee go,
Till I Thy Name, Thy Nature know.

What though my shrinking flesh complain,
  And murmur to contend so long?
I rise superior to my pain;
  When I am weak, then I am strong:
And when my all of strength shall fail,
I shall with the GOD-MAN prevail.

My strength is gone; my nature dies;
  I sink beneath Thy weighty hand;
Faint to revive, and fall to rise;
  I fall, and yet by faith I stand:
I stand, and will not let Thee go,
Till I Thy Name, Thy Nature know.

Yield to me now, for I am weak,
  But confident in self-despair;
Speak to my heart, in blessings speak,
  Be conquer'd by my instant prayer!
Speak, or Thou never hence shalt move,—
And tell me, if Thy Name is Love?

—'Tis Love! 'tis Love! Thou diedst for me!
I hear Thy whisper in my heart!
The morning breaks, the shadows flee;
Pure universal Love Thou art!
To me, to all, Thy bowels move;
Thy Nature and Thy Name is Love!

My prayer hath power with God; the grace
Unspeakable I now receive;
Through faith I see Thee face to face,
I see Thee face to face, and live:
In vain I have not wept and strove;
Thy Nature and Thy Name is Love.

I know Thee, Saviour, Who Thou art;
Jesus, the feeble sinner's Friend!
Nor wilt Thou with the night depart,
But stay, and love me to the end!
Thy mercies never shall remove—
Thy Nature and Thy Name is Love!

The Sun of Righteousness on me
Hath rose, with healing in His wings;
Wither'd my nature's strength, from Thee
My soul its life and succour brings;
My help is all laid up above;
Thy Nature, and Thy Name, is Love.

Contented now upon my thigh
I halt, till life's short journey end;
All helplessness, all weakness, I
On Thee alone for strength depend;
Nor have I power from Thee to move;
Thy Nature, and Thy Name, is Love.

Lame as I am, I take the prey,
  Hell, earth, and sin, with ease o'ercome
I leap for joy, pursue my way,
  And as a bounding hart fly home—
Through all eternity to prove,
Thy Nature and Thy Name is Love!

235 *'Times without Number have I pray'd'*

TIMES without number have I pray'd,
  'This only once forgive';
Relapsing, when Thy hand was stay'd,
  And suffer'd me to live:—

Yet now the kingdom of Thy peace,
  LORD, to my heart restore;
Forgive my vain repentances,
  And bid me sin no more.

236 *'Still, O Lord, for Thee I tarry'*

STILL, O LORD, for Thee I tarry,
  Full of sorrows, sins, and wants;
Thee, and all thy Saints I weary
  With my sad but vain complaints;
Sawn asunder by temptation,
  Tortur'd by distracting care,
Kill'd by doubts' severe vexation,
  Sorer evil than despair.

Will the fight be never over?
  Will the balance never turn?
Still 'twixt life and death I hover,
  Bear what is not to be borne;

Who can bear a wounded spirit?
  Whither must my spirit go?
Shall I Heaven or Hell inherit?
  Let me die my doom to know.

All in vain for death I languish,
  Death from his pursuer flies:
Still I feel the gnawing anguish,
  Feel the worm that never dies:
Still in horrid expectation
  Like the damn'd in Hell I groan,
Envy them their swift damnation,
  Fearful to enhance my own.

Jesus, see thy fallen creature,
  Fallen at thy feet I lie,
Act according to thy nature,
  Bid the sinner live or die;
Of my pain fill up the measure,
  If Thou canst no more forgive:
If Thou in my life hast pleasure,
  Speak, and now my soul shall live.

237 *'Christ, Whose Glory fills the Skies'*

CHRIST, Whose glory fills the skies,
  Christ, the true, the only Light,
Sun of Righteousness, arise,
  Triumph o'er the shades of night!
Day-spring from on high, be near!
Day-star, in my heart appear!

Dark and cheerless is the morn
  Unaccompanied by Thee;
Joyless is the day's return,
  Till Thy mercy's beams I see;
Till they inward light impart,
Glad my eyes, and warm my heart.

Visit then this soul of mine,
  Pierce the gloom of sin and grief!
Fill me, Radiancy Divine,
  Scatter all my unbelief!
More and more Thyself display,
Shining to the perfect day!

238 *'Gentle Jesus, meek and mild'*

GENTLE Jesus, meek and mild,
  Look upon a little child;
Pity my simplicity,
Suffer me to come to Thee.

Fain I would to Thee be brought;
Dearest God, forbid it not:
Give me, dearest God, a place
In the kingdom of Thy grace.

Put Thy hands upon my head,
Let me in Thine arms be stayed;
Let me lean upon Thy breast,
Lull me, lull me, Lord, to rest.

Hold me fast in Thy embrace,
Let me see Thy smiling face.
Give me, Lord, Thy blessing give;
Pray for me, and I shall live.

CHARLES WESLEY

. . . .

Lamb of God, I look to Thee;
Thou shalt my Example be;
Thou art gentle, meek and mild,
Thou wast once a little Child.

Fain I would be as Thou art;
Give me Thy obedient heart.
Thou art pitiful and kind;
Let me have Thy loving mind.

Meek and lowly may I be;
Thou art all humility.
Let me to my betters bow;
Subject to Thy parents Thou.

Let me above all fulfil
God my heavenly Father's will;
Never His good Spirit grieve,
Only to his glory live.

Thou didst live to God alone,
Thou didst never seek Thine own;
Thou Thyself didst never please.
God was all Thy happiness.

Loving Jesu, gentle Lamb,
In Thy gracious hands I am,
Make me, Saviour, what Thou art,
Live Thyself within my heart.

PHILIP SKELTON

1707–1787

239 *'To God, ye Choir above'*

TO GOD, ye choir above, begin
  A hymn so loud and strong
That all the universe may hear
  And join the grateful song.

Praise Him, thou sun, Who dwells unseen
  Amidst transcendent light,
Where thy refulgent orb would seem
  A spot, as dark as night.

Thou silver moon, ye host of stars,
  The universal song
Through the serene and silent night
  To listening worlds prolong.

Sing Him, ye distant worlds and suns,
  From whence no travelling ray
Hath yet to us, through ages past,
  Had time to make its way.

Assist, ye raging storms, and bear
  On rapid wings His praise,
From north to south, from east to west,
  Through heaven, and earth, and seas.

Exert your voice, ye furious fires
  That rend the watery cloud,
And thunder to this nether world
  Your Maker's words aloud.

PHILIP SKELTON

Ye works of God, that dwell unknown
Beneath the rolling main;
Ye birds, that sing among the groves,
And sweep the azure plain;

Ye stately hills, that rear your heads,
And towering pierce the sky;
Ye clouds, that with an awful pace
Majestic roll on high;

Ye insects small, to which one leaf
Within its narrow sides
A vast extended world displays,
And spacious realms provides;

Ye race, still less than these, with which
The stagnant water teems,
To which one drop, however small,
A boundless ocean seems;

—Whate'er ye are, where'er ye dwell,
Ye creatures great or small,
Adore the Wisdom, praise the Power,
That made and governs all.

JAMES MERRICK

1720–1769

240 *The Ignorance of Man*

BEHOLD yon new-born infant, griev'd
With hunger, thirst, and pain;
That asks to have the wants reliev'd,
It knows not to explain.

Aloud the speechless suppliant cries,
  And utters, as it can,
The woes that in its bosom rise,
  And speaks its nature man.

That infant, whose advancing hour
  Life's various sorrows try,
(Sad proof of sin's transmissive power)
  That infant, Lord, am I.

A childhood yet my thoughts confess,
  Though long in years mature;
Unknowing whence I feel distress,
  And where, or what its cure.

Author of good! to Thee I turn;
  Thy ever-wakeful eye
Alone can all my wants discern,
  Thy hand alone supply.

O let Thy fear within me dwell,
  Thy love my footsteps guide:
That love shall vainer loves expel,
  That fear all fears beside.

And O, by error's force subdu'd,
  Since oft my stubborn will,
Preposterous, shuns the latent good,
  And grasps the specious ill;

Not to my wish, but to my want,
  Do Thou Thy gifts apply:
Unask'd, what good Thou knowest, grant
  What ill, though ask'd, deny.

CHRISTOPHER SMART

1722–1771

241 *From 'A Song to David'*

O DAVID, highest in the list
Of worthies, on God's ways insist,
The genuine word repeat;
Vain are the documents of men,
And vain the flourish of the pen
That keeps the fool's conceit.

Praise above all—for praise prevails;
Heap up the measure, load the scales,
And good to goodness add:
The gen'rous soul her Saviour aids,
But peevish obloquy degrades;
The Lord is great and glad.

For Adoration all the ranks
Of angels yield eternal thanks,
And David in the midst;
With God's good poor, which, last and least
In man's esteem, thou to thy feast,
O blessed bridegroom, bidst.

For Adoration seasons change,
And order, truth, and beauty range,
Adjust, attract, and fill:
The grass the polyanthus cheques;
And polish'd porphyry reflects,
By the descending rill.

Rich almonds colour to the prime
For Adoration; tendrils climb,
        And fruit-trees pledge their gems;
And Ivis with her gorgeous vest,
Builds for her eggs her cunning nest,
        And bell-flowers bow their stems.

With vinous syrup cedars spout;
From rocks pure honey gushing out,
        For Adoration springs;
All scenes of painting crowd the map
Of nature; to the mermaid's pap
        The scaled infant clings.

The spotted ounce and playsome cubs
Run rustling 'mongst the flow'ring shrubs,
        And lizards feed the moss;
For Adoration beasts embark,
While waves upholding halcyon's ark
        No longer roar and toss.

While Israel sits beneath his fig,
With coral root and amber sprig
        The wean'd adventurer sports;
Where to the palm the jasmine cleaves,
For Adoration 'mong the leaves
        The gale his peace reports.

Increasing days their reign exalt,
Nor in the pink and mottled vault
        Th' opposing spirits tilt;
And, by the coasting reader spy'd,
The silverlings and crusions glide
        For Adoration gilt.

For Adoration rip'ning canes
And cocoa's purest milk detains
 The western pilgrim's staff;
Where rain in clasping bough inclos'd,
And vines with oranges dispos'd,
 Embower the social laugh.

Now labour his reward receives,
For Adoration counts his sheaves
 To peace, her bounteous prince;
The nect'rine his strong tint imbibes,
And apples of ten thousand tribes,
 And quick peculiar quince.

The wealthy crops of whit'ning rice
'Mongst thyine woods and groves of spice,
 For Adoration grow;
And, marshall'd in the fenced land,
The peaches and pomegranates stand,
 Where wild carnations blow.

The laurels with the winter strive;
The crocus burnishes alive
 Upon the snow-clad earth.
For Adoration myrtles stay
To keep the garden from dismay,
 And bless the sight from dearth.

The pheasant shows his pompous neck;
And ermine, jealous of a speck,
 With fear eludes offence:
The sable, with his glossy pride,
For Adoration is descried,
 Where frosts the wave condense.

The cheerful holly, pensive yew,
And holy thorn, their trim renew;
The squirrel hoards his nuts:
All creatures batten o'er their stores,
And careful nature all her doors
For Adoration shuts.

For Adoration, David's Psalms
Lift up the heart to deeds of alms;
And he, who kneels and chants,
Prevails his passions to control,
Finds meat and med'cine to the soul,
Which for translation pants.

For Adoration, beyond match,
The scholar bulfinch aims to catch
The soft flute's iv'ry touch;
And, careless on the hazel spray,
The daring redbreast keeps at bay
The damsel's greedy touch.

For Adoration, in the skies,
The Lord's philosopher espies
The dog, the ram, and rose;
The planet's ring, Orion's sword;
Nor is his greatness less ador'd
In the vile worm that glows.

For Adoration on the strings
The western breezes work their wings,
The captive ear to soothe—
Hark! 'tis a voice—how still, and small—
That makes the cataract to fall,
Or bids the sea be smooth.

CHRISTOPHER SMART

For Adoration, incense comes
From bezoar, and Arabian gums,
And from the civet's fur:
But as for prayer, or ere it faints,
Far better is the breath of saints
Than galbanum or myrrh.

For Adoration, from the down
Of damsons to th' anana's crown,
God sends to tempt the taste;
And while the luscious zest invites
The sense, that in the scene delights,
Commands desire be chaste.

For Adoration, all the paths
Of grace are open, all the baths
Of purity refresh;
And all the rays of glory beam
To deck the man of God's esteem,
Who triumphs o'er the flesh.

For Adoration, in the dome
Of Christ, the sparrows find a home;
And on his olives perch:
The swallow also dwells with thee,
O man of God's humility,
Within his Saviour's Church.

Sweet is the dew that falls betimes,
And drops upon the leafy limes;
Sweet Hermon's fragrant air:
Sweet is the lily's silver bell,
And sweet the wakeful tapers smell
That watch for early prayer.

Sweet the young nurse, with love intense,
Which smiles o'er sleeping innocence;
    Sweet when the lost arrive:
Sweet the musician's ardour beats,
While his vague mind 's in quest of sweets,
    The choicest flowers to hive.

Sweeter in all the strains of love,
The language of thy turtle-dove,
    Pair'd to thy swelling chord;
Sweeter with ev'ry grace endued,
The glory of thy gratitude,
    Respir'd unto the Lord.

Strong is the horse upon his speed;
Strong in pursuit the rapid glede,
    Which makes at once his game;
Strong the tall ostrich on the ground;
Strong through the turbulent profound
    Shoots xiphias to his aim.

Strong is the lion—like a coal
His eyeball—like a bastion's mole
    His chest against the foes:
Strong the gier-eagle on his sail,
Strong against tide th' enormous whale
    Emerges, as he goes.

But stronger still in earth and air,
And in the sea, the man of prayer,
    And far beneath the tide;
And in the seat to faith assign'd,
Where ask is have, where seek is find,
    Where knock is open wide.

Beauteous the fleet before the gale;
Beauteous the multitudes in mail,
　　Rank'd arms, and crested heads:
Beauteous the garden's umbrage mild,
Walk, water, meditated wild,
　　And all the bloomy beds.

Beauteous the moon full on the lawn;
And beauteous, when the veil 's withdrawn,
　　The virgin to her spouse:
Beauteous the temple, deck'd and fill'd,
When to the heav'n of heav'ns they build
　　Their heart-directed vows.

Beauteous, yea beauteous more than these,
The Shepherd King upon his knees,
　　For his momentous trust;
With wish of infinite conceit,
For man, beast, mute, the small and great,
　　And prostrate dust to dust.

Precious the bounteous widow's mite;
And precious, for extreme delight,
　　The largess from the churl:
Precious the ruby's blushing blaze,
And alba's blest imperial rays,
　　And pure cerulean pearl.

Precious the penitential tear;
And precious is the sigh sincere;
　　Acceptable to God;
And precious are the winning flowers,
In gladsome Israel's feast of bowers,
　　Bound on the hallow'd sod.

More precious that diviner part
Of David, e'en the Lord's own heart,
Great, beautiful, and new:
In all things where it was intent,
In all extremes, in each event,
Proof—answering true to true.

Glorious the sun in mid career;
Glorious th' assembled fires appear;
Glorious the comet's train:
Glorious the trumpet and alarm;
Glorious th' Almighty's stretch'd-out arm;
Glorious th' enraptured main:

Glorious the northern lights astream;
Glorious the song, when God 's the theme;
Glorious the thunder's roar:
Glorious hosannah from the den;
Glorious the catholic amen;
Glorious the martyr's gore:

Glorious—more glorious is the crown
Of Him, that brought salvation down
By meekness, call'd thy Son;
Thou that stupendous truth believ'd,
And now the matchless deed 's achieved,
Determin'd, dar'd, and done.

JOHN NEWTON 1725–1807

242 *'How sweet the Name of Jesus sounds'*

HOW sweet the Name of JESUS sounds
In a believer's ear!
It soothes his sorrows, heals his wounds,
And drives away his fear!

It makes the wounded spirit whole
  And calms the troubled breast;
'Tis manna to the hungry soul,
  And to the weary, rest.

Dear Name! the rock on which I build,
  My shield and hiding-place,
My never-failing treasury, fill'd
  With boundless stores of grace,—

By Thee my prayers acceptance gain,
  Although with sin defiled;
Satan accuses me in vain,
  And I am own'd a Child.

Weak is the effort of my heart,
  And cold my warmest thought;
But, when I see Thee as Thou art,
  I'll praise Thee as I ought.

Till then, I would Thy love proclaim
  With every fleeting breath;
And may the music of Thy Name
  Refresh my soul in death!

243 *'In Evil long I took Delight'*

IN evil long I took delight,
  Unawed by shame or fear,
Till a new object struck my sight,
  And stopp'd my wild career:
I saw One hanging on a Tree
  In agonies and blood,
Who fix'd His languid eyes on me,
  As near His Cross I stood.

Sure never till my latest breath
  Can I forget that look:
It seem'd to charge me with His death,
  Though not a word He spoke:
My conscience felt and own'd the guilt,
  And plunged me in despair;
I saw my sins His Blood had spilt,
  And help'd to nail Him there.

Alas! I knew not what I did!
  But now my tears are vain:
Where shall my trembling soul be hid?
  For I the LORD have slain!
—A second look He gave, which said,
  'I freely all forgive;
This Blood is for thy ransom paid;
  I die, that thou may'st live.'

Thus, while His death my sin displays
  In all its blackest hue,
Such is the mystery of grace,
  It seals my pardon too.
With pleasing grief, and mournful joy,
  My spirit now is fill'd,
That I should such a life destroy,—
  Yet live by Him I kill'd!

WILLIAM COWPER 1731–1800

244 *'Oh! for a closer Walk with God'*

OH! for a closer walk with GOD,
  A calm and heav'nly frame;
A light to shine upon the road
  That leads me to the Lamb!

Where is the blessedness I knew
  When first I saw the LORD?
Where is the soul-refreshing view
  Of JESUS, and his word?

What peaceful hours I once enjoy'd!
  How sweet their mem'ry still!
But they have left an aching void,
  The world can never fill.

Return, O holy Dove, return,
  Sweet messenger of rest;
I hate the sins that made thee mourn,
  And drove thee from my breast.

The dearest idol I have known,
  Whate'er that idol be;
Help me to tear it from thy throne,
  And worship only thee.

So shall my walk be close with GOD,
  Calm and serene my frame;
So purer light shall mark the road
  That leads me to the Lamb.

245 *'The Lord will Happiness divine'*

THE LORD will happiness divine
  On contrite hearts bestow:
Then tell me, gracious GOD, is mine
  A contrite heart, or no?

I hear, but seem to hear in vain,
  Insensible as steel;
If ought is felt, 'tis only pain,
  To find I cannot feel.

I sometimes think myself inclin'd
  To love thee, if I could;
But often feel another mind,
  Averse to all that's good.

My best desires are faint and few,
  I fain would strive for more;
But when I cry, 'My strength renew,'
  Seem weaker than before.

Thy saints are comforted I know,
  And love thy house of pray'r;
I therefore go where others go,
  But find no comfort there.

Oh make this heart rejoice, or ache;
  Decide this doubt for me;
And if it be not broken, break,
  And heal it, if it be.

246 *'My former Hopes are fled'*

MY former hopes are fled,
  My terror now begins;
I feel, alas! that I am dead
In trespasses and sins.

Ah, whither shall I fly?
I hear the thunder roar;
The law proclaims destruction nigh,
And vengeance at the door.

When I review my ways,
I dread impending doom;
But sure, a friendly whisper says,
'Flee from the wrath to come.'

I see, or think I see,
A glimm'ring from afar;
A beam of day that shines for me,
To save me from despair.

Fore-runner of the sun,
It marks the Pilgrim's way;
I'll gaze upon it while I run
And watch the rising day.

247 *'O Lord, my best Desire fulfil'*

O LORD, my best desire fulfil,
  And help me to resign
Life, health, and comfort to thy will,
  And make thy pleasure mine.

Why should I shrink at thy command,
  Whose love forbids my fears?
Or tremble at the gracious hand
  That wipes away my tears?

No, rather let me freely yield
  What most I prize to thee;
Who never hast a good withheld,
  Or wilt withhold from me.

Thy favor, all my journey thro',
   Thou art engag'd to grant;
What else I want, or think I do,
   'Tis better still to want.

Wisdom and mercy guide my way,
   Shall I resist them both?
A poor blind creature of a day,
   And crush'd before the moth!

But ah! my inward spirit cries,
   Still bind me to thy sway;
Else the next cloud that vails my skies,
   Drives all these thoughts away.

248 *From 'The Task'*

I WAS a stricken deer, that left the herd
Long since; with many an arrow deep infixt
My panting side was charg'd, when I withdrew
To seek a tranquil death in distant shades.
There was I found by one who had himself
Been hurt by th' archers. In his side he bore,
And in his hands and feet, the cruel scars.
With gentle force soliciting the darts,
He drew them forth, and heal'd, and bade me live.
Since then, with few associates, in remote
And silent woods I wander, far from those
My former partners of the peopled scene;
With few associates, and not wishing more.

WILLIAM COWPER

249 *Lines on a Bill of Mortality, 1790*

HE who sits from day to day,
  Where the prison'd lark is hung,
Heedless of his loudest lay,
  Hardly knows that he has sung.

Where the watchman in his round
  Nightly lifts his voice on high,
None, accustom'd to the sound,
  Wakes the sooner for his cry.

So your verse-man I, and clerk,
  Yearly in my song proclaim
Death at hand—yourselves his mark—
  And the foe's unerring aim.

Duly at my time I come,
  Publishing to all aloud—
Soon the grave must be your home,
  And your only suit a shroud.

But the monitory strain,
  Oft repeated in your ears,
Seems to sound too much in vain,
  Wins no notice, wakes no fears.

Can a truth, by all confess'd
  Of such magnitude and weight,
Grow, by being oft express'd,
  Trivial as a parrot's prate?

Pleasure's call attention wins,
  Hear it often as we may;
New as ever seem our sins,
  Though committed ev'ry day.

Death and Judgement, Heav'n and Hell—
   These alone, so often heard,
No more move us than the bell
   When some stranger is interr'd.

Oh then, ere the turf or tomb
   Cover us from ev'ry eye,
Spirit of instruction, come;
   Make us learn that we must die.

AUGUSTUS MONTAGUE TOPLADY

1740–1778

250 *'Rock of Ages'*

ROCK of Ages, cleft for me,
Let me hide myself in Thee!
Let the water and the blood
From Thy riven side which flow'd,
Be of sin the double cure,
Cleanse me from its guilt and power.

Not the labours of my hands
Can fulfil Thy law's demands;
Could my zeal no respite know,
Could my tears for ever flow,
All for sin could not atone;
Thou must save, and Thou alone.

Nothing in my hand I bring;
Simply to Thy Cross I cling;
Naked, come to Thee for dress;
Helpless, look to Thee for grace;
Foul, I to the Fountain fly;
Wash me, Saviour, or I die!

While I draw this fleeting breath,
When my eyestrings break in death,
When I soar through tracts unknown,
See Thee on Thy Judgement-throne;
Rock of Ages, cleft for me,
Let me hide myself in Thee!

251 *'Ah! give me, Lord, the single eye'*

AH! give me, LORD, the single eye,
  Which aims at nought but Thee:
I fain would live, and yet not I—
  But JESUS live in me.

Like Noah's dove, no rest I find
  But in Thy ark of peace;
Thy cross, the balance of my mind;
  Thy wounds, my hiding-place.

In vain the tempter spreads the snare,
  If Thou my keeper art;
—Get thee behind me, GOD is near,
  My Saviour takes my part!

On Him my spirit I recline,
  Who put my nature on;
His light shall in my darkness shine,
  And guide me to His throne.

252 *'Lord! it is not Life to live'*

LORD! it is not life to live,
  If Thy presence Thou deny;
LORD! if Thou Thy presence give,
  'Tis no longer death—to die.

Source and Giver of repose,
Singly from Thy smile it flows;
Peace and happiness are Thine,—
Mine they are, if Thou art mine.

253 *'Deathless Principle, arise'*

DEATHLESS principle, arise;
Soar thou native of the skies.
Pearl of price by Jesus bought,
To his glorious likeness wrought,
Go to shine before his throne;
Deck his mediatorial crown;
Go, his triumphs to adorn;
Made for God, to God return.

Lo, he beckons from on high!
Fearless to his presence fly:
Thine the merit of his blood;
Thine the righteousness of God.

Angels, joyful to attend,
Hov'ring, round thy pillow bend;
Wait to catch the signal giv'n,
And escort thee quick to heav'n.

Is thy earthly house distrest?
Willing to retain her guest?
'Tis not thou, but she, must die:
Fly, celestial tenant, fly.
Burst thy shackles, drop thy clay,
Sweetly breathe myself away:
Singing, to thy crown remove;
Swift of wing, and fir'd with love.

Shudder not to pass the stream:
Venture all thy care on him;
Him, whose dying love and pow'r
Still'd its tossing, hush'd its roar.
Safe is the expanded wave;
Gentle as a summer's eve:

Not one object of his care
Ever suffer'd shipwreck there.
See the haven full in view?
Love divine shall bear thee through.
Trust to that propitious gale:
Weigh thy anchor, spread thy sail.

Saints in glory perfect made,
Wait thy passage through the shade:
Ardent for thy coming o'er,
See, they throng the blissful shore.
Mount, their transports to improve:
Join the longing choir above:
Swiftly to their wish be giv'n:
Kindle higher joy in heav'n.
Such the prospects that arise
To the dying Christian's eyes!
Such the glorious vista Faith
Opens through the shades of death.

GEORGE CRABBE

1754-1832

254 *Resurrection*

THE wintry winds have ceased to blow,
And trembling leaves appear;
And fairest flowers succeed the snow,
And hail the infant year.

So, when the world and all its woes
  Are vanish'd far away,
Fair scenes and wonderful repose
  Shall bless the new-born day,—

When, from the confines of the grave,
  The body too shall rise;
No more precarious passion's slave,
  Nor error's sacrifice.

'Tis but a sleep—and Sion's king
  Will call the many dead:
'Tis but a sleep—and then we sing,
  O'er dreams of sorrow fled.

Yes!—wintry winds have ceased to blow,
  And trembling leaves appear,
And Nature has her types to show
  Throughout the varying year.

WILLIAM BLAKE

1757–1827

255 ### *The Divine Image*

TO Mercy, Pity, Peace, and Love
  All pray in their distress;
And to these virtues of delight
Return their thankfulness,

For Mercy, Pity, Peace, and Love
Is God, our Father dear,
And Mercy, Pity, Peace, and Love
Is man, His child and care.

For Mercy has a human heart,
Pity a human face,
And Love, the human form divine,
And Peace, the human dress.

Then every man, of every clime,
That prays in his distress,
Prays to the human form divine,
Love, Mercy, Pity, Peace.

And all must love the human form,
In heathen, Turk, or Jew;
Where Mercy, Love, and Pity dwell
There God is dwelling too.

256

Night

THE sun descending in the west,
The evening star does shine;
The birds are silent in their nest,
And I must seek for mine.
The moon, like a flower,
In heaven's high bower,
With silent delight
Sits and smiles on the night.

Farewell, green fields and happy groves,
Where flocks have took delight.
Where lambs have nibbled, silent moves
The feet of angels bright;
Unseen they pour blessing,
And joy without ceasing,
On each bud and blossom,
And each sleeping bosom.

They look in every thoughtless nest,
Where birds are cover'd warm;
They visit caves of every beast,
To keep them all from harm.
If they see any weeping
That should have been sleeping,
They pour sleep on their head,
And sit down by their bed.

When wolves and tigers howl for prey,
They pitying stand and weep;
Seeking to drive their thirst away,
And keep them from the sheep.
But if they rush dreadful,
The angels, most heedful,
Receive each mild spirit,
New worlds to inherit.

And there the lion's ruddy eyes
Shall flow with tears of gold,
And pitying the tender cries,
And walking round the fold,
Saying 'Wrath, by His meekness,
And, by His health, sickness
Is driven away
From our immortal day.

'And now beside thee, bleating lamb,
I can lie down and sleep;
Or think on Him who bore thy name,
Graze after thee and weep.

For, wash'd in life's river,
My bright mane for ever
Shall shine like the gold
As I guard o'er the fold.'

257 *The Lamb*

LITTLE Lamb, who made thee?
Dost thou know who made thee?
Gave thee life, and bid thee feed,
By the stream and o'er the mead;
Gave thee clothing of delight,
Softest clothing, woolly, bright;
Gave thee such a tender voice,
Making all the vales rejoice?
Little Lamb, who made thee?
Dost thou know who made thee?

Little Lamb, I'll tell thee,
Little Lamb, I'll tell thee:
He is callèd by thy name,
For He calls Himself a Lamb.
He is meek, and He is mild;
He became a little child.
I a child, and thou a lamb,
We are callèd by His name.
Little Lamb, God bless thee!
Little Lamb, God bless thee!

258 *The Little Black Boy*

MY mother bore me in the southern wild,
And I am black, but O! my soul is white;
White as an angel is the English child,
But I am black, as if bereav'd of light.

My mother taught me underneath a tree,
And, sitting down before the heat of day,
She took me on her lap and kissèd me,
And, pointing to the east, began to say:

'Look on the rising sun,—there God does live,
And gives His light, and gives His heat away;
And flowers and trees and beasts and men receive
Comfort in morning, joy in the noonday.

'And we are put on earth a little space,
That we may learn to bear the beams of love;
And these black bodies and this sunburnt face
Is but a cloud, and like a shady grove.

'For when our souls have learn'd the heat to bear,
The cloud will vanish; we shall hear His voice,
Saying: "Come out from the grove, My love and care,
And round My golden tent like lambs rejoice." '

Thus did my mother say, and kissèd me;
And thus I say to little English boy.
When I from black and he from white cloud free,
And round the tent of God like lambs we joy,

I'll shade him from the heat, till he can bear
To lean in joy upon our Father's knee;
And then I'll stand and stroke his silver hair,
And be like him, and he will then love me.

259 *To Tirzah*

WHATE'ER is born of mortal birth
Must be consumèd with the earth,
To rise from generation free:
Then what have I to do with thee?

The sexes sprung from shame and pride,
Blow'd in the morn; in evening died;
But Mercy chang'd death into sleep;
The sexes rose to work and weep.

Thou, Mother of my mortal part,
With cruelty didst mould my heart,
And with false self-deceiving tears
Didst bind my nostrils, eyes, and ears;

Didst close my tongue in senseless clay,
And me to mortal life betray:
The death of Jesus set me free:
Then what have I to do with thee?

260 *From 'The Everlasting Gospel'*

JESUS was sitting in Moses' chair,
They brought the trembling woman there.
Moses commands she be stoned to death,
What was the sound of Jesus' breath?
He laid His hand on Moses' law:
The Ancient Heavens, in silent awe
Writ with curses from pole to pole,
All away began to roll:
The Earth trembling and naked lay
In secret bed of mortal clay,
On Sinai felt the hand divine
Putting back the bloody shrine,
And she heard the breath of God
As she heard by Eden's flood:
'Good and evil are no more!
Sinai's trumpets, cease to roar!

Cease, finger of God, to write!
The Heavens are not clean in thy sight.
Thou art good, and thou alone;
Nor may the sinner cast one stone.
To be good only, is to be
A God or else a Pharisee.
Thou Angel of the Presence Divine
That didst create this body of mine,
Wherefore hast thou writ these laws
And created Hell's dark jaws?
My presence I will take from thee:
A cold leper thou shalt be.
Tho' thou wast so pure and bright
That Heaven was impure in thy sight,
Tho' thy oath turn'd Heaven pale,
Tho' thy covenant built Hell's jail,
Tho' thou didst all to chaos roll
With the serpent for its soul,
Still the breath Divine does move
And the breath Divine is love.
Mary, fear not! Let me see
The Seven Devils that torment thee:
Hide not from my sight thy sin,
That forgiveness thou may'st win.
Has no man condemned thee?'
'No man, Lord.' 'Then what is he
Who shall accuse thee? Come ye forth,
Fallen fiends of heav'nly birth
That have forgot your ancient love
And driven away my trembling dove.
You shall bow before her feet;
You shall lick the dust for meat; . . .'

261 *'Mock on, mock on, Voltaire, Rousseau'*

MOCK on, mock on, Voltaire, Rousseau;
Mock on, mock on; 'tis all in vain!
You throw the sand against the wind,
And the wind blows it back again.

And every sand becomes a gem
Reflected in the beams divine;
Blown back they blind the mocking eye,
But still in Israel's paths they shine.

The Atoms of Democritus
And Newton's Particles of Light
Are sands upon the Red Sea shore,
Where Israel's tents do shine so bright.

262 *'My Spectre around me Night and Day'*

I

MY Spectre around me night and day
Like a wild beast guards my way;
My Emanation far within
Weeps incessantly for my sin.

II

'A fathomless and boundless deep,
There we wander, there we weep;
On the hungry craving wind
My Spectre follows thee behind.

III

'He scents thy footsteps in the snow,
Wheresoever thou dost go,
Thro' the wintry hail and rain.
When wilt thou return again?

IV

'Dost thou not in pride and scorn
Fill with tempests all my morn,
And with jealousies and fears
Fill my pleasant nights with tears?

V

'Seven of my sweet loves thy knife
Has bereavèd of their life.
Their marble tombs I built with tears,
And with cold and shuddering fears.

VI

'Seven more loves weep night and day
Round the tombs where my loves lay,
And seven more loves attend each night
Around my couch with torches bright.

VII

'And seven more loves in my bed
Crown with wine my mournful head,
Pitying and forgiving all
Thy transgressions great and small.

VIII

'When wilt thou return and view
My loves, and them to life renew?
When wilt thou return and live?
When wilt thou pity as I forgive?'

IX

'Never, never, I return:
Still for victory I burn.
Living, thee alone I'll have;
And when dead I'll be thy grave.

X

'Thro' the Heaven and Earth and Hell
Thou shalt never, never quell:
I will fly and thou pursue:
Night and morn the flight renew.'

XI

'Till I turn from Female love
And root up the Infernal Grove,
I shall never worthy be
To step into Eternity.

XII

'And, to end thy cruel mocks,
Annihilate thee on the rocks,
And another form create
To be subservient to my fate.

XIII

'Let us agree to give up love,
And root up the Infernal Grove;
Then shall we return and see
The worlds of happy Eternity.

XIV

'And throughout all Eternity
I forgive you, you forgive me.
As our dear Redeemer said:
"This the Wine, and this the Bread."'

WILLIAM WORDSWORTH

1770–1850

263 *Inside of King's College Chapel, Cambridge*

TAX not the royal Saint with vain expense,
With ill-matched aims the Architect who planned—
Albeit labouring for a scanty band
Of white-robed Scholars only—this immense
And glorious Work of fine intelligence!
Give all thou canst; high Heaven rejects the lore
Of nicely-calculated less or more;
So deemed the man who fashioned for the sense
These lofty pillars, spread that branching roof
Self-poised, and scooped into ten thousand cells,
Where light and shade repose, where music dwells
Lingering—and wandering on as loth to die;
Like thoughts whose very sweetness yieldeth proof
That they were born for immortality.

264 *Devotional Incitements*

WHERE will they stop, those breathing Powers,
The Spirits of the new-born flowers?
They wander with the breeze, they wind
Where'er the streams a passage find;
Up from their native ground they rise
In mute aerial harmonies;

From humble violet—modest thyme—
Exhaled, the essential odours climb,
As if no space below the sky
Their subtle flight could satisfy:
Heaven will not tax our thoughts with pride
If like ambition be *their* guide.

Roused by this kindliest of May-showers,
The spirit-quickener of the flowers,
That with moist virtue softly cleaves
The buds, and freshens the young leaves,
The birds pour forth their souls in notes
Of rapture from a thousand throats—
Here checked by too impetuous haste,
While there the music runs to waste,
With bounty more and more enlarged,
Till the whole air is overcharged;
Give ear, O Man! to their appeal,
And thirst for no inferior zeal,
Thou, who canst *think*, as well as feel.

Mount from the earth; aspire! aspire!
So pleads the town's cathedral quire,
In strains that from their solemn height
Sink, to attain a loftier flight;
While incense from the altar breathes
Rich fragrance in embodied wreaths;
Or, flung from swinging censer, shrouds
The taper-lights, and curls in clouds
Around angelic Forms, the still
Creation of the painter's skill,
That on the service wait concealed
One moment, and the next revealed.

—Cast off your bonds, awake, arise,
And for no transient ecstasies!
What else can mean the visual plea
Of still or moving imagery—
The iterated summons loud,
Not wasted on the attendant crowd,
Nor wholly lost upon the throng
Hurrying the busy streets along?

Alas! the sanctities combined
By art to unsensualise the mind
Decay and languish; or, as creeds
And humours change, are spurned like weeds:
The priests are from their altars thrust;
Temples are levelled with the dust;
And solemn rites and awful forms
Founder amid fanatic storms.
Yet evermore, through years renewed
In undisturbed vicissitude
Of seasons balancing their flight
On the swift wings of day and night,
Kind Nature keeps a heavenly door
Wide open for the scattered Poor.
Where flower-breathed incense to the skies
Is wafted in mute harmonies;
And ground fresh-cloven by the plough
Is fragrant with a humbler vow;
Where birds and brooks from leafy dells
Chime forth unwearied canticles,
And vapours magnify and spread
The glory of the sun's bright head—
Still constant in her worship, still

Conforming to the eternal Will,
Whether men sow or reap the fields,
Divine monition Nature yields,
That not by bread alone we live,
Or what a hand of flesh can give;
That every day should leave some part
Free for a sabbath of the heart:
So shall the seventh be truly blest,
From morn to eve, with hallowed rest.

SAMUEL TAYLOR COLERIDGE

1772–1834

265 *A Christmas Carol*

THE shepherds went their hasty way,
  And found the lowly stable-shed
Where the Virgin-Mother lay:
  And now they checked their eager tread,
For to the Babe, that at her bosom clung,
A Mother's song the Virgin-Mother sung.

They told her how a glorious light,
  Streaming from a heavenly throng,
Around them shone, suspending night!
  While sweeter than a mother's song,
Blest Angels heralded the Saviour's birth,
Glory to God on high! and Peace on Earth.

She listened to the tale divine,
  And closer still the Babe she pressed;
And while she cried, the Babe is mine!
  The milk rushed faster to her breast:
Joy rose within her, like a summer's morn;
Peace, Peace on Earth! the Prince of Peace is born.

Thou Mother of the Prince of Peace,
  Poor, simple, and of low estate!
That strife should vanish, battle cease,
  O why should this thy soul elate?
Sweet Music's loudest note, the Poet's story,—
Didst thou ne'er love to hear of fame and glory?

And is not War a youthful king,
  A stately Hero clad in mail?
Beneath his footsteps laurels spring;
  Him Earth's majestic monarchs hail
Their friend, their playmate! and his bold bright eye
Compels the maiden's love-confessing sigh.

'Tell this in some more courtly scene,
  To maids and youths in robes of state!
I am a woman poor and mean,
  And therefore is my soul elate.
War is a ruffian, all with guilt defiled,
That from the agèd father tears his child!

'A murderous fiend, by fiends adored,
  He kills the sire and starves the son;
The husband kills, and from her board
  Steals all his widow's toil had won;
Plunders God's world of beauty; rends away
All safety from the night, all comfort from the day.

'Then wisely is my soul elate,
  That strife should vanish, battle cease:
I'm poor and of a low estate,
  The Mother of the Prince of Peace.
Joy rises in me, like a summer's morn:
Peace, Peace on Earth! the Prince of Peace is born.'

266 *Hymn before Sunrise in the Vale of Chamouni*

HAST thou a charm to stay the morning-star
In his steep course? So long he seems to pause
On thy bald awful head, O sovran BLANC,
The Arve and Arveiron at thy base
Rave ceaselessly; but thou, most awful Form!
Risest from forth thy silent sea of pines,
How silently! Around thee and above
Deep is the air and dark, substantial, black,
An ebon mass: methinks thou piercest it,
As with a wedge! But when I look again,
It is thine own calm home, thy crystal shrine,
Thy habitation from eternity!
O dread and silent Mount! I gazed upon thee,
Till thou, still present to the bodily sense,
Didst vanish from my thought: entranced in prayer
I worshipped the Invisible alone.

Yet, like some sweet beguiling melody,
So sweet, we know not we are listening to it,
Thou, the meanwhile, wast blending with my Thought,
Yea, with my Life and Life's own secret joy:
Till the dilating Soul, enrapt, transfused,
Into the mighty vision passing,—there
As in her natural form, swelled vast to Heaven!

Awake, my soul! not only passive praise
Thou owest! not alone these swelling tears,
Mute thanks and secret ecstasy! Awake,
Voice of sweet song! Awake, my heart, awake!
Green vales and icy cliffs, all join my Hymn.

Thou first and chief, sole sovereign of the Vale!
O struggling with the darkness all the night,
And visited all night by troops of stars,
Or when they climb the sky or when they sink:
Companion of the morning-star at dawn,
Thyself Earth's rosy star, and of the dawn
Co-herald: wake, O wake, and utter praise!
Who sank thy sunless pillars deep in Earth?
Who filled thy countenance with rosy light?
Who made thee parent of perpetual streams?

And you, ye five wild torrents fiercely glad!
Who called you forth from night and utter death,
From dark and icy caverns called you forth,
Down those precipitous, black, jaggèd rocks,
For ever shattered and the same for ever?
Who gave you your invulnerable life,
Your strength, your speed, your fury, and your joy,
Unceasing thunder and eternal foam?
And who commanded (and the silence came),
Here let the billows stiffen, and have rest?

Ye Ice-falls! ye that from the mountain's brow
Adown enormous ravines slope amain—
Torrents, methinks, that heard a mighty voice,
And stopped at once amid their maddest plunge!
Motionless torrents! silent cataracts!
Who made you glorious as the Gates of Heaven
Beneath the keen full moon? Who bade the sun
Clothe you with rainbows? Who, with living flowers
Of loveliest blue, spread garlands at your feet?—
God! let the torrents, like a shout of nations,

Answer! and let the ice-plains echo, God!
God! sing ye meadow-streams with gladsome voice!
Ye pine-groves, with your soft and soul-like sounds!
And they too have a voice, yon piles of snow,
And in their perilous fall shall thunder, God!

Ye living flowers that skirt the eternal frost!
Ye wild goats sporting round the eagle's nest!
Ye eagles, play-mates of the mountain-storm!
Ye lightnings, the dread arrows of the clouds!
Ye signs and wonders of the element!
Utter forth God, and fill the hills with praise!

Thou too, hoar Mount! with thy sky-pointing peaks,
Oft from whose feet the avalanche, unheard,
Shoots downward, glittering through the pure serene
Into the depth of clouds, that veil thy breast—
Thou too again, stupendous Mountain! thou
That as I raise my head, awhile bowed low
In adoration, upward from thy base
Slow travelling with dim eyes suffused with tears,
Solemnly seemest, like a vapoury cloud,
To rise before me—Rise, O ever rise,
Rise like a cloud of incense from the Earth!
Thou kingly Spirit throned among the hills,
Thou dread ambassador from Earth to Heaven,
Great Hierarch! tell thou the silent sky,
And tell the stars, and tell yon rising sun
Earth, with her thousand voices, praises God.

267 *Epitaph on himself*

STOP, Christian passer-by!—Stop, child of God,
And read with gentle breast. Beneath this sod
A poet lies, or that which once seem'd he.
O, lift one thought in prayer for S. T. C.;
That he who many a year with toil of breath
Found death in life, may here find life in death!
Mercy for praise—to be forgiven for fame
He ask'd, and hoped, through Christ. Do thou the same!

REGINALD HEBER

1783–1826

268 *'By cool Siloam's shady Rill'*

BY cool Siloam's shady rill
How sweet the lily grows!
How sweet the breath beneath the hill
Of Sharon's dewy rose!

Lo, such the child whose early feet
The paths of peace have trod;
Whose secret heart, with influence sweet,
Is upward drawn to God.

By cool Siloam's shady rill
The lily must decay;
The rose that blooms beneath the hill
Must shortly fade away.

And soon, too soon, the wintry hour
Of man's maturer age
Will shake the soul with sorrow's power,
And stormy passion's rage.

O Thou, Whose infant feet were found
  Within Thy Father's shrine!
Whose years, with changeless virtue crown'd,
  Were all alike Divine;

Dependent on Thy bounteous breath,
  We seek Thy grace alone,
In childhood, manhood, age, and death,
  To keep us still Thine own!

HENRY HART MILMAN

1791–1868

269 *The Holy Field*

BENEATH our feet and o'er our head
  Is equal warning given;
Beneath us lie the countless dead,
  Above us is the Heaven!

Their names are graven on the stone,
  Their bones are in the clay;
And ere another day is done,
  Ourselves may be as they.

Death rides on every passing breeze,
  He lurks in every flower;
Each season has its own disease,
  Its peril every hour.

Our eyes have seen the rosy light
  Of youth's soft cheek decay,
And Fate descend in sudden night
  On manhood's middle day.

Our eyes have seen the steps of age
Halt feebly towards the tomb;
And yet shall earth our hearts engage,
And dreams of days to come?

Turn, mortal, turn! thy danger know;
Where'er thy foot can tread
The earth rings hollow from below,
And warns thee of her dead!

Turn, Christian, turn! thy soul apply
To truths divinely given;
The bones that underneath thee lie
Shall live for Hell or Heaven!

JOHN KEBLE

1792–1866

270 *'Fill high the Bowl'*

'FILL high the bowl, and spice it well, and pour
The dews oblivious: for the Cross is sharp,
The Cross is sharp, and He
Is tenderer than a lamb.

'He wept by Lazarus' grave—how will He bear
This bed of anguish? and His pale weak form
Is worn with many a watch
Of sorrow and unrest.

'His sweat last night was as great drops of blood,
And the sad burthen press'd Him so to earth,
The very torturers paus'd
To help Him on His way.

JOHN KEBLE

'Fill high the bowl, benumb His aching sense
With medicin'd sleep.'—O awful in Thy woe!
        The parching thirst of death
        Is on Thee, and Thou triest

The slumb'rous potion bland, and wilt not drink:
Not sullen, nor in scorn, like haughty man
        With suicidal hand
        Putting his solace by:

But as at first Thine all-pervading look
Saw from Thy Father's bosom to th' abyss,
        Measuring in calm presage
        The infinite descent;

So to the end, though now of mortal pangs
Made heir, and emptied of Thy glory awhile,
        With unaverted eye
        Thou meetest all the storm.

Thou wilt feel all, that Thou mayst pity all;
And rather wouldst Thou wrestle with strong pain,
        Than overcloud Thy soul,
        So clear in agony,

Or lose one glimpse of Heaven before the time.
O most entire and perfect sacrifice,
        Renew'd in every pulse
        That on the tedious Cross

Told the long hours of death, as, one by one,
The life-strings of that tender heart gave way;
        E'en sinners, taught by Thee,
        Look Sorrow in the face,

And bid her freely welcome, unbeguil'd
By false kind solaces, and spells of earth:—
    And yet not all unsooth'd:
    For when was Joy so dear,

As the deep calm that breath'd '*Father, forgive*',
Or, '*Be with Me in Paradise to-day*'?
    And, though the strife be sore,
    Yet in His parting breath

Love masters Agony; the soul that seem'd
Forsaken, feels her present God again,
    And in her Father's arms
    Contented dies away.

271 *'Red o'er the Forest'*

RED o'er the forest peers the setting sun,
  The line of yellow light dies fast away
That crown'd the eastern copse: and chill and dun
  Falls on the moor the brief November day.

Now the tir'd hunter winds a parting note,
  And Echo bids good-night from every glade;
Yet wait awhile, and see the calm leaves float
  Each to his rest beneath their parent shade.

How like decaying life they seem to glide!
  And yet no second spring have they in store,
But where they fall, forgotten to abide
  Is all their portion, and they ask no more.

Soon o'er their heads blithe April airs shall sing,
  A thousand wild-flowers round them shall unfold,
The green buds glisten in the dews of Spring,
  And all be vernal rapture as of old.

Unconscious they in waste oblivion lie,
  In all the world of busy life around
No thought of them; in all the bounteous sky
  No drop, for them, of kindly influence found.

Man's portion is to die and rise again—
  Yet he complains, while these unmurmuring part
With their sweet lives, as pure from sin and stain,
  As his when Eden held his virgin heart.

And haply half unblam'd his murmuring voice
  Might sound in Heaven, were all his second life
Only the first renew'd—the heathen's choice,
  A round of listless joy and weary strife.

For dreary were this earth, if earth were all,
  Tho' brighten'd oft by dear Affection's kiss;—
Who for the spangles wears the funeral pall?
  But catch a gleam beyond it, and 'tis bliss.

Heavy and dull this frame of limbs and heart,
  Whether slow creeping on cold earth, or borne
On lofty steed, or loftier prow, we dart
  O'er wave or field: yet breezes laugh to scorn

Our puny speed, and birds, and clouds in heaven,
  And fish, like living shafts that pierce the main,
And stars that shoot through freezing air at even—
  Who but would follow, might he break his chain?

And thou shalt break it soon; the grovelling worm
  Shall find his wings, and soar as fast and free
As his transfigur'd Lord with lightning form
  And snowy vest—such grace He won for thee,

JOHN KEBLE

When from the grave He sprang at dawn of morn,
   And led through boundless air thy conquering road,
Leaving a glorious track, where saints, new-born,
   Might fearless follow to their blest abode.

But first, by many a stern and fiery blast
   The world's rude furnace must thy blood refine,
And many a gale of keenest woe be pass'd,
   Till every pulse beat true to airs divine,

Till every limb obey the mounting soul,
   The mounting soul, the call by Jesus given.
He who the stormy heart can so control,
   The laggard body soon will waft to Heaven.

JOHN CLARE

1793–1864

272 *The Stranger*

WHEN trouble haunts me, need I sigh?
   No, rather smile away despair;
For those have been more sad than I,
   With burthens more than I could bear;
Aye, gone rejoicing under care
Where I had sunk in black despair.

When pain disturbs my peace and rest,
   Am I a hopeless grief to keep,
When some have slept on torture's breast
   And smiled as in the sweetest sleep,
Aye, peace on thorns, in faith forgiven,
And pillowed on the hope of heaven?

JOHN CLARE

Though low and poor and broken down,
  Am I to think myself distrest?
No, rather laugh where others frown
  And think my being truly blest;
For others I can daily see
More worthy riches worse than me.

Aye, once a stranger blest the earth
  Who never caused a heart to mourn,
Whose very voice gave sorrow mirth—
  And how did earth his worth return?
It spurned him from its lowliest lot,
The meanest station owned him not;

An outcast thrown in sorrow's way,
  A fugitive that knew no sin,
Yet in lone places forced to stray—
  Men would not take the stranger in.
Yet peace, though much himself he mourned,
Was all to others he returned.

. . . .

His presence was a peace to all,
  He bade the sorrowful rejoice.
Pain turned to pleasure at his call,
  Health lived and issued from his voice.
He healed the sick and sent abroad
The dumb rejoicing in the Lord.

The blind met daylight in his eye,
  The joys of everlasting day;
The sick found health in his reply;
  The cripple threw his crutch away.
Yet he with troubles did remain
  And suffered poverty and pain.

Yet none could say of wrong he did,
   And scorn was ever standing by;
Accusers by their conscience chid,
   When proof was sought, made no reply.
Yet without sin he suffered more
Than ever sinners did before.

WILLIAM BARNES

1801–1886

273 *Vo'k a-comen into Church*

THE church do zeem a touchèn zight,
   When vo'k, a-comèn in at door,
Do softly tread the long-aïled vloor
Below the pillar'd arches' height,
   Wi' bells a-pealèn,
   Vo'k a-kneelèn,
Hearts a-healèn, wi' the love
An' peäce a-zent em vrom above.

An' there, wi' mild an' thoughtvul feäce,
      Wi' downcast eyes, an' vaïces dum',
      The wold an' young do slowly come,
An' teäke in stillness each his pleäce,
         A-zinkèn slowly,
         Kneelèn lowly,
Seekèn holy thoughts alwone,
In pray'r avore their Meäker's throne.

An' there be sons in youthvul pride,
      An' fathers weak, wi' years an' païn,
      An' daughters in their mother's traïn,
The tall wi' smaller at their zide;

Heads in murnèn
Never turnèn,
Cheäks a-burnèn, wi' the het
O' youth, an' eyes noo tears do wet.

There friends do settle, zide by zide,
The knower speechless to the known;
Their vaïce is there vor God alwone,
To flesh an' blood their tongues be tied.
Grief a-wringèn,
Jaÿ a-zingèn,
Pray'r a-bringèn welcome rest
So softly to the troubled breast.

274 *Withstanders*

WHEN weakness now do strive wi' might
In struggles ov' an e'thly trial,
Might mid overcome the right,
An' truth be turn'd by might's denial;
Withstanders we ha' mwost to feär,
If selfishness do wring us here,
Be souls a-holdèn in their hand
The might an' riches o' the land.

But when the wicked, now so strong,
Shall stan' vor judgment, peäle as ashes,
By the souls that rued their wrong,
Wi' tears a-hangèn on their lashes—
Then withstanders they shall deäre
The leäst ov' all to meet wi' there,
Mid be the helpless souls that now
Below their wrongvul might mid bow.

Sweet childern o' the dead, bereft
  Ov all their goods by guile an' forgèn;
Souls o' driven sleäves that left
  Their weäry limbs a-mark'd by scourgèn;
They that God ha' call'd to die
Vor a truth ageän the worold's lie,
An' they that groan'd an' cried in vaïn,
A-bound by foes' unrighteous chaïn.

The maïd that selfish craft led on
  To sin, an' left wi' hope a-blighted;
Starvèn workmen, thin an' wan,
  Wi' hopeless leäbour ill requited;
Souls a-wrong'd, an' call'd to vill
Wi' dread, the men that used em ill,—
When might shall yield to right as pliant
As a dwarf avore a giant.

When there, at last, the good shall glow
  In starbright bodies lik' their Seäviour,
Vor all their flesh noo mwore mid show
  The marks o' man's unkind beheäviour:
Wi' speechless tongue, an' burnèn cheäk,
The strong shall bow avore the weäk,
An' vind that helplessness, wi' right,
Is strong beyond all e'thly might.

JOHN HENRY NEWMAN

1801–1890

275 From 'The Dream of Gerontius'

(i)

ANGEL OF THE AGONY

JESU! by that shuddering dread which fell on Thee;
Jesu! by that cold dismay which sicken'd Thee;
Jesu! by that pang of heart which thrill'd in Thee;
Jesu! by that mount of sins which crippled Thee;
Jesu! by that sense of guilt which stifled Thee;
Jesu! by that innocence which girdled Thee;
Jesu! by that sanctity which reign'd in Thee;
Jesu! by that Godhead which was one with Thee;
Jesu! spare these souls which are so dear to Thee,
Who in prison, calm and patient, wait for Thee;
Hasten, Lord, their hour, and bid them come to Thee,
To that glorious Home, where they shall ever gaze on Thee.

(ii)

THE SOUL BEFORE GOD

Take me away, and in the lowest deep
There let me be,
And there in hope the lone night-watches keep,
Told out for me.
There, motionless and happy in my pain,
Lone, not forlorn,—
There will I sing my sad perpetual strain,
Until the morn.

There will I sing, and soothe my stricken breast,
Which ne'er can cease
To throb, and pine, and languish, till possest
Of its Sole Peace.
There will I sing my absent Lord and Love:—
Take me away,
That sooner I may rise, and go above,
And see Him in the truth of everlasting day.

(*iii*)

ANGEL

Softly and gently, dearly-ransom'd soul,
In my most loving arms I now enfold thee,
And, o'er the penal waters, as they roll,
I poise thee, and I lower thee, and hold thee,

And carefully I dip thee in the lake,
And thou, without a sob or a resistance,
Dost through the flood thy rapid passage take,
Sinking deep, deeper, into the dim distance.

Angels, to whom the willing task is given,
Shall tend, and nurse, and lull thee, as thou liest;
And Masses on the earth, and prayers in heaven,
Shall aid thee at the Throne of the Most Highest.

Farewell, but not for ever! brother dear,
Be brave and patient on thy bed of sorrow;
Swiftly shall pass thy night of trial here,
And I will come and wake thee on the morrow.

276 *The Trance of Time*

Felix, qui potuit rerum cognoscere causas,
Atque metus omnes, et inexorabile fatum
Subjecit pedibus, strepitumque Acherontis avari!

IN childhood, when with eager eyes
The season-measured year I view'd,
All, garb'd in fairy guise,
Pledged constancy of good.

Spring sang of heaven; the summer flowers
Bade me gaze on, and did not fade;
Even suns o'er autumn's bowers
Heard my strong wish, and stay'd.

They came and went, the short-lived four;
Yet, as their varying dance they wove,
To my young heart each bore
Its own sure claim of love.

Far different now;—the whirling year
Vainly my dizzy eyes pursue;
And its fair tints appear
All blent in one dusk hue.

Why dwell on rich autumnal lights,
Spring-time, or winter's social ring?
Long days are fire-side nights,
Brown autumn is fresh spring.

Then what this world to thee, my heart?
Its gifts nor feed thee nor can bless.
Thou hast no owner's part
In all its fleetingness.

The flame, the storm, the quaking ground,
  Earth's joy, earth's terror, naught is thine;
    Thou must but hear the sound
      Of the still voice divine.

O priceless art! O princely state!
  E'en while by sense of change opprest,
    Within to antedate
      Heaven's Age of fearless rest.

ROBERT STEPHEN HAWKER

1804–1875

277

Aishah Schechinah

A SHAPE, like folded light, embodied air,
  Yet wreathed with flesh, and warm;
All that of heaven is feminine and fair,
  Moulded in visible form.

She stood, the Lady Schēchĭnăh of earth,
  A chancel for the sky;
Where woke, to breath and beauty, God's own birth,
  For men to see Him by.

Round her, too pure to mingle with the day,
  Light, that was life, abode;
Folded within her fibres meekly lay
  The link of boundless God.

So linked, so blent, that when, with pulse fulfilled,
  Moved but that infant hand,
Far, far away, His conscious Godhead thrilled,
  And stars might understand.

Lo! where they pause, with intergathering rest,
The Threefold and the One!
And lo! He binds them to her Orient breast,
His Manhood girded on.

The Zone, where two glad worlds for ever meet,
Beneath that bosom ran:—
Deep in that womb, the conquering Paraclete
Smote Godhead on to man!

Sole scene among the stars; where, yearning, glide,
The Threefold and the One:
Her God upon her lap: the Virgin-Bride,
Her Awful Child: her Son.

278 *The Southern Cross*

THREE ancient men in Bethlehem's cave,
With awful wonder stand:
A voice had called them from their grave,
In some far Eastern land.

They lived: they trod the former earth,
When the old waters swelled,
The ark, that womb of second birth,
Their house and lineage held.

Pale Japhet bows the knee with gold,
Bright Sem sweet incense brings,
And Cham the myrrh his fingers hold;
Lo! the three Orient kings.

Types of the total earth, they hailed
The signal's starry frame;
Shuddering with second life, they quailed
At the Child Jesu's Name.

Then slow the Patriarchs turned and trod,
  And this their parting sigh:
'Our eyes have seen the living God,
  And now—once more to die.'

279 *King Arthur's Waes-hael*

THE RUBRIC

When the brown bowl is filled for yule, let the dome or upper half be set on; then let the waes-haelers kneel one by one and draw up the wine with their reeds through the two bosses at the rim. Let one breath only be drawn by each of the morice for his waes-hael.

The rounded shape of the bowl for waes-hael was intended to recall the image of a mother's breast; and thus it was meant, with a touching simplicity, to blend the thought of our Christmas gladness with the earliest nurture of the child Jesus.

WAES-HAEL for the knight and dame!
  O! merry be their dole;
Drink-hael! in Jesu's name
  We fill the tawny bowl;
But cover down the curving crest,
Mould of the Orient Lady's breast.

Waes-hael! yet lift no lid:
  Drain ye the reeds for wine!
Drink-hael! the milk was hid
  That soothed that Babe divine,
Hushed, as this hollow channel flows,
He drew the balsam from the rose.

Waes-hael! thus glowed the breast
  Where a God yearned to cling;
Drink-hael! so Jesu pressed
  Life from its mystic spring;
Then hush, and bend in reverent sigh,
And breathe the thrilling reeds for wine.

Waes-hael! in shadowy scene,
  Lo! Christmas children we;
Drink-hael! behold we lean
  At a far Mother's knee:
To dream, that thus her bosom smiled,
And learn the lip of Bethlehem's child.

ELIZABETH BARRETT BROWNING

1806–1861

280 *Patience taught by Nature*

'O DREARY life,' we cry, 'O dreary life!'
And still the generations of the birds
Sing through our sighing, and the flocks and herds
Serenely live while we are keeping strife
With Heaven's true purpose in us, as a knife
Against which we may struggle! ocean girds
Unslackened the dry land, savannah-swards
Unweary sweep,—hills watch, unworn; and rife
Meek leaves drop yearly from the forest-trees,
To show above the unwasted stars that pass
In their old glory. O thou God of old,
Grant me some smaller grace than comes to these!—
But so much patience as a blade of grass
Grows by, contented through the heat and cold.

RICHARD CHENEVIX TRENCH

1807–1886

281

God our Refuge

IF there had anywhere appeared in space
 Another place of refuge where to flee,
Our hearts had taken refuge in that place,
  And not with Thee.

For we against creation's bars had beat
 Like prisoned eagles, through great worlds had sought
Though but a foot of ground to plant our feet,
  Where Thou wert not.

And only when we found in earth and air,
 In heaven or hell, that such might nowhere be—
That we could not flee from Thee anywhere,
  We fled to Thee.

HORATIUS BONAR

1808–1889

282

'Thy Way, not mine'

THY way, not mine, O Lord,
 However dark it be!
Lead me by Thine own hand,
 Choose out the path for me.

Smooth let it be or rough,
 It will be still the best;
Winding or straight, it leads
 Right onward to Thy rest.

I dare not choose my lot;
 I would not, if I might;
Choose Thou for me, my GOD;
 So shall I walk aright.

The kingdom that I seek
   Is Thine; so let the way
That leads to it be Thine;
   Else I must surely stray.

Take Thou my cup, and it
   With joy or sorrow fill,
As best to Thee may seem;
   Choose Thou my good and ill;

Choose Thou for me my friends,
   My sickness or my health;
Choose Thou my cares for me,
   My poverty or wealth.

Not mine, not mine the choice,
   In things or great or small;
Be Thou my guide, my strength,
   My wisdom, and my all!

ALFRED TENNYSON, LORD TENNYSON

1809–1892

283 *St. Agnes' Eve*

DEEP on the convent-roof the snows
   Are sparkling to the moon:
My breath to heaven like vapour goes:
   May my soul follow soon!
The shadows of the convent-towers
   Slant down the snowy sward,
Still creeping with the creeping hours
   That lead me to my Lord:

Make Thou my spirit pure and clear
  As are the frosty skies,
Or this first snowdrop of the year
  That in my bosom lies.

As these white robes are soil'd and dark,
  To yonder shining ground;
As this pale taper's earthly spark,
  To yonder argent round;
So shows my soul before the Lamb,
  My spirit before Thee;
So in mine earthly house I am,
  To that I hope to be.
Break up the heavens, O Lord! and far,
  Thro' all yon starlight keen,
Draw me, thy bride, a glittering star,
  In raiment white and clean.

He lifts me to the golden doors;
  The flashes come and go;
All heaven bursts her starry floors,
  And strows her lights below,
And deepens on and up! the gates
  Roll back, and far within
For me the Heavenly Bridegroom waits,
  To make me pure of sin.
The sabbaths of Eternity,
  One sabbath deep and wide—
A light upon the shining sea—
  The Bridegroom with his bride!

284 *'Strong Son of God'*

STRONG Son of God, immortal Love,
    Whom we, that have not seen thy face,
    By faith, and faith alone, embrace,
Believing where we cannot prove;

Thine are these orbs of light and shade;
    Thou madest Life in man and brute;
    Thou madest Death; and lo, thy foot
Is on the skull which thou hast made.

Thou wilt not leave us in the dust:
    Thou madest man, he knows not why;
    He thinks he was not made to die;
And thou hast made him: thou art just.

Thou seemest human and divine,
    The highest, holiest manhood, thou:
    Our wills are ours, we know not how;
Our wills are ours, to make them thine.

Our little systems have their day;
    They have their day and cease to be:
    They are but broken lights of thee,
And thou, O Lord, art more than they.

We have but faith: we cannot know;
    For knowledge is of things we see;
    And yet we trust it comes from thee,
A beam in darkness: let it grow.

Let knowledge grow from more to more,
    But more of reverence in us dwell;
    That mind and soul, according well,
May make one music as before,

But vaster. We are fools and slight;
    We mock thee when we do not fear:
    But help thy foolish ones to bear;
Help thy vain worlds to bear thy light.

Forgive what seem'd my sin in me;
    What seem'd my worth since I began;
    For merit lives from man to man,
And not from man, O Lord, to thee.

Forgive my grief for one removed,
    Thy creature, whom I found so fair.
    I trust he lives in thee, and there
I find him worthier to be loved.

Forgive these wild and wandering cries,
    Confusions of a wasted youth;
    Forgive them where they fail in truth,
And in thy wisdom make me wise.

In Memoriam A. H. H.

ROBERT BROWNING

1812–1889

285 *Saul*

SAID Abner, 'At last thou art come! Ere I tell, ere thou speak,
Kiss my cheek, wish me well!' Then I wished it, and did kiss his cheek.
And he, 'Since the King, O my friend, for thy countenance sent,
Neither drunken nor eaten have we; nor until from this tent
Thou return with the joyful assurance the King liveth yet,
Shall our lip with the honey be bright, with the water be wet.

For out of the black mid-tent's silence, a space of three days,
Not a sound hath escaped to thy servants, of prayer or of
praise,
To betoken that Saul and the Spirit have ended their strife,
And that, faint in his triumph, the monarch sinks back upon
life.

II

Yet now my heart leaps, O beloved! God's child, with His
dew
On thy gracious gold hair, and those lilies still living and blue
Just broken to twine round thy harpstrings, as if no wild
heat
Were now raging to torture the desert!'

III

Then I, as was meet,
Knelt down to the God of my fathers, and rose on my feet,
And ran o'er the sand burnt to powder. The tent was
unlooped;
I pulled up the spear that obstructed, and under I stooped;
Hands and knees on the slippery grasspatch, all withered and
gone,
That extends to the second enclosure, I groped my way on
Till I felt where the foldskirts fly open. Then once more I
prayed,
And opened the foldskirts and entered, and was not afraid,
But spoke, 'Here is David, thy servant!' And no voice
replied.
At the first I saw nought but the blackness; but soon I
descried

A something more black than the blackness—the vast the upright
Main prop which sustains the pavilion: and slow into sight
Grew a figure against it, gigantic and blackest of all:
Then a sunbeam, that burst thro' the tent-roof, showed Saul.

IV

He stood as erect as that tent-prop; both arms stretched out wide
On the great cross-support in the centre, that goes to each side;
He relaxed not a muscle, but hung there, as, caught in his pangs
And waiting his change, the king-serpent all heavily hangs,
Far away from his kind, in the pine, till deliverance come
With the spring-time,—so agonized Saul, drear and stark, blind and dumb.

V

Then I tuned my harp,—took off the lilies we twine round its chords
Lest they snap 'neath the stress of the noontide—those sunbeams like swords!
And I first played the tune all our sheep know, as, one after one,
So docile they come to the pen-door, till folding be done.
They are white and untorn by the bushes, for lo, they have fed
Where the long grasses stifle the water within the stream's bed;
And now one after one seeks its lodging, as star follows star
Into eve and the blue far above us,—so blue and so far!

VI

—Then the tune, for which quails on the cornland will each leave his mate
To fly after the player; then, what makes the crickets elate,
Till for boldness they fight one another: and then, what has weight
To set the quick jerboa a-musing outside his sand house—
There are none such as he for a wonder, half bird and half mouse!
God made all the creatures and gave them our love and our fear,
To give sign, we and they are His children, one family here.

VII

Then I played the help-tune of our reapers, their wine-song, when hand
Grasps at hand, eye lights eye in good friendship, and great hearts expand
And grow one in the sense of this world's life.—And then, the last song
When the dead man is praised on his journey—'Bear, bear him along
With his few faults shut up like dead flowerets! are balm-seeds not here
To console us? The land has none left such as he on the bier.
Oh, would we might keep thee, my brother!'—And then, the glad chaunt
Of the marriage,—first go the young maidens, next, she whom we vaunt
As the beauty, the pride of our dwelling.—And then, the great march
Wherein man runs to man to assist him and buttress an arch

Nought can break; who shall harm them, our friends?—
Then, the chorus intoned
As the Levites go up to the altar in glory enthroned.
But I stopped here—for here in the darkness, Saul groaned.

VIII

And I paused, held my breath in such silence, and listened apart;
And the tent shook, for mighty Saul shuddered—and sparkles 'gan dart
From the jewels that woke in his turban at once with a start—
All its lordly male-sapphires, and rubies courageous at heart.
So the head—but the body still moved not, still hung there erect.
And I bent once again to my playing, pursued it unchecked,
As I sang,—

IX

'Oh, our manhood's prime vigour! no spirit feels waste,
Not a muscle is stopped in its playing, nor sinew unbraced.
Oh, the wild joys of living! the leaping from rock up to rock—
The strong rending of boughs from the fir-tree,—the cool silver shock
Of the plunge in a pool's living water,—the hunt of the bear,
And the sultriness showing the lion is couched in his lair.
And the meal—the rich dates yellowed over with gold dust divine,
And the locust's-flesh steeped in the pitcher! the full draught of wine,
And the sleep in the dried river-channel where bulrushes tell
That the water was wont to go warbling so softly and well.

How good is man's life, the mere living! how fit to employ
All the heart and the soul and the senses, for ever in joy!
Hast thou loved the white locks of thy father, whose sword
  thou didst guard
When he trusted thee forth with the armies, for glorious
  reward?
Didst thou see the thin hands of thy mother, held up as
  men sung
The low song of the nearly-departed, and heard her faint
  tongue
Joining in while it could to the witness, "Let one more attest,
I have lived, seen God's hand thro' a lifetime, and all was
  for best!"
Then they sung thro' their tears in strong triumph, not much
  —but the rest.
And thy brothers, the help and the contest, the working
  whence grew
Such result as, from seething grape-bundles, the spirit strained
  true!
And the friends of thy boyhood—that boyhood of wonder
  and hope,
Present promise, and wealth of the future beyond the eye's
  scope,—
Till lo, thou art grown to a monarch; a people is thine;
And all gifts, which the world offers singly, on one head
  combine!
On one head, all the beauty and strength, love and rage (like
  the throe
That, a-work in the rock, helps its labour and lets the gold go),
High ambition and deeds which surpass it, fame crowning
  it,—all
Brought to blaze on the head of one creature—King Saul!'

x

And lo, with that leap of my spirit,—heart, hand, harp and voice,
Each lifting Saul's name out of sorrow, each bidding rejoice
Saul's fame in the light it was made for—as when, dare I say,
The Lord's army, in rapture of service, strains through its array,
And upsoareth the cherubim-chariot—'Saul!' cried I, and stopped,
And waited the thing that should follow. Then Saul, who hung propped
By the tent's cross-support in the centre, was struck by his name.
Have ye seen when Spring's arrowy summons goes right to the aim,
And some mountain, the last to withstand her, that held (he alone,
While the vale laughed in freedom and flowers) on a broad bust of stone
A year's snow bound about for a breast-plate,—leaves grasp of the sheet?
Fold on fold all at once it crowds thunderously down to his feet,
And there fronts you, stark, black, but alive yet, your mountain of old,
With his rents, the successive bequeathing of ages untold—
Yea, each harm got in fighting your battles, each furrow and scar
Of his head thrust 'twixt you and the tempest—all hail, there they are!
Now again to be softened with verdure, again hold the nest
Of the dove, tempt the goat and its young to the green on its crest

For their food in the ardours of summer! One long shudder thrilled
All the tent till the very air tingled, then sank and was stilled
At the King's self left standing before me, released and aware.
What was gone, what remained? all to traverse 'twixt hope and despair;
Death was past, life not come: so he waited. Awhile his right hand
Held the brow, helped the eyes left too vacant forthwith to remand
To their place what new objects should enter: 'twas Saul as before.
I looked up and dared gaze at those eyes, nor was hurt any more
Than by slow pallid sunsets in autumn, ye watch from the shore,
At their sad level gaze o'er the ocean—a sun's slow decline
Over hills which, resolved in stern silence, o'erlap and entwine
Base with base to knit strength more intense: so, arm folded in arm
O'er the chest whose slow heavings subsided.

XI

What spell or what charm,
(For, awhile there was trouble within me) what next should I urge
To sustain him where song had restored him?—Song filled to the verge
His cup with the wine of this life, pressing all that it yields
Of mere fruitage, the strength and the beauty! Beyond, on what fields,

Glean a vintage more potent and perfect to brighten the eye
And bring blood to the lip, and commend them the cup they
    put by?
He saith, 'It is good'; still he drinks not: he lets me praise life,
Gives assent, yet would die for his own part.

XII

Then fancies grew rife
Which had come long ago on the pastures, when round me
    the sheep
Fed in silence—above, the one eagle wheeled slow as in sleep;
And I lay in my hollow, and mused on the world that might
    lie
'Neath his ken, though I saw but the strip 'twixt the hill and
    the sky:
And I laughed—'Since my days are ordained to be passed
    with my flocks,
Let me people at least, with my fancies, the plains and the
    rocks,
Dream the life I am never to mix with, and image the show
Of mankind as they live in those fashions I hardly shall know!
Schemes of life, its best rules and right uses, the courage that
    gains,
And the prudence that keeps what men strive for.' And
    now these old trains
Of vague thought came again; I grew surer; so, once more
    the string
Of my harp made response to my spirit, as thus—

XIII

'Yea, my King,'
I began—'thou dost well in rejecting mere comforts that
    spring

From the mere mortal life held in common by man and by brute:
In our flesh grows the branch of this life, in our soul it bears fruit.
Thou hast marked the slow rise of the tree,—how its stem trembled first
Till it passed the kid's lip, the stag's antler; then safely outburst
The fan-branches all round; and thou mindest when these too, in turn
Broke a-bloom and the palm-tree seemed perfect: yet more was to learn,
Ev'n the good that comes in with the palm-fruit. Our dates shall we slight,
When their juice brings a cure for all sorrow? or care for the plight
Of the palm's self whose slow growth produced them? Not so! stem and branch
Shall decay, nor be known in their place, while the palm-wine shall staunch
Every wound of man's spirit in winter. I pour thee such wine.
Leave the flesh to the fate it was fit for! the spirit be thine!
By the spirit, when age shall o'ercome thee, thou still shalt enjoy
More indeed, than at first when inconscious, the life of a boy.
Crush that life, and behold its wine running! each deed thou hast done
Dies, revives, goes to work in the world; until e'en as the sun
Looking down on the earth, though clouds spoil him, though tempests efface,
Can find nothing his own deed produced not, must everywhere trace

The results of his past summer-prime,—so, each ray of thy will,
Every flash of thy passion and prowess, long over, shall thrill
Thy whole people the countless, with ardour, till they too give forth
A like cheer to their sons, who in turn, fill the South and the North
With the radiance thy deed was the germ of. Carouse in the Past!
But the license of age has its limit; thou diest at last:
As the lion when age dims his eyeball, the rose at her height,
So with man—so his power and his beauty for ever take flight.
No! again a long draught of my soul-wine! look forth o'er the years—
Thou hast done now with eyes for the actual; begin with the seer's!
Is Saul dead? in the depth of the vale make his tomb—bid arise
A grey mountain of marble heaped four-square, till, built to the skies,
Let it mark where the great First King slumbers: whose fame would ye know?
Up above see the rock's naked face, where the record shall go
In great characters cut by the scribe,—Such was Saul, so he did;
With the sages directing the work, by the populace chid,—
For not half, they'll affirm, is comprised there! Which fault to amend,
In the grove with his kind grows the cedar, whereon they shall spend
(See, in tablets 'tis level before them) their praise, and record
With the gold of the graver, Saul's story,—the statesman's great word

Side by side with the poet's sweet comment. The river 's
a-wave
With smooth paper-reeds grazing each other when prophet-
winds rave:
So the pen gives unborn generations their due and their part
In thy being! Then, first of the mighty, thank God that
thou art!'

XIV

And behold while I sang . . . But O Thou who didst grant
me that day,
And before it not seldom hast granted Thy help to essay
Carry on and complete an adventure,—my Shield and my
Sword
In that act where my soul was Thy servant, Thy word was
my word,—
Still be with me, who then at the summit of human en-
deavour
And scaling the highest, man's thought could, gazed hopeless
as ever
On the new stretch of Heaven above me—till, mighty to save,
Just one lift of Thy hand cleared that distance—God's
throne from man's grave!
Let me tell out my tale to its ending—my voice to my heart
Which can scarce dare believe in what marvels last night I
took part,
As this morning I gather the fragments, alone with my sheep,
And still fear lest the terrible glory evanish like sleep!
For I wake in the grey dewy covert, while Hebron upheaves
The dawn struggling with night on his shoulder, and Kidron
retrieves
Slow the damage of yesterday's sunshine.

XV

I say then,—my song
While I sang thus, assuring the monarch, and ever more strong
Made a proffer of good to console him—he slowly resumed
His old motions and habitudes kingly. The right hand replumed
His black locks to their wonted composure, adjusted the swathes
Of his turban, and see—the huge sweat that his countenance bathes,
He wipes off with the robe; and he girds now his loins as of yore,
And feels slow for the armlets of price, with the clasp set before.
He is Saul, ye remember in glory,—ere error had bent
The broad brow from the daily communion; and still, though much spent
Be the life and the bearing that front you, the same, God did choose,
To receive what a man may waste, desecrate, never quite lose.
So sank he along by the tent-prop till, stayed by the pile
Of his armour and war-cloak and garments, he leaned there awhile,
And so sat out my singing,—one arm round the tent-prop, to raise
His bent head, and the other hung slack—till I touched on the praise
I foresaw from all men in all times, to the man patient there;
And thus ended, the harp falling forward. Then first I was 'ware

That he sat, as I say, with my head just above his vast knees
Which were thrust out on each side around me, like oak roots which please
To encircle a lamb when it slumbers. I looked up to know
If the best I could do had brought solace: he spoke not, but slow
Lifted up the hand slack at his side, till he laid it with care
Soft and grave, but in mild settled will, on my brow: thro' my hair
The large fingers were pushed, and he bent back my head, with kind power—
All my face back, intent to peruse it, as men do a flower.
Thus held he me there with his great eyes that scrutinized mine—
And oh, all my heart how it loved him! but where was the sign?
I yearned—'Could I help thee, my father, inventing a bliss,
I would add to that life of the Past, both the Future and this;
I would give thee new life altogether, as good, ages hence,
As this moment,—had love but the warrant, love's heart to dispense!'

XVI

Then the truth came upon me. No harp more—no song more! outbroke—

XVII

'I have gone the whole round of Creation: I saw and I spoke!
I, a work of God's hand for that purpose, received in my brain
And pronounced on the rest of His handwork—returned Him again

His creation's approval or censure: I spoke as I saw.
I report, as a man may of God's work—all 's love, yet all 's law!
Now I lay down the judgeship He lent me. Each faculty tasked
To perceive Him, has gained an abyss, where a dewdrop was asked.
Have I knowledge? confounded it shrivels at Wisdom laid bare.
Have I forethought? how purblind, how blank, to the Infinite Care!
Do I task any faculty highest, to image success?
I but open my eyes,—and perfection, no more and no less,
In the kind I imagined, full-fronts me, and God is seen God
In the star, in the stone, in the flesh, in the soul and the clod.
And thus looking within and around me, I ever renew
(With that stoop of the soul which in bending upraises it too)
The submission of Man's nothing-perfect to God's All-Complete,
As by each new obeisance in spirit, I climb to His feet!
Yet with all this abounding experience, this Deity known,
I shall dare to discover some province, some gift of my own.
There's a faculty pleasant to exercise, hard to hoodwink,
I am fain to keep still in abeyance, (I laugh as I think)
Lest, insisting to claim and parade in it, wot ye, I worst
E'en the Giver in one gift.—Behold! I could love if I durst!
But I sink the pretension as fearing a man may o'ertake
God's own speed in the one way of love: I abstain for love's sake.
—What, my soul? see thus far and no farther? when doors great and small,

Nine-and-ninety flew ope at our touch, should the hundredth appal?
In the least things, have faith, yet distrust in the greatest of all?
Do I find love so full in my nature, God's ultimate gift,
That I doubt His own love can compete with it? here, the parts shift?
Here, the creature surpass the Creator, the end, what Began?—
Would I fain in my impotent yearning do all for this man,
And dare doubt He alone shall not help him, who yet alone can?
Would it ever have entered my mind, the bare will, much less power,
To bestow on this Saul what I sang of, the marvellous dower
Of the life he was gifted and filled with? to make such a soul,
Such a body, and then such an earth for insphering the whole?
And doth it not enter my mind (as my warm tears attest)
These good things being given, to go on, and give one more, the best?
Ay, to save and redeem and restore him, maintain at the height
This perfection,—succeed with life's dayspring, death's minute of night?
Interpose at the difficult minute, snatch Saul, the mistake,
Saul, the failure, the ruin he seems now,—and bid him awake
From the dream, the probation, the prelude, to find himself set
Clear and safe in new light and new life,—a new harmony yet
To be run, and continued, and ended—who knows?—or endure!
The man taught enough by life's dream, of the rest to make sure;

By the pain-throb, triumphantly winning intensified bliss,
And the next world's reward and repose, by the struggles
in this.

XVIII

'I believe it! 'tis Thou, God, that givest, 'tis I who receive:
In the first is the last, in Thy will is my power to believe.
All 's one gift: Thou canst grant it moreover, as prompt to my
prayer
As I breathe out this breath, as I open these arms to the air.
From Thy will, stream the worlds, life and nature, thy dread
Sabaoth:
I will?—the mere atoms despise me! why am I not loth
To look that, even that in the face too? why is it I dare
Think but lightly of such impuissance? what stops my
despair?
This;—'tis not what man Does which exalts him, but what
man Would do!
See the King—I would help him but cannot, the wishes fall
through.
Could I wrestle to raise him from sorrow, grow poor to
enrich,
To fill up his life, starve my own out, I would—knowing
which,
I know that my service is perfect. Oh, speak through me now!
Would I suffer for him that I love? So wouldst Thou—so
wilt Thou!
So shall crown Thee the topmost, ineffablest, uttermost
crown—
And Thy love fill infinitude wholly, nor leave up nor down
One spot for the creature to stand in! It is by no breath,
Turn of eye, wave of hand, that salvation joins issue with
death!

As Thy Love is discovered almighty, almighty be proved
Thy power, that exists with and for it, of being Beloved!
He who did most, shall bear most; the strongest shall stand the most weak.
'Tis the weakness in strength, that I cry for! my flesh, that I seek
In the Godhead! I seek and I find it. O Saul, it shall be
A Face like my face that receives thee; a Man like to me,
Thou shalt love and be loved by, for ever: a Hand like this hand
Shall throw open the gates of new life to thee! See the Christ stand!'

XIX

I know not too well how I found my way home in the night.
There were witnesses, cohorts about me, to left and to right,
Angels, powers, the unuttered, unseen, the alive, the aware—
I repressed, I got through them as hardly, as strugglingly there,
As a runner beset by the populace famished for news—
Life or death. The whole earth was awakened, hell loosed with her crews;
And the stars of night beat with emotion, and tingled and shot
Out in fire the strong pain of pent knowledge: but I fainted not,
For the Hand still impelled me at once and supported, suppressed
All the tumult, and quenched it with quiet, and holy behest,
Till the rapture was shut in itself, and the earth sank to rest.
Anon at the dawn, all that trouble had withered from earth—
Not so much, but I saw it die out in the day's tender birth;

In the gathered intensity brought to the grey of the hills;
In the shuddering forests' new awe; in the sudden wind-thrills;
In the startled wild beasts that bore off, each with eye sidling still
Though averted with wonder and dread; in the birds stiff and chill
That rose heavily, as I approached them, made stupid with awe!
E'en the serpent that slid away silent,—he felt the new Law.
The same stared in the white humid faces upturned by the flowers;
The same worked in the heart of the cedar, and moved the vine-bowers:
And the little brooks witnessing murmured, persistent and low,
With their obstinate, all but hushed voices—'E'en so, it is so!'

286 *A Death in the Desert*

[SUPPOSED of Pamphylax the Antiochene:
It is a parchment, of my rolls the fifth,
Hath three skins glued together, is all Greek,
And goeth from *Epsilon* down to *Mu*:
Lies second in the surnamed Chosen Chest,
Stained and conserved with juice of terebinth,
Covered with cloth of hair, and lettered *Xi*,
From Xanthus, my wife's uncle, now at peace:
Mu and *Epsilon* stand for my own name,
I may not write it, but I make a cross
To show I wait His coming, with the rest,
And leave off here: beginneth Pamphylax.]

I said, 'If one should wet his lips with wine,
And slip the broadest plantain leaf we find,
Or else the lappet of a linen robe,
Into the water-vessel, lay it right,
And cool his forehead just above the eyes,
The while a brother, kneeling either side,
Should chafe each hand and try to make it warm,—
He is not so far gone but he might speak.'

This did not happen in the outer cave,
Nor in the secret chamber of the rock,
Where, sixty days since the decree was out,
We had him, bedded on a camel-skin,
And waited for his dying all the while;
But in the midmost grotto: since noon's light
Reached there a little, and we would not lose
That last of what might happen on his face.

I at the head, and Xanthus at the feet,
With Valens and the Boy, had lifted him,
And brought him from the chamber in the depths,
And laid him in the light where we might see:
For certain smiles began about his mouth,
And his lids moved, presageful of the end.

Beyond, and half way up the mouth o' the cave,
The Bactrian convert, having his desire,
Kept watch, and made pretence to graze a goat
That gave us milk, on rags of various herb,
Plantain and quitch, the rocks' shade keeps alive:
So that if any thief or soldier passed,
(Because the persecution was aware)
Yielding the goat up promptly with his life,

Such man might pass on, joyful at a prize,
Nor care to pry into the cool o' the cave.
Outside was all noon and the burning blue.

'Here is wine,' answered Xanthus,—dropped a drop;
I stooped and placed the lap of cloth aright,
Then chafed his right hand, and the Boy his left:
But Valens had bethought him, and produced
And broke a ball of nard, and made perfume.
Only, he did—not so much wake, as—turn
And smile a little, as a sleeper does
If any dear one call him, touch his face—
And smiles and loves, but will not be disturbed.

Then Xanthus said a prayer, but still he slept:
It is the Xanthus that escaped to Rome,
Was burned, and could not write the chronicle.

Then the Boy sprang up from his knees, and ran,
Stung by the splendour of a sudden thought,
And fetched the seventh plate of graven lead
Out of the secret chamber, found a place,
Pressing with finger on the deeper dints,
And spoke, as 'twere his mouth proclaiming first,
'I am the Resurrection and the Life.'

Whereat he opened his eyes wide at once,
And sat up of himself, and looked at us;
And thenceforth nobody pronounced a word:
Only, outside, the Bactrian cried his cry
Like the lone desert-bird that wears the ruff,
As signal we were safe, from time to time.

First he said, 'If a friend declared to me,
This my son Valens, this my other son,
Were James and Peter,—nay, declared as well
This lad was very John,—I could believe:
—Could, for a moment, doubtlessly believe:
So is myself withdrawn into my depths,
The soul retreated from the perished brain
Whence it was wont to feel and use the world
Through these dull members, done with long ago.
Yet I myself remain; I feel myself:
And there is nothing lost. Let be, awhile!'

[This is the doctrine he was wont to teach,
How divers persons witness in each man,
Three souls which make up one soul: first, to wit,
A soul of each and all the bodily parts,
Seated therein, which works, and is what Does,
And has the use of earth, and ends the man
Downward: but, tending upward for advice,
Grows into, and again is grown into
By the next soul, which, seated in the brain,
Useth the first with its collected use,
And feeleth, thinketh, willeth,—is what Knows:
Which, duly tending upward in its turn,
Grows into, and again is grown into
By the last soul, that uses both the first,
Subsisting whether they assist or no,
And, constituting man's self, is what Is—
And leans upon the former, makes it play,
As that played off the first: and, tending up,
Holds, is upheld by, God, and ends the man
Upward in that dread point of intercourse,
Nor needs a place, for it returns to Him.

What Does, what Knows, what Is; three souls, one man.
I give the glossa of Theotypas.]

And then, 'A stick, once fire from end to end;
Now, ashes save the tip that holds a spark!
Yet, blow the spark, it runs back, spreads itself
A little where the fire was: thus I urge
The soul that served me, till it task once more
What ashes of my brain have kept their shape,
And these make effort on the last o' the flesh,
Trying to taste again the truth of things—'
(He smiled)—'their very superficial truth;
As that ye are my sons, that it is long
Since James and Peter had release by death,
And I am only he, your brother John,
Who saw and heard, and could remember all.
Remember all! It is not much to say.
What if the truth broke on me from above
As once and oft-times? Such might hap again:
Doubtlessly He might stand in presence here,
With head wool-white, eyes flame, and feet like brass,
The sword and the seven stars, as I have seen—
I who now shudder only and surmise
"How did your brother bear that sight and live?"

'If I live yet, it is for good, more love
Through me to men: be nought but ashes here
That keep awhile my semblance, who was John,—
Still, when they scatter, there is left on earth
No one alive who knew (consider this!)
—Saw with his eyes and handled with his hands
That which was from the first, the Word of Life.
How will it be when none more saith "I saw"?

'Such ever was love's way: to rise, it stoops.
Since I, whom Christ's mouth taught, was bidden teach,
I went, for many years, about the world,
Saying "It was so; so I heard and saw,"
Speaking as the case asked: and men believed.
Afterward came the message to myself
In Patmos isle; I was not bidden teach,
But simply listen, take a book and write,
Nor set down other than the given word,
With nothing left to my arbitrament
To choose or change: I wrote, and men believed.
Then, for my time grew brief, no message more,
No call to write again, I found a way,
And, reasoning from my knowledge, merely taught
Men should, for love's sake, in love's strength, believe;
Or I would pen a letter to a friend
And urge the same as friend, nor less nor more:
Friends said I reasoned rightly, and believed.
But at the last, why, I seemed left alive
Like a sea-jelly weak on Patmos strand,
To tell dry sea-beach gazers how I fared
When there was mid-sea, and the mighty things;
Left to repeat, "I saw, I heard, I knew,"
And go all over the old ground again,
With Antichrist already in the world,
And many Antichrists, who answered prompt
"Am I not Jasper as thyself art John?
Nay, young, whereas through age thou mayest forget:
Wherefore, explain, or how shall we believe?"
I never thought to call down fire on such,
Or, as in wonderful and early days,
Pick up the scorpion, tread the serpent dumb;

But patient stated much of the Lord's life
Forgotten or misdelivered, and let it work:
Since much that at the first, in deed and word,
Lay simply and sufficiently exposed,
Had grown (or else my soul was grown to match,
Fed through such years, familiar with such light,
Guarded and guided still to see and speak)
Of new significance and fresh result;
What first were guessed as points, I now knew stars,
And named them in the Gospel I have writ.
For men said, "It is getting long ago":
"Where is the promise of His coming?"—asked
These young ones in their strength, as loth to wait,
Of me who, when their sires were born, was old.
I, for I loved them, answered, joyfully,
Since I was there, and helpful in my age;
And, in the main, I think such men believed.
Finally, thus endeavouring, I fell sick,
Ye brought me here, and I supposed the end,
And went to sleep with one thought that, at least,
Though the whole earth should lie in wickedness,
We had the truth, might leave the rest to God.
Yet now I wake in such decrepitude
As I had slidden down and fallen afar,
Past even the presence of my former self,
Grasping the while for stay at facts which snap,
Till I am found away from my own world,
Feeling for foot-hold through a blank profound,
Along with unborn people in strange lands,
Who say—I hear said or conceive they say—
"Was John at all, and did he say he saw?
Assure us, ere we ask what he might see!"

'And how shall I assure them? Can they share
—They, who have flesh, a veil of youth and strength
About each spirit, that needs must bide its time,
Living and learning still as years assist
Which wear the thickness thin, and let man see—
With me who hardly am withheld at all,
But shudderingly, scarce a shred between,
Lie bare to the universal prick of light?
Is it for nothing we grow old and weak,
We whom God loves? When pain ends, gain ends too.
To me, that story—ay, that Life and Death
Of which I wrote "it was"—to me, it is;
—Is, here and now: I apprehend nought else.
Is not God now i' the world His power first made?
Is not His love at issue still with sin,
Closed with and cast and conquered, crucified
Visibly when a wrong is done on earth?
Love, wrong, and pain, what see I else around?
Yea, and the Resurrection and Uprise
To the right hand of the throne—what is it beside,
When such truth, breaking bounds, o'erfloods my soul,
And, as I saw the sin and death, even so
See I the need yet transiency of both,
The good and glory consummated thence?
I saw the Power; I see the Love, once weak,
Resume the Power: and in this word "I see",
Lo, there is recognized the Spirit of both
That, moving o'er the spirit of man, unblinds
His eye and bids him look. These are, I see;
But ye, the children, His beloved ones too,
Ye need,—as I should use an optic glass
I wondered at erewhile, somewhere i' the world,

It had been given a crafty smith to make;
A tube, he turned on objects brought too close,
Lying confusedly insubordinate
For the unassisted eye to master once:
Look through his tube, at distance now they lay,
Become succinct, distinct, so small, so clear!
Just thus, ye needs must apprehend what truth
I see, reduced to plain historic fact,
Diminished into clearness, proved a point
And far away: ye would withdraw your sense
From out eternity, strain it upon time,
Then stand before that fact, that Life and Death,
Stay there at gaze, till it dispart, dispread,
As though a star should open out, all sides,
And grow the world on you, as it is my world.

'For life, with all it yields of joy and woe,
And hope and fear,—believe the aged friend,—
Is just our chance o' the prize of learning love,
How love might be, hath been indeed, and is;
And that we hold thenceforth to the uttermost
Such prize despite the envy of the world,
And, having gained truth, keep truth: that is all.
But see the double way wherein we are led,
How the soul learns diversely from the flesh!
With flesh, that hath so little time to stay,
And yields mere basement for the soul's emprise,
Expect prompt teaching. Helpful was the light,
And warmth was cherishing and food was choice
To every man's flesh, thousand years ago,
As now to yours and mine; the body sprang
At once to the height, and stayed: but the soul,—no!

Since sages who, this noontide, meditate
In Rome or Athens, may descry some point
Of the eternal power, hid yestereve;
And as thereby the power's whole mass extends,
So much extends the æther floating o'er,
The love that tops the might, the Christ in God.
Then, as new lessons shall be learned in these
Till earth's work stop and useless time run out,
So duly, daily, needs provision be
For keeping the soul's prowess possible,
Building new barriers as the old decay,
Saving us from evasion of life's proof,
Putting the question ever, "Does God love,
And will ye hold that truth against the world?"
Ye know there needs no second proof with good
Gained for our flesh from any earthly source:
We might go freezing, ages,—give us fire,
Thereafter we judge fire at its full worth,
And guard it safe through every chance, ye know!
That fable of Prometheus and his theft,
How mortals gained Jove's fiery flower, grows old
(I have been used to hear the pagans own)
And out of mind; but fire, howe'er its birth,
Here is it, precious to the sophist now
Who laughs the myth of Æschylus to scorn,
As precious to those satyrs of his play,
Who touched it in gay wonder at the thing.
While were it so with the soul,—this gift of truth
Once grasped, were this our soul's gain safe, and sure
To prosper as the body's gain is wont,—
Why, man's probation would conclude, his earth
Crumble; for he both reasons and decides,

Weighs first, then chooses: will he give up fire
For gold or purple once he knows its worth?
Could he give Christ up were His worth as plain?
Therefore, I say, to test man, shift the proofs,
Nor may he grasp that fact like other fact,
And straightway in his life acknowledge it,
As, say, the indubitable bliss of fire.
Sigh ye, "It had been easier once than now"?
To give you answer I am left alive;
Look at me who was present from the first!
Ye know what things I saw; then came a test,
My first, befitting me who so had seen:
"Forsake the Christ thou sawest transfigured, Him
Who trod the sea and brought the dead to life?
What should wring this from thee?"—ye laugh and ask.
What wrung it? Even a torchlight and a noise,
The sudden Roman faces, violent hands,
And fear of what the Jews might do! Just that,
And, it is written, "I forsook and fled":
There was my trial, and it ended thus.
Ay, but my soul had gained its truth, could grow:
Another year or two,—what little child,
What tender woman that had seen no least
Of all my sights, but barely heard them told,
Who did not clasp the cross with a light laugh,
Or wrap the burning robe round, thanking God?
Well, was truth safe for ever, then? Not so.
Already had begun the silent work
Whereby truth, deadened of its absolute blaze,
Might need love's eye to pierce the o'erstretched doubt:
Teachers were busy, whispering "All is true
As the aged ones report; but youth can reach

Where age gropes dimly, weak with stir and strain,
And the full doctrine slumbers till to-day."
Thus, what the Roman's lowered spear was found,
A bar to me who touched and handled truth,
Now proved the glozing of some new shrewd tongue,
This Ebion, this Cerinthus or their mates,
Till imminent was the outcry "Save us Christ!"
Whereon I stated much of the Lord's life
Forgotten or misdelivered, and let it work.
Such work done, as it will be, what comes next?
What do I hear say, or conceive men say,
"Was John at all, and did he say he saw?
Assure us, ere we ask what he might see!"

'Is this indeed a burthen for late days,
And may I help to bear it with you all,
Using my weakness which becomes your strength?
For if a babe were born inside this grot,
Grew to a boy here, heard us praise the sun,
Yet had but yon sole glimmer in light's place,—
One loving him and wishful he should learn,
Would much rejoice himself was blinded first
Month by month here, so made to understand
How eyes, born darkling, apprehend amiss:
I think I could explain to such a child
There was more glow outside than gleams he caught,
Ay, nor need urge "I saw it, so believe!"
It is a heavy burthen you shall bear
In latter days, new lands, or old grown strange,
Left without me, which must be very soon.
What is the doubt, my brothers? Quick with it!
I see you stand conversing, each new face,

Either in fields, of yellow summer eves,
On islets yet unnamed amid the sea;
Or pace for shelter 'neath a portico
Out of the crowd in some enormous town
Where now the larks sing in a solitude;
Or muse upon blank heaps of stone and sand
Idly conjectured to be Ephesus:
And no one asks his fellow any more
"Where is the promise of His coming?" but
"Was He revealed in any of His lives,
As Power, as Love, as Influencing Soul?"

'Quick, for time presses, tell the whole mind out,
And let us ask and answer and be saved!
My book speaks on, because it cannot pass;
One listens quietly, nor scoffs but pleads:
"Here is a tale of things done ages since;
What truth was ever told the second day?
Wonders, that would prove doctrine, go for nought.
Remains the doctrine, love; well, we must love,
And what we love most, power and love in one,
Let us acknowledge on the record here,
Accepting these in Christ: must Christ then be?
Has He been? Did not we ourselves make Him?
Our mind receives but what it holds, no more.
First of the love, then; we acknowledge Christ—
A proof we comprehend His love, a proof
We had such love already in ourselves,
Knew first what else we should not recognize.
'Tis mere projection from man's inmost mind,
And, what he loves, thus falls reflected back,
Becomes accounted somewhat out of him;

He throws it up in air, it drops down earth's,
With shape, name, story added, man's old way.
How prove you Christ came otherwise at least?
Next try the power: He made and rules the world:
Certes there is a world once made, now ruled,
Unless things have been ever as we see.
Our sires declared a charioteer's yoked steeds
Brought the sun up the east and down the west,
Which only of itself now rises, sets,
As if a hand impelled it and a will,
Thus they long thought, they who had will and hands:
But the new question's whisper is distinct,
Wherefore must all force needs be like ourselves?
We have the hands, the will; what made and drives
The sun is force, is law, is named, not known,
While will and love we do know; marks of these,
Eye-witnesses attest, so books declare—
As that, to punish or reward our race,
The sun at undue times arose or set
Or else stood still: what do not men affirm?
But earth requires as urgently reward
Or punishment to-day as years ago,
And none expects the sun will interpose:
Therefore it was mere passion and mistake,
Or erring zeal for right, which changed the truth.
Go back, far, farther, to the birth of things;
Ever the will, the intelligence, the love,
Man's!—which he gives, supposing he but finds,
As late he gave head, body, hands and feet,
To help these in what forms he called his gods.
First, Jove's brow, Juno's eyes were swept away
But Jove's wrath, Juno's pride continued long;

As last, will, power, and love discarded these,
So law in turn discards power, love, and will.
What proveth God is otherwise at least?
All else, projection from the mind of man!"

'Nay, do not give me wine, for I am strong,
But place my gospel where I put my hands.

'I say that man was made to grow, not stop;
That help, he needed once, and needs no more,
Having grown up but an inch by, is withdrawn:
For he hath new needs, and new helps to these.
This imports solely, man should mount on each
New height in view; the help whereby he mounts,
The ladder-rung his foot has left, may fall,
Since all things suffer change save God the Truth.
Man apprehends Him newly at each stage
Whereat earth's ladder drops, its service done;
And nothing shall prove twice what once was proved.
You stick a garden-plot with ordered twigs
To show inside lie germs of herbs unborn,
And check the careless step would spoil their birth;
But when herbs wave, the guardian twigs may go,
Since should ye doubt of virtues, question kinds,
It is no longer for old twigs ye look,
Which proved once underneath lay store of seed,
But to the herb's self, by what light ye boast,
For what fruit's signs are. This book's fruit is plain,
Nor miracles need prove it any more.
Doth the fruit show? Then miracles bade 'ware
At first of root and stem, saved both till now
From trampling ox, rough boar and wanton goat.
What? Was man made a wheelwork to wind up,

And be discharged, and straight wound up anew?
No!—grown, his growth lasts; taught, he ne'er forgets:
May learn a thousand things, not twice the same.

'This might be pagan teaching: now hear mine.

'I say, that as the babe, you feed awhile,
Becomes a boy and fit to feed himself,
So, minds at first must be spoon-fed with truth:
When they can eat, babe's nurture is withdrawn.
I fed the babe whether it would or no:
I bid the boy or feed himself or starve.
I cried once, "That ye may believe in Christ,
Behold this blind man shall receive his sight!"
I cry now, "Urgest thou, *for I am shrewd*
And smile at stories how John's word could cure—
Repeat that miracle and take my faith?"
I say, that miracle was duly wrought
When, save for it, no faith was possible.
Whether a change were wrought i' the shows o' the world,
Whether the change came from our minds which see
Of the shows o' the world so much as and no more
Than God wills for His purpose,—(what do I
See now, suppose you, there where you see rock
Round us?)—I know not; such was the effect,
So faith grew, making void more miracles
Because too much: they would compel, not help.
I say, the acknowledgment of God in Christ
Accepted by thy reason, solves for thee
All questions in the earth and out of it,
And has so far advanced thee to be wise.
Wouldst thou unprove this to re-prove the proved?
In life's mere minute, with power to use that proof,

Leave knowledge and revert to how it sprung?
Thou hast it; use it and forthwith, or die!

'For I say, this is death and the sole death,
When a man's loss comes to him from his gain,
Darkness from light, from knowledge ignorance,
And lack of love from love made manifest;
A lamp's death when, replete with oil, it chokes;
A stomach's when, surcharged with food, it starves.
With ignorance was surety of a cure.
When man, appalled at nature, questioned first
"What if there lurk a might behind this might?"
He needed satisfaction God could give,
And did give, as ye have the written word:
But when he finds might still redouble might,
Yet asks, "Since all is might, what use of will?"
—Will, the one source of might,—he being man
With a man's will and a man's might, to teach
In little how the two combine in large,—
That man has turned round on himself and stands,
Which in the course of nature is, to die.

'And when man questioned, "What if there be love
Behind the will and might, as real as they?"—
He needed satisfaction God could give,
And did give, as ye have the written word:
But when, beholding that love everywhere,
He reasons, "Since such love is everywhere,
And since ourselves can love and would be loved,
We ourselves make the love, and Christ was not,"—
How shall ye help this man who knows himself,
That he must love and would be loved again,
Yet, owning his own love that proveth Christ,

Rejecteth Christ through very need of Him?
The lamp o'erswims with oil, the stomach flags
Loaded with nurture, and that man's soul dies.

'If he rejoin, "But this was all the while
A trick; the fault was, first of all, in thee,
Thy story of the places, names and dates,
Where, when and how the ultimate truth had rise,
—Thy prior truth, at last discovered none,
Whence now the second suffers detriment.
What good of giving knowledge if, because
Of the manner of the gift, its profit fail?
And why refuse what modicum of help
Had stopped the after-doubt, impossible
I' the face of truth—truth absolute, uniform?
Why must I hit of this and miss of that,
Distinguish just as I be weak or strong,
And not ask of thee and have answer prompt,
Was this once, was it not once?—then and now
And evermore, plain truth from man to man.
Is John's procedure just the heathen bard's?
Put question of his famous play again
How for the ephemerals' sake, Jove's fire was filched,
And carried in a cane and brought to earth:
The fact is in the fable, cry the wise,
Mortals obtained the boon, so much is fact,
Though fire be spirit and produced on earth.
As with the Titan's, so now with thy tale:
Why breed in us perplexity, mistake,
Nor tell the whole truth in the proper words?"

'I answer, Have ye yet to argue out
The very primal thesis, plainest law,

—Man is not God but hath God's end to serve,
A master to obey, a course to take,
Somewhat to cast off, somewhat to become?
Grant this, then man must pass from old to new,
From vain to real, from mistake to fact,
From what once seemed good, to what now proves best.
How could man have progression otherwise?
Before the point was mooted "What is God?"
No savage man inquired "What am myself?"
Much less replied, "First, last, and best of things."
Man takes that title now if he believes
Might can exist with neither will nor love,
In God's case—what he names now Nature's Law—
While in himself he recognizes love
No less than might and will: and rightly takes.
Since if man prove the sole existent thing
Where these combine, whatever their degree,
However weak the might or will or love,
So they be found there, put in evidence,
He is as surely higher in the scale
Than any might with neither love nor will,
As life, apparent in the poorest midge,
When the faint dust-speck flits, ye guess its wing,
Is marvellous beyond dead Atlas' self:
I give such to the midge for resting-place!
Thus, man proves best and highest—God, in fine,
And thus the victory leads but to defeat,
The gain to loss, best rise to the worst fall,
His life becomes impossible, which is death.

'But if, appealing thence, he cower, avouch
He is mere man, and in humility

Neither may know God nor mistake himself;
I point to the immediate consequence
And say, by such confession straight he falls
Into man's place, a thing nor God nor beast,
Made to know that he can know and not more:
Lower than God who knows all and can all,
Higher than beasts which know and can so far
As each beast's limit, perfect to an end,
Nor conscious that they know, nor craving more;
While man knows partly but conceives beside,
Creeps ever on from fancies to the fact,
And in this striving, this converting air
Into a solid he may grasp and use,
Finds progress, man's distinctive mark alone,
Not God's, and not the beasts': God is, they are,
Man partly is and wholly hopes to be.
Such progress could no more attend his soul
Were all it struggles after found at first
And guesses changed to knowledge absolute,
Than motion wait his body, were all else
Than it the solid earth on every side,
Where now through space he moves from rest to rest.
Man, therefore, thus conditioned, must expect
He could not, what he knows now, know at first;
What he considers that he knows to-day,
Come but to-morrow, he will find mis-known;
Getting increase of knowledge, since he learns
Because he lives, which is to be a man,
Set to instruct himself by his past self:
First, like the brute, obliged by facts to learn,
Next, as man may, obliged by his own mind,
Bent, habit, nature, knowledge turned to law.

God's gift was that man should conceive of truth
And yearn to gain it, catching at mistake,
As midway help till he reach fact indeed.
The statuary ere he mould a shape
Boasts a like gift, the shape's idea, and next
The aspiration to produce the same;
So, taking clay, he calls his shape thereout,
Cries ever "Now I have the thing I see":
Yet all the while goes changing what was wrought,
From falsehood like the truth, to truth itself.
How were it had he cried "I see no face,
No breast, no feet i' the ineffectual clay?"
Rather commend him that he clapped his hands,
And laughed "It is my shape and lives again!"

'Enjoyed the falsehood, touched it on to truth,
Until yourselves applaud the flesh indeed
In what is still flesh-imitating clay.
Right in you, right in him, such way be man's!
God only makes the live shape at a jet.
Will ye renounce this pact of creatureship?
The pattern on the Mount subsists no more,
Seemed awhile, then returned to nothingness;
But copies, Moses strove to make thereby,
Serve still and are replaced as time requires:
By these, make newest vessels, reach the type!
If ye demur, this judgment on your head,
Never to reach the ultimate, angels' law,
Indulging every instinct of the soul
There where law, life, joy, impulse are one thing!

'Such is the burthen of the latest time.
I have survived to hear it with my ears,

Answer it with my lips: does this suffice?
For if there be a further woe than such,
Wherein my brothers struggling need a hand
So long as any pulse is left in mine,
May I be absent even longer yet,
Plucking the blind ones back from the abyss,
Though I should tarry a new hundred years!'

But he was dead: 'twas about noon, the day
Somewhat declining: we five buried him
That eve, and then, dividing, went five ways,
And I, disguised, returned to Ephesus.

By this, the cave's mouth must be filled with sand.
Valens is lost, I know not of his trace;
The Bactrian was but a wild, childish man,
And could not write nor speak, but only loved:
So, lest the memory of this go quite,
Seeing that I to-morrow fight the beasts,
I tell the same to Phœbas, whom believe
For many look again to find that face,
Beloved John's to whom I ministered,
Somewhere in life about the world; they err:
Either mistaking what was darkly spoke
At ending of his book, as he relates,
Or misconceiving somewhat of this speech
Scattered from mouth to mouth, as I suppose.
Believe ye will not see him any more
About the world with his divine regard!
For all was as I say, and now the man
Lies as he lay once, breast to breast with God.

[Cerinthus read and mused; one added this:

'If Christ, as thou affirmest, be of men
Mere man, the first and best but nothing more,—
Account Him, for reward of what He was,
Now and for ever, wretchedest of all.
For see; Himself conceived of life as love,
Conceived of love as what must enter in,
Fill up, make one with His each soul He loved:
Thus much for man's joy, all men's joy for Him.
Well, He is gone, thou sayest, to fit reward.
But by this time are many souls set free,
And very many still retained alive:
Nay, should His coming be delayed awhile,
Say, ten years longer (twelve years, some compute)
See if, for every finger of thy hands,
There be not found, that day the world shall end,
Hundreds of souls, each holding by Christ's word
That He will grow incorporate with all,
With me as Pamphylax, with him as John,
Groom for each bride! Can a mere man do this?
Yet Christ saith, this He lived and died to do.
Call Christ, then, the illimitable God,
Or lost!'

But 'twas Cerinthus that is lost.]

JOHN MASON NEALE

1818–1866

287 *'Light's glittering Morn'*

LIGHT'S glittering morn bedecks the sky;
Heaven thunders forth its victor-cry;
The glad earth shouts her triumph high,
And groaning hell makes wild reply;

While He, the King, the mighty King,
Despoiling death of all its sting,
And, trampling down the powers of night,
Brings forth His ransom'd Saints to light.

His tomb of late the threefold guard
Of watch and stone and seal had barr'd;
But now, in pomp and triumph high,
He comes from death to victory.

The pains of hell are loosed at last;
The days of mourning now are past;
An Angel robed in light hath said,
'The Lord is risen from the dead.'

CHARLES KINGSLEY

1819–1875

288 *Drifting Away*

A Fragment

THEY drift away. Ah, God! they drift for ever.
I watch the stream sweep onward to the sea,
Like some old battered buoy upon a roaring river,
Round whom the tide-waifs hang—then drift to sea.

I watch them drift—the old familiar faces,
Who fished and rode with me, by stream and wold,
Till ghosts, not men, fill old beloved places,
And, ah! the land is rank with churchyard mold.

I watch them drift—the youthful aspirations,
Shores, landmarks, beacons, drift alike.

. . . .

I watch them drift—the poets and the statesmen;
The very streams run upward from the sea.

. . . .

Yet overhead the boundless arch of heaven
Still fades to night, still blazes into day.

. . . .

Ah, God! My God! Thou wilt not drift away.

MATTHEW ARNOLD

1822–1888

289

Rugby Chapel

COLDLY, sadly descends
The autumn evening. The Field
Strewn with its dank yellow drifts
Of wither'd leaves, and the elms,
Fade into dimness apace,
Silent;—hardly a shout
From a few boys late at their play!
The lights come out in the street,
In the school-room windows; but cold,
Solemn, unlighted, austere,
Through the gathering darkness, arise
The Chapel walls, in whose bound
Thou, my father! art laid.

There thou dost lie, in the gloom
Of the autumn evening. But ah!
That word, *gloom*, to my mind
Brings thee back in the light
Of thy radiant vigour again!
In the gloom of November we pass'd
Days not of gloom at thy side;

Seasons impair'd not the ray
Of thine even cheerfulness clear.
Such thou wast; and I stand
In the autumn evening, and think
Of bygone autumns with thee.

Fifteen years have gone round
Since thou arosest to tread,
In the summer morning, the road
Of death, at a call unforeseen,
Sudden. For fifteen years,
We who till then in thy shade
Rested as under the boughs
Of a mighty oak, have endured
Sunshine and rain as we might,
Bare, unshaded, alone,
Lacking the shelter of thee.

O strong soul, by what shore
Tarriest thou now? For that force,
Surely, has not been left vain!
Somewhere, surely, afar,
In the sounding labour-house vast
Of being, is practised that strength,
Zealous, beneficent, firm!

Yes, in some far-shining sphere,
Conscious or not of the past,
Still thou performest the word
Of the Spirit in whom thou dost live,
Prompt, unwearied, as here!
Still thou upraisest with zeal
The humble good from the ground,

Sternly repressest the bad.
Still, like a trumpet, dost rouse
Those who with half-open eyes
Tread the border-land dim
'Twixt vice and virtue; reviv'st,
Succourest;—this was thy work,
This was thy life upon earth.

What is the course of the life
Of mortal men on the earth?—
Most men eddy about
Here and there—eat and drink,
Chatter and love and hate,
Gather and squander, are raised
Aloft, are hurl'd in the dust,
Striving blindly, achieving
Nothing; and, then they die—
Perish; and no one asks
Who or what they have been,
More than he asks what waves
In the moonlit solitudes mild
Of the midmost Ocean, have swell'd,
Foam'd for a moment, and gone.

And there are some, whom a thirst
Ardent, unquenchable, fires,
Not with the crowd to be spent,
Not without aim to go round
In an eddy of purposeless dust,
Effort unmeaning and vain.
Ah yes, some of us strive
Not without action to die
Fruitless, but something to snatch

From dull oblivion, nor all
Glut the devouring grave!
We, we have chosen our path—
Path to a clear-purposed goal,
Path of advance! but it leads
A long, steep journey, through sunk
Gorges, o'er mountains in snow!
Cheerful, with friends, we set forth;
Then, on the height, comes the storm!
Thunder crashes from rock
To rock, the cataracts reply;
Lightnings dazzle our eyes;
Roaring torrents have breach'd
The track, the stream-bed descends
In the place where the wayfarer once
Planted his footstep—the spray
Boils o'er its borders; aloft,
The unseen snow-beds dislodge
Their hanging ruin;—alas,
Havoc is made in our train!
Friends who set forth at our side
Falter, are lost in the storm!
We, we only, are left!
With frowning foreheads, with lips
Sternly compress'd, we strain on,
On—and at nightfall, at last,
Come to the end of our way,
To the lonely inn 'mid the rocks;
Where the gaunt and taciturn Host
Stands on the threshold, the wind
Shaking his thin white hairs—
Holds his lantern to scan

Our storm-beat figures, and asks:
Whom in our party we bring?
Whom we have left in the snow?
Sadly we answer: We bring
Only ourselves; we lost
Sight of the rest in the storm.
Hardly ourselves we fought through,
Stripp'd, without friends, as we are.
Friends, companions, and train
The avalanche swept from our side.

But thou would'st not *alone*
Be saved, my father! *alone*
Conquer and come to thy goal,
Leaving the rest in the wild.
We were weary, and we
Fearful, and we, in our march,
Fain to drop down and to die.
Still thou turnedst, and still
Beckonedst the trembler, and still
Gavest the weary thy hand!
If, in the paths of the world,
Stones might have wounded thy feet,
Toil or dejection have tried
Thy spirit, of that we saw
Nothing! to us thou wert still
Cheerful, and helpful, and firm.
Therefore to thee it was given
Many to save with thyself;
And, at the end of thy day,
O faithful shepherd! to come,
Bringing thy sheep in thy hand.

And through thee I believe
In the noble and great who are gone;
Pure souls honour'd and blest
By former ages, who else—
Such, so soulless, so poor,
Is the race of men whom I see—
Seem'd but a dream of the heart,
Seem'd but a cry of desire.
Yes! I believe that there lived
Others like thee in the past,
Not like the men of the crowd
Who all round me to-day
Bluster or cringe, and make life
Hideous, and arid, and vile;
But souls temper'd with fire,
Fervent, heroic, and good,
Helpers and friends of mankind.

Servants of God!—or sons
Shall I not call you? because
Not as servants ye knew
Your Father's innermost mind,
His, who unwillingly sees
One of his little ones lost—
Yours is the praise, if mankind
Hath not as yet in its march
Fainted, and fallen, and died!

See! in the rocks of the world
Marches the host of mankind,
A feeble, wavering line.
Where are they tending?—A God
Marshall'd them, gave them their goal.—
Ah, but the way is so long!

Years they have been in the wild!
Sore thirst plagues them; the rocks,
Rising all round, overawe.
Factions divide them; their host
Threatens to break, to dissolve.
Ah, keep, keep them combined!
Else, of the myriads who fill
That army, not one shall arrive!
Sole they shall stray; in the rocks
Labour for ever in vain,
Die one by one in the waste.

Then, in such hour of need
Of your fainting, dispirited race,
Ye, like angels, appear,
Radiant with ardour divine.
Beacons of hope, ye appear!
Languor is not in your heart,
Weakness is not in your word,
Weariness not on your brow.
Ye alight in our van; at your voice,
Panic, despair, flee away.
Ye move through the ranks, recall
The stragglers, refresh the outworn,
Praise, re-inspire the brave.
Order, courage, return.
Eyes rekindling, and prayers,
Follow your steps as ye go.
Ye fill up the gaps in our files,
Strengthen the wavering line,
Stablish, continue our march,
On, to the bound of the waste,
On, to the City of God.

COVENTRY PATMORE

1823–1896

290

Faint yet pursuing

HEROIC Good, target for which the young
Dream in their dreams that every bow is strung,
And, missing, sigh
Unfruitful, or as disbelievers die,
Thee having miss'd, I will not so revolt,
But lowlier shoot my bolt,
And lowlier still, if still I may not reach,
And my proud stomach teach
That less than highest is good, and may be high.
An even walk in life's uneven way,
Though to have dreamt of flight and not to fly
Be strange and sad,
Is not a boon that's given to all who pray.
If this I had
I'd envy none!
Nay, trod I straight for one
Year, month or week,
Should Heaven withdraw, and Satan me amerce
Of power and joy, still would I seek
Another victory with a like reverse;
Because the good of victory does not die,
As dies the failure's curse,
And what we have to gain
Is, not one battle, but a weary life's campaign.
Yet meaner lot being sent
Should more than me content;
Yea, if I lie
Among vile shards, though born for silver wings,
In the strong flight and feathers gold
Of whatsoever heavenward mounts and sings

I must by admiration so comply
That there I should my own delight behold.
Yea, though I sin each day times seven,
And dare not lift the fearfullest eyes to Heaven,
Thanks must I give
Because that seven times are not eight or nine,
And that my darkness is all mine,
And that I live
Within this oak-shade one more minute even,
Hearing the winds their Maker magnify.

291 *Remembered Grace*

SINCE succour to the feeblest of the wise
Is charge of nobler weight
Than the security
Of many and many a foolish soul's estate,
This I affirm,
Though fools will fools more confidently be:
Whom God does once with heart to heart befriend,
He does so till the end:
And having planted life's miraculous germ,
One sweet pulsation of responsive love,
He sets him sheer above,
Not sin and bitter shame
And wreck of fame,
But Hell's insidious and more black attempt,
The envy, malice, and pride,
Which men who share so easily condone
That few ev'n list such ills as these to hide.
From these unalterably exempt
Through the remember'd grace

Of that divine embrace,
Of his sad errors none,
Though gross to blame,
Shall cast him lower than the cleansing flame,
Nor make him quite depart
From the small flock named 'after God's own heart,'
And to themselves unknown.
Nor can he quail
In faith, nor flush nor pale
When all the other idiot people spell
How this or that new Prophet's word belies
Their last high oracle;
But constantly his soul
Points to its pole
Ev'n as the needle points, and knows not why;
And, under the ever-changing clouds of doubt,
When others cry,
'The stars, if stars there were,
Are quench'd and out!'
To him, uplooking t'ward the hills for aid,
Appear, at need display'd,
Gaps in the low-hung gloom, and, bright in air,
Orion or the Bear.

292 *To the Unknown Eros*

WHAT rumour'd heavens are these
Which not a poet sings,
O, Unknown Eros? What this breeze
Of sudden wings
Speeding at far returns of time from interstellar space
To fan my very face,

And gone as fleet,
Through delicatest ether feathering soft their solitary beat,
With ne'er a light plume dropp'd, nor any trace
To speak of whence they came, or whither they depart?
And why this palpitating heart,
This blind and unrelated joy,
This meaningless desire,
That moves me like the Child
Who in the flushing darkness troubled lies,
Inventing lonely prophecies,
Which even to his Mother mild
He dares not tell;
To which himself is infidel;
His heart not less on fire
With dreams impossible as wildest Arab Tale,
(So thinks the boy,)
With dreams that turn him red and pale,
Yet less impossible and wild
Than those which bashful Love, in his own way and hour,
Shall duly bring to flower?
O, Unknown Eros, sire of awful bliss,
What portent and what Delphic word,
Such as in form of snake forebodes the bird,
Is this?
In me life's even flood
What eddies thus?
What in its ruddy orbit lifts the blood,
Like a perturbed moon of Uranus,
Reaching to some great world in ungauged darkness hid;
And whence
This rapture of the sense
Which, by thy whisper bid,

Reveres with obscure rite and sacramental sign
A bond I know not of nor dimly can divine;
This subject loyalty which longs
For chains and thongs
Woven of gossamer and adamant,
To bind me to my unguess'd want,
And so to lie,
Between those quivering plumes that thro' fine ether pant,
For hopeless, sweet eternity?
What God unhonour'd hitherto in songs,
Or which, that now
Forgettest the disguise
That Gods must wear who visit human eyes,
Art Thou?
Thou art not Amor; or, if so, yon pyre,
That waits the willing victim, flames with vestal fire;
Nor mooned Queen of maids; or, if thou'rt she,
Ah, then, from Thee
Let Bride and Bridegroom learn what kisses be!
In what veil'd hymn
Or mystic dance
Would he that were thy Priest advance
Thine earthly praise, thy glory limn?
Say, should the feet that feel thy thought
In double-center'd circuit run,
In that compulsive focus, Nought,
In this a furnace like the sun;
And might some note of thy renown
And high behest
Thus in enigma be expressed:
'There lies the crown

Which all thy longing cures.
Refuse it, Mortal, that it may be yours!
It is a Spirit, though it seems red gold;
And such may no man, but by shunning, hold.
Refuse it, till refusing be despair;
And thou shalt feel the phantom in thy hair.'

293 *Legem tuam dilexi*

THE 'Infinite'. Word horrible! at feud
With life, and the braced mood
Of power and joy and love;
Forbidden, by wise heathen ev'n, to be
Spoken of Deity,
Whose Name, on popular altars, was 'The Unknown,'
Because, or ere It was reveal'd as One
Confined in Three,
The people fear'd that it might prove
Infinity,
The blazon which the devils desired to gain;
And God, for their confusion, laugh'd consent;
Yet did so far relent,
That they might seek relief, and not in vain,
In dashing of themselves against the shores of pain.
Nor bides alone in hell
The bond-disdaining spirit boiling to rebel.
But for compulsion of strong grace,
The pebble in the road
Would straight explode,
And fill the ghastly boundlessness of space.
The furious power,
To soft growth twice constrain'd in leaf and flower,

Protests, and longs to flash its faint self far
Beyond the dimmest star.
The same
Seditious flame,
Beat backward with reduplicated might,
Struggles alive within its stricter term,
And is the worm.
And the just Man does on himself affirm
God's limits, and is conscious of delight,
Freedom and right;
And so His Semblance is, Who, every hour,
By day and night,
Buildeth new bulwarks 'gainst the Infinite.
For, ah, who can express
How full of bonds and simpleness
Is God,
How narrow is He,
And how the wide, waste field of possibility
Is only trod
Straight to His homestead in the human heart,
And all His art
Is as the babe's that wins his Mother to repeat
Her little song so sweet!
What is the chief news of the Night?
Lo, iron and salt, heat, weight and light
In every star that drifts on the great breeze!
And these
Mean Man,
Darling of God, Whose thoughts but live and move
Round him; Who woos his will
To wedlock with His own, and does distil
To that drop's span

The attar of all rose-fields of all love!
Therefore the soul select assumes the stress
Of bonds unbid, which God's own style express
Better than well,
And aye hath, cloister'd, borne,
To the Clown's scorn,
The fetters of the threefold golden chain:
Narrowing to nothing all his worldly gain;
(Howbeit in vain;
For to have nought
Is to have all things without care or thought!)
Surrendering, abject, to his equal's rule,
As though he were a fool,
The free wings of the will;
(More vainly still;
For none knows rightly what 'tis to be free
But only he
Who, vow'd against all choice, and fill'd with awe
Of the ofttimes dumb or clouded Oracle,
Does wiser than to spell,
In his own suit, the least word of the Law!)
And, lastly, bartering life's dear bliss for pain;
But evermore in vain;
For joy (rejoice ye Few that tasted have!)
Is Love's obedience
Against the genial laws of natural sense,
Whose wide, self-dissipating wave,
Prison'd in artful dykes,
Trembling returns and strikes
Thence to its source again,
In backward billows fleet,
Crest crossing crest ecstatic as they greet,

Thrilling each vein,
Exploring every chasm and cove
Of the full heart with floods of honied love,
And every principal street
And obscure alley and lane
Of the intricate brain
With brimming rivers of light and breezes sweet
Of the primordial heat;
Till, unto view of me and thee,
Lost the intense life be,
Or ludicrously display'd, by force
Of distance; as a soaring eagle, or a horse
On far-off hillside shewn,
May seem a gust-driv'n rag or a dead stone.
Nor by such bonds alone—
But more I leave to say,
Fitly revering the Wild Ass's bray,
Also his hoof,
Of which, go where you will, the marks remain
Where the religious walls have hid the bright reproof.

294 *To the Body*

CREATION'S and Creator's crowning good;
Wall of infinitude;
Foundation of the sky,
In Heaven forecast
And long'd for from eternity,
Though laid the last;
Reverberating dome,
Of music cunningly built home
Against the void and indolent disgrace
Of unresponsive space;

Little, sequester'd pleasure-house
For God and for his Spouse;
Elaborately, yea, past conceiving, fair,
Since, from the graced decorum of the hair,
Ev'n to the tingling, sweet
Soles of the simple, earth-confiding feet,
And from the inmost heart
Outwards unto the thin
Silk curtains of the skin,
Every least part
Astonish'd hears
And sweet replies to some like region of the spheres;
Form'd for a dignity prophets but darkly name,
Lest shameless men cry 'Shame!'
So rich with wealth conceal'd
That Heaven and Hell fight chiefly for this field;
Clinging to everything that pleases thee
With indefectible fidelity;
Alas, so true
To all thy friendships that no grace
Thee from thy sin can wholly disembrace;
Which thus 'bides with thee as the Jebusite,
That, maugre all God's promises could do,
The chosen People never conquer'd quite;
Who therefore lived with them,
And that by formal truce and as of right,
In metropolitan Jerusalem.
For which false fealty
Thou needs must, for a season, lie
In the grave's arms, foul and unshriven,
Albeit, in Heaven,
Thy crimson-throbbing Glow

Into its old abode aye pants to go,
And does with envy see
Enoch, Elijah, and the Lady, she
Who left the lilies in her body's lieu.
O, if the pleasures I have known in thee
But my poor faith's poor first-fruits be,
What quintessential, keen, ethereal bliss
Then shall be his
Who has thy birth-time's consecrating dew
For death's sweet chrism retain'd,
Quick, tender, virginal, and unprofaned!

295 *Deliciae Sapientiae de Amore*

LOVE, light for me
Thy ruddiest blazing torch,
That I, albeit a beggar by the Porch
Of the glad Palace of Virginity,
May gaze within, and sing the pomp I see;
For, crown'd with roses all,
'Tis there, O Love, they keep thy festival!
But first warn off the beatific spot
Those wretched who have not
Even afar beheld the shining wall,
And those who, once beholding, have forgot,
And those, most vile, who dress
The charnel spectre drear
Of utterly dishallow'd nothingness
In that refulgent fame,
And cry, Lo, here!
And name
The Lady whose smiles inflame

The sphere.
Bring, Love, anear,
And bid be not afraid
Young Lover true, and love-foreboding Maid,
And wedded Spouse, if virginal of thought;
For I will sing of nought
Less sweet to hear
Than seems
A music in their half-remember'd dreams.
The magnet calls the steel:
Answers the iron to the magnet's breath;
What do they feel
But death!
The clouds of summer kiss in flame and rain,
And are not found again;
But the heavens themselves eternal are with fire
Of unapproach'd desire,
By the aching heart of Love, which cannot rest,
In blissfullest pathos so indeed possess'd.
O, spousals high;
O, doctrine blest,
Unutterable in even the happiest sigh;
This know ye all
Who can recall
With what a welling of indignant tears
Love's simpleness first hears
The meaning of his mortal covenant,
And from what pride comes down
To wear the crown
Of which 'twas very heaven to feel the want.
How envies he the ways
Of yonder hopeless star,

And so would laugh and yearn
With trembling lids eterne,
Ineffably content from infinitely far
Only to gaze
On his bright Mistress's responding rays,
That never know eclipse;
And, once in his long year,
With praeternuptial ecstacy and fear,
By the delicious law of that ellipse
Wherein all citizens of ether move,
With hastening pace to come
Nearer, though never near,
His Love
And always inaccessible sweet Home;
There on his path doubly to burn,
Kiss'd by her doubled light
That whispers of its source,
The ardent secret ever clothed with Night,
Then go forth in new force
Towards a new return,
Rejoicing as a Bridegroom on his course!
This know ye all;
Therefore gaze bold,
That so in you be joyful hope increas'd,
Thorough the Palace portals, and behold
The dainty and unsating Marriage-Feast.
O, hear
Them singing clear
'Cor meum et caro mea' round the 'I am',
The Husband of the Heavens, and the Lamb
Whom they for ever follow there that kept,
Or, losing, never slept

Till they reconquer'd had in mortal fight
The standard white.
O, hear
From the harps they bore from Earth, five-strung, what music springs,
While the glad Spirits chide
The wondering strings!
And how the shining sacrificial Choirs,
Offering for aye their dearest hearts' desires,
Which to their hearts come back beatified,
Hymn, the bright aisles along,
The nuptial song,
Song ever new to us and them, that saith,
'Hail Virgin in Virginity a Spouse!'
Heard first below
Within the little house
At Nazareth;
Heard yet in many a cell where brides of Christ
Lie hid, emparadised,
And where, although
By the hour 'tis night,
There's light,
The Day still lingering in the lap of snow.
Gaze and be not afraid
Ye wedded few that honour, in sweet thought
And glittering will,
So freshly from the garden gather still
The lily sacrificed;
For ye, though self-suspected here for nought,
Are highly styled
With the thousands twelve times twelve of undefiled.
Gaze and be not afraid

Young Lover true and love-foreboding Maid.
The full Moon of deific vision bright
Abashes nor abates
No spark minute of Nature's keen delight,
'Tis there your Hymen waits!
There where in courts afar, all unconfused, they crowd,
As fumes the starlight soft
In gulfs of cloud,
And each to the other, well-content,
Sighs oft,
"'Twas this we meant!'
Gaze without blame
Ye in whom living Love yet blushes for dead shame.
There of pure Virgins none
Is fairer seen,
Save One,
Than Mary Magdalene.
Gaze without doubt or fear
Ye to whom generous Love, by any name, is dear.
Love makes the life to be
A fount perpetual of virginity;
For, lo, the Elect
Of generous Love, how named soe'er, affect
Nothing but God,
Or mediate or direct,
Nothing but God,
The Husband of the Heavens:
And who Him love, in potence great or small
Are, one and all,
Heirs of the Palace glad,
And inly clad
With the bridal robes of ardour virginal.

RICHARD WILTON

1827–1903

296 *Hymn to the Holy Spirit*

COME, Holy Dove,
Descend on silent pinion,
Brood o'er my sinful soul with patient love,
Till all my being owns Thy mild dominion.

Round yon sad Tree
With frequent circles hover,
That in my glorious Surety I may see
Grace to redeem and righteousness to cover.

On wings of peace
Bring from that precious Altar
The Blood which bids the storms of conscience cease,
And blots out all the debt of the defaulter.

Spirit of Grace,
Reveal in me my Saviour,
That I may gaze upon His mirrored Face,
Till I reflect it in my whole behaviour.

Oh, let me hear
Thy soft, low voice controlling
My devious steps with intimations clear,
With comforts manifold my heart consoling.

Let that sweet sound
To holy deeds allure me,
With heavenly echoes make my spirit bound,
And of my Home in Paradise assure me.

Come, Holy Dove,
Guide me to yon bright portal,
Where I shall see the Saviour whom I love,
And enter on the joys which are immortal.

DANTE GABRIEL ROSSETTI

1828–1882

297 *Ave*

MOTHER of the Fair Delight,
Thou handmaid perfect in God's sight,
Now sitting fourth beside the Three,
Thyself a woman-Trinity,—
Being a daughter borne to God,
Mother of Christ from stall to rood,
And wife unto the Holy Ghost:—
Oh when our need is uttermost,
Think that to such as death may strike
Thou once wert sister sisterlike!
Thou headstone of humanity,
Groundstone of the great Mystery,
Fashioned like us, yet more than we!

Mind'st thou not (when June's heavy breath
Warmed the long days in Nazareth,)
That eve thou didst go forth to give
Thy flowers some drink that they might live
One faint night more amid the sands?
Far off the trees were as pale wands
Against the fervid sky: the sea
Sighed further off eternally
As human sorrow sighs in sleep.
Then suddenly the awe grew deep,

As of a day to which all days
Were footsteps in God's secret ways:
Until a folding sense, like prayer,
Which is, as God is, everywhere,
Gathered about thee; and a voice
Spake to thee without any noise,
Being of the silence:—'Hail,' it said,
'Thou that art highly favourèd;
The Lord is with thee here and now;
Blessed among all women thou.'

Ah! knew'st thou of the end, when first
That Babe was on thy bosom nurs'd?—
Or when He tottered round thy knee
Did thy great sorrow dawn on thee?—
And through His boyhood, year by year
Eating with Him the Passover,
Didst thou discern confusedly
That holier sacrament, when He,
The bitter cup about to quaff,
Should break the bread and eat thereof?—
Or came not yet the knowledge, even
Till on some day forecast in Heaven
His feet passed through thy door to press
Upon His Father's business?—
Or still was God's high secret kept?

Nay, but I think the whisper crept
Like growth through childhood. Work and play,
Things common to the course of day,
Awed thee with meanings unfulfill'd;
And all through girlhood, something still'd

Thy senses like the birth of light,
When thou hast trimmed thy lamp at night
Or washed thy garments in the stream;
To whose white bed had come the dream
That He was thine and thou wast His
Who feeds among the field-lilies.
O solemn shadow of the end
In that wise spirit long contain'd!
O awful end! and those unsaid
Long years when It was Finishèd!

Mind'st thou not (when the twilight gone
Left darkness in the house of John,)
Between the naked window-bars
That spacious vigil of the stars?—
For thou, a watcher even as they,
Wouldst rise from where throughout the day
Thou wroughtest raiment for His poor
And, finding the fixed terms endure
Of day and night which never brought
Sounds of His coming chariot,
Wouldst lift through cloud-waste unexplor'd
Those eyes which said, 'How long, O Lord?'
Then that disciple whom He loved,
Well heeding, haply would be moved
To ask thy blessing in His name;
And that one thought in both, the same
Though silent, then would clasp ye round
To weep together,—tears long bound,
Sick tears of patience, dumb and slow.
Yet, 'Surely I come quickly,'—so
He said, from life and death gone home.
Amen: even so, Lord Jesus, come!

But oh! what human tongue can speak
That day when death was sent to break
From the tir'd spirit, like a veil,
Its covenant with Gabriel
Endured at length unto the end?
What human thought can apprehend
That mystery of motherhood
When thy Beloved at length renew'd
The sweet communion severèd,—
His left hand underneath thine head
And His right hand embracing thee?—
Lo! He was thine, and this is He!

Soul, is it Faith, or Love, or Hope,
That lets me see her standing up
Where the light of the Throne is bright?
Unto the left, unto the right,
The cherubim, arrayed, conjoint,
Float inward to a golden point,
And from between the seraphim
The glory issues for a hymn.
O Mary Mother, be not loth
To listen,—thou whom the stars clothe,
Who seëst and mayst not be seen!
Hear us at last, O Mary Queen!
Into our shadow bend thy face,
Bowing thee from the secret place,
O Mary Virgin, full of grace!

298 *'Our Lady of the Rocks'*

MOTHER, is this the darkness of the end,
The Shadow of Death? and is that outer sea
Infinite imminent Eternity?

And does the death-pang by man's seed sustain'd
In Time's each instant cause thy face to bend
  Its silent prayer upon the Son, while he
  Blesses the dead with his hand silently
To his long day which hours no more offend?

Mother of grace, the pass is difficult,
  Keen as these rocks, and the bewildered souls
    Throng it like echoes, blindly shuddering through.
  Thy name, O Lord, each spirit's voice extols,
    Whose peace abides in the dark avenue
Amid the bitterness of things occult.

CHRISTINA GEORGINA ROSSETTI

1830–1894

299 *'If only'*

IF I might only love my God and die!
  But now He bids me love Him and live on,
  Now when the bloom of all my life is gone,
The pleasant half of life has quite gone by.
My tree of hope is lopped that spread so high;
  And I forget how summer glowed and shone,
  While autumn grips me with its fingers wan,
And frets me with its fitful windy sigh.
When autumn passes then must winter numb,
  And winter may not pass a weary while,
    But when it passes spring shall flower again:
  And in that spring who weepeth now shall smile,
    Yea, they shall wax who now are on the wane,
Yea, they shall sing for love when Christ shall come.

300 *Who shall deliver me?*

GOD strengthen me to bear myself;
That heaviest weight of all to bear,
Inalienable weight of care.

All others are outside myself;
I lock my door and bar them out,
The turmoil, tedium, gad-about.

I lock my door upon myself,
And bar them out; but who shall wall
Self from myself, most loathed of all?

If I could once lay down myself,
And start self-purged upon the race
That all must run! Death runs apace.

If I could set aside myself,
And start with lightened heart upon
The road by all men overgone!

God harden me against myself,
This coward with pathetic voice
Who craves for ease, and rest, and joys:

Myself, arch-traitor to myself;
My hollowest friend, my deadliest foe,
My clog whatever road I go.

Yet One there is can curb myself,
Can roll the strangling load from me,
Break off the yoke and set me free.

301 *Mother Country*

OH what is that country
  And where can it be,
Not mine own country,
  But dearer far to me?
Yet mine own country,
  If I one day may see
Its spices and cedars,
  Its gold and ivory.

As I lie dreaming
  It rises, that land:
There rises before me
  Its green golden strand,
With its bowing cedars
  And its shining sand;
It sparkles and flashes
  Like a shaken brand.

Do angels lean nearer
  While I lie and long?
I see their soft plumage
  And catch their windy song,
Like the rise of a high tide
  Sweeping full and strong;
I mark the outskirts
  Of their reverend throng.

Oh what is a king here,
  Or what is a boor?
Here all starve together,
  All dwarfed and poor;

Here Death's hand knocketh
  At door after door,
He thins the dancers
  From the festal floor.

Oh what is a handmaid,
  Or what is a queen?
All must lie down together
  Where the turf is green,
The foulest face hidden,
  The fairest not seen;
Gone as if never,
  They had breathed or been.

Gone from sweet sunshine
  Underneath the sod,
Turned from warm flesh and blood
  To senseless clod,
Gone as if never
  They had toiled or trod,
Gone out of sight of all
  Except our God.

Shut into silence
  From the accustomed song,
Shut into solitude
  From all earth's throng,
Run down tho' swift of foot,
  Thrust down tho' strong;
Life made an end of,
  Seemed it short or long.

Life made an end of,
  Life but just begun,
Life finished yesterday,
  Its last sand run;
Life new-born with the morrow,
  Fresh as the sun:
While done is done for ever;
  Undone, undone.

And if that life is life,
  This is but a breath,
The passage of a dream
  And the shadow of death;
But a vain shadow
  If one considereth;
Vanity of vanities,
  As the Preacher saith.

302 *'In the bleak mid-winter'*

IN the bleak mid-winter
  Frosty wind made moan,
Earth stood hard as iron,
  Water like a stone;
Snow had fallen, snow on snow,
  Snow on snow,
In the bleak mid-winter
  Long ago.

Our God, Heaven cannot hold Him,
  Nor earth sustain;
Heaven and earth shall flee away
  When He comes to reign:

In the bleak mid-winter
  A stable-place sufficed
The Lord God Almighty
  Jesus Christ.

Enough for Him, whom cherubim
  Worship night and day,
A breastful of milk
  And a mangerful of hay;
Enough for Him, whom angels
  Fall down before,
The ox and ass and camel
  Which adore.

Angels and archangels
  May have gathered there,
Cherubim and seraphim
  Thronged the air;
But only His mother
  In her maiden bliss
Worshipped the Belovèd
  With a kiss.

What can I give Him,
  Poor as I am?
If I were a shepherd
  I would bring a lamb,
If I were a Wise Man
  I would do my part,—
Yet what I can I give Him,
  Give my heart.

303 *Marvel of Marvels*

MARVEL of marvels, if I myself shall behold
With mine own eyes my King in his city of gold;
Where the least of lambs is spotless white in the fold,
Where the least and last of saints in spotless white is stoled,
Where the dimmest head beyond a moon is aureoled.
O saints, my belovèd, now mouldering to mould in the mould,
Shall I see you lift your heads, see your cerements unroll'd,
See with these very eyes? who now in darkness and cold
Tremble for the midnight cry, the rapture, the tale untold,—
The Bridegoom cometh, cometh, his Bride to enfold!

Cold it is, my belovèd, since your funeral bell was toll'd:
Cold it is, O my King, how cold alone on the wold!

304 *'None other Lamb'*

NONE other Lamb, none other Name,
None other Hope in heaven or earth or sea,
None other Hiding-place from guilt and shame,
None beside Thee.

My faith burns low, my hope burns low
Only my heart's desire cries out in me
By the deep thunder of its want and woe
Cries out to Thee.

Lord, Thou art Life tho' I be dead,
Love's Fire Thou art, however cold I be:
Nor heaven have I, nor place to lay my head,
Nor home, but Thee.

305 *Shadows To-day*

SHADOWS to-day, while shadows show God's Will.
Light were not good except He sent us light.
Shadows to-day, because this day is night
Whose marvels and whose mysteries fulfil
Their course and deep in darkness serve Him still.
Thou dim aurora, on the extremest height
Of airy summits, wax not overbright;
Refrain thy rose, refrain thy daffodil.
Until God's Word go forth to kindle thee
And garland thee and bid thee stoop to us,
Blush in the heavenly choirs and glance not down:
To-day we race in darkness for a crown,
In darkness for beatitude to be,
In darkness for the city luminous.

306 *'Heaven is not far'*

HEAVEN is not far, tho' far the sky
Overarching earth and main.
It takes not long to love and die,
Die, revive, and rise again.
Not long: how long? Oh long re-echoing song!
O Lord, how long?

307 *Paradise*

ONCE in a dream I saw the flowers
That bud and bloom in Paradise;
More fair they are than waking eyes
Have seen in all this world of ours.

And faint the perfume-bearing rose,
  And faint the lily on its stem,
And faint the perfect violet
    Compared with them.

I heard the songs of Paradise:
  Each bird sat singing in his place;
  A tender song so full of grace
It soared like incense to the skies.
Each bird sat singing to his mate
  Soft cooing notes among the trees:
The nightingale herself were cold
    To such as these.

I saw the fourfold River flow,
  And deep it was, with golden sand;
  It flowed between a mossy land
Which murmured music grave and low.
It hath refreshment for all thirst,
  For fainting spirits strength and rest:
Earth holds not such a draught as this
    From east to west.

The Tree of Life stood budding there,
  Abundant with its twelvefold fruits;
  Eternal sap sustains its roots,
Its shadowing branches fill the air.
Its leaves are healing for the world,
  Its fruit the hungry world can feed,
Sweeter than honey to the taste
    And balm indeed.

I saw the gate called Beautiful;
And looked, but scarce could look, within
I saw the golden streets begin,
And outskirts of the glassy pool.
Oh harps, oh crowns of plenteous stars,
Oh green palm-branches many-leaved—
Eye hath not seen, nor ear hath heard,
Nor heart conceived.

I hope to see these things again,
But not as once in dreams by night;
To see them with my very sight,
And touch, and handle, and attain:
To have all Heaven beneath my feet
For narrow ways that once they trod;
To have my part with all the Saints,
And with my God.

308 *A Better Resurrection*

I HAVE no wit, no words, no tears;
My heart within me like a stone
Is numbed too much for hopes or fears;
Look right, look left, I dwell alone;
I lift mine eyes, but dimmed with grief
No everlasting hills I see;
My life is in the falling leaf:
O Jesus, quicken me.

My life is like a faded leaf,
My harvest dwindled to a husk;
Truly my life is void and brief
And tedious in the barren dusk;

My life is like a frozen thing,
No bud nor greenness can I see:
Yet rise it shall—the sap of Spring;
O Jesus, rise in me.

My life is like a broken bowl,
A broken bowl that cannot hold
One drop of water for my soul
Or cordial in the searching cold;
Cast in the fire the perished thing,
Melt and remould it, till it be
A royal cup for Him my King:
O Jesus, drink of me.

309 *Lord, grant us Calm*

LORD, grant us calm, if calm can set forth Thee;
Or tempest, if a tempest set Thee forth;
Wind from the east or west or south or north,
Or congelation of a silent sea,
With stillness of each tremulous aspen tree.

Still let fruit fall, or hang upon the tree;
Still let the east and west, the south and north,
Curb in their winds, or plough a thundering sea;
Still let the earth abide to set Thee forth,
Or vanish like a smoke to set forth Thee.

310 *'I will accept'*

I WILL accept thy will to do and be,
Thy hatred and intolerance of sin,
Thy will at least to love, that burns within
And thirsteth after Me:

So will I render fruitful, blessing still,
The germs and small beginnings in thy heart,
Because thy will cleaves to the better part.—
Alas, I cannot will.

Dost not thou will, poor soul? Yet I receive
The inner unseen longings of the soul,
I guide them turning towards Me; I control
And charm hearts till they grieve:
If thou desire, it yet shall come to pass,
Though thou but wish indeed to choose My love;
For I have power in earth and heaven above.—
I cannot wish, alas!

What, neither choose nor wish to choose? and yet
I still must strive to win thee and constrain:
For thee I hung upon the cross in pain,
How then can I forget?
If thou as yet dost neither love, nor hate,
Nor choose, nor wish,—resign thyself, be still
Till I infuse love, hatred, longing, will.—
I do not deprecate.

311 *Eve*

'WHILE I sit at the door
Sick to gaze within
Mine eye weepeth sore
For sorrow and sin:
As a tree my sin stands
To darken all lands;
Death is the fruit it bore.

'How have Eden bowers grown
Without Adam to bend them!
How have Eden flowers blown
Squandering their sweet breath
Without me to tend them!
The Tree of Life was ours,
Tree twelvefold-fruited,
Most lofty tree that flowers,
Most deeply rooted:
I chose the tree of death.

'Hadst thou but said me nay,
Adam, my brother,
I might have pined away;
I, but none other:
God might have let thee stay
Safe in our garden,
By putting me away
Beyond all pardon.

'I, Eve, sad mother
Of all who must live,
I, not another
Plucked bitterest fruit to give
My friend, husband, lover—
O wanton eyes run over;
Who but I should grieve?—
Cain hath slain his brother:
Of all who must die mother,
Miserable Eve!'

Thus she sat weeping,
Thus Eve our mother,
Where one lay sleeping
Slain by his brother.
Greatest and least
Each piteous beast
To hear her voice
Forgot his joys
And set aside his feast.

The mouse paused in his walk
And dropped his wheaten stalk;
Grave cattle wagged their heads
In rumination;
The eagle gave a cry
From his cloud station;
Larks on thyme beds
Forbore to mount or sing;
Bees drooped upon the wing;
The raven perched on high
Forgot his ration;
The conies in their rock,
A feeble nation,
Quaked sympathetical;
The mocking-bird left off to mock;
Huge camels knelt as if
In deprecation;
The kind hart's tears were falling;
Chattered the wistful stork;
Dove-voices with a dying fall
Cooed desolation
Answering grief by grief.

Only the serpent in the dust
Wriggling and crawling
Grinned an evil grin and thrust
His tongue out with its fork.

312 *Before the Beginning*

BEFORE the beginning Thou hast foreknown the end,
  Before the birthday the death-bed was seen of Thee:
Cleanse what I cannot cleanse, mend what I cannot mend,
  O Lord All-Merciful, be merciful to me.

While the end is drawing near I know not mine end;
  Birth I recall not, my death I cannot foresee:
O God, arise to defend, arise to befriend,
  O Lord All-Merciful, be merciful to me.

RICHARD WATSON DIXON

1833–1900

313 *Rapture: an Ode*

WHAT is this?
  The white and crumbling clouds leave bare the blue;
Shines out the central sun with golden hue;
And all the fruit-trees, rolling blossom-boughed,
Are white and billowy as the rolling cloud.
The warm beam bedded sleeps upon the trees,
The springing thickets and the gorse-bound leas;
Sleeps where I lie at ease,
Pulling the ruby orchis and the pale
Half-withered cowslip from the hill-side grass,
Midway the brow that overhangs the vale,
Where the sleepy shadows pass,
And the sunbeam sleeps till all is grown
Into one burning sapphire stone,
All air, all earth, each violet-deepened zone.

It sleeps and broods upon the moss-mapped stone,
The thready mosses and the plumy weeds;
Numbers the veined flowers one after one,
Their colours and their leaves and ripening seeds:
Above, around, its influence proceeds;
It tracks in gleams the stream through crowding bush,
And beds of sworded flags and bearded rush,
Where slow it creeps along the lower ground;
The ridges far above are all embrowned,
The golden heavens over all are ploughed
In furrows of fine tissue that abound,
And melting fragments of the whitest cloud.

Ah, what is this, that now with sated eyes
And humming ears the soul no more descries?
Drawn back upon the spirit all the sense
Becomes intelligence;
And to be doubly now unfolded feels
That which itself reveals;
Double the world of all that may appear
To eye or hand or ear;
Double the soul of that which apprehends
By that which sense transcends.

For deep the cave of human consciousness;
The thoughts, like light, upon its depths may press,
Seeking and finding wonders numberless;
But never may they altogether pierce
The hollow gloom so sensitive and fierce
Of the deep bosom: far the light may reach,
There is a depth unreached; in clearest speech
There is an echo from an unknown place:
And in the dim, unknown, untrodden space

RICHARD WATSON DIXON

Our life is hidden; were we all self-known,
No longer should we live; a wonder shown
Is wonderful no more; and being flies
For ever from its own self-scrutinies.
Here is the very effort of the soul
To keep itself unmingled, safe, and whole
In changes and the flitting feints of sense:
Here essence holds a calm and sure defence;
It is a guarded shrine and sacred grove,
A fountain hidden where no foot may rove,
A further depth within a sounded sea;
A mirror 'tis from hour to hour left free
By things reflected: and because 'tis so,
Therefore the outer world and all its show
Is as the music of the upper wave
To the deep Ocean in his sunken cave;
A part of its own self, yet but its play,
Which doth the sunbeam and the cloud convey
To central deeps, where in an awful shade
The stormless heart receives the things conveyed,
Knowing the cloud by darkness, and the light
By splendours dying through the infinite.

And being such the soul doth recognize
The doubleness of nature, that there lies
A soul occult in Nature, hidden deep
As lies the soul of man in moveless sleep.
And like a dream
Broken in circumstance and foolish made,
Through which howe'er the future world doth gleam,
And floats a warning to the gathered thought,
Like to a dream,

Through sense and all by sense conveyed,
Into our soul the shadow of that soul
Doth float.
Then are we lifted up erect and whole
In vast confession to that universe
Perceived by us: our soul itself transfers
Thither by instinct sure; it swiftly hails
The mighty spirit similar; it sails
In the divine expansion; it perceives
Tendencies glorious, distant; it enweaves
Itself with excitations more than thought
Unto that soul unveiled and yet unsought.

Ye winds and clouds of light,
Ye lead the soul to God;
The new-born soul that height
With rapturous foot hath trod,
And is received of God:
God doth the soul receive
Which mounts toward Him, and alone would dwell
With Him; though finite with the Infinite,
Though finite, rising with a might
Like to infinitude.
Gently receiving such He doth dispel
All solitary horror with delight,
Honouring the higher mood.

For though the soul pants with fierce ecstasy
The unattainable to grasp, to be
For ever mingled with infinity;
And this in vain, since God Himself withdraws
From human knowledge, e'en as its own laws

Seclude the soul from sense;
Yet not from love He hies;
From love God never flies.
Love is the soul's best sense, which God descries,
Which bares the covert of intelligence:
And, honouring in love the higher mood,
With lovely joys He fills the solitude
Of His own presence, whither trusting Him
The soul hath mounted: lo, it might have found
Utter destruction on this higher ground,
Tenuity of air and swooning dim
For lack of breath; but now it finds hereby
A lovely vesture of infinity,
And ecstasies that nourish ecstasy.
God giveth love to love, and ministers
Substance to substance; life to life He bears.

Therefore, ye winds and ye
High moving clouds of light,
Ye rivers running free,
Thou glory of the sea,
Thou glory of the height,
The gleam beside the bush,
The tremble of the rush,
To me made manifest,
The beauty of the flower
In summer's sunny power,
Portions of entity supreme ye be,
And motions massed upon eternal rest.

Broad breezes, clouds of light,
Thither ye lead the soul,
To this most sacred height
Above the sacred whole:

The azure world is not so fair,
The azure world and all the circling air,
As that true spiritual kingdom known
Unto the spirit only and alone;
  Thither the soul ye bear,
  Oh winds and clouds of light.

Ye winds and clouds of light,
  That bear the soul to God;
The new-born soul that height
  By ecstasy hath trod.

WILLIAM MORRIS

1834–1896

314 *Outlanders, whence come ye last?*

OUTLANDERS, whence come ye last?
  The snow in the street and the wind on the door.
Through what green sea and great have ye passed?
  Minstrels and maids, stand forth on the floor.

From far away, O masters mine,
  The snow in the street and the wind on the door.
We come to bear you goodly wine:
  Minstrels and maids, stand forth on the floor.

From far away we come to you,
  The snow in the street and the wind on the door.
To tell of great tidings strange and true:
  Minstrels and maids, stand forth on the floor.

News, news of the Trinity,
  The snow in the street and the wind on the door.
And Mary and Joseph from over the sea:
  Minstrels and maids, stand forth on the floor.

For as we wandered far and wide,
  The snow in the street and the wind on the door.
What hap do ye deem there should us betide?
  Minstrels and maids, stand forth on the floor.

Under a bent when the night was deep,
  The snow in the street and the wind on the door.
There lay three shepherds tending their sheep:
  Minstrels and maids, stand forth on the floor.

'O ye shepherds, what have ye seen,
  The snow in the street and the wind on the door,
To slay your sorrow and heal your teen?'
  Minstrels and maids, stand forth on the floor.

'In an ox-stall this night we saw,
  The snow in the street and the wind on the door,
A Babe and a maid without a flaw.'
  Minstrels and maids, stand forth on the floor.

'There was an old man there beside,
  The snow in the street and the wind on the door,
His hair was white and his hood was wide.'
  Minstrels and maids, stand forth on the floor.

'And as we gazed this thing upon,
  The snow in the street and the wind on the door,
Those twain knelt down to the Little One.'
  Minstrels and maids, stand forth on the floor.

'And a marvellous song we straight did hear,
  The snow in the street and the wind on the door,
That slew our sorrow and healed our care.'
  Minstrels and maids, stand forth on the floor.

News of a fair and a marvellous thing,
  The snow in the street and the wind on the door.
Nowell, nowell, nowell, we sing!
  Minstrels and maids, stand forth on the floor.

ROBERT WILLIAMS BUCHANAN

1841–1901

315 *Judas Iscariot*

'TWAS the soul of Judas Iscariot,
  Strange, and sad, and tall,
Stood all alone at dead of night
  Before a lighted hall.

And the wold was white with snow,
  And his foot-marks black and damp,
And the ghost of the silvern Moon arose,
  Holding her yellow lamp.

And the icicles were on the eaves,
  And the walls were deep with white,
And the shadows of the guests within
  Pass'd on the window light.

The shadows of the wedding guests
  Did strangely come and go,
And the body of Judas Iscariot
  Lay stretch'd along the snow.

The body of Judas Iscariot
  Lay stretched along the snow;
'Twas the soul of Judas Iscariot
  Ran swiftly to and fro.

To and fro, and up and down,
He ran so swiftly there,
As round and round the frozen Pole
Glideth the lean white bear.

. . . 'Twas the Bridegroom sat at the table-head,
And the lights burnt bright and clear—
'Oh, who is that,' the Bridegroom said,
'Whose weary feet I hear?'

'Twas one looked from the lighted hall
And answer'd soft and slow,
'It is a wolf runs up and down
With a black track in the snow.

The Bridegroom in his robe of white
Sat at the table-head—
'Oh, who is that who moans without?'
The blessèd Bridegroom said.

'Twas one look'd from the lighted hall,
And answer'd fierce and low,
' 'Tis the soul of Judas Iscariot
Gliding to and fro.'

'Twas the soul of Judas Iscariot
Did hush itself and stand,
And saw the Bridegroom at the door
With a light in his hand.

The Bridegroom stood in the open door,
And he was clad in white,
And far within the Lord's Supper
Was spread so broad and bright.

The Bridegroom shaded his eyes and look'd,
  And his face was bright to see—
'What dost thou here at the Lord's Supper
  With thy body's sins?' said he.

'Twas the soul of Judas Iscariot
  Stood black, and sad, and bare—
'I have wander'd many nights and days;
  There is no light elsewhere.'

'Twas the wedding guests cried out within,
  And their eyes were fierce and bright—
'Scourge the soul of Judas Iscariot
  Away into the night!'

The Bridegroom stood in the open door,
  And he waved hands still and slow,
And the third time that he waved his hands
  The air was thick with snow.

And of every flake of falling snow,
  Before it touch'd the ground,
There came a dove, and a thousand doves
  Made sweet sound.

'Twas the body of Judas Iscariot
  Floated away full fleet,
And the wings of the doves that bare it off
  Were like its winding-sheet.

'Twas the Bridegroom stood at the open door,
  And beckon'd, smiling sweet;
'Twas the soul of Judas Iscariot
  Stole in, and fell at his feet.

'The Holy Supper is spread within,
   And the many candles shine,
And I have waited long for thee
   Before I pour'd the wine!'

The supper wine is pour'd at last,
   The lights burn bright and fair,
Iscariot washes the Bridegroom's feet,
   And dries them with his hair.

FREDERIC WILLIAM HENRY MYERS

1843–1901

316 *Surrender to Christ*

SEE, when a fireship in mid ocean blazes
   Lone on the battlefields a swimmer stands,
Looks for a help, and findeth none, and raises
   High for a moment melancholy hands;

Then the sad ship, to her own funeral flaring,
   Holds him no longer in her arms, for he
Simple and strong and desolate and daring
   Leaps to the great embraces of the sea.

So when around me for my soul's affrighting,
   Madly red-litten of the woe within,
Faces of men and deeds of their delighting
   Stare in a lurid cruelty of sin,

Thus as I weary me and long and languish,
   Nowise availing from that pain to part,—
Desperate tides of the whole world's anguish
   Forced through the channels of a single heart,—

Then let me feel how infinite around me
Floats the eternal peace that is to be,
Rush from the demons, for my King has found me,
Leap from the universe and plunge in Thee!

GERARD MANLEY HOPKINS

1844–1889

317 *The Wreck of the Deutschland*

Part I

THOU mastering me
God! giver of breath and bread;
World's strand, sway of the sea;
Lord of living and dead;
Thou hast bound bones and veins in me, fastened me flesh,
And after it almost unmade, what with dread,
Thy doing: and dost thou touch me afresh?
Over again I feel thy finger and find thee.

I did say yes
O at lightning and lashed rod;
Thou heardst me truer than tongue confess
Thy terror, O Christ, O God;
Thou knowest the walls, altar and hour and night:
The swoon of a heart that the sweep and the hurl of thee trod
Hard down with a horror of height:
And the midriff astrain with leaning of, laced with fire of stress.

The frown of his face
Before me, the hurtle of hell
Behind, where, where was a, where was a place?
I whirled out wings that spell

And fled with a fling of the heart to the heart of the Host.
My heart, but you were dovewinged, I can tell,
Carrier-witted, I am bold to boast,
To flash from the flame to the flame then, tower from the grace to the grace.

I am soft sift
In an hourglass—at the wall
Fast, but mined with a motion, a drift,
And it crowds and it combs to the fall;
I steady as a water in a well, to a poise, to a pane,
But roped with, always, all the way down from the tall
Fells or flanks of the voel, a vein
Of the gospel proffer, a pressure, a principle, Christ's gift.

I kiss my hand
To the stars, lovely-asunder
Starlight, wafting him out of it; and
Glow, glory in thunder;
Kiss my hand to the dappled-with-damson west:
Since, tho' he is under the world's splendour and wonder,
His mystery must be instressed, stressed;
For I greet him the days I meet him, and bless when I understand.

Not out of his bliss
Springs the stress felt
Nor first from heaven (and few know this)
Swings the stroke dealt—
Stroke and a stress that stars and storms deliver,
That guilt is hushed by, hearts are flushed by and melt—
But it rides time like riding a river
(And here the faithful waver, the faithless fable and miss).

It dates from day
Of his going in Galilee;
Warm-laid grave of a womb-life grey;
Manger, maiden's knee;
The dense and the driven Passion, and frightful sweat;
Thence the discharge of it, there its swelling to be,
Though felt before, though in high flood yet—
What none would have known of it, only the heart, being
hard at bay,

Is out with it! Oh,
We lash with the best or worst
Word last! How a lush-kept plush-capped sloe
Will, mouthed to flesh-burst,
Gush!—flush the man, the being with it, sour or sweet,
Brim, in a flash, full!—Hither then, last or first,
To hero of Calvary, Christ's feet—
Never ask if meaning it, wanting it, warned of it—men go.

Be adored among men,
God, three-numberèd form;
Wring thy rebel, dogged in den,
Man's malice, with wrecking and storm.
Beyond saying sweet, past telling of tongue,
Thou art lightning and love, I found it, a winter and warm;
Father and fondler of heart thou hast wrung:
Hast thy dark descending and most art merciful then.

With an anvil-ding
And with fire in him forge thy will
Or rather, rather then, stealing as Spring
Through him, melt him but master him still:

Whether at once, as once at a crash Paul,
Or as Austin, a lingering-out sweet skill,
Make mercy in all of us, out of us all
Mastery, but be adored, but be adored King.

318 *God's Grandeur*

THE world is charged with the grandeur of God.
It will flame out, like shining from shook foil;
It gathers to a greatness, like the ooze of oil
Crushed. Why do men then now not reck his rod?
Generations have trod, have trod, have trod;
And all is seared with trade; bleared, smeared with toil;
And wears man's smudge and shares man's smell: the soil
Is bare now, nor can foot feel, being shod.

And for all this, nature is never spent;
There lives the dearest freshness deep down things;
And though the last lights off the black West went
Oh, morning, at the brown brink eastward, springs—
Because the Holy Ghost over the bent
World broods with warm breast and with ah! bright wings.

319 *The Starlight Night*

LOOK at the stars! look, look up at the skies!
O look at all the fire-folk sitting in the air!
The bright boroughs, the circle-citadels there!
Down in dim woods the diamond delves! the elves'-eyes!
The grey lawns cold where gold, where quickgold lies!
Wind-beat whitebeam! airy abeles set on a flare!
Flake-doves sent floating forth at a farmyard scare!—
Ah well! it is all a purchase, all is a prize.

Buy then! bid then!—What?—Prayer, patience, alms, vows.
Look, look: a May-mess, like on orchard boughs!
  Look! March-bloom, like on mealed-with-yellow sallows!
These are indeed the barn; withindoors house
The shocks. This piece-bright paling shuts the spouse
  Christ home, Christ and his mother and all his hallows.

320 *Spring*

NOTHING is so beautiful as spring—
  When weeds, in wheels, shoot long and lovely and lush;
  Thrush's eggs look little low heavens, and thrush
Through the echoing timber does so rinse and wring
The ear, it strikes like lightnings to hear him sing;
  The glassy peartree leaves and blooms, they brush
  The descending blue; that blue is all in a rush
With richness; the racing lambs too have fair their fling.

What is all this juice and all this joy?
  A strain of the earth's sweet being in the beginning
In Eden garden.—Have, get, before it cloy,
  Before it cloud, Christ, lord, and sour with sinning,
Innocent mind and Mayday in girl and boy,
  Most, O maid's child, thy choice and worthy the winning.

321 *The Lantern out of Doors*

SOMETIMES a lantern moves along the night,
  That interests our eyes. And who goes there?
  I think; where from and bound, I wonder, where,
With, all down darkness wide, his wading light?

Men go by me whom either beauty bright
  In mould or mind or what not else makes rare:
  They rain against our much-thick and marsh air
Rich beams, till death or distance buys them quite.

Death or distance soon consumes them: wind
  What most I may eye after, be in at the end
I cannot, and out of sight is out of mind.

Christ minds; Christ's interest, what to avow or amend
  There, éyes them, heart wánts, care haúnts, foot fóllows kínd,
Their ránsom, théir rescue, ánd first, fást, last friénd.

322 *The Candle Indoors*

SOME candle clear burns somewhere I come by.
I muse at how its being puts blissful back
With yellowy moisture mild night's blear-all black,
Or to-fro tender trambeams truckle at the eye.
By that window what task what fingers ply,
I plod wondering, a-wanting, just for lack
Of answer the eagerer a-wanting Jessy or Jack
There, God to aggrándise, God to glorify.—

Come you indoors, come home; your fading fire
Mend first and vital candle in close heart's vault:
You there are master, do your own desire;
What hinders? Are you beam-blind, yet to a fault
In a neighbour deft-handed? are you that liar
And, cast by conscience out, spendsavour salt?

323 *The Blessed Virgin Compared to the Air we Breathe*

WILD air, world-mothering air,
Nestling me everywhere,
That each eyelash or hair
Girdles; goes home betwixt
The fleeciest, frailest-flixed
Snowflake; that's fairly mixed
With, riddles, and is rife
In every least thing's life;
This needful, never spent,
And nursing element;
My more than meat and drink,
My meal at every wink;
This air, which, by life's law,
My lung must draw and draw
Now but to breathe its praise,
Minds me in many ways
Of her who not only
Gave God's infinity
Dwindled to infancy
Welcome in womb and breast,
Birth, milk, and all the rest
But mothers each new grace
That does now reach our race—
Mary Immaculate,
Merely a woman, yet
Whose presence, power is
Great as no goddess's
Was deemèd, dreamèd; who
This one work has to do—

Let all God's glory through,
God's glory which would go
Through her and from her flow
Off, and no way but so.

I say that we are wound
With mercy round and round
As if with air: the same
Is Mary, more by name.
She, wild web, wondrous robe,
Mantles the guilty globe,
Since God has let dispense
Her prayers his providence:
Nay, more than almoner,
The sweet alms' self is her
And men are meant to share
Her life as life does air.
If I have understood,
She holds high motherhood
Towards all our ghostly good
And plays in grace her part
About man's beating heart,
Laying, like air's fine flood,
The deathdance in his blood;
Yet no part but what will
Be Christ our Saviour still.
Of her flesh he took flesh:
He does take fresh and fresh,
Though much the mystery how,
Not flesh but spirit now
And makes, O marvellous!
New Nazareths in us,

Where she shall yet conceive
Him, morning, noon, and eve;
New Bethlems, and he born
There, evening, noon, and morn—
Bethlem or Nazareth,
Men here may draw like breath
More Christ and baffle death;
Who, born so, comes to be
New self and nobler me
In each one and each one
More makes, when all is done,
Both God's and Mary's Son.
  Again, look overhead
How air is azurèd;
O how! nay do but stand
Where you can lift your hand
Skywards: rich, rich it laps
Round the four fingergaps.
Yet such a sapphire-shot,
Charged, steepèd sky will not
Stain light. Yea, mark you this:
It does no prejudice.
The glass-blue days are those
When every colour glows,
Each shape and shadow shows.
Blue be it: this blue heaven
The seven or seven times seven
Hued sunbeam will transmit
Perfect, not alter it.
Or if there does some soft,
On things aloof, aloft,
Bloom breathe, that one breath more

Earth is the fairer for.
Whereas did air not make
This bath of blue and slake
His fire, the sun would shake,
A blear and blinding ball
With blackness bound, and all
The thick stars round him roll
Flashing like flecks of coal,
Quartz-fret, or sparks of salt,
In grimy vasty vault.
  So God was god of old:
A mother came to mould
Those limbs like ours which are
What must make our daystar
Much dearer to mankind;
Whose glory bare would blind
Or less would win man's mind.
Through her we may see him
Made sweeter, not made dim,
And her hand leaves his light
Sifted to suit our sight.

  Be thou then, O thou dear
Mother, my atmosphere;
My happier world, wherein
To wend and meet no sin;
Above me, round me lie
Fronting my froward eye
With sweet and scarless sky;
Stir in my ears, speak there
Of God's love, O live air,
Of patience, penance, prayer:

World-mothering air, air wild,
Wound with thee, in thee isled,
Fold home, fast fold thy child.

324 *'Thou art indeed just'*

THOU art indeed just, Lord, if I contend
With thee; but, sir, so what I plead is just.
Why do sinners' ways prosper? and why must
Disappointment all I endeavour end?
 Wert thou my enemy, O thou my friend,
How wouldst thou worse, I wonder, than thou dost
Defeat, thwart me? Oh, the sots and thralls of lust
Do in spare hours more thrive than I that spend,
Sir, life upon thy cause. See, banks and brakes
Now, leavèd how thick! lacèd they are again
With fretty chervil, look, and fresh wind shakes
Them; birds build—but not I build; no, but strain,
Time's eunuch, and not breed one work that wakes.
Mine, O thou lord of life, send my roots rain.

325 *'Carrion Comfort'*

NOT, I'll not, carrion comfort, Despair, not feast on thee;
Not untwist—slack they may be—these last strands of man
In me ór, most weary, cry *I can no more*. I can;
Can something, hope, wish day come, not choose not to be.
But ah, but O thou terrible, why wouldst thou rude on me

Thy wring-world right foot rock? lay a lionlimb against me? scan
With darksome devouring eyes my bruisèd bones? and fan,
O in turns of tempest, me heaped there; me frantic to avoid thee and flee?

Why? That my chaff might fly; my grain lie, sheer and clear.
Nay in all that toil, that coil, since (seems) I kissed the rod,
Hand rather, my heart lo! lapped strength, stole joy, would laugh, chéer.
Cheer whom though? the hero whose heaven-handling flung me, fóot tród
Me? or me that fought him? O which one? is it each one? That night, that year
Of now done darkness I wretch lay wrestling with (my God!) my God.

ROBERT BRIDGES

(*See also* No. 352.) 1844–1930

326 *Noel: Christmas Eve, 1913*

Pax hominibus bonae voluntatis

A FROSTY Christmas Eve
when the stars were shining
Fared I forth alone
where westward falls the hill,
And from many a village
in the water'd valley
Distant music reach'd me
peals of bells aringing:
The constellated sounds
ran sprinkling on earth's floor
As the dark vault above
with stars was spangled o'er.

Then sped my thought to keep
  that first Christmas of all
When the shepherds watching
  by their folds ere the dawn
Heard music in the fields
  and marveling could not tell
Whether it were angels
  or the bright stars singing.

Now blessed be the tow'rs
  that crown England so fair
That stand up strong in prayer
  unto God for our souls:
Blessed be their founders
  (said I) an' our country folk
Who are ringing for Christ
  in the belfries to-night
With arms lifted to clutch
  the rattling ropes that race
Into the dark above
  and the mad romping din.

But to me heard afar
  it was starry music
Angels' song, comforting
  as the comfort of Christ
When he spake tenderly
  to his sorrowful flock:
The old words came to me
  by the riches of time
Mellow'd and transfigured
  as I stood on the hill
Heark'ning in the aspect
  of th' eternal silence.

DIGBY MACKWORTH DOLBEN

1848–1867

327 *'I asked for Peace'*

I ASKED for Peace—
My sins arose,
And bound me close,
I could not find release.

I asked for Truth—
My doubts came in,
And with their din
They wearied all my youth.

I asked for Love—
My lovers failed,
And griefs assailed
Around, beneath, above.

I asked for Thee—
And Thou didst come
To take me home
Within Thy Heart to be.

328 *'Come to me, beloved'*

COME to me, Belovèd,
Babe of Bethlehem;
Lay aside Thy Sceptre
And Thy Diadem.

Come to me, Belovèd;
Light and healing bring;
Hide my sin and sorrow
Underneath Thy wing.

Bid all fear and doubting
From my soul depart,
As I feel the beating
Of Thy Human Heart.

Look upon me sweetly
With Thy Human Eyes
With Thy Human Finger
Point me to the skies.

Safe from earthly scandal
My poor spirit hide
In the utter stillness
Of Thy wounded Side.

Guide me, ever guide me,
With Thy piercèd Hand,
Till I reach the borders
Of the pleasant land.

Then, my own Belovèd,
Take me home to rest;
Whisper words of comfort;
Lay me on Thy Breast.

Show me not the Glory
Round about Thy Throne;
Show me not the flashes
Of Thy jewelled Crown.

Hide me from the pity
Of the Angels' Band,
Who ever sing Thy praises,
And before Thee stand.

Hide me from the glances
Of the Seraphin,—
They, so pure and spotless,
I, so stained with sin.

Hide me from S. Michael
With his flaming sword:—
Thou can'st understand me,
O my Human Lord!

Jesu, my Belovèd,
Come to me alone;
In Thy sweet embraces
Make me all Thine own.

By the quiet waters,
Sweetest Jesu, lead;
'Mid the virgin lilies,
Purest Jesu, feed.

Only Thee, Belovèd,
Only Thee, I seek.
Thou, the Man Christ Jesus,
Strength in flesh made weak.

MICHAEL FIELD

(Katharine Bradley, 1846–1914, and Edith Cooper, 1862–1913)

329 *'Where the blessed Feet have trod'*

NOT alone in Palestine those blessed Feet have trod,
For I catch their print,
I have seen their dint
On a plot of chalky ground,
Little villas dotted round;

On a sea-worn waste,
Where a priest, in haste,
Passeth with the Blessèd Sacrament to one dying, frail,
Through the yarrow, past the tamarisk, and the plaited snail:
Bright upon the grass I see
Bleeding Feet of Calvary—
And I worship, and I clasp them round!
On this bit of chalky, English ground,
Jesu, Thou art found: my God I hail,
My Lord, my God!

330 *Aridity*

O SOUL, canst thou not understand
Thou art not left alone,
As a dog to howl and moan
His master's absence? Thou art as a book
Left in a room that He forsook,
But returns to by and by,
A book of His dear choice,—
That quiet waiteth for His Hand,
That quiet waiteth for His Eye,
That quiet waiteth for His Voice.

ALICE MEYNELL

1847–1922

331 *In Portugal, 1912*

AND will they cast the altars down,
Scatter the chalice, crush the bread?
In field, in village, and in town
He hides an unregarded head;

Waits in the corn-lands far and near,
Bright in His sun, dark in His frost,
Sweet in the vine, ripe in the ear—
Lonely unconsecrated Host.

In ambush at the merry board,
The Victim lurks unsacrificed;
The mill conceals the harvest's Lord,
The wine-press holds the unbidden Christ.

332 *The Crucifixion*

OH, man's capacity
For spiritual sorrow, corporal pain!
Who has explored the deepmost of that sea,
With heavy links of a far-fathoming chain?

That melancholy lead,
Let down in guilty and in innocent hold,
Yet into childish hands deliverèd,
Leaves the sequestered floor unreached, untold.

One only has explored
The deepmost; but He did not die of it.
Not yet, not yet He died. Man's human Lord
Touched the extreme; it is not infinite.

But over the abyss
Of God's capacity for woe He stayed
One hesitating hour; what gulf was this?
Forsaken He went down, and was afraid.

FRANCIS THOMPSON

1859–1907

333 *The Hound of Heaven*

I FLED Him, down the nights and down the days;
  I fled Him, down the arches of the years;
I fled Him, down the labyrinthine ways
  Of my own mind; and in the mist of tears
I hid from Him, and under running laughter.
        Up vistaed hopes I sped;
        And shot, precipitated,
Adown Titanic glooms of chasmed fears,
  From those strong Feet that followed, followed after.
        But with unhurrying chase,
        And unperturbèd pace,
    Deliberate speed, majestic instancy,
        They beat—and a Voice beat
        More instant than the Feet—
    'All things betray thee, who betrayest Me.'

          I pleaded, outlaw-wise,
  By many a hearted casement, curtained red,
    Trellised with intertwining charities;
  (For, though I knew His love Who followèd,
          Yet was I sore adread
  Lest, having Him, I must have naught beside)
  But, if one little casement parted wide,
    The gust of His approach would clash it to:
    Fear wist not to evade, as Love wist to pursue.
  Across the margent of the world I fled,
    And troubled the gold gateways of the stars,
    Smiting for shelter on their clangèd bars;
          Fretted to dulcet jars

And silvern chatter the pale ports o' the moon.
I said to Dawn: Be sudden—to Eve: Be soon;
With thy young skiey blossoms heap me over
From this tremendous Lover—
Float thy vague veil about me, lest He see!
I tempted all His servitors, but to find
My own betrayal in their constancy,

In faith to Him their fickleness to me,
Their traitorous trueness, and their loyal deceit.
To all swift things for swiftness did I sue;
Clung to the whistling mane of every wind.
But whether they swept, smoothly fleet,
The long savannahs of the blue;
Or whether, Thunder-driven,
They clanged his chariot 'thwart a heaven,
Plashy with flying lightnings round the spurn o' their feet:—
Fear wist not to evade as Love wist to pursue.
Still with unhurrying chase,
And unperturbèd pace,
Deliberate speed, majestic instancy,
Came on the following Feet,
And a Voice above their beat—
'Naught shelters thee, who wilt not shelter Me.'

I sought no more that after which I strayed
In face of man or maid;
But still within the little children's eyes
Seems something, something that replies,
They at least are for me, surely for me!
I turned me to them very wistfully;
But just as their young eyes grew sudden fair
With dawning answers there,

Their angel plucked them from me by the hair.
'Come then, ye other children, Nature's—share
With me' (said I) 'your delicate fellowship;
Let me greet you lip to lip,
Let me twine with you caresses,
Wantoning
With our Lady-Mother's vagrant tresses,
Banqueting
With her in her wind-walled palace,
Underneath her azured daïs,
Quaffing, as your taintless way is,
From a chalice
Lucent-weeping out of the dayspring.'
So it was done:
I in their delicate fellowship was one—
Drew the bolt of Nature's secrecies.
I knew all the swift importings
On the wilful face of skies;
I knew how the clouds arise
Spumèd of the wild sea-snortings;
All that's born or dies
Rose and drooped with; made them shapers
Of mine own moods, or wailful or divine;
With them joyed and was bereaven.
I was heavy with the even,
When she lit her glimmering tapers
Round the day's dead sanctities.
I laughed in the morning's eyes.
I triumphed and I saddened with all weather,
Heaven and I wept together,
And its sweet tears were salt with mortal mine;
Against the red throb of its sunset-heart

I laid my own to beat,
And share commingling heat;
But not by that, by that, was eased my human smart.
In vain my tears were wet on Heaven's grey cheek.
For ah! we know not what each other says,
These things and I; in sound *I* speak—
Their sound is but their stir, they speak by silences.
Nature, poor stepdame, cannot slake my drouth;
Let her, if she would owe me,
Drop yon blue bosom-veil of sky, and show me
The breasts o' her tenderness:
Never did any milk of hers once bless
My thirsting mouth.
Nigh and nigh draws the chase,
With unperturbèd pace,
Deliberate speed, majestic instancy;
And past those noisèd Feet
A Voice comes yet more fleet—
'Lo! naught contents thee, who content'st not Me.'

Naked I wait Thy love's uplifted stroke!
My harness piece by piece Thou hast hewn from me,
And smitten me to my knee;
I am defenceless utterly.
I slept, methinks, and woke,
And, slowly gazing, find me stripped in sleep.
In the rash lustihead of my young powers,
I shook the pillaring hours
And pulled my life upon me; grimed with smears,
I stand amid the dust o' the mounded years—
My mangled youth lies dead beneath the heap.
My days have crackled and gone up in smoke,

Have puffed and burst as sun-starts on a stream.
        Yea, faileth now even dream
The dreamer, and the lute the lutanist;
Even the linked fantasies, in whose blossomy twist
I swung the earth a trinket at my wrist,
Are yielding; cords of all too weak account
For earth with heavy griefs so overplussed.
        Ah! is Thy love indeed
A weed, albeit an amaranthine weed,
Suffering no flowers except its own to mount?
        Ah! must—
        Designer infinite!—
Ah! must Thou char the wood ere Thou canst limn with it?
My freshness spent its wavering shower i' the dust;
And now my heart is as a broken fount,
Wherein tear-drippings stagnate, spilt down ever
        From the dank thoughts that shiver
Upon the sighful branches of my mind.
        Such is; what is to be?
The pulp so bitter, how shall taste the rind?
I dimly guess what Time in mists confounds;
Yet ever and anon a trumpet sounds
From the hid battlements of Eternity;
Those shaken mists a space unsettle, then
Round the half-glimpsèd turrets slowly wash again.
        But not ere him who summoneth
        I first have seen, enwound
With glooming robes purpureal, cypress-crowned;
His name I know, and what his trumpet saith.
Whether man's heart or life it be which yields
        Thee harvest, must Thy harvest-fields
        Be dunged with rotten death?

Now of that long pursuit
Comes on at hand the bruit;
That Voice is round me like a bursting sea:
'And is thy earth so marred,
Shattered in shard on shard?
Lo, all things fly thee, for thou fliest Me!
Strange, piteous, futile thing!
Wherefore should any set thee love apart?
Seeing none but I makes much of naught' (He said),
'And human love needs human meriting:
How hast thou merited—
Of all man's clotted clay the dingiest clot?
Alack, thou knowest not
How little worthy of any love thou art!
Whom wilt thou find to love ignoble thee,
Save Me, save only Me?
All which I took from thee I did but take,
Not for thy harms,
But just that thou might'st seek it in My arms.
All which thy child's mistake
Fancies as lost, I have stored for thee at home:
Rise, clasp My hand, and come!'

Halts by me that footfall:
Is my gloom, after all,
Shade of His hand, outstretched caressingly?
'Ah, fondest, blindest, weakest,
I am He Whom thou seekest!
Thou dravest love from thee, who dravest Me.'

334 *The Kingdom of God*

'In no Strange Land'

O WORLD invisible, we view thee,
O world intangible, we touch thee,
O world unknowable, we know thee,
Inapprehensible, we clutch thee!

Does the fish soar to find the ocean,
The eagle plunge to find the air—
That we ask of the stars in motion
If they have rumour of thee there?

Not where the wheeling systems darken,
And our benumbed conceiving soars!—
The drift of pinions, would we hearken,
Beats at our own clay-shuttered doors.

The angels keep their ancient places;—
Turn but a stone, and start a wing!
'Tis ye, 'tis your estrangèd faces,
That miss the many-splendoured thing.

But (when so sad thou canst not sadder)
Cry;—and upon thy so sore loss
Shall shine the traffic of Jacob's ladder
Pitched betwixt Heaven and Charing Cross.

Yea, in the night, my Soul, my daughter,
Cry,—clinging Heaven by the hems;
And lo, Christ walking on the water
Not of Gennesareth, but Thames!

MARY ELIZABETH COLERIDGE

1861–1907

335 *'There was no Place found'*

ONE night, as dreaming on my bed I lay,
I saw the whole world die and pass away.

Young men and old, true lover and fair maid
Passed, in an endless passing, unafraid.

And as they went, each to his radiant home,
They hailed me after, calling to me, 'Come!'

Some sought a land of living light, where none
Remembers more the shining of the sun.

Some sought a land of living light, and there
Longed for the dark, to hide their bright despair.

At last I lay upon the ground alone.
No voice; the empty silence cried, 'Begone!'

Then I arose and turned about to flee.
On either hand there was no place for me.

The shining ones said sadly, 'All too late!
None enter Heaven but through the narrow gate.'

The fiery ones said sadly, 'All too fast!
There is no need of Hell, while Earth shall last.'

336 *'I saw a Stable'*

I SAW a stable, low and very bare,
  A little child in a manger.
The oxen knew Him, had Him in their care,
  To men He was a stranger.
The safety of the world was lying there,
  And the world's danger.

MARY COLERIDGE

337 'Lord of the Winds'

LORD of the winds, I cry to Thee,
I that am dust,
And blown about by every gust
I fly to Thee.

Lord of the waters, unto Thee I call.
I that am weed upon the waters borne,
And by the waters torn,
Tossed by the waters, at Thy feet I fall.

LIONEL JOHNSON

1867–1902

338 Te Martyrum Candidatus

AH, see the fair chivalry come, the companions of Christ!
White Horsemen, who ride on white horses, the Knights of God!
They, for their Lord and their Lover who sacrificed
All, save the sweetness of treading, where He first trod!

These, through the darkness of death, the dominion of night,
Swept, and they woke in white places at morning tide:
They saw with their eyes, and sang for joy of the sight,
They saw with their eyes the Eyes of the Crucified.

Now, whithersoever He goeth, with Him they go:
White Horsemen, who ride on white horses, oh, fair to see!
They ride, where the Rivers of Paradise flash and flow,
White Horsemen, with Christ their Captain: for ever He!

JOSEPH HILAIRE BELLOC

b. 1870

339 'Because my faltering Feet'

BECAUSE my faltering feet may fail to dare
The first descendant of the steps of Hell
Give me the Word in time that triumphs there.
I too must pass into the misty hollow
Where all our living laughter stops: and hark!
The tiny stuffless voices of the dark
Have called me, called me, till I needs must follow:
Give me the Word and I'll attempt it well.

Say it 's the little winking of an eye
Which in that issue is uncurtained quite;
A little sleep that helps a moment by
Between the thin dawn and the large daylight.
Ah! tell me more than yet was hoped of men;
Swear that 's true now, and I'll believe it then.

340 The Prophet lost in the hills at Evening

STRONG God which made the topmost stars
To circulate and keep their course,
Remember me; whom all the bars
Of sense and dreadful fate enforce.

Above me in your heights and tall,
Impassable the summits freeze,
Below the haunted waters call
Impassable beyond the trees.

I hunger and I have no bread.
  My gourd is empty of the wine.
Surely the footsteps of the dead
  Are shuffling softly close to mine!

It darkens. I have lost the ford.
  There is a change on all things made.
The rocks have evil faces, Lord,
  And I am awfully afraid.

Remember me: the Voids of Hell
  Expand enormous all around.
Strong friend of souls, Emmanuel,
  Redeem me from accursed ground.

The long descent of wasted days,
  To these at last have led me down;
Remember that I filled with praise
The meaningless and doubtful ways
  That lead to an eternal town.

I challenged and I kept the Faith,
  The bleeding path alone I trod;
It darkens. Stand about my wraith,
  And harbour me—almighty God.

GILBERT KEITH CHESTERTON

1874–1936

341 *King Alfred answers the Danes*

'WHEN God put man in a garden
  He girt him with a sword,
And sent him forth a free knight
  That might betray his lord;

'He brake Him and betrayed Him,
  And fast and far he fell,
Till you and I may stretch our necks
  And burn our beards in hell.

'But though I lie on the floor of the world,
  With the seven sins for rods,
I would rather fall with Adam
  Than rise with all your gods.

'What have the strong gods given?
  Where have the glad gods led?
When Guthrum sits on a hero's throne
  And asks if he is dead?

'Sirs, I am but a nameless man,
  A rhymester without home,
Yet since I come of the Wessex clay
  And carry the cross of Rome,

'I will even answer the mighty earl
  That asked of Wessex men
Why they be meek and monkish folk,
And bow to the White Lord's broken yoke;
What sign have we save blood and smoke?
  Here is my answer then.

'That on you is fallen the shadow,
  And not upon the Name;
That though we scatter and though we fly,
And you hang over us like the sky,
You are more tired of victory,
  Than we are tired of shame.

'That though you hunt the Christian man
   Like a hare on the hill-side,
The hare has still more heart to run
   Than you have heart to ride.

'That though all lances split on you,
   All swords be heaved in vain,
We have more lust again to lose
   Than you to win again.

'Your lord sits high in the saddle,
   A broken-hearted king,
But our king Alfred, lost from fame,
Fallen among foes or bonds of shame,
In I know not what mean trade or name,
   Has still some song to sing;

'Our monks go robed in rain and snow,
   But the heart of flame therein,
But you go clothed in feasts and flames,
   When all is ice within;

'Nor shall all iron dooms make dumb
   Men wondering ceaselessly,
If it be not better to fast for joy
   Than feast for misery.

'Nor monkish order only
   Slides down, as field to fen,
All things achieved and chosen pass,
As the White Horse fades in the grass,
   No work of Christian men.

'Ere the sad gods that made your gods
  Saw their sad sunrise pass,
The White Horse of the White Horse Vale,
That you have left to darken and fail,
  Was cut out of the grass.

'Therefore your end is on you,
  Is on you and your kings,
Not for a fire in Ely fen,
Not that your gods are nine or ten,
But because it is only Christian men
  Guard even heathen things.

'For our God hath blessed creation,
  Calling it good. I know
What spirit with whom you blindly band
Hath blessed destruction with his hand;
Yet by God's death the stars shall stand
  And the small apples grow.'

Ballad of the White Horse.

342 *Hymn for the Church Militant*

GREAT God, that bowest sky and star,
  Bow down our towering thoughts to thee,
And grant us in a faltering war
  The firm feet of humility.

Lord, we that snatch the swords of flame,
  Lord, we that cry about Thy ear,
We too are weak with pride and shame,
  We too are as our foemen are.

Yea, we are mad as they are mad,
   Yea, we are blind as they are blind,
Yea, we are very sick and sad
   Who bring good news to all mankind.

The dreadful joy Thy Son has sent
   Is heavier than any care;
We find, as Cain his punishment,
   Our pardon more than we can bear.

Lord, when we cry Thee far and near
   And thunder through all lands unknown
The gospel into every ear,
   Lord, let us not forget our own.

Cleanse us from ire of creed or class,
   The anger of the idle kings;
Sow in our souls, like living grass,
   The laughter of all lowly things.

CHARLES WILLIAMS

b. 1886

343 ### *At the 'Ye that do truly'*

NOW are our prayers divided, now
   Must you go lonelily, and I;
For penitence shall disallow
Communion and propinquity.

Together we commandments heard,
Paid tithes together and professed:
Now mourns a solitary word
Where solitary deeds transgressed.

CHARLES WILLIAMS

Averted be that head of grace,
And turned those melancholy eyes
To weep, within a narrow place
And shadow of iniquities.

Farewell! we may no more be kind,
Nor either ease the other's breath;
Death shall our marriage vows unbind,
Death, and this sharp foretaste of death.

Farewell! before this hour is done
We shall have met or missed, my dear,
In a remoter union,
But now the solitudes are here.

THOMAS STEARNS ELIOT

b. 1888

344 *From 'Ash Wednesday'*

(i)

BECAUSE I do not hope to turn again
Because I do not hope
Because I do not hope to turn
Desiring this man's gift and that man's scope
I no longer strive to strive towards such things
(Why should the agèd eagle stretch its wings?)
Why should I mourn
The vanished power of the usual reign?

Because I do not hope to know again
The infirm glory of the positive hour
Because I do not think
Because I know I shall not know

The one veritable transitory power
Because I cannot drink
There, where trees flower, and springs flow, for there is
    nothing again

Because I know that time is always time
And place is always and only place
And what is actual is actual only for one time
And only for one place

I rejoice that things are as they are and
I renounce the blessèd face
And renounce the voice
Because I cannot hope to turn again
Consequently I rejoice, having to construct something
Upon which to rejoice

And pray to God to have mercy upon us
And I pray that I may forget
These matters that with myself I too much discuss
Too much explain
Because I do not hope to turn again
Let these words answer
For what is done, not to be done again
May the judgement not be too heavy upon us

Because these wings are no longer wings to fly
But merely vans to beat the air
The air which is now thoroughly small and dry
Smaller and dryer than the will
Teach us to care and not to care
Teach us to sit still.

Pray for us sinners now and at the hour of our death
Pray for us now and at the hour of our death.

(ii)

If the lost word is lost, if the spent word is spent
If the unheard, unspoken
Word is unspoken, unheard;
Still is the unspoken word, the Word unheard,
The Word within a word, the Word within
The world and for the world;
And the light shone in darkness and
Against the World the unstilled world still whirled
About the centre of the silent Word.

O my people, what have I done unto thee.

Where shall the word be found, where will the word
Resound? Not here, there is not enough silence
Not on the sea or on the islands, not
On the mainland, in the desert or the rain land,
For those who walk in darkness
Both in the day time and in the night time
The right time and the right place are not here
No place of grace for those who avoid the face
No time to rejoice for those who walk among noise and deny
the voice.

Will the veiled sister pray for
Those who walk in darkness, who chose thee and oppose
thee,
Those who are torn on the horn between season and season,
time and time, between
Hour and hour, word and word, power and power, those
who wait

In darkness? Will the veiled sister pray
For children at the gate
Who will not go away and cannot pray:
Pray for those who chose and oppose

O my people, what have I done unto thee.

Will the veiled sister between the slender
Yew trees pray for those who offend her
And are terrified and cannot surrender
And affirm before the world and deny between the rocks
In the last desert between the last blue rocks
The desert in the garden the garden in the desert
Of drouth, spitting from the mouth the withered apple-seed.

O my people.

345 *A Song for Simeon*

LORD, the Roman hyacinths are blooming in bowls and
The winter sun creeps by the snow hills;
The stubborn reason has made stand.
My life is light, waiting for the death wind,
Like a feather on the back of my hand.
Dust in sunlight and memory in corners
Wait for the wind that chills towards the dead land.

Grant us thy peace.
I have walked many years in this city,
Kept faith and fast, provided for the poor,
Have given and taken honour and ease.
There went never any rejected from my door.

Who shall remember my house, where shall live my children's
children
When the time of sorrow is come?
They will take to the goat's path, and the fox's home,
Fleeing from the foreign faces and the foreign swords.

Before the time of cords and scourges and lamentation
Grant us thy peace.
Before the stations of the mountain of desolation,
Before the certain hour of maternal sorrow,
Now at this birth season of decease,
Let the Infant, the still unspeaking and unspoken Word,
Grant Israel's consolation
To one who has eighty years and no to-morrow.

According to thy word.
They shall praise Thee and suffer in every generation
With glory and derision,
Light upon light, mounting the saints' stair.
Not for me the martyrdom, the ecstasy of thought and prayer,
Not for me the ultimate vision.
Grant me thy peace
(And a sword shall pierce thy heart,
Thine also).
I am tired with my own life and the lives of those after me,
I am dying in my own death and the deaths of those after me.
Let thy servant depart,
Having seen thy salvation.

346 *From 'The Rock'*

(i)

I have known two worlds, I have known two worlds of
  death.
All that you suffer, I have suffered before.
Does the spring change, does the bird's wing change, does the
  fly alter
Its purpose since the amber-time, the old time?
There shall always be the Church and the World
And the Heart of Man
Shivering and fluttering between them, choosing and chosen,
Valiant, ignoble, dark, and full of light
Swinging between Hell Gate and Heaven Gate.
And the Gates of Hell shall not prevail.
Darkness now, then
  Light.

(ii)

In the beginning GOD created the world. Waste and void.
Waste and void. And darkness was upon the face of the
  deep.
And when there were men, in their various ways, they
  struggled in torment towards GOD
Blindly and vainly, for man is a vain thing, and man without
  GOD is a seed upon the wind: driven this way and that,
  and finding no place of lodgement and germination.
They followed the light and the shadow, and the light led
  them forward to light and the shadow led them to
  darkness,

Worshipping snakes or trees, worshipping devils rather than nothing: crying for life beyond life, for ecstasy not of the flesh.
Waste and void. Waste and void. And darkness on the face of the deep.

And the Spirit moved upon the face of the water.
And men who turned towards the light and were known of the light
Invented the Higher Religions; and the Higher Religions were good
And led men from light to light, to knowledge of Good and Evil.
But their light was ever surrounded and shot with darkness
As the air of temperate seas is pierced by the still dead breath of the Arctic Current;
And they came to an end, a dead end stirred with a flicker of life,
And they came to the withered ancient look of a child that has died of starvation.
Prayer wheels, worship of the dead, denial of this world, affirmation of rites with forgotten meanings
In the restless wind-whipped sand, or the hills where the wind will not let the snow rest.
Waste and void. Waste and void. And darkness on the face of the deep.

Then came, at a predetermined moment, a moment in time and of time,
A moment not out of time, but in time, in what we call history: transecting, bisecting the world of time, a moment in time but not like a moment of time,

A moment in time but time was made through that moment:
  for without the meaning there is no time, and that
  moment of time gave the meaning.
Then it seemed as if men must proceed from light to light,
  in the light of the Word,
Through the Passion and Sacrifice saved in spite of their
  negative being;
Bestial as always before, carnal, self-seeking as always before,
  selfish and purblind as ever before,
Yet always struggling, always reaffirming, always resuming
  their march on the way that was lit by the light;
Often halting, loitering, straying, delaying, returning, yet
  following no other way.
But it seems that something has happened that has never
  happened before: though we know not just when, or
  why, or how, or where.
Men have left GOD not for other gods, they say, but for no
  god; and this has never happened before
That men both deny gods and worship gods, professing first
  Reason,
And then Money, and Power, and what they call Life, or
  Race, or Dialectic.
The Church disowned, the tower overthrown, the bells up-
  turned, what have we to do
But stand with empty hands and palms turned upwards
In an age which advances progressively backwards?

(iii)

O Light Invisible, we praise Thee!
Too bright for mortal vision.
O Greater Light, we praise Thee for the less

THOMAS STEARNS ELIOT

The eastern light our spires touch at morning,
The light that slants upon our western doors at evening,
The twilight over stagnant pools at batflight,
Moon light and star light, owl and moth light,
Glow-worm glowlight on a grassblade.
O Light Invisible, we worship Thee!

We thank Thee for the lights that we have kindled,
The light of altar and of sanctuary;
Small lights of those who meditate at midnight
And lights directed through the coloured panes of windows
And light reflected from the polished stone,
The gilded carven wood, the coloured fresco.
Our gaze is submarine, our eyes look upward
And see the light that fractures through unquiet water.
We see the light but see not whence it comes.
O Light Invisible, we glorify Thee!

In our rhythm of earthly life we tire of light. We are glad when the day ends, when the play ends; and ecstasy is too much pain.
We are children quickly tired: children who are up in the night and fall asleep as the rocket is fired; and the day is long for work or play.
We tire of distraction or concentration, we sleep and are glad to sleep,
Controlled by the rhythm of blood and the day and the night and the seasons.
And we must extinguish the candle, put out the light and relight it;
Forever must quench, forever relight the flame.

Therefore we thank Thee for our little light, that is dappled with shadow.
We thank Thee who hast moved us to building, to finding, to forming at the ends of our fingers and beams of our eyes.
And when we have built an altar to the Invisible Light, we may set thereon the little lights for which our bodily vision is made.
And we thank Thee that darkness reminds us of light.
O Light Invisible, we give Thee thanks for Thy great glory!

WILLIAM FORCE STEAD

b. 1889

347 *From 'Uriel'*

(i)

Reach forth Thy hand!
Sunder the clouds, for we have lost our way;
Reach forth Thy hand and guide us thro' this darkness.
Thou in Thy wisdom having dwelt in us,
Thou wilt not with Thy kindred heart condemn us
To know Thee once, once only, and only a little,
Nor wilt Thou in Thy justice, when our hearts
Respond, and long to know Thee more and more,
Wither us into dust and nothingness.
A homeless dog looked up to me, as I
Look up to Thee, he came and trusted me,
Tho' strange my ways to him past finding out;
Strange are Thy ways to me, but I am glad
We three are kinsmen, and Thou art to me
As I am to the friendship-craving beast.

We trust; but then the freezing shadow falls,
Our vision fails, we cannot understand;
Even the Heart of the World, nailed to the Cross,
Cried out, 'Forsaken!'—but never was forsaken;
He died, He lives, with nothing lost, all gained.

I see Thee putting forth Thy hand to write
A crimson line above the western hills,
And here, in night's cottage, we detained can tell
Where Thy great sun, in strength undimmed, rides on
Beyond the cloud-thatched eaves of dying day.

(Pt. V, section 1.)

(ii)

Praise, then, to Uriel, who in unlikely places,
The drab, the scarred, the flesh-pot Mammon Land,
By striking silvery chords within us, startles
The torpor of self-content, wakens desires
Not to be satisfied as men appease
Hunger of food or sex or market gain;
Praise, then, to Uriel, who in unlikely places
Wakens the unsuspected otherness
That lives to give, not to receive, and flowers
In loveliness of carven stone and marble,
When men build outwardly the hidden intent
Of Uriel in their hearts. So did they build
When fairer than the moon upon the hills
White over Athens the Parthenon arose,
And many a sea-girt island snowed the water
With gleam of fluted shaft and sculptured frieze.
From age to age, and land to land, Thy light
Dawned in the mind, and moved men's hearts and hands,

Until from hearts enlarged and willing hands,
Moving as Thou didst move within them, came
Thy inward image visibly issuing forth
In Notre-Dame, in Peter's Dome and Paul's.
O Uriel, I have walked in these amazed
To find they opened into Thee,—amazed
At earth's transfiguration: stone that lay
Inert and meaningless, here lifted up,
Climbing and soaring after Thee, or taught
To stand in pillared strength, or wreathed in knots
Of clustered thought, or arched in endless prayer;
Inert and meaningless, crude stone transformed,
Under the hand of man, Uriel guiding,
With vista after vista into Thee,
Ever enduring beautiful Spirit serene.
Amazed I saw, for I had thought that Thou
Delightest only to reveal Thyself
In native growth of wood and field; but here
Thou buildest Thyself a temple made with hands,
As truly Thy native budding forth as any
Meadow blossom, or mountain oak or pine;
Built of Thine own, but under human hands,
Thou both in outward world and inward soul
Immanent, only in one made visible,
Or as the other traces out these lines
Of our desire in Thy revealed design.
We enter and we recognize ourselves
Raised to our pure ideal, and in it find
Promptings of destiny; mine to achieve
This loftiness and this unbroken peace,
Peace not of death, but purpose long upheld,
And balance well adjusted, well sustained;

WILLIAM FORCE STEAD

My body from the earth, mine to achieve
This ordered beauty; out in the rasping street,
Chaos jolts on and jars; here Worship dwells,
Confident, self-collected, self-secure;
Unresting Time finds here his resting-place,
Unchanged, yet not monotonously the same,
For here the morning and the evening lights
Have their interpretation; mine to attain
This varied constancy; mine to achieve
Such friendship as these walls,—tho' self-contained,
Not life-excluding, for other lives come in,
As to their centre, give their best, receive
More than they give, and strengthened go their way.
Here noon is darkened, that the inward eye
May shine; the outward sun, shorn of his glare,
Delayed by coloured panes, glows glorified.
Darkness and shadows are but wings that veil
Thy burning point of brightness over-bright.
There, in the Sanctuary, where all lines converge,
There, in the darkness, where the angels tremble,
Thou, beyond time, yet, in Thy Tabernacle,
Dwellest in time, and Thou, beyond all space,
Without circumference, art drawn into a point,—
Thou meaning and Thou secret of the whole!
So may I find Thee burning in my heart,
As there, the witness to Thy Presence, swung
High on a golden chain in quiet darkness,
All night Thy dedicated lamp burns on.

(Pt. IV, section 3.)

FREDEGOND SHOVE

b. 1889

348 *The New Ghost*

'And he casting away his garment rose and came to Jesus.'

AND he cast it down, down, on the green grass,
Over the young crocuses, where the dew was—
He cast the garment of his flesh that was full of death,
And like a sword his spirit showed out of the cold sheath.

He went a pace or two, he went to meet his Lord,
And, as I said, his spirit looked like a clean sword,
And seeing him the naked trees began shivering,
And all the birds cried out aloud as it were late spring.

And the Lord came on, He came down, and saw
That a soul was waiting there for Him, one without flaw,
And they embraced in the churchyard where the robins play,
And the daffodils hang their heads, as they burn away.

The Lord held his head fast, and you could see
That He kissed the unsheathed ghost that was gone free—
As a hot sun, on a March day, kisses the cold ground;
And the spirit answered, for he knew well that his peace was found.

The spirit trembled, and sprang up at the Lord's word—
As on a wild, April day, springs up a small bird—
So the ghost's feet lifting him up, he kissed the Lord's cheek,
And for the greatness of their love neither of them could speak.

But the Lord went then, to show him the way,
Over the young crocuses, under the green may
That was not quite in flower yet—to a far-distant land;
And the ghost followed, like a naked cloud holding the sun's hand.

RUTH PITTER

b. 1897

349 *A Solemn Meditation*

THESE discords and these warring tongues are gales
Of the great autumn: how shall winter be?
Of love, of summer speak not; rather pray
That in the warmer vales
Some may survive: that some winged seeds may flee
Into the mountains far away,
That such may see
Their spring, and spread their green in unimagined day.

Think not that I complain, that I must go
Under the ground, unblossomed, unfulfilled;
Though our stem freeze, in the earth's bosom I
And you sleep: under snow
We shall be saved, though winter blow so wild
That not a tree remain under the sky:
This hydra life will not take no,
More withering now, more blossoming by and by.

It goes down to the nadir: never fear,
Down to the dark, go down, as deep as hell:
The swift fall wings the ascent: close eyes
And hurl head down and sheer
Into the black of life unfathomable;
Down to the nethermost dive: the prize
Only to him who the night-hemisphere
Can girdle like the sun: gone! it is well.

Naked upon the bosom of my God,
Bereft of all save the Unmanifest,
My blossom nipped and my leaf shorn,
In the great bitter dark I touch his breast:

Praise him that I was born,
Cast in the utter gulf those rags and weeds,
My ruined hopes, my summer's short delight,
And my abortive deeds,
Even as children leave their toys at night.

Perusing death with these shade-coloured eyes,
I have surprised the secret of the strong,
Drunk of the nether springs of fearlessness;
Stolen the knowledge of the wise:
Seen where the great rocks and glooms among
The rubied treasure burns in its recess;
Fallen, have fought and thrust
My way to where the immortal lies enwombed in dust.

Then Alleluia all my gashes cry;
My woe springs up and flourishes from the tomb
In her Lord's likeness terrible and fair;
Knowing her root, her blossom in the sky
She rears: now flocking to her branches come
The paradisal birds of upper air,
Which Alleluia cry, and cry again,
And death from out the grave replies Amen.

350 *Help, Good Shepherd*

TURN not aside, Shepherd, to see
How bright the constellations are,
Hanging in heaven, or on the tree;
The skyborn or terrestrial star

Brood not upon; the waters fleet,
Willows, or thy crown-destined thorn,
Full of her rubies, as is meet,
Or whitening in the eye of morn,

Pause not beside: shepherds' delight,
The pipe and tabor in the vale,
And mirthful watchfires of a night,
And herdsman's rest in wattled pale,

Forsake, though dearly earned: and still
Sound with thy crook the darkling flood,
Still range the sides of shelvy hill
And call about in underwood:

For on the hill are many strayed,
Some held in thickets plunge and cry,
And the deep waters make us afraid.
Come then and help us, or we die.

351 *To J. S. Collis*

LIVE unlamenting though obscure remaining:
be as the bird that in the desolate places
feeds her two young, and man-unheard is heard still
to her God crying.

Die unaccursed though the universal
curse be abroad: for of her God remembered
though the world burn, the spirit as a bird shall
flee to her mountain.

ROBERT BRIDGES

1844–1930

(*See also* No. 326.)

352 *From 'The Testament of Beauty'*

'TWAS at thatt hour of beauty when the setting sun
squandereth his cloudy bed with rosy hues, to flood
his lov'd works as in turn he biddeth them Good-night;
and all the towers and temples and mansions of men
face him in bright farewell, ere they creep from their pomp
naked beneath the darkness;—while to mortal eyes
'tis given, ifso they close not of fatigue, nor strain
at lamplit tasks—'tis given, as for a royal boon
to beggarly outcasts in homeless vigil, to watch
where uncurtain'd behind the great windows of space
Heav'n's jewel'd company circleth unapproachably—
'Twas at sunset that I, fleeing to hide my soul
in refuge of beauty from a mortal distress,
walk'd alone with the Muse in her garden of thought,
discoursing at liberty with the mazy dreams
that came wavering pertinaciously about me; as when
the small bats, issued from their hangings, flitter o'erhead
thru' the summer twilight, with thin cries to and fro
hunting in muffled flight atween the stars and flowers.
Then fell I in strange delusion, illusion strange to tell;
for as a man who lyeth fast asleep in his bed
may dream he waketh, and that he walketh upright
pursuing some endeavour in full conscience—so 'twas
with me; but contrawise; for being in truth awake
methought I slept and dreamt; and in thatt dream methought
I was telling a dream; nor telling was I as one
who, truly awaked from a true sleep, thinketh to tell
his dream to a friend, but for his scant remembrances
findeth no token of speech—it was not so with me;

for my tale was my dream and my dream the telling,
and I remember wondring the while I told it
how I told it so tellingly. And yet now 'twould seem
that Reason inveigled me with her old orderings;
as once when she took thought to adjust theology,
peopling the inane that vex'd her between God and man
with a hierarchy of angels; like those asteroids
wherewith she later fill'd the gap 'twixt Jove and Mars.
Verily by Beauty it is that we come at WISDOM,
yet not by Reason at Beauty: and now with many words
pleasing myself betimes I am fearing lest in the end
I play the tedious orator who maundereth on
for lack of heart to make an end of his nothings.
Wherefor as when a runner who hath run his round
handeth his staff away, and is glad of his rest,
here break I off, knowing the goal was not for me
the while I ran on telling of what cannot be told.

For not the Muse herself can tell of Goddes love;
which cometh to the child from the Mother's embrace,
an Idea spacious as the starry firmament's
inescapable infinity of radiant gaze,
that fadeth only as it outpasseth mortal sight:
and this direct contact is 't with eternities,
this springtide miracle of the soul's nativity
that oft hath set philosophers adrift in dream;
which thing Christ taught, when he set up a little child
to teach his first Apostles and to accuse their pride,
saying, *Unless ye shall receive it as a child,*
ye cannot enter into the kingdom of heaven.
So thru'out all his young mental apprenticehood
the child of very simplicity, and in the grace

and beauteous attitude of infantine wonder,
is apt to absorb Ideas in primal purity,
and by the assimilation of thatt immortal food
may build immortal life; but ever with the growth
of understanding, as the sensible images
are more and more corrupt, troubled by questioning thought,
or with vainglory alloy'd, 'tis like enough the boy
in prospect of his manhood wil hav cast to th' winds
his Baptism with his Babyhood; nor might he escape
the fall of Ev'ryman, did not a second call
of nature's Love await him to confirm his Faith
or to revoke him if he is wholly lapsed therefrom.
And so mighty is this second vision, which cometh
in puberty of body and adolescence of mind
that, forgetting his Mother, he calleth it 'first Love';
for it mocketh at suasion or stubbornness of heart,
as the oceantide of the omnipotent Pleasur of God,
flushing all avenues of life, and unawares
by thousandfold approach forestalling its full flood
with divination of the secret contacts of Love,—
of faintest ecstacies aslumber in Nature's calm,
like thought in a closed book, where some poet long since
sang his throbbing passion to immortal sleep—with coy
tenderness delicat as the shifting hues
that sanctify the silent dawn with wonder-gleams,
whose evanescence is the seal of their glory,
consumed in self-becoming of eternity;
til every moment as it flyeth, cryeth 'Seize!
Seize me ere I die! I am the Life of Life.'
'Tis thus by near approach to an eternal presence
man's heart with divine furor kindled and possess'd
falleth in blind surrender; and finding therewithal

in fullest devotion the full reconcilement
betwixt his animal and spiritual desires,
such welcome hour of bliss standeth for certain pledge
of happiness perdurable: and coud he sustain
this great enthusiasm, then the unbounded promise
would keep fulfilment; since the marriage of true minds
is thatt once fabled garden, amidst of which was set
the single Tree that bore such med'cinable fruit
that if man ate thereof he should liv for ever.
  Friendship is in loving rather than in being lov'd,
which is its mutual benediction and recompense;
and tho' this be, and tho' love is from lovers learn'd,
it springeth none the less from the old essence of self.
No friendless man ('twas well said) can be truly himself;
what a man looketh for in his friend and findeth,
and loving self best, loveth better than himself,
is his own better self, his live lovable idea,
flowering by expansion in the loves of his life.
  And in the nobility of our earthly friendships
we hav all grades of attainment, and the best may claim
perfection of kind; and so, since ther be many bonds
other than breed (friendships of lesser motiv, found
even in the brutes) and since our politick is based
on actual association of living men, 'twil come
that the spiritual idea of Friendship, the huge
vastidity of its essence, is fritter'd away
in observation of the usual habits of men;
as happ'd with the great moralist, where his book saith
that ther can be no friendship betwixt God and man
because of their unlimited disparity.
  From this dilemma of pagan thought, this poison of faith,
Man-soul made glad escape in the worship of Christ;

for his humanity is God's Personality,
and communion with him is the life of the soul.
  Of which living ideas (when in the struggle of thought
harden'd by language they became symbols of faith)
Reason builded her maze, wherefrom none should escape.
wandering intent to map and learn her tortuous clews,
chanting their clerkly creed to the high-echoing stones
of their hand-fashion'd temple: but the Wind of heav'n
bloweth where it listeth, and Christ yet walketh the earth,
and talketh still as with those two disciples once
on the road to Emmaus—where they walk and are sad;
whose vision of him then was his victory over death,
thatt resurrection which all his lovers should share,
who in loving him had learn'd the Ethick of happiness;
whereby they too should come where he was ascended
to reign over men's hearts in the Kingdom of God.
  Our happiest earthly comradeships hold a foretaste
of the feast of salvation and by thatt virtue in them
provoke desire beyond them to out-reach and surmount
their humanity in some superhumanity
and ultimat perfection: which, howe'er 'tis found
or strangely imagin'd, answereth to the need of each
and pulleth him instinctivly as to a final cause.
Thus unto all who hav found their high ideal in Christ,
Christ is to them the essence discern'd or undiscern'd
of all their human friendships; and each lover of him
and of his beauty must be as a bud on the Vine
and hav participation in him; for Goddes love
is unescapable as nature's environment,
which if a man ignore or think to thrust it off
he is the ill-natured fool that runneth blindly on death.
  This Individualism is man's true Socialism.

This is the rife Idea whose spiritual beauty
multiplieth in communion to transcendant might.
This is thatt excelent way whereon if we wil walk
all things shall be added unto us—thatt Love which inspired
the wayward Visionary in his dóctrinal ode
to the three christian Graces, the Church's first hymn
and only deathless athanasian creed,—the which
'except a man believe he cannot be savèd'.
This is the endearing bond whereby Christ's company
yet holdeth together on the truth of his promise
that he spake of his great pity and trust in man's love,
Lo, I am with you always ev'n to the end of the world.
Truly the Soul returneth the body's loving
where it hath won it . . . and God so loveth the world . . .
and in the fellowship of the friendship of Christ
God is seen as the very self-essence of love,
Creator and mover of all as activ Lover of all,
self-express'd in not-self, without which no self were.
In thought whereof is neither beginning nor end
nor space nor time; nor any fault nor gap therein
'twixt self and not-self, mind and body, mother and child,
'twixt lover and loved, God and man: but ONE ETERNAL
in the love of Beauty and in the selfhood of Love.

iv. 1268–1446.

INDEX
OF AUTHORS
AND FIRST LINES

INDEX OF AUTHORS

The references are to the numbers of the poems.

INDEX OF AUTHORS

INDEX OF FIRST LINES

INDEX OF FIRST LINES

INDEX OF FIRST LINES

INDEX OF FIRST LINES

INDEX OF FIRST LINES

INDEX OF FIRST LINES

INDEX OF FIRST LINES

INDEX OF FIRST LINES

INDEX OF FIRST LINES